Cello

Kate Kennedy is one of the foremost critics of twentieth-century music of her generation. She has published widely, including *The Silent Morning: Culture and the Armistice, 1918*, *Literary Britten*, *Lives of Houses* and *Dweller in Shadows: A Life of Ivor Gurney* (selected by the Royal Philharmonic Society as the best writing on music in 2021). She is a Supernumerary Fellow of Wolfson College, Oxford, Director of the Oxford Centre for Life-writing, Director of the Centre for the Study of Women Composers, Director of the Museum of Music History, and a Fellow of the Royal Historical Society.

ALSO BY KATE KENNEDY

Dweller in Shadows: A life of Ivor Gurney
(Princeton University Press, 2021)

Lives of Houses (Co-ed. Hermione Lee,
Princeton University Press, 2020)

*Literary Britten: Words and Music in Benjamin Britten's
Vocal Works*
(ed., Boydell and Brewer, 2018)

The Silent Morning: Culture, Memory and the Armistice
(Co-ed. Trudi Tate, Manchester University Press, 2014)

KATE KENNEDY

Cello

A Journey Through Silence to Sound

HEAD
of ZEUS

An Apollo Book

First published in the UK in 2024 by Head of Zeus Ltd,
part of Bloomsbury Publishing Plc

9 7 5 3 2 4 6 8

A catalogue record for this book is available from the British Library.

ISBN (HB): 9781803287034
ISBN (E): 9781803287010

Cover design: Meg Shepherd
Maps: Jeff Edwards

Endpapers: Pál Hermann's cello concerto, first movement.
Reproduced by kind permission of the family of Pál Hermann.

Printed and bound in Great Britain by CPI Group (UK) Ltd,
Croydon CR0 4YY

Bloomsbury Publishing Plc
50 Bedford Square, London, WC1B 3DP, UK
Bloomsbury Publishing Ireland Limited,
29 Earlsfort Terrace, Dublin 2, D02 AY28, Ireland

HEAD OF ZEUS LTD
First Floor East, 5–8 Hardwick Street, London EC1R 4RG

To find out more about our authors and books visit www.headofzeus.com
For product safety related questions contact productsafety@bloomsbury.com

To Alison Hennegan

In memory of Renato Zanettovich,
the violinist of the Trieste Piano Trio,
and of Tik Weevers

To a 'Cellist

Centaur is man and stallion, gloriously
Pasturing masterless on plains of air,
A merman wears his raiment of the sea
And sphynx takes all the desert for her lair:
Part human creatures, in equal part still free
In the beasts' world that half their bodies share.
Musician, hand to bow grafted in equal mastery,
Goes like an angel where no mortal dare.

Composite being, man's intelligence
and tautened strings on wooden shell, sets free
Voice beyond speech or words' close boundary
To shape a world in logic of pure sense,
To comprehend beyond experience
Silence and sound in measured harmony.

(Ursula Wood)

Contents

3rd Movement – Silence

4th Movement – Sound

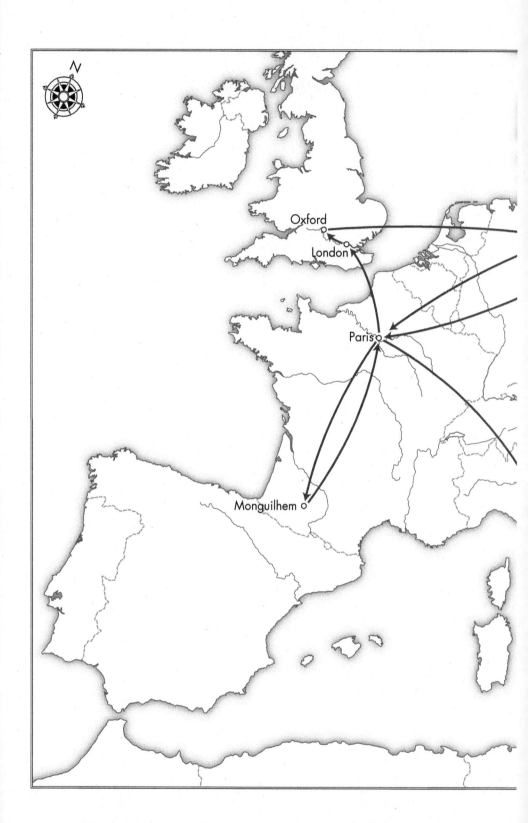

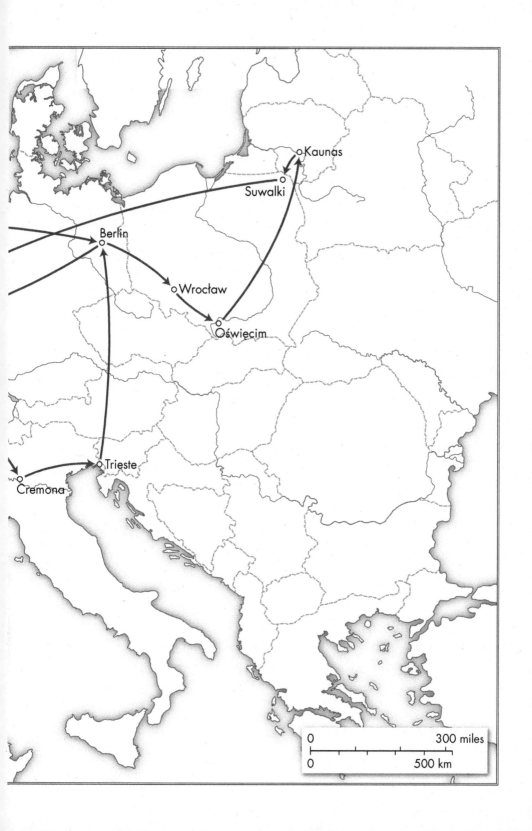

Prelude

What better instrument than a cello, half thunder, half prayer, to listen to the world?[1] But what if that instrument falls silent? When I was fifteen I won a scholarship to study at Wells Cathedral School, a specialist music school in Somerset. It meant swapping my inner-city home for medieval architecture, and surrounding myself with some of the best young players of my generation. I had wanted to be a cellist for as long as I could remember, and this was the nearest I could get to heaven. I sat in my practice room for hours, with the sounds of my friends hammering away at pianos and virtuosic string studies mingling in the central staircase. I got up at 6 a.m. to play scales, practised at lunchtime and returned to my cello after lessons. After a year or so, as my stamina improved, I played for longer and longer. I attempted harder repertoire, mastering as many concertos as I could. In my practice room I discovered the fireworks of Dvořák, the frenetic drive and nerviness of Shostakovich and the melancholy of Bloch. But above all I fell deeply and forever in love with Elgar's Cello Concerto, the breathless hush of its slow movement and the lonely solemnity of the great melody of the first movement. I had entered a world in which I knew I belonged, and I never wanted to leave.

One evening a year later, as I was preparing for a major competition, I pushed myself too far. I was playing some demanding study involving endless trills, working my weaker fourth and fifth fingers too hard, when something felt as if it had snapped in my forearm, and I felt a burning pain shoot down between wrist and elbow. At first I was simply shocked. When it hadn't got better after a day or two I started to panic. When, many weeks later, I still could not write or play, I was thin to the point of anorexia and numb with frustration. The school sent me to all the specialists they could, but no one offered a conclusive diagnosis, or any treatment that proved effective.

In the meantime, the months passed. I spent the days sitting in lessons, unable to write, and the evenings wandering the cobbled streets of Wells like a ghost, my arm in a sling. The concerto opportunities, recitals and competitions I'd been preparing for came and went.

Although I could not play, I still had to find something to do with the hours of practice time allotted to me as a music student. I would take my cello to my usual practice room and sit with it, place my copy of the Bach Cello Suites on the stand in front of me. Just looking at the music for the Elgar made me want to cry, so that stayed firmly in my music case. But Bach was different. In silence I imagined exactly how it would feel to play each note: what bowing patterns I would choose, whether one note would have more or less stress than another, where the emphases fell in each phrase. This fantastical music-making, dipping in and out of silence, my silence, seemed to lend itself perfectly only to the Bach Suites. When I tried it with a sonata, it felt more like a one-way conversation. Each silent suite was real to me, and after a few weeks of this eccentric practising, I could, had I been able to, have played most of them from memory.

When I wasn't sitting with my instrument, I was punishing myself for my own stupidity. My technique had probably not been secure enough for the demands I was placing on it, and I had never heard of tendonitis. But now it was too late. What was I if I wasn't a cellist? It was the quality that defined me, my one calling card. I lost so much weight I was made to attend weekly weigh-ins with the school nurse, which I got round by filling my pockets with stones in advance. Each week I simply added another stone or two. My subterfuge didn't work for very long. Eventually, my parents were summoned to be told I needed to be hospitalized, and I realized I had to make a decision. I decided to live, even if that meant a future without my cello.

I did eventually manage to continue to study the cello, and I play professionally, although the struggle with my injury continues, and is a constant limitation. As I recovered a little of the use of my arm, with a combination of physiotherapy and rest, I found that I could build up my stamina very gradually by playing early music that made fewer demands on my permanently weak arm, so I performed on a baroque cello, forgoing the Romantic and twentieth-century repertoire that I had loved. But the limitations my injury imposed have forced me to explore other ways to express my passion for music, and for that I'm grateful. I've written books and opera libretti, and talk about music on the radio and concert platforms. But what I haven't ever done until now is try to understand my complicated relationship with the instrument that was my first love.

The catalyst for this book was a photoshoot. I needed an up-to-date picture for appearances at literary and music festivals, and so booked a session in a studio near to my home. I was shifted about, asked to turn, fold my arms, smile, look serious. It was rather fun, a bit exposing, a bit awkward. After

a while the photographer suggested I get my cello and see what images of playing might look like through the camera. I remonstrated – I didn't see myself primarily as a cellist any more. But, in the face of his enthusiasm, I fetched it and sat in front of the blank screen, improvising and playing snatches of Bach. The photographer became much more animated, snapping away. 'This is it!' he said. 'Perfect.' In that moment, observed, the lens pointing at both my instrument and me, I began to understand something I had only half sensed until then. Away from my cello, my shadow was missing. Without it I felt exposed, my silhouette incomplete. But with my instrument I was protected, and entirely happy within my own skin.

During that photoshoot I realized that I needed to find out what the cello, and its absence, had meant to other cellists, in order to start to understand what it meant to me.

And so began a journey across Europe, a journey in and out of silence and music to uncover the stories of cellists and their instruments. I found new ways of looking and listening to the instrument, exploring it in every way, often in the company of other cellists, and these encounters are recorded in the eight interludes in this book. Over the course of my research, I found that four cellists in particular became important to me. And so, just as a cello's voice is divided across four strings, each with its own colour and character, so this is a journey of four parts, following four players and their instruments: Pál Hermann, Lise Cristiani, Anita Lasker-Wallfisch and Amedeo Baldovino.

Pál Hermann (1902–1944) was a Jewish cellist and composer who was celebrated in his lifetime, but was murdered by the Nazis. When he was arrested, his cello (made by Nicolò Gagliano (c.1730–1787)) was rescued, but has subsequently been lost. Lise Cristiani (c.1824–1853), the first female cello soloist, is hardly remembered today.[2] She took what is now the world's most valuable Stradivari cello on a fatal exploration of the furthest parts of Siberia. Anita Lasker-Wallfisch (b. 1925–) survived the Auschwitz and Bergen-Belsen concentration camps only because she was an exceptional cellist, and the camp orchestra needed a bass line. During her persecution in her home town of Breslau, her cello made by Lorenzo Ventapane (1780–1843) was lost. Finally, I followed the adventures of the Stradivari cello of 1711 known as the 'Mara'. Amedeo Baldovino (1916–1998), the cellist in the Trieste Piano Trio, was the owner of the 'Mara' during the 1960s. On tour between Buenos Aires and Uruguay, the trio and their instruments were involved in a shipwreck. Forced to jump into the water, the trio survived, but their instruments were washed away.

With my own cello as my travelling companion, we drew around us a community of players, both historic and contemporary. As I delved deeper into their stories I found that

Pál Hermann and Anita Lasker-Wallfisch.

Amedeo Baldovino and
Lise Cristiani.

they were woven together by absences and silence, but also by resilience, survival and sound. Their experiences are very different from mine, but we all share a passionate connection to our cellos. I hoped that learning about their relationship to their instruments might help me, in turn, to understand my own.

1st *Movement* – *Cello*

... tautened strings on wooden shell, sets free
Voice beyond speech or words' close boundary

(from Ursula Wood, 'To a 'Cellist')

Oxford

I'm standing in the workshop of Oxford Violins, on an afternoon in October 2021. As the sound of cello playing resonates around, my eyes fall on the workbench in front of me. There is a cello, held in a brace; its 'top' (as the wooden front of the instrument is known) is off, and a cloth is draped around it like a surgical gown, protecting its modesty. Above the window hang rows of bridges like carved washing on a metal line. The violin bridges look to my cellist's eye as if they should belong in a doll's house. On the bare plaster walls are scrawled phone numbers and names, and around them yellowing newspaper clips with photographs of violins are glued (probably by instrument varnish). Coffee is made on the Primus camping stove, which adds a pleasing smell of gas to the glue and dust, and it's hard to know where to put a coffee cup down, as the benches are strewn with scrolls, necks and the ribs of instruments. It is, in short, a ramshackle, wood-shaving-filled paradise.

Instrument maker Bruno Guastalla and I are testing ourselves, trying to tell the difference between the sound of two cellos. We both have our backs to the room. From the doorway come crashing the opening chords of the Elgar Cello Concerto. We listen, straining into the sound as if we're leaning into a strong wind. 'And now this one...' calls cellist Nick Roberts from the other room. A slight scuffle as he puts down the cello he's just been playing and picks up another.

Bruno Guastalla at his workbench in the
Oxford Violin shop.

Again, the Elgar. It sounds different, certainly, but does it
sound better?

Bruno frowns. My mind forms sentences as I listen, trying
to capture the qualities of the two different sounds in inadequate phrases. One is more 'present', perhaps? One might
be richer, with more depth; the other has more immediacy,
more focus, what we might describe as 'blade' in the sound.
As I rehearse my opinions, I am conscious that I am shaping
sound, moulding it in imagination just as Bruno carves his
instruments on the workbench in front of me. But am I right?
Nick comes bounding in, grinning, eager to know which cello
we preferred. He had been playing two instruments. First, his
own treasured cello, made by the Milanese luthier Giovanni
Grancino, one of the great Italian makers who were at their

zenith at the end of the seventeenth century. The other is a brash, chestnut-coloured cello, so new that the varnish is barely dry. It's like a stately home competing with a boxy little new-build. But in Nick's hands, from another room, can we tell which is which?

Bruno is intense and dark, a brilliant craftsman and an 'amateur' in the true, sixteenth-century French meaning of the word: a real *lover* of the cello. In his lilting European accent, he had earlier explained to us how every cello eventually takes on the character of its player. The resonance of the wood alters, just a little, when an instrument is repeatedly played in particular ways. After thousands of hours of practice in the hands of one owner, it is not the same instrument. It takes on the imprint of its player like a finger in wax, and is shaped by their partnership, just as its strengths and weaknesses will dictate how the cellist plays. Nick has been the cellist of the Coull Quartet for twenty four years. His Grancino, after decades of string quartet repertoire, will hold within the grain of its glossy body the essence of his playing: the solid, rich sound that he makes as he supports the other three players.

Any cello with a history hums with audible ghosts; but a new cello is a *tabula rasa*, with no history to hold, no memories in its sound, no repetitious practice inscribed on its body. It can take years before a new instrument has grown fully into its wooden skin.[1]

As the first few notes of Nick's playing floated through the open door, Bruno and I decided that we were listening to the pedigree Grancino, with its great richness of sound. On the instant of deciding, I felt that I could see it in his arms, and once I had that image, the sound I believed I heard had subtly taken on a different quality, shaping itself to fit my theory. Once confident that I was hearing hundreds of years of history, it was impossible to be objective. Bruno had had the same experience. But we had both guessed wrong. It was the modern, nameless cello, with its sound not yet opened up.

From only a short distance, we had mistaken a stallion for a new-born foal. So now we are most perplexed, and Nick is highly amused.

'If', I ask Nick, 'you can make two instruments of vastly different quality sound the same (albeit from a distance), then why bother with a superb cello, and all the cost and responsibility it entails?'

'A great instrument allows you to become yourself, to experience what it is to realize your musical voice with no barriers, and let it flourish,' he explains. 'When you then go back to an average instrument, you take the glimpse of paradise you've experienced, and everything you've learnt about yourself as a player back with you, and work much harder to try to get back to that point, but it's running to stand still.' A really good instrument frees you up to be as musical as you like. It lets you sing. So while to the outside observer, if your technique is good enough and you're an experienced player, the overall sound might be similar, the feeling for the player is not. As Nick puts it, 'Perhaps it's like being trapped in a bad marriage – it might look all right from the outside, but you play despite the instrument, not in partnership with it.'

Some elements of a player's relationship to their instrument are private. There is a distinction between hearing music and making music, between public and personal. What the experience feels like to Nick, and what we hear are not the same. If I am to understand anything about my own relationship to my cello, I need to fathom this ineffable connection between instrument and player, the secret, silent negotiations that shape the music.

෴

I could have listened all day to Nick, now reunited with his Grancino, but I have a train to catch, the first of many that will take me across Europe on a journey to find out about the partnerships between instruments and their players. Some are relationships that have been destroyed, through accident or war; in some cases the cellos are lost. I hope, if only by telling the stories of their premature absences, in some way to restore their silences with sound. After a quick second Nescafé peppered with wood dust, I say my goodbyes to Nick and Bruno, sling my cello on my back and head off through the autumnal colours of the tree-lined Banbury Road, and across St Giles. I turn right by the columns of the neoclassical palace of objects known as the Ashmolean Museum and nod to its collection of Stradivari and Amati violins nestled in their glass cases on an upper floor. A few minutes later I roll my suitcase past the hundreds of bicycles, up the ramp and onto the concourse of Oxford station.

Once settled on the train to London, my cello propped up against the seat next to me, I can begin to think about the journey we have begun. This trip across Europe to trace the journeys of my four cellists and their instruments had been planned from the comfort and safety of my study, my maps and itineraries spread out across the desk and spilling onto the floor. The cellists I will follow had faced any number of perilous and extreme situations, including the destruction and loss of their instruments. I, however, hope to be in no more danger than risking bed bugs in cheap hotels. But as my cello and I move towards the suburbs of London, I suddenly feel rather alone. Raindrops start to track their way across the carriage windows in thin fingers, and I notice I have wrapped the strap of my cello case around my wrist. We belong together; this is one cello that will not disappear.

Berlin I

From the iron pillars and glass of St Pancras, through the autumnal greens and browns of Kent, the train rushes into the Channel Tunnel. After what seems no time at all, the flat expanse of the French countryside is suddenly upon us; then, just as seamlessly, station names change to Flemish, then German. Eventually, after Cologne, we turn north, then north-east, until factories and flats begin to replace the fields. Nine hours after I left London, my train pulls into Berlin.

Berlin is the one place where my four cellists' lives converge. Lise Cristiani, Amedeo Baldovino, Pál Hermann and Anita Lasker-Wallfisch never met, but across a period of a hundred years they all stayed within a few miles of each other, even performed on the same stages. Lise was at the height of her fame when, as a young woman, she visited Berlin in 1845–6, touring Europe with her Stradivari. The child prodigy Amedeo frequently performed on the same stages from the age of fifteen, during the 1930s and 40s.[2] Pál made his home here, studying and performing in Berlin between 1923 and 1933. And Anita studied here in 1938, until the rise of fascism made it impossible for her to stay. If I can find echoes of these cellists anywhere, Berlin seems to be a good starting point. It is a city loud with their absence.

∾

I arrive at what my phone claims is the address of my rented accommodation late in the evening, although I can't see the apartment. A message pings onto the screen with a series of instructions worthy of the most innovative of treasure hunts. I must walk up the road and find an Italian restaurant, looking around the street near it for an abandoned child's bike. Attached to the bike is a box. If I type in the code I will find a key. It takes me half an hour to identify the bike, concealed behind many others, which I can't get past with a suitcase and cello. It is now dark and starting to rain. The key box won't open. I pull at it, bang it on things, and eventually it creaks open enough for me to prise out a rusty key with my fingernails. Then I fail to find the apartment block, which is neither numbered nor in the least evident. I accost a waiter outside the Italian restaurant and ask, in woeful German, if he can help me. He stares, points at my cello case, enquires in broken English as to whether I have my boyfriend in there, and then laughs uproariously. If I had had the energy, or indeed the language skills, I could have told him how, while there obviously isn't a human in the case, I am nonetheless partnered to the object that inhabits this large humanoid container which I carry on my back. But it is now pouring with rain, the cello case's straps are digging into my shoulders, and I'm thinking about crying.

Welcome to Berlin.

⌇

Verena Alves meets me at a nearby café early the next morning. She is the archivist for the Berlin Philharmonic Orchestra, and a smiling, calm presence, with wavy brown hair and a beret. She has offered to help me find my way across the city, to locate the places in which my cellists played. Although she herself moved to Berlin twenty years ago, she still observes the city and its relationship to its history with the objective interest of a foreigner. She pulls a map from her rucksack. 'Here,' she says triumphantly. 'This is what we're looking for. Not the Berlin you see here' (she gestures at the world outside the large windows of the café), 'but the Berlin that Lise Cristiani knew in the 1800s, and that Pál, Amedeo and Anita knew before the war.' I look closely at the map. It has been compiled as a research project, a meta-map, if such a thing exists, to mark the location of the concert halls and music societies of Berlin as they were before it was bombed, rebuilt and then carved in half by the wall. Few of the many musical landmarks shown here exist today. It is a map of memories and absences, particularly apt for a city haunted by the lives and the places that are no longer there. Layers of erased history, which music, perhaps, has a peculiar power to connect and restore.

Walking past the nearby Pierre Boulez Saal, we see a quote on a poster from the man himself: *Man sollte das Konzert grundsätzlich als Kommunikationsmittel betrachten, als lebendigen Kontakt zwischen aktiven Personen, seien sie Hörende oder Schaffende* ('One should essentially see concerts as a means of communication, as animated contact between active participants, be they listeners or creators'). I am hoping to find my own version of this 'animated contact' that Boulez experiences. The connections between player and audience happen at the moment of performance, but the act of making music in a place leaves its resonance across time, like the shadows marked on our map, for others to hear.

Verena takes me to a neat, white classical building, the Maxim Gorki Theater. Between 1827 and 1943 this place was the Singakademie. It is the oldest concert hall in Berlin, and one of the few buildings we're visiting that all four of my cellists would have recognized. Lise Cristiani performed here in April 1846; Amedeo Baldovino played a Haydn concerto with the Berlin Philharmonic here on 14 November 1931; and Pál Hermann performed with his baroque trio here in the late 1920s and early 1930s.[3] Pál might well have known about Baldovino's concert and attended, curious to see another cellist who, like himself, was being hailed as an internationally renowned prodigy. When the teenage Anita Lasker studied in Berlin in 1938, she spent many hours wandering the city, and would have known the concert hall, which was one of the great musical landmarks of pre-war Berlin. Four years after she left, the Singakademie was almost completely destroyed in an Allied air raid. When it was rebuilt it became the theatre we are now standing outside. I'd hoped to look inside, and perhaps even to play on its stage, but today it is shut. With Verena's encouragement I get my cello out and perch on the wall outside to play a little of the Haydn that

Outside the Singakademie.

Amedeo performed here, the wind whipping at my bow. It's something between an eccentric tribute and busking. I stop when a builder glowers at me from a window of a nearby terrapin hut, and we move hastily on.

Next we walk to the Konzerthaus, the other venue at which Lise Cristiani made her triumphant two-concert Berlin debut, though when she performed here, and until the end of the First World War, it was still called the Königliches Schauspielhaus – the King's Theatre. With its vast stone steps leading high up to its entrance, it is set proudly in the centre of a huge neoclassical square, Gendarmenmarkt. Built at the end of the seventeenth century, when one fifth to a quarter of the population of Berlin was French, the 'gendarme' of the square's name reflects the city's dual nationality. On one side of the Konzerthaus is the French church; on the other, its twin, the German church (in which

Pál Hermann performed in 1928[4]). Like the Maxim Gorki Theater, the Königliches Schauspielhaus only gives the appearance of age. It too was destroyed during the war, and was left for many years as a ruin. It was only in the 1980s that it became a concert hall once more, when the German Democratic Republic entered into a competition with West Berlin and spent an uncharacteristic amount of money restoring it. In a reconstruction of the opulence that would have greeted the young Lise Cristiani, it is now once again dazzlingly full of chandeliers, sculptures and paintings of severe-looking composers, with every conceivable surface covered in gilt or velvet.

In 1846 Lise performed here to an audience curious to see one of the first female cellists. The whole spectacle was carefully choreographed. Nowadays, cellists usually walk on stage with their cellos, but Lise could not have been expected to make her entrance clutching so unwieldy an instrument, so her Stradivari was placed on the stage ready for her. There was a certain logic to her cello making the first appearance. The audience settled in their seats, wondering what this young lady would look like, whether the performance they would witness would be sublime or ridiculous, or anything in between. Alone on stage, Lise's Stradivari eyed them aslant, or as one critic put it, the cello was 'already melancholically propped up against a chair and staring out at the audience with her long, slit F-hole eyes'.[5] The ruse enabled the audience to get used to the idea of a woman with a cello, easing them in gently by introducing the instrument before Lise herself.

This description of the mute, melancholy female form, waiting to be animated by its player, is compelling and strikingly strange. Yet it was fairly common in the 1700s for objects to be imbued with life, and that legacy would have lingered into the early 1800s. There is, for instance, a whole body of literature that tells the story of life in London through the progress of a coat, or the life story of a penny. These objects very often talk, and have opinions on the society in which they find themselves, or on their current owner.[6] Why not a cello, quietly alive, capable of telling us about society at that time, its attitudes to gender, and culture?

Can a cello be melancholic, can it gaze at 'her' audience? I like to think so. Anthropologist Ivan Gaskell writes that 'those who would see into the life of things cannot confine themselves to the taxonomic domains of biology, for there is life in senses numinous or sacred, well beyond their confines'.[7] There is life too – or, if not life, then perhaps shadows – preserved in the map that Verena and I are following, with its silent concert halls and indications of buildings that turn out to be office blocks, or forbidding edifices of steel and glass.

I do not know whether Pál Hermann ever performed at the Konzerthaus, but according to the handful of dog-eared concert programmes in my possession, he played at least twice in the Bechstein-Saal, in 1926 and 1927, and so this is our next destination.[8] According to our map, the Bechstein Hall used to be located at Linkstraße 42, on Mendelssohn-Bartholdy Park, near Potsdamer Platz. Verena leads the way, and I emerge from the U-Bahn expecting, as promised, a park – or at the very least a verdant area, with the odd flowerbed. Instead, we are confronted with a narrow strip of grass raised inexplicably into miniature green pyramids, flanked by great multi-storey buildings. On the right is a millennial glass building designed by Richard Rogers, architect of the Pompidou Centre. The Bechstein Hall would have been somewhere near this building, but it is impossible to tell where. Like Pál Hermann himself, it has vanished.

Berlin II – Pál Hermann

Pál Hermann had made his home in Berlin in 1923, after completing his studies in his native Hungary. He was born in Budapest on 27 March 1902, into a middle-class family who valued culture highly. Pál's parents were Jewish, although they were not observant and did not attend synagogue. Jews were so integrated in his home town of Budapest that singling them out as different would have been absurd. And yet, Pál's Jewishness would come to define him.

Pál's parents sent him to piano lessons and gave him a cello as soon as he started to show an interest in music. By the time he was fifteen he had made so much progress that they took him to the ornate marble halls of the nearby Royal National Hungarian Academy of Music (now the Franz Liszt Academy). The professors agreed that this young boy did indeed have considerable potential, and he began seven years of study there, as both cellist and composer.

It was a golden time for the academy, and the teenage Pál found himself surrounded by great names. Béla Bartók and Zoltán Kodály presided over the composition students, and their musical influence haunts Pál's later works. His fellow students were equally inspiring. The friendships he formed at the academy went on to become the musical partnerships that defined his career. The virtuoso violinist Zoltán Székely was a year younger than Pál, and they became close friends. In amongst the academy's archives are lists of student performances from 1919 and 1920. Pál Hermann and Zoltán Székely are always together, performing Beethoven quartets and trios, duos by Brahms, or chamber pieces by Mendelssohn and Liszt.

Pál and Zoltán toured Europe throughout the 1920s, writing for each other and performing their own compositions, amongst other challenging contemporary repertoire.

Pál Hermann and Zoltán Székely.

Pál's playing first attracted serious attention when he performed Kodály's Sonata for Solo Cello (opus 8) in Vienna
for the Society for the Private Performance of Music, at
the invitation of the eminent composer Arnold Schoenberg.
After a second performance at the International Society for
Contemporary Music concerts in Salzburg in 1923, he was
well on the way to becoming one of the most exciting young
string players in Europe.

Decades later, Pál's daughter Corrie paid an impromptu
visit to Zoltán Székely in Canada. The interview was filmed,
and makes for moving viewing. Zoltán is ninety years old,
bird-like and frail. Corrie asks him what he remembers of her
father. He is thoughtful for a moment. 'He always took life
lightly,' he says, with slow deliberation. He uses the Dutch

word *vlot*. There's no direct equivalent in English. It suggests fluidity and fluency, but not aimless drifting – rather a form of easy-going energy: light, quick and humorous. I'm reminded of Alexander Pope, who wrote 'True ease in writing comes from Art, not Chance, / As those move easiest who have learn'd to dance.'[9] Pál Hermann's playing, and his composition, both deeply informed by technique and craftsmanship, were *vlot*. They danced.

During the war, Pál's handwritten music manuscripts had been stored away carefully in a box in Corrie's family home, ready for his return. They remained there until very recently – safe, but unplayed. If the facts of his life had been different, his work would be well known, programmed in chamber music festivals and recitals alongside Bartók or Kodály. But instead, his work is only now being rediscovered, after a seventy-year silence. In a quiet corner of a café I open my laptop and play Verena some of the recent recordings of Pál Hermann's orchestral and chamber works. His music is fiendishly difficult. It is full of rhythm and vivacity, combining the driving motor of Hungarian folk music with a haunting simplicity and nostalgia.

When I had first played his cello works myself, I found, overwhelmingly, that this was a man whose own technique was simply formidable. On the cello he was, as Pope would have had it, someone who could 'move easiest'. His instrument was an opportunity, not a barrier, and he wrote some of the most difficult music in the repertoire for himself. His solo writing often feels as if there are at least two instruments playing at any one time, the single player entwining different melodic lines and harmonies together, often playing two or three strings simultaneously. Like Bach's, his music is conceived on multiple planes; it is as if one instrument isn't enough for him.

As Verena and I look through some of the many concert programmes and reviews I have brought to Berlin, it becomes clear that it was predominantly contemporary music for which Pál Hermann was known. In the 1920s we find him taking the colourful special effects of the Debussy Cello Sonata and Kodály's Solo Cello Sonata around Europe. The reviews in various European papers give an idea of the response his playing elicited. One critic in Budapest, listening to his debut there on 12 December 1923, hails the 'already world-famous Hungarian cello genius'.[10] The normally cynical critics at the Salzburg Festival are in raptures over 'Pál Hermann – the Hungarian Casals', a title that is echoed by a reviewer in Rotterdam.[11] This comparison with Pablo Casals, the great Catalan cellist, seems to have stuck. To be likened to one of the greatest cellists of all time, before Pál had reached his twenty-first birthday, was no mean achievement. As Verena translates for me, we find that the German critics tell us, again and again, how impressive and fluent his playing was, how technically superb. In the course of 1923 alone he performed to rapturous acclaim in Berlin, Dresden, Budapest, New York, Rotterdam and London. In short, Pál Hermann was an international phenomenon, even before he had finished studying.

⮀

These reviews praise Pál's tone, but in the early 1920s it was one he created despite, rather than because of, the instrument he played (I am reminded of Nick Roberts back in Oxford, coaxing quality sound from a student cello). It was only in 1928 that Pál acquired the cello that would be his life partner, an instrument with a particularly luminous, golden tone, made by Nicolò Gagliano (c.1730–87). Nicolò was the eldest son of Alessandro Gagliano, founder of the dynasty of distinguished luthiers who were based in Naples between 1700 and 1860.[12] Pál Hermann's Gagliano cello is an integral part of his story, and what happened to it after his death has become nothing short of a personal obsession of mine.

The Gagliano had been given to Pál in 1928, when he and Zoltán were on tour in London. He had damaged his own cello one evening by dancing with it at a party after a house concert in London. It is a detail of his life that captivates me. I imagine this long-limbed, whimsical young man twirling his cello round the room like a dance partner. The laughter, the music... and then a drink spills, the glass smashes – the varnish is stained – disaster!

The morning after the party, Pál needed to get his instrument repaired. He chose to entrust his wine-stained cello to the great London instrument dealer and maker W. E. Hill & Sons. His appearance in the Hills' workshop on Saturday 20 February 1926 received a disdainful mention in Arthur Frederick Hill's workshop diary:

> Paul Hermann called with his instrument as it had met with a slight accident. It is one of the most ordinary German type with no individuality, but he makes it sound well, because, through use, he has become accustomed to it and as a result produces the best obtainable tone from the cello.

The Hill brothers were notoriously hard to please, and most string players, however famous, meet with disdain in the pages of their diaries, so this admission of Pál's skill is tantamount to acknowledging him as a genius.

The Hills' workshop quickly repaired the damage to the stained varnish of Pál's 'ordinary' German cello. By a curious coincidence, I was to discover that, only twenty years before, the same workshops based in Ealing had removed wine stains from another instrument that would feature in my travels: the anything-but-ordinary 'Mara' Stradivari.[13] In fact, as it turned out, wine stains were far from the worst thing to befall the 'Mara', and it would not be the last time it would find itself on the workbench at W. E. Hill & Sons. But that story is for later.

The fateful house concert had been hosted by a wealthy Dutch couple, Jaap de Graaff and Louise Bachiene. Something about the talented, feckless cellist and his duo partner, Székely, appealed to de Graaff and Bachiene, and they decided to support them both by buying them instruments worthy of their abilities. In 1928 the couple purchased a cello for Pál. It is possible that he would have selected the Gagliano cello himself, as the relationship between player and instrument is so deeply personal, but there is no record of where the instrument was obtained. While it was not uncommon for patrons to invest in instruments for talented young soloists, an £800 cello was an impressive gift for a cash-strapped young graduate to receive. Jaap de Graaff wrote a document stating that it was to be understood as an extended loan, and that Pál would start to pay it back when he could afford to do so. Both parties must have known

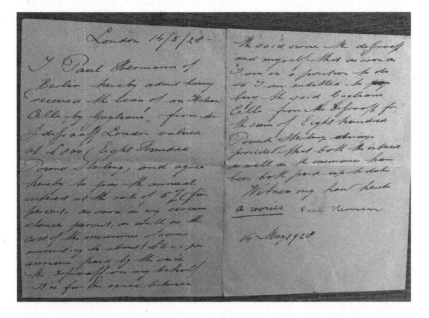

Jaap de Graaff and Pál Hermann's 1928 agreement.

that there was little or no chance of his ever being able to afford the repayment. Pál's daughter Corrie believes that this arrangement was intended to preserve her father's dignity and was a measure of his new patron's sensitivity to the fact that her father would otherwise not have allowed himself to accept such an expensive gift.

Jaap de Graaff and Louise Bachiene also purchased a Stradivari violin in 1928, for Székely: the 'Michelangelo' Stradivari of 1718, now known as the 'Michelangelo, Székely'. Both players and their instruments were inseparable for the rest of their careers. There is no recording of the two playing together, but Pál's 'Grand' Second Duo for violin and cello, written two years after they took ownership of their new instruments, is a musical snapshot of their sounds and styles. The piece, composed for a recital at the Wigmore Hall in London, was premiered within a short walk of Jaap de Graaff's home. It was as great a gesture of thanks as a young musician could make to a generous patron. De Graaff would have heard his Stradivari and Gagliano enter in a flash of confident chords. The instruments are in partnership throughout, with the intensity and exuberance that characterized the players themselves.

Shortly after he left London, Pál Hermann embarked on a recital tour across the Netherlands. One of his concerts happened to take place in Amsterdam. Louise Bachiene and Jaap de Graaff had a young, musical niece called Ada Weevers, who lived in Amersfoort, near Utrecht. Louise had written to Ada to tell her all about the genial and prodigiously talented cellist they had discovered, encouraging her to go to Amsterdam to hear him play, and to meet him after the concert. Ada and Pál quickly found they had more in common than a mutual fondness for her uncle and aunt; he began to visit Amersfoort whenever his schedule would allow. It soon became clear to Ada that her future lay with Pál, so she withdrew from her medical degree at Amsterdam

University. She married Pál in the town hall in Amersfoort on 29 September 1931, and moved with her new husband to Berlin.

Pál Hermann and Ada Weevers, 1929/1930.

Pál relinquished his rented bachelor rooms to find a flat for his new wife. As soon as they had moved in, Ada wrote home to her brother Jaap on their own headed notepaper. Their new address was Riehlstraße 2, a middle-class residential street of apartment blocks in the Charlottenburg area of Berlin. Ada wrote of her delight when her new husband managed to obtain a Bechstein grand piano for her to play. Her letters to Jaap describe the many house concerts she and Pál attended. The music that excited Pál was avant-garde, and more likely to be performed in smaller venues than in concert halls. Ada attended a concert in the enormous house of a bank director, featuring contemporary music that used quartertones. Pál knew about a third of the guests and presented Ada to 'a lot of ladies with a lot of make-up'. She was introduced to 'a very nice little man with a bald head', who was in fact Paul Hindemith, and she was amused when he remarked to 'Páli' (as she called her husband) that 'you are lucky to have more hair than I'. Another concert was hosted by a man who, Ada noted, 'has a beautiful house and a unique wife', adding, 'It would be better to be able to write that conversely.' Erich Mendelsohn was a distinguished German architect who would flee the Nazis in 1933; Luise, his 'unique' wife, was a cellist, studying with Pál.[14]

In the late summer of 1932, the year before Hitler seized power, Ada and Pál brought their tiny baby daughter up the stairs to the flat in Riehlstraße that was to be her home. Corrie (short for Cornelia) had been born on 4 August in Ada's family house in the Netherlands. After a few weeks of getting to grips with feeding and the lack of sleep, Ada, Pál and Corrie were ready to begin their life as a family of three in Berlin.

༄

When Pál Hermann had left Budapest for Berlin back in 1923, he was already 'a very outstanding artist, and one of the first in his field', but he must have felt that there was more he could learn.[15] One of the few people who could help him was the German cellist Hugo Becker, with whom he studied until 1929. Many of Becker's other pupils went on to significant international careers, including Beatrice Harrison (who made the first recordings of Elgar's Cello Concerto), Gregor Piatigorsky and Paul Grümmer, the cellist of the Busch Quartet.

A supreme technician, Becker was developing a formidable, streamlined cello technique that allowed the instrument to be played with as few unnatural demands on the body

Pál and Corrie, on their Berlin apartment balcony.

as possible. These developments helped to shift perceptions of the cello from something cumbersome and awkward, primarily limited to sentimentality and nostalgia, to a soloistic instrument capable of as much virtuosity and intensity of expression as the violin. The exercises Becker published are still used today to hone students' technique. I grew up on them, alongside the equally gruelling studies by Piatti and Grützmacher. To young cellists, their names are as familiar as old friends. The only name missing from the family tree of great technicians is that of Pál Hermann. Now, as I return to their exercises, an experience that at its best is meditative, at worst, more punishment than music-making, I feel a little closer to Pál. I trace my fingers in the patterns that he, like so many other cello students, would have known by heart. I can imagine him working through them in his lessons with Becker, the eager, dark-haired young Hungarian and the be-whiskered German, his moustache cultivated into horizontal points, like a miniature cello bow balanced across his upper lip.

Hugo Becker owned two Stradivari cellos. One of these has been known as the 'Becker' ever since; the other, which he had played when he was Pál's age, shaping his formidable technique, was the 'Cristiani'. I knew that Lise Cristiani and Pál Hermann had both walked the streets and played in the concert halls of Paris and Berlin, a century apart. I had no idea that, via his teacher, there was a direct connection between Lise's cello and Pál. The instruments and players I am following are holding hands (or rather, touching bows) across time.

⁓

Since 1929 Pál had taught at a newly formed music school in Neukölln, a deprived area of south-east Berlin, as a cello and – probably – composition teacher. In those days the school was known as the Volksmusikschule Neukölln but, having changed location a number of times since the war, it is now the Musikschule Paul Hindemith. It was a project born of a particular moment in German politics of the interwar period, when left-wing idealism and the arts briefly met and flourished, before being extinguished (along with many of the brilliant Jewish musicians at the forefront of the movement). Pál Hermann joined the school only two years after it was founded, becoming one of twenty staff, who also included Paul Hindemith amongst their number. They taught shop workers, labourers and children, introducing them to folk music, singing, composition and the philosophy behind music. One of the first public music schools in Berlin, it was the vision of its director, the violinist and composer Ernst-Lothar von Knorr.[16] In the 1930s, pupils were entitled to lessons on merit, rather than on their ability to pay, and the school's professors survived more on vision and enthusiasm than on salary, leaving them obliged to stage regular fund-raising concerts to keep the institution going.

Knorr was to become a friend of Pál's, and they formed a baroque ensemble, the Berliner Cembalo Trio, together with Walter Drwenski, harpsichordist and organist of the Kaiser Wilhelm Gedächtniskirche. They recorded and performed trio sonatas by Buxtehude, Krieger and Handel, at a time when very few musicians experimented with 'authentic' baroque performance. I had wondered whether it was these musicians in Berlin who sparked Pál's interest in baroque music, but there are concert programmes showing that, back in the early 1920s, he had already chosen to perform Handel alongside Kodály and other contemporary composers. The two interests had developed side by side, and now he had found companions with whom he could explore baroque repertoire in depth. Studying with Bach scholar Dr Ludwig Landshoff, they gave chamber concerts almost every week in the Bach Hall or in the Singakademie. One audience member was Albert Einstein, who, alongside being one of the greatest names in modern science, was a skilled violinist. He invited the trio to perform in his house on several occasions, and Knorr remembered that Einstein played chamber music in this 'culturally attractive circle', alongside Pál Hermann and the violinist Fritz Kreisler.[17]

Although Pál broadcast frequently both on European radio stations and on the BBC, it is hard to find recordings of his playing. But one or two LPs of the baroque trio exist. When I first managed to obtain one of these records, the experience of hearing him play for the very first time elicited a physical reaction. I had read and thought so much about this man, but never heard him play. It was like listening to a ghost. Above all, it was the vulnerability of his sound that moved me: evidently so vivacious at the point of recording, but now seeming so fragile as it intermittently breaks through the aquatic sounds of the warped old record. The experience was the aural equivalent of trying to reach someone from whom one is separated by a pane of smudgy glass. But even from these imperfect recordings it's clear that Pál was a player interested in exploring the timbres of the cello, finding different colours and shapes to fit the architecture of the dance-like baroque phrasing. A photograph of one of these recording sessions exists, with Pál looking delightfully wry, perched on a table above the other musicians, who are clustered in a motley assemblage around a huge gramophone horn protruding from the wall, recording the sound. Pál's daughter Corrie remembers him talking about his frustration that the cello couldn't be heard properly and suggesting the precarious table arrangement himself.[18]

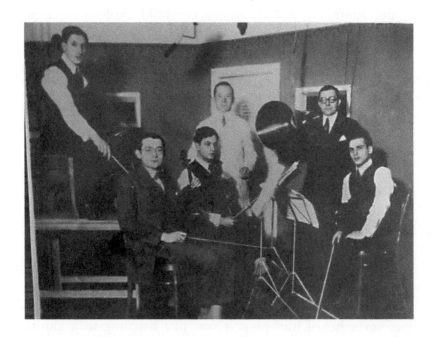

Since leaving Budapest, Pál Hermann had stood out for his brilliance, sensitivity and musicianship. But just as he was establishing his reputation, anti-Jewish laws imposed from 1933 onwards made it increasingly difficult for him to perform in public. She could not have known it at the time, but Ada's observations on her new life in Berlin had reflected a world of German-Jewish intellectual and musical culture that was doomed to come to an abrupt end. Over the next few years, scores of Jewish musicians and their patrons would leave the city, if they were lucky enough not to be arrested. Pál's colleagues at the music school were aware that their left-wing, pro-Jewish allegiances were exposing them – and the school – to danger. The Volksmusikschule in Neukölln stood for everything the Nazis disliked, and within a few years of Hitler becoming chancellor the social experiment was over. After the Reichstag fire of February 1933, Hindemith emigrated; many other Jewish musicians fled. One teacher, Rudolph Bartel, continued to conduct the Socialist Workers Youth Orchestra, until he was arrested in 1934 and held in Lichtenburg concentration camp for a year. Only the deputy director, pianist Hans Boettcher, succeeded in maintaining the social community of the school and protecting it against Nazi interference for a time, until, in the last months of the war, he was drafted into the *Volkssturm* and was killed fighting.[19]

Pál Hermann watched as the atmosphere of hostility increased month by month. Knorr tried to keep him in his position at the music school, and years later their mutual friend Hans-Erich Riebensahm (who would later become an accompanist to the baritone Dietrich Fischer-Dieskau) remembered how grateful Pál had been at the time for Knorr's support.[20] Ironically, while Knorr could not save him, his friendship with Pál may well have saved his own career. Knorr joined the Nazi party in 1942, but his pre-war efforts to help his friend were to be cited in 1947, as part of his own character defence in an Allied court.

❧

Within a year of Corrie's birth, life in Berlin had become intolerable for her father. To many citizens of Berlin, he was no longer a celebrated cellist or composer, but a Jew first and foremost. Probably, like so many others, he had not even begun to imagine the extent of the horrors that were to come. Perhaps he believed that a country with as deep and rich a musical heritage as Germany would not turn on its musicians. But what he could no longer ignore was the evidence that the same people who had recently applauded his playing in the press and praised him at the stage door after his concerts now seemed intent on hounding Jews from the country. By the summer of 1933, he decided he had no choice but to pack up the flat in Riehlstraße and leave Germany. Pál and Ada travelled with one-year-old Corrie, the Gagliano cello and whatever else they could salvage from their apartment, to find safety with Jaap de Graaff, Louise Bachiene and the rest of Ada's family at their large beach house in Ouddorp. The trip to the Dutch seaside was an annual event, but this year they knew that they would not return to their apartment in the autumn.

The house was the property of Louise and Jaap. When Pál had first met them they had built a rich and cultured life around themselves in London as philanthropists and patrons of the arts, but they missed the many members of their family who were all living either in France or in Holland. So they decided to buy a holiday house in Ouddorp on the delta island of Goeree-Overflakkee, where the family could stay and could walk across the flat fields to the tall brick lighthouse and the kilometres of white sand that edged the island. From its purchase in 1914 onwards, the house became the focus of the extended family's annual holidays. With the exception of the war years, Corrie would spend every summer there. Later on she would take me there so I could see it for myself, and together we would find the visitors' book that she had signed every year, her handwriting childish at first but then gradually taming itself. We would look back through the names before her birth, amongst the Bachienes and de Graaffs, to see her mother Ada Weevers' neat signature. One year, around the time of Ada's engagement to Pál, his stylish signature appears next to hers. Soon after, she signs herself Ada Hermann.

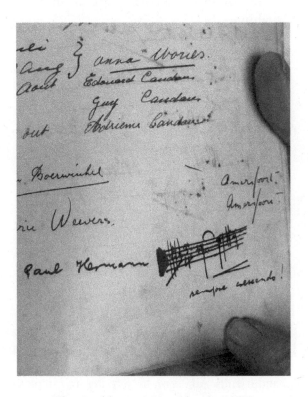

The Ouddorp visitors' book, 1937.
Here Pál writes 'sempre crescendo!'

For Pál and Ada, the darkness of their life in the German capital must have seemed a world away from the tranquillity of the Dutch countryside. There are a couple of photographs of this time, showing a handsome, slender young couple, Pál in a patterned jumper and baggy mid-calf trousers leaning backwards into a haystack, arms folded, smiling proprietorially down at his family, while Ada, in short sleeves with her plaited blonde hair tightly wound round her head, kneels on a picnic rug, holding the hands of a chubby baby Corrie, steadying her on her feet. Another photograph shows Pál smiling out at us from the beach, surrounded by young women, one of whom is Ada. They are all in bathing suits, running, laughing.

Pál and friends. Ada is on his left, her hair in plaits.

A few days after these photographs were taken, the family was engulfed in personal tragedy. Ada and a group of friends had gone to the beach for the day. She and one of her cousins were enjoying a swim when they were caught in a rip tide. They were rescued and pulled to shore by their friends, but Ada had inhaled so much water she was only half alive. The next few months were a nightmare of hospital visits, grief and confusion. Pál visited Ada as often as he could, sitting by her bed in the hospital in The Hague as she gradually lost strength and weight. On one of these occasions, he wrote of being much comforted by his colleague, the soprano Maartje Offers, who sang Brahms lieder to him between hospital visits. Perennially optimistic, Pál wrote to Ada's sister Loes that the fact that Ada was coughing blood was probably a good sign, as it might clear her lungs. Sometimes Pál and Ada talked, but more often they sat together in silence. By October 1933 the silence was final. On 20 October Ada died of exhaustion and pneumonia.

I ask Corrie what she remembers of her mother. She smiles, but her answer is, of necessity, well polished and sadly impersonal. She was little over a year old at the time, and can only rehearse what she has been told, bland phrases that can hardly do justice to a life that had been erased too early. Corrie has been told that Ada loved her family very much, was a dutiful daughter and devoted to Pál. She was obviously intelligent and studious but, as was the convention of the time, had given up her ambition to become a doctor to make her home with her new husband. Beyond these stock images of a conventional, kindly girl, there is nothing left, other than the flashes of wit and observant curiosity that we find in the few letters of hers that survive.

Ada's death left Pál alone at a time when he had no income and no proper home. The Dutch Musicians' Union had a policy to offer work only to Dutch performers, leaving him no possibility of earning a living in the Netherlands. He managed through convoluted means to obtain a visa to work in Brussels in order to take the post of cellist with the Gertler Quartet. Despite the turmoil of his personal life, and the political situation around him, he enjoyed his time with the group, performing and broadcasting his own string quartet alongside works by Haydn, Beethoven and Hindemith. The exposure his compositions were receiving meant that other ensembles, such as the world-class Pro Arte Quartet, were becoming aware of his work, and wanting to perform it. By early 1934 the quartet had toured to Venice and other Italian cities, as well as Amsterdam, Budapest and Marseilles. Pál could travel all over Europe, but as a Jew he could not go back to Germany, and, as a single parent, he could not bring up a toddler while touring and living in hotels. He took little Corrie to Ada's parents in Amersfoort, where Ada's younger sister Loes was to be her guardian. Corrie would grow up with her relatives, in her mother's family home. Pál was adored by the family, and came to stay whenever work permitted, but he would always remain a visitor.

Pál's cheap accommodation in Brussels was not home, and he had few of his belongings around him. Without Ada and Corrie, his cello was all that was familiar, and its voice alone broke the silence in his rented rooms. It was a desperately lonely time. In August 1934, ten months after Ada's death, he wrote a song setting of a poem by Paul Valéry. The text he chose, 'La Ceinture', ends:

Absent, present... Je suis bien seul,
Et sombre, ô suave linceul!

(Absent, present... I am all alone,
and in the gloom, our gentle shroud!)

He dedicated the song to Ada's sister Loes as a gesture of solidarity in their shared grief. As he mourned for his wife, and now for his absent daughter, he found himself growing ever closer to Loes. She was the nearest link to Ada herself, and she and the little ad hoc family he had left behind in Amersfoort came to embody all he had lost. Pál's side of the 1933–4 correspondence with Loes survives, although her replies are lost. They are the writings of a man in exile. The boundaries between loss and love are very porous, and in his loneliness Pál began to imagine himself a part of their world once more, falling in love as much with the idea of the domesticity and security he had so abruptly lost as with Loes herself. His gift of 'La Ceinture' was an articulation of the sorrow that brought them closer together, but it was also a love song.

∿

Corrie's cousin (known as 'Tik') and her parents, Jan and Hinke Weevers, visited the beach house at Ouddorp every year, making the journey up from their village of Monguilhem, to the west of Toulouse. Corrie was delighted to be reunited annually with her French cousin, who, in age, was practically her twin. As an only child, being able to play with Tik out in the countryside around the house was a holiday in itself, and Corrie learnt her first French words from her. Pál would join them as regularly as he could, romping with his daughter and Tik on the beach and in the gardens, and gathering with the others for the big family meals. But always there was the claims of the cello on his time. Pál would practise for hours every day, and Corrie remembers how he would shut the door when he didn't want to be distracted. Desperate to be close to her father on his visits, she recalls her childish anger at what must have felt like rejection. A cloud passes over Corrie's face as she recalls her envy of his cello, which, accompanying Pál everywhere, would have felt his touch far more than his little daughter ever did. The cello is now lost, but I find myself wondering what it would mean to restore the instrument to her now, after all these years, for her to touch the polished wood her father had known more intimately than any human body.

∿

Every year, the family assembled outside the beach house in Ouddorp for a photograph. Taken in 1939, on this occasion

the group smiling at the camera have gathered to celebrate
Jaap and Louise's thirty-seventh wedding anniversary. An urn
of arum lilies has been placed in the front, for added formal-
ity. Tik is at the front on the left, a doll on her knees, and
Corrie is on the right, frowning in the sun, her pigtails tied
back with large ribbons. Pál is in the back row. Tik's father
Jan, strikingly blond, peeps out from behind the others. Loes,
Corrie's surrogate mother, is on the right. Jaap de Graaff sits
at the centre of the photograph, presiding over his family like
a benign monarch. He is dressed in plus fours, a beret at a
slant on his head, and a large, dark flower in his buttonhole.
He is not smiling but his face is kindly, and he is linking arms
with a little boy, Tik's brother, who stands leaning in towards
him. His wife, Louise Bachiene, in pearls and patterned cardi-
gan, sits on his other side.

Once the war was declared and the borders had closed, the
house at Ouddorp was left empty until the Nazis requisitioned
it, when it became the *Kommandantur* (headquarters) for the
island. When the family were finally able to return to it in

1945, they were horrified at what they found. The soldiers had set fire to the house before their departure. It was not until 1952, after the payment of a large war damages grant, that the family were able to regroup there once more for the traditional photograph, taken this time on Corrie's birthday. The two pigtailed little girls of the pre-war photograph, Corrie and Tik, are now twenty and about to start university. There are two notable absences. One is Jaap de Graaff, the head of the family and owner of the house, who had died in 1947. The other is Pál Hermann.

INTERLUDE

Gazing at the Cello I

While with an eye made quiet by the power
Of harmony, and the deep power of joy,
We see into the life of things.

(from William Wordsworth, 'Lines Composed
a Few Miles above Tintern Abbey')

'Prop up your cello and simply look at it', instructs Evangeline Benedetti in her book *Cello, Bow and You*. She advocates observing our cellos in very much the same terms as we might observe our own bodies, calmly centring ourselves by drawing our attention to our different body parts from the head downwards, focusing on our breathing. As we look at our cellos, we are meditating our way around a beautifully proportioned wooden torso. It is no longer in our arms, but balanced, standing alone, away from our embrace. We must simply sit and look at it, learning to be attentive to its curvaceous perfection, its wrinkles and idiosyncrasies.

The exquisite shape is undeniably the first attribute we see, followed by the colour and the patina of the varnish, breathtakingly beautiful, expressions of the maker's artistry and skill tinged by that magical mystique brought about by time. The symmetry of the F holes grabs our attention. These cut-outs resemble the letter f as it was written many years ago. The bridge, the tailpiece, the fingerboard come to our attention as we move our eyes around the instrument. Looking at the whole instrument, the rounded, figure-of-eight-like shape of this beautifully proportioned body, we see a true work of art.[21]

The cello is art, observed at a distance, but where does the observer stop and the instrument start? Does it need us, and the emotion we pour into it?

The critic Susan Sontag writes that 'Contemplation, strictly speaking, entails self-forgetfulness on the part of the spectator: an object worthy of contemplation is one which, in effect, annihilates the perceiving subject. [...] In principle, the audience may not even add its thought. All objects, rightly perceived, are already full.'[22]

All this, before we even ask it to talk to us.

It is possible to appreciate a great instrument as a work of supreme craftsmanship, like a sculpture, or a masterfully crafted and inlaid cabinet. We don't require a sound from it to form an opinion, or to be in awe in its presence. But its appearance does not remain static – it can shift in and out of focus, from familiar to absurdly strange. The great Russian-American cellist Gregor Piatigorsky once, and only once, tried to combine conducting and playing in one concert. He was quite pleased with the overture, his first ever attempt at conducting, but, when he went to fetch his Stradivari for the concerto, 'I faced my instrument in the backstage room almost in confusion, as if it were a piece of furniture I had never seen before.'[23] His perspective had shifted, and what to him had looked like an object utterly familiar while he had been exclusively a cellist, now looked alien and disconcerting.

The language that we use to describe a cello is often as revealing of the instrument's semi-mythical status as it is descriptive of what we see. Cellos can, for instance, be fiery in appearance, the patterns flickering across their wood referred to as 'flames'.[24] A fiery cello is a possibility we can entertain as plausible in spite of the fact that it would actually go up in a puff of smoke like seasoned kindling. (One thinks of William Dewey in Thomas Hardy's poem 'Friends Beyond', who says 'Ye mid burn the wold bass-viol that I set such vallie by.')

My first cello teacher once ran into her burning house, pregnant, to rescue her instrument. It was a controversial but instinctive impulse: she would no more leave her cello than she would a baby. The image of it has stayed with me since childhood. I remember sitting wide-eyed in my lesson as she told me, sneaking glances at her cello in the hope of seeing scorch marks. In my mind at least, there is a continuum between her cello being rescued from the flames, and the ingrained fiery patterns that often lick the body of a cello. Is it a phoenix, rising untouchable from ashes? Or something devilish? My own first cello had flames flickering from its central joint like stripes. I used to call it 'Tiger', and I like to think that I had Blake in mind, and imagined my cello, sinuous and powerful, stalking fierily through the forests of the night. But it was probably given its name for the prosaic reason that its back was orange and stripy.

When we pick up our instrument and play it, the cello resonates through our breastbone, and our heart beats through the cello. It is a hollow organ, placed against other such organs: the heart, stomach, lungs. It is made to work, and the air in it to move, powered by the strokes of the bow, its breath. We must breathe to play, to oxygenate our muscles, to impel the bow, to shape the phrases.

Without raising the eyebrows of anyone who objects to the anthropomorphizing of instruments, we can safely say of a cello that it is evidence of the presence of a human mind operating at the time of fabrication. A cello is, in short, both in and part of culture, and history. An object so resonant with meaning that it can reflect ourselves and our society, functioning both as a mirror and as a portal into the past.

Cellos (and other stringed instruments, for that matter) have a human anatomy: neck, shoulders, head and ribs, back, belly, body. Even the soundpost (the word for the little piece of wood inside the body of the instrument that is held in tension between the back and front) translates in French, Italian and Spanish as the 'soul' of the instrument. Most stringed instruments have elements of the symmetry of human form, and an anatomical vocabulary to match, but only the cello is the same size as the person playing it. In fact the 'cello' is an actual, named body shape. One can be blessed (or not, depending on how you feel about it) with a pear-shaped figure, or a cello-shaped torso, and must dress accordingly. Human cellos are big-breasted and big-hipped, with a short waist, curvaceous and sensuous. (Fashion experts advise us that a cello-shaped woman should go for halterneck dresses with a wide belt, as their best look.)

However, while a cello figure might look good in a dress, the instrument itself is an androgynous dichotomy between the tenor and baritone voices and a female form. Justus Johann Friedrich Dotzauer said in 1826 that 'the sound of the cello's A and D strings are heart-melting, and have a character flattering to the ear. It is in this register, which corresponds to the tenor voice, that the artist, filled with emotion, is capable of speaking to the heart.' So a cello might 'sound' male, despite resembling a woman. Ethnomusicologist Regula Quereshi cites an example of an instrument that has come to be gendered through association: the Indian sarangi (a type of bowed lute) was used to accompany courtesans singing. Quereshi found that now, to those with a sense of its cultural heritage, it sounds female. Its history has dictated its gender.[25]

In southern India, wealthy families might encourage their daughters to learn to play the vina – an instrument rather like a cello. It is a kind of lute that carries associations of graceful femininity. This is because it not only resembles the female form but was said to have been created actively to represent it. Lord Shiva modelled it on his wife, the goddess Parvati. Its slender neck represents her body, and two gourds, in which the air resonates, stand in for her breasts.

The cello's representative abilities extend beyond binary gender – far beyond the human form, in fact. Piatigorsky described how it can signify almost anything.

> The cello can be a perfect breath of death, as in the concluding notes of Richard Strauss's *Don Quixote*. Of Hindemith's Variations on 'A Frog He Went A-Courting', a critic said that the cello had no trouble whatever in turning into a bullfrog. Napoleon, listening to the famous cellist Duport, is supposed to have said, 'You have made an ox sound like a nightingale.' The cello's gift of metaphor and personification ranges from swan, clown, king, horse, or courtesan. As for me, the violoncello is a part of all things, and a central substance of this universe.[26]

Whether their cellos are male or female (or an ox or a swan, for that matter), it seems that, in the minds of players, there is often no real correlation between the player's gender and the one that they ascribe to their instrument. Pablo Casals's instrument was definitely male. 'I have played my cello more than half a century,' he said. 'He is my companion. And I love him, and he loves me, yes. He loves me, and he sounds well to make me happy.'

I put the question to British soloist Steven Isserlis. 'What is your cello to you?'

He didn't hesitate: 'My cello is my alter ego. I think it's male, just because of the lowness of the voice. I know it's female and curvaceous, but I don't like to think of my cello in erotic terms, as I spend so long with it between my legs! It's my spiritual alter ego.'

Julian Lloyd Webber felt his cello was his best friend. He told me how, when he owned the Stradivari known as the 'Barjansky', he 'tried to keep it comfortable, like a person'. The Portuguese cellist Guilhermina Suggia asked for her Stradivari to be placed on her bed alongside her as she died. It was her companion in life and in death, sharing the most intensely lonely experience a human can endure.

When we imbue objects with personality and enmesh them in what we might call 'a texture of social relationships', we give them a form of social agency.[27] This anthropomorphism isn't exclusive to the cello of course. Maxim Vengerov describes his relationship with his Stradivari violin (the 'Kreutzer' of 1727) as a marriage. On the other hand, when American violinist Nathan Milstein decided to change instruments, things got positively steamy: 'My love for this violin did not diminish. It was just that after years with a sparkling, eager blonde, I came to feel that I should turn to a more sombre and perhaps quieter and more composed, sedate brunette.'[28] In some cultures, the sexual affair between Milstein and his violin is pushed much further. Ritual flutes from Papua New Guinea, for instance, are played in pairs by a man and a woman, the man using a particular 'hocketing' technique, supposed to mimic sex.[29] When Piatigorsky showed a friend a photograph of him 'tenderly embracing' two cellos, the friend exclaimed: 'WHAT is it? A menage a trois? Bigamy? A harem?' Piatigorsky goes on to observe that: 'The cello in Russian is a "she." But where the cello is concerned, linguistic definitions mean little. For instance, although in English the cello is an "it", when Beatrice Harrison, the English cellist, spoke to me about her instrument, she cried out, "I love him."'[30]

Anthropologist Ivan Gaskell writes that 'Those who would see into the life of things cannot confine themselves to the taxonomic domains of biology, for there is life, in senses numinous or sacred, well beyond their confines.'[31] Beyond Western culture, it is far more frequent for inanimate objects to be endowed with life. At the same time, objects are created to represent humans, a vicarious life-giving.

Can a cello have a life, or are we simply lacking in imagination, transforming everything we see into object-versions of ourselves, transcribing our alive-ness onto the things around us? I undertook an international poll of cellists to establish whether anthropomorphizing their instruments was as common as I suspected. I found that, for every cellist who was sure the very idea was utterly ridiculous, there were many others who played a 'Charlie', a 'Gretel', a 'Godiva', an 'Alfred' or a 'Julie'. What was most striking was the strength of feeling, on both sides of the debate.[32]

We can learn something of the relationship of the player to their instrument from the way they describe their cello. Depending on the player, their instrument might variously be a beloved pet animal, a child, a spouse, a body-double or body extension, or an alter ego. We can specifically gender our instruments by carving on them likenesses of body parts. The scrolls of certain stringed instruments – viols, for instance – are sometimes carved like heads. In fact, whole families of viols are precisely that – families – their nodding wooden heads peering over the shoulders of their players. No wonder we anthropomorphize our cellos, their modern-day successors. In other instances, we use the weighty reliability of the male of our species to reassure ourselves that society is in good hands – bells such as Big Ben in London and Old Tom in Oxford are rarely if ever flighty females. In other cultures the gendering is a little more subtle. Instruments can be made from specifically gendered trees: the warlike Kweli drum from Chad, in East Africa, is made from male acacia trees. Other instruments blur the boundaries of gender. The Tibetan Damaru drum is most disturbingly androgynous, being made from two human skulls – a man's and a woman's.

Cellists are physically altered by their cello playing, or so Piatigorsky maintains:

> It has been said that many a profession leaves its imprint on a man's character – even his appearance. [...] A cellist too is quite unmistakable. There is a touch of nostalgia that can be recognized like a scar, left from a long battle – often a losing one – against the odds of his instrument. His melancholic disposition is particularly apparent when he has to perform something spirited and gay, often found in passages written in such awkward positions as to make them sound sad enough for tears.[33]

When I was a student at the Royal College of Music, there was a porter who manned the front desk, and prided himself on guessing, just by looking at them, what instrument the students who came into the building played (this game only worked, of course, when they were not carrying their instrument cases). He was invariably right, and could spot a clarinettist, opera singer or violinist from a mile off. Although I wasn't aware of the cellists looking particularly mournful, he identified my friends and me without hesitation.

Paris I – Lise Cristiani

November 2021

After ten days in Berlin, Verena and I part company at the Hauptbahnhof. The next stop on my journey is Paris, where I am on the trail of Lise Cristiani. She had caused a sensation when she had toured across Europe with her cello in her early twenties. She was internationally famous during her lifetime, but now she is remembered only through the name of her cello, and the dedication of one particular cello-and-piano piece by Mendelssohn, a 'Song without Words'.[34] It was here in Paris, on St Valentine's Day in 1845, that Lise made her debut. Before this point, very few women had played the cello professionally, and only one name is really known at all: that of Therese-Rosalie Pain (1773–1859). Pain performed at the beginning of the nineteenth century, but only in private salons, never as the central attraction on a public stage.[35] At the time of her debut, Lise Cristiani was seventeen: the same age as I was when I began to play professionally in public. I indirectly owe my choice of instrument to her trailblazing, for it was her pan-European touring that introduced the very idea of the female cellist. What I find so fascinating about her concert career, as I piece together the snippets of reviews, is that, even in the course of a few years, she seems to have turned her particular brand of playing from a novelty into a blueprint for future female cellists.

As my train slows its pace and we approach the Gare de l'Est, I gather up my cello ready to head towards the site of the Salle Herz, the concert hall in which Lise's cello was first seen and heard in her hands. The Salle was in the ninth arrondissement, a few blocks back from the busiest shop-ping streets around the Boulevard Haussmann. A short walk from Métro Notre-Dame-de-Lorette and close to the Palais Garnier, it is a distinguished area, with ornately carved town houses exuding wealth and grandeur. The road on which the hall was built, Rue de la Victoire, is a narrow side street, over-shadowed by the height of its buildings on either side. It is hard to know exactly where the hall was, but it definitely isn't there now. Henri Herz, the pianist who built it using the wealth from his successful piano workshop to create his own venue, lived above his hall at no. 38.[36] But at some point the street was renumbered, and 38 merged into 48. Now it's an impersonal marble-clad office building, with glass doors and a spacious, deserted entrance hall. I stand outside for a while, but there's absolutely no sign of life on a Saturday, and it doesn't look like the kind of place that would take kindly to a woman with a cello on her back wanting to poke around inside. However, it's hard to believe that such an important hall has vanished so entirely. Lise's debut was only one of the historic events to take place within its gold-painted, candlelit walls. Hector Berlioz premiered compositions there, such as his overture *Le Carnaval romain* on 18 January 1844, and the oratorio *L'Enfance du Christ* a decade later. Surely it merits at least a small plaque? But after my experience with the map of lost concert halls in Berlin, I should know better. There is an alternative world of forgotten music and lost sound under the stones of most cities.

> The day before yesterday, in the Salle Herz we heard Miss Lise Cristiani – a young and [beautiful] person with an inspired manner. [...] Miss Cristiani possesses a distinguished style, a rare talent for performance and what is better still, that deep sensitivity and artistic hallmark which are only seen among a few of the finest women.[37]

The Salle Herz (or Salle des concerts Herz, to give it its full, and romantic-sounding, name) was once a large recital hall, capable of seating over 650, and had opened only seven years before Lise played there. It closed for a year of repairs in 1885, but when it reopened the following year, another competing hall had been built (oddly enough named after another Herz – this time the Salle Philippe Herz). When Henri Herz died in 1888, his Salle Herz became financially unviable without the driving force of its founder. There is some uncertainty about when it was actually demolished, but as I stand outside the building that has replaced it, I see that the portico boasts the following words carved into its central stone: 'Compagnie d'Assurances, fondée en 1881'. The growth of the insurance company necessitated a bigger building, and the site of the Salle Herz proved to be the ideal location.

To one side of the building is the huge and ornate Synagogue de la Victoire, but on the other side is a gateway leading from the pavement to a courtyard behind what is now the offices that replaced Salle Herz. The arched wooden doors, designed for a horse and carriage, are ajar, so I step inside, to see if there are any further clues. As I do so, a caretaker with a mop and bucket walks out of a side door. I explain in questionable French what it is I'm doing here, and I show him a lithograph of Lise Cristiani. He studies it carefully and, to my surprise, disappears back into the doorway, returning with a plastic chair. 'Here, why don't you play?' So I do. I play *Prière* and *Bolero* by Offenbach, Donizetti's plaintive tenor aria 'Una furtiva lagrima' and Schubert's gently lilting lied 'Ständchen', all of which Lise had adapted as her cello repertoire for her debut.

An exclusive gathering took place last Friday at the Salle de Herz as Miss Cristiani set aflutter the strings of her 'cello, with which she is so seductive. Sometimes she moves you to tears, sometimes harmonious tones warm your heart; whether it be a lively Iberian bolero, a sweetly inspiring romance, a thought, a feeling. Miss Cristiani was met with a frenzy of well-deserved applause.[38]

The caretaker isn't moved to tears or indeed a frenzy of applause, but he does tap his foot as he fills his bucket from the outside tap. He listens for a bit, then quietly continues to mop the tiles around me, whistling along through his teeth, and nodding at me every now and then for encouragement, as if it were the most natural thing in the world to have a cellist appear from nowhere to play to him as he goes about his business.

❧

Lise Cristiani had grown up Lise (or Elise) Barbier, the surname of the grandparents who looked after her following the premature deaths of her parents. But she returned to her baptismal name of 'Chrétien', changing it to the modishly Italianate 'Cristiani' for her debut. Lise's grandfather Nicolas-Alexandre Barbier and uncle Jules-Paul were active members of the arts world in Paris in the 1840s, and were well aware that spectacle attracted audiences.[39] If they could exploit her youth and attractiveness to catch the public's interest, they would all stand to benefit financially. Having decided that – although she was musical – the young Lise was never going to excel at the piano or as a singer, they decided to present her to the world as the first female concert cellist.

Her grandfather apparently alighted on this idea while looking at German paintings of musicians in a Paris art gallery, noting that, in art at least, the image of a woman with a cello seemed to be acceptable (after all, St Cecilia herself was supposed to have played the bass viol). This may have been the actual inspiration for his granddaughter's career, or it may be fabrication, to lend legitimacy to his marketing experiment. Either way, he rightly anticipated that art was the only frame of reference for a female cellist at the time – the phenomenon that became cellist Lise Cristiani stepped straight out of a canvas.[40] Having made up his mind as to her career, her grandfather immediately set about putting his plan into action. Bernard Benazet, a cellist with the Italian Theatre Orchestra, was hired to give lessons to the fourteen-year-old Lise. They fell out after only a year of instruction, but just three years later, an impossibly short time for even a prodigy to master an instrument to a high level, Lise was deemed ready for her debut at the Salle Herz. Her outfit for the occasion was a white dress, appropriately befitting a virginal St Cecilia. One review even mockingly fantasized a kind of tableau vivant modelled on a painting:

> What one must advise Mademoiselle Cristiani is to play on the violoncello to her admirers, who must be numerous, a tender, gentle A minor romance on the A string, to raise her eyes to heaven like Saint Cecilia in the face of martyrdom, and her success will be pyramidal; she will find the model of that religious, poetic and musical pose in a very beautiful painting by a famous Italian master.[41]

In the few reviews that survive of Lise's concerts, the same preoccupations dominate. She is an ornament, feminine and diverting, flirting with her instrument in beguiling and becoming gestures as she caressed and stroked the strings. It's hard, in fact, to get any sound that will carry out of a cello with caressing and stroking – even the most basic bow stroke is a more muscular and committed gesture, and yet, in the hands of a young woman, the movement has become something sexual.

Cristiani made her appearance in the Parisian musical world with her brand fully fledged, clearly having decided to meet and exceed expectations of the male gaze. However, the irony at the heart of her career was that her perfectly feminine presentation as the first female cellist had been determined by the men in her family. As I wade through the reviews of distracted male critics who were unable to tear themselves away from descriptions of her winsome appearance, I find that I am no nearer a sense of her as a person, let alone an objective appraisal of her as a musician. What I *do* learn is that she is judged against the gendered preconceptions of what a cello should sound like, and the impossibility of a woman's playing being able to fit into that masculine template.

> Mademoiselle Cristiani is a young, tall person, pretty, even beautiful [...] We do not quite know how to tell her: that the affectation, the mannerisms, the fancied glissandi, the feeble and doubtful intonation are not at all in keeping with the character of the violoncello; and we can hardly encourage her to handle this instrument generously and seriously; for instance, to tackle the low strings with force instead of meowing the prières and boleros like a pretty white kitten – knowing that all this is hardly befitting the fair sex.[42]

Lise Cristiani cannot win. She must not play like a man, but when she plays like a woman (or even a mewing kitten, apparently), she must be criticized for it, as the cello is inherently masculine, and she is denaturing it by daring to impose her feline affectations on this manly instrument. Even this is not straightforward, however. Another critic maintains that the cello is, obviously, a female instrument; in fact, a female cellist is altogether more natural – sexier even – than a woman with a violin:

> The character of the violoncello with its soft, wailing, touchingly mellow tone is certainly more feminine than the shrill, wildly effervescent violin, which one has heard played by ladies, and what should give the cello an undeniable advantage over all musical instruments in the eyes of the ladies, is that it has the advantage of allowing the executor (or executrix) the most graceful posture, on the whole the most elegant, rounded

movements of the arm and the most advantageous, natural, eye-catching placement of a beautiful hand.[43]

Clearly not all the men thrown into a frenzy at the sight of a teenage girl with a cello found it monstrous. Later, when she played in Berlin, another male critic found her sex to be part of her appeal:

> I was myself witness to the striking impression her personality and her playing, which are difficult to separate one from the other, have upon the audience. Whether she be a fervent artist producing soft and soulful tones on the 'cello, or a mischievous young girl stirring in the confines of the home, it is the magic of pure femininity which has bestowed a companion charm upon both the artist and the girl.[44]

Lithograph image of Lise Cristiani from the
Wiener Illustrierte Theaterzeitung, 10 May 1845.

There are only a few images of Lise Cristiani. One lithograph in particular was splashed all over Paris and Berlin
in advance of her appearances there. It was the carefully
curated equivalent of a publicity photo. Many attended her
concerts with the expectation that a girl with a cello would
be an ugly, inelegant sight. She had to prove that she was not
a freak show, and she appears generally to have succeeded.
In the words of the critic of the *Allgemeine Musikalische
Zeitung*: 'First of all, it should be noted that the expectation
of seeing an unattractive spectacle, which many had certainly harboured, was completely refuted.'[45] The following
year, he added:

> A cellist from Paris – pretty and young – [...] must be an
> exciting and interesting phenomenon. We have already read
> a lot about her original appearance, and even seen her picture
> taken in Paris, which she placed in every Berlin postcard shop
> after her arrival in the form of a tasteful lithograph.[46]

Predictably, as the first female solo cellist, Lise met with
both enthusiasm and opposition, with opinion equally
divided as to whether she was any good. Some critics describe
an international soloist, others find an attractive young girl,
famous simply for her novelty value. And then there's the
topic of perennial fascination (for male critics at least): did
she or did she not open her legs? Side-saddle or full-frontal
cello playing – which was it? The obsession with what went
on under her voluminous skirts may be prurient, but the
question of what method women used to play the cello is an
important one in our search for understanding the cultural
significance of cello playing.

> Most of the audience thought it must look a little frivolous,
> having completely forgotten that Cristiani was a lady and wore
> a flowing dress for her special purpose, which concealed all the

contours of her body, and that it must therefore necessarily look much prettier and more graceful when a lady kneels around the violoncello than when a man does.[47]

The artist who created her portrait has depicted the folds of her gown very carefully, to make the protrusion of a knee impossible to detect accurately. What goes on below the waist is a secret, and not for us to know. Above stairs, her collar is high and demure, her face serious but beautiful. She is, in short, beyond criticism, not done up like a doll, or overtly sexualized, but deliberately respectable and elegant. The focus of the etching is the cello, Lise looking away in profile, too modest to fix us with her gaze. She poses as if listening to her own music and inviting us to do the same, presenting the instrument as the focus. Her gender is not the point – her Stradivari is.

∾

Lise Cristiani was as much a spectacle as she was a cellist, and her playing was part of the act. She seems to have fully understood that to choose robust, full-blooded pieces, or to play aggressively or even vigorously, would have been too transgressive to meet with approval. She deliberately devised a repertoire, technique and sound that allowed her to forge for herself a specifically feminine niche.

The reviews reveal two things: both how difficult it was for her to find favour, and how skilfully she trod a path between the misogyny and the adoration. I scoured them for phrases that might shed light on the choices she made as to how to play, and found the same words recurring. Her playing is (almost obsessively) 'soft', then often elegiac, skilful, graceful, plaintive, heart-touching, with pleasant, singing tone (for the sceptical this might be whiny, or too light). 'Ease' and 'grace' crop up with regularity (for the more spiteful, her facility is a 'frivolous' ease).

Lise selected pieces that would make the cello sing, usually set within the range of the female vocal register. 'The virtuoso almost completely avoids the use of the two lowest strings. On the contrary, she almost always plays only on the two highest strings and uses the harmonics so often that the character of the instrument is almost completely blurred.' Was she consciously creating a mezzo-soprano repertoire for her instrument? Yes, it may be a cello, she seems to be saying, but my billowing skirts mask its relationship to my body, and, although it's made of wood, it's really a feminine, curvaceous wooden mezzo.

Her choices of programme are oddly unvaried, by today's standards, deliberately missing out the flashy and furious that would give a recital a change of pace. Instead, she almost invariably chose lyrical, technically undemanding, graceful pieces. 'She has a beautiful cantabile, often very expressive, an unconstrained, light bowing and quiet agility on her instrument. The more energetic expression is far from her, of course, because it is the masculine one.'[48]

I can gain a physical sense of what it would have been to play like Lise, as her repertoire choices of slow arias and lieder dictate playing with an unhurried legato lyricism, but it is next to impossible to find an objective account of her as a musician from the reviews. One of them summarizes the conflict even in the minds of the critics themselves:

Now that the general hysteria has passed, we realize as we look at it in the cold light of day, that we were ourselves left cold. This is because, say those who understand such things, Miss Cristiani has neither the mental gifts, nor poetic inspiration, that her playing, when considered from a position of elevated musical sensitivity, lacks character, energy and insistence. In short, they say that Miss Cristiani is one of those artistic phenomena who owe their appeal to their physical appearance. Other people who understand these things, claim that Miss

Cristiani is a prodigy, that her 'cello sings a siren's song like that of Malibran, that her technique could compete with that of Servais or Romberg, and so on. The truth will doubtless lie somewhere between these two verdicts.[49]

Regardless of her actual abilities as a musician, Lise Cristiani was obliged to navigate a world in which reviewers and audiences were either obsessed with her appearance or determined to 'out' her as talentless, and merely a curiosity. In Paris, the hype surrounding her performances was bound to elicit a furious backlash from the straight-laced men who saw themselves as the custodians of decency. A woman cellist? Where would the madness end? 'After Cristiani's progress', wrote one indignant critic, 'it should no longer surprise us if tomorrow a lady plays the French horn, the viola or even the timpani.'[50]

൭

Lise's debut at Salle Herz was such a huge success that she was soon receiving invitations to play across Paris and beyond. She made so much money from all these engagements that she was able to replace her average cello with the Stradivari that would take her name. Turning down other provincial French engagements, she travelled straight to Vienna, then on to Linz, Regensburg, Baden-Baden and Leipzig, where she performed at the Gewandhaus in 1845. Felix Mendelssohn was in the audience. Shortly afterwards, he wrote the 'Song without Words' that bears his dedication to her.[51] The piece is not only a tribute to her, but an artist's impression. He has captured her style. It is vocal, gentle, without bravura, elegant, with harmonics. It is 'soft' (that dreadful word again), and relies on the top two strings of the cello. The fault-finding of the critics helps us towards a definition of her style, and with their adjectives in mind it becomes obvious that Mendelssohn has embodied Lise's sound in his writing.[52] She performed it frequently, and it became her calling card, specific only to her, as it remained unpublished until 1868. By then, both she and Mendelssohn had died.

Reading the critics' phrases again, as they struggle to artic-ulate the gender confusion that Lise's playing elicits, I find Mendelssohn's 'Song without Words' weaving through my mind. Perhaps, if the fiendishly difficult repertoire that Pál Hermann championed ninety years later had existed, and the society of her day would have permitted her to play it, she might have swapped her elegant, wafting tones for a physical performance style more natural to a woman who was later to demonstrate extraordinary stamina and determination. But even Jacqueline du Pré, first amongst the gutsy female cel-lists, ran into the same problems that Lise foresaw before her debut on 14 February 1845. Du Pré, adored by many, also faced criticism for playing that was too sensuous and embod-ied making love to her instrument. She was too earthy, too natural. The carefully constructed distance that Lise Cristiani maintained between herself and her cello through her clothes and her repertoire choices was precisely what allowed her to survive, and to make a living. There was to be no passionate lovemaking in Lise's performances, merely a chaste kiss on the hand.

However, while Lise's body is a world away from Jacqueline du Pré's ecstatic entwining with her cello, she does seem to mirror her instrument – the curves of its wooden torso finding a parallel in the language with which her playing is so frequently described. Her physical relationship to the instru-ment is frequently imagined in terms of its shape: her bowing arm is sophisticated and curvaceous ('the bowing shows us the wavy lines, which a beautiful hand can make quite grace-fully and elegantly'), her tone soft, warm and rounded, like the cello's smooth contours.[53]

Lise Cristiani's rise to fame was meteoric. From her Parisian debut until her death, she would be travelling, always with

'Monseigneur Stradivarius' (as she called 'him') by her side. What had begun as an arranged marriage between cello and player evolved over the course of her all-too-short career into a passionate love match. I am reminded of the Berlin reviewer fascinated by her Stradivari, alone on the concert platform, looking at the audience through 'melancholic' F-hole eyes: the instrument, before the woman, taking centre stage. Where does Lise Cristiani stop and the cello begin? Alongside Mendelssohn's music, Lise's Stradivari is one of the few traces that remain of her once celebrated life; her cello itself is an embodiment of a 'Song without Words', bearing witness, and making wordless connections across time and continents.

Paris II – Pál Hermann

Lise Cristiani's story is not the only reason I am in Paris. I am also here on the trail of Pál Hermann, who moved to France in 1937. Soon I will be standing, cello in one hand, a bundle of letters in the other, outside some apartments in the seventeenth arrondissement. I have only the fact that Pál wrote a handful of Parisian addresses as his temporary residences on his correspondence to make these buildings stand out in my imagination from the identical apartments on either side. Their anonymity is representative of his story, as in an odd parallel to Lise Cristiani before him, his life and career have been almost completely erased. I don't know what it is I want these addresses to say to me, but I feel that, if I walk these streets, carrying my cello on the routes he would have taken with his, I can keep pace with him, momentarily. The ripples through time in which he existed might once more be stirred up, even for a moment.

After leaving Germany in 1933, Pál, Ada and Corrie went back to the safety of Ada's family in the Netherlands, living in Ouddorp and Amersfoort. But after Ada's death, and with no permission to earn a living in the Netherlands, Pál moved alone to Brussels and then on to Paris in 1937. Perhaps he intended to settle here, in the belief that conditions in Paris were better for Jewish musicians than elsewhere in Europe. The move was very much in keeping with patterns of Jewish migration at the time. Despite the lingering stain of the Dreyfus Affair, which had dominated French political life at the turn of the century and revealed the ingrained anti-Semitism lurking beneath the surface in institutions such as the military and the police, France was still welcoming to Jewish immigrants in the years leading up to the Second World War. So many Frenchmen had died in the previous war that immigration was seen as a way of filling holes in the job market and rebuilding the shattered economy. The Parisian arts scene was characterized by its diversity and multi-nationalism, which became part of its exoticism and charm. As it happened, Paris was to be the last city in which Pál would be celebrated, and have a prominent role to play in the world of performance.

It's not easy to piece together Pál Hermann's movements during this period of his career. I have my handful of addresses but little else. Before I can pull together the fragmentary traces of his life in Paris, I need to compile every anecdote, family photograph and review, in order to trace his story. And to help me piece the snippets of information together, his ninety-year-old daughter Corrie is coming to join me.

᠕

As I wait at the Gare du Nord for Corrie's train to arrive, a fine snow starts to fall. Eddying in little whirls through the glass doors and carried into the station on people's boots, it turns quickly to a muddy slush. Corrie is coming from Holland, bringing with her the little bundle of manuscripts that are all she has of the father she last saw when she was seven years old. Her train slows to a stop and she springs out, setting an impressive pace, wheeled suitcase bumping along behind her. Corrie Hermann is a formidable woman, in the best possible sense. Highly intelligent and cultured, she is at home speaking in French, English or Dutch. She combines a kindly, no-nonsense pragmatism – reflective of her two careers as doctor and politician – with a contagious enthusiasm and zest for adventure. It is hard to believe she is not at least ten years younger than she is.

Once we've settled into our hotel, which is close to the opera house at Bastille, we set to work. Corrie spreads out all the manuscripts she has brought with her: black and white photographs of Pál and Ada; concert programmes in a variety of European languages from the 1920s and 30s; yellowing newspaper reviews; postcards and letters in Pál's neat handwriting from all over Europe; and finally, a handful of letters from the 1950s – the official correspondence Corrie herself received when trying to find out what had happened to her father during the war. As we stumble through a mixture of Dutch, German and French translations, Corrie and I begin to find the clues we need about his Parisian life in exile from Nazi Berlin.

By the time Pál and Ada Hermann arrived at Ouddorp for the summer of 1933, only two of Pál's compositions had been published.[54] He had frequently played his works with chamber ensembles, and performed his duos with Székely, but in the midst of all the international touring there had been no time – and no obvious necessity – to publish his manuscripts. As a result, in correspondence and concert programmes there are mentions of pieces he performed that are now lost. I had initially assumed that he might have left them in Berlin, but amongst Corrie's documents we find a letter from October 1933 to her aunt Loes, in which Pál talks of a performance in Brussels that will include his duo, his string quartet and a solo cello sonata. Today, only the duo's whereabouts is known. Corrie and I find a programme from a London performance the year before, in which he performed the missing cello sonata. It gives an intriguing clue to the nature of the work, which bears the rather lonely title 'Sonata for 'Cello Alone', and has an intriguing set of movements: Prelude, Lute and Finale.[55]

Corrie's personal memories of her father are of his annual visits to the family summer residence at Ouddorp, and his frequent trips to her grandparents' house in Amersfoort. She never went to Paris while her father was living there, so this is a voyage of discovery for us both. We are reliant on Pál's post-cards and letters from Paris to provide clues to his itinerant, unsettled existence here, moving from one rented apartment or room to another. From the addresses on Corrie's docu-ments we see that between 1937 and 1939 he lived in at least three different homes: 7 Rue Philibert Delorme, 26 Rue de Lübeck and 7 Rue Alfred Bruneau.

The shadows are lengthening on the pavements outside our hotel by the time Corrie and I are ready to begin our journey. We settle ourselves in a taxi, and Corrie explains to the driver what it is we're doing. She leans back to whisper to me conspiratorially: 'I hope this isn't a red hare.' It's her fabu-lous variant on the more familiar 'red herring' – and a phrase I hope will catch on. As we drive, I wonder what it is we're both looking for, and whether we can indeed find it. I hardly expect to discover a plaque, or to be ushered into a flat that would have been exactly as Pál had left it (although either would be fantastic). We are mapping him, pinning down his life on a plan of Paris, perhaps in the hope of finding the imprint of him, the traces of his impression on this city. But travelling these streets, I start to wonder whether the journey is more an act of creativity than discovery, whether we're in fact creating a shadow for Pál Hermann by giving shape and form to the memories Corrie does not have of his life in Paris. Somehow, by taking her to the streets that were familiar to him, I can offer her some new thoughts, some fresh memories, many years after her childhood ones have settled into a carefully curated mental photograph album – cherished, but full of gaps and silences.

◡

Our first destination is Rue Philibert Delorme, a narrow, one-way avenue, sandwiched between shop-lined boulevards and lined by imposing blocks of white modernist apartments, which would have been state of the art in the 1930s. Pál lived at no. 7, according to two postcards from July and September 1938. It may well have been here that he wrote his 1938 harpsichord composition for Marcelle de Lacour, an instrumentalist who, like Pál, toured Europe combining historic repertoire with new compositions. As well as Pál Hermann's piece, dedicated to her 'avec toute mon admiration', she had work written for her by Francis Poulenc and Bohuslav Martinů. As we discover these connections with some of the most distinguished musicians of the era, it is impossible not to wonder how different Pál's fate might have been had the German invasion not intervened. Perhaps he would have been offered a position at the Paris Conservatoire, like de Lacour, teaching baroque as well as contemporary music, providing him with a steady income and putting an end to his unsettled lifestyle.

Corrie and I stand silently outside the great building that includes apartment no. 7. There is no answer when we ring the bell. Eventually, someone comes out of the front door, giving us a searching look. We return to the waiting taxi, and head from south to north for the second address: 26 Rue de Lübeck. Situated in one of the richest arrondissements of Paris, the sixteenth, Rue de Lübeck is dominated by buildings dating from the 1860s and the Belle Époque, but the architecture of no. 26 is modernist – a curving 1920s block of white flats. Pál's rental choices may have been driven by financial constraint, but these buildings don't look run down or particularly cheap. It feels more likely to have been an expression of his personality; the man who premiered so much modern music, and wrote it himself, seemed to be most at home amongst modernist buildings.

Rue de Lübeck turns out to be only a short walk from one of the venues he performed in: the Salle de la Revue Musicale, at no. 70 Avenue Kléber near the Arc de Triomphe. In Pál Hermann's day it was a private venue, possibly in some great patron's home, particularly dedicated to performances of new music. It is a grand, double-fronted terraced mansion, which, as we find out, now houses a café in the bottom right-hand corner.

Back to the taxi, and on we go, across Place d'Iéna, past the Chaillot National Theatre. Our taxi driver is getting into the spirit of the search now. At each of our new destinations he jumps out with me to ring on doorbells and enquire in neighbouring shops. He wants to know all about Pál Hermann, and Corrie is happy to oblige, telling him about her father in impeccable French. I look out of the window at Paris in the deepening glow of evening, the energy and excitement of the place as it puts away the concerns of the day and begins to reinvent itself for the night. I picture Pál living right at the very heart of it all, walking these streets with his cello case at his side, lonely and bereaved, but nourished by the new musical colleagues he was acquiring, and the performance opportunities Paris afforded.

'Rue Alfred Bruneau!' announces our driver. We leave Corrie in the car as it's now raining, and he and I locate no. 7, another large, white, modern building. This is probably where Pál was living when, in 1939, he wrote 'Ophélie', an elaborate song for soprano and orchestra, although he did not finish the orchestration and only a piano version survives.[56] Having spent as long outside as seems reasonable in the wet, and acknowledging that there are no further clues, we make our way back through the rain-soaked streets. Our driver is now so invested in our story that he has found a recording of Pál's *Suite for Recorders* on Spotify. The woody, hollow purity of the recorders wafts ethereally around the car, accompanied by the swish of wet tyres. Corrie is sitting quietly, hands clasped together. I can't tell whether she is enjoying the music or not. She is usually very matter of fact, almost forthright, but now I can't quite read her mood. We sit side by side, lost in our own thoughts, watching the rain fall through the streetlights on either side of the wide boulevard.

﹏

During the summer of 1939 it had been difficult for Pál to get a visa to visit Holland, as the international situation rapidly deteriorated. He finally worked round all the regulations in time to reach Corrie to celebrate her seventh birthday on 4 August. There was tremendous excitement at his impending arrival at the beach house in Ouddorp. When Corrie's aunt Loes drove in her little two-seater car to pick him up from the ferry that joined the island to mainland Rotterdam, Corrie was allowed to accompany her, and remembers her father sitting in the 'dickie seat' (as she puts it) of the two-seater, his long legs curled round his cello, his hair streaming in the wind.

One particular memory from this visit seems to stand out for Corrie and she returns to it repeatedly in our conversations. Her father had brought a birthday copy of the French children's story *Babar the Elephant* with him to Ouddorp, and she was delighted with it. *Babar* had been written eight years before by Jean de Brunhoff, for his own children. Pál read to Corrie how a hunter killed Babar's mother in his presence and the little elephant ran away to the city. Corrie remembers the book as her first stumbling attempt to read French, guided by her father. For her, it is infused with his voice, an imaginary world they briefly shared together. If there were parallels with her own loss of her mother, she chose not to think of them.

Corrie can still vividly recall the laughter and sense of

celebration during these precious days with her father. But there was also a dim feeling of foreboding hanging over the summer of 1939. She remembers the sudden departure of relatives who would ordinarily have stayed to swim and enjoy the house for the whole summer. Corrie believes that her father's visits to Ouddorp during those years in exile in Brussels and Paris must have been like stepping back into the life that had been taken from him. She tells me that, growing up, she was very aware that she didn't have a regular father who lived with her like the other girls, but she remembers the intensity of her joy during those longed-for reunions. Pál would play games with her, was full of jokes and fun, and always brought her new toys and books. Eighty years later, she still has dolls and bears that he brought her: permanent physical representatives of a father who could not remain with her. Corrie's face lights up as she recalls these presents, so resonant with memory, and still so important. There had been one doll in particular, made from a luxurious brown velvet and wonderfully tactile. She had beads and a skirt of feathers, and was called Joséphine. Pál had seen the dancer Joséphine Baker perform in Paris, possibly even met her, and a little of the cosmopolitan glamour of Paris had filtered back to his daughter in rural Holland through this much-adored doll. Only a few weeks after her father boarded the little ferry to return to Paris once more, France was to declare war on Germany, the fighting began in eastern Europe, and all borders were closed. Corrie was left with her doll and her new book, but she would no longer have her father's lap to sit on, or his quietly spoken translation of the trickier French words.

～

Just before Germany's invasion of Poland, and in the last weeks of the post still being delivered to other countries, Pál sent Corrie the second volume of *Babar*. It reached her, when he could not. Back at the hotel, as we look back through the letters Corrie has brought me, she shows me her final letter from her father. Writing from Paris on 16 January 1940, he thanks her for the picture she has drawn him of Celeste, Babar's wife, the elephant queen. He is very impressed by her drawing skills, he tells her, and how much she has developed, and assures her he will keep the picture with him forever, to remind him of her. 'But surely, the legs are too thin for an elephant?!'

Pál would have read the reports in the papers as the French invasion of the Saarland failed and the few troops involved began to retreat. It was already obvious that it was only a matter of time before the Germans invaded, and the possibility of France resisting for long was slim. Some of the concert halls began to close, and the shops in the boulevards boarded up their windows. However, despite the atmosphere of increasing uncertainty, new music societies continued to programme concerts. These societies provided a much-needed community, as well as performance opportunities. The Triton Society, which had booked Pál with Székely and the Hungarian Quartet in the early 1930s, was one such. They promoted new French music but were equally committed to supporting immigrant composers.[57] During their seven years of activity, they hosted 120 premieres across 55 concerts.[58] The French composer Darius Milhaud was on its board, and asked Pál to perform his first cello concerto, written in 1934. The performance was scheduled for February 1940. There is no mention of the location of this concert on Corrie's scraps of programmes and postcards. However, a bit of digging in archives shows that the society held their concerts in l'École Normale de Musique, a music school for teachers as well as performers. In 1927 it had moved into a Belle Époque mansion in the seventeenth arrondissement. Two years later, a 500-seat concert hall was added, named the Salle Cortot after the pianist (and Vichy collaborator) Alfred Cortot, who was the college's principal. It was a prime venue for performance, with an exceptional acoustic. It was here that Pál would have performed Milhaud's concerto, one of the last performances in Paris for them both: Milhaud fled the city only months later, and managed to escape to America.

The Salle Cortot.

The Salle Cortot is on the Rue Cardinet, only a short walk from the modern flats of the Rue Philibert Delorme where Pál was living in 1938. On our second day in Paris, I take Corrie to the hall to admire its art deco interior. While we couldn't enter any of her father's apartments, here we can step sideways straight into a world that was just as he would have known it. This was the stage that marked Pál's last truly public appearance, and the hall has hardly changed since. We are told by the receptionist that we're only allowed in if we're going to the student concert that lunchtime, so we acquire two tickets and take our seats. A very young and enthusiastic baritone and a terrified-looking pianist entertain a thinly spread audience, and we look around the hall at our leisure. The Salle Cortot has the same gentle art deco curved balconies as Pál's apartment blocks, all rounded edges like the sloping shoulders of a cello. The hall is almost entirely made from wood, with carved columns and a chamber music-sized stage with a shiny Steinway at the centre. Narrow, rounded wooden seats flip down for the audience, curving round in rows to embrace the stage. Even the stage itself is a wooden curve, concave at the back, giving the impression of the performers being in the body of a stringed instrument.

The baritone has finished, the collective spell is broken, and the internationally familiar murmur of an emptying concert hall begins. Soon only Corrie and I are left alone in the hall. She has a quiet word with one of the student stewards, who closes the door, and I quickly take my cello out of its case. I want to play the Milhaud concerto, even just a few bars of it, on the spot where most likely no one has played it since Pál Hermann. I know that when I sit down to play, I will share with him the same extra-sensory awareness of the acoustic, listening to the cello's sound as it travels around the hall. This is something that will not have changed since he listened for the same quality of sound, made the same calculations as to how quietly he could play and still be heard, eighty years ago.

As soon as I touch the bow on the strings, I can tell the acoustic is superb. Back in the late 1930s, Pál's rendition of the Milhaud, a work almost as new as the hall and spiritually in keeping with it, would have been electrifying. Every nuance and every note would have been audible. I play some of the slow movement, my notes echoing his. The phrases spiral around the room, resonating with the wooden curves of the interior, mirroring the movement of the air within my cello. Perhaps, in that crisp, alive acoustic, there is something woven into the air still, into the fabric of the building itself, of Pál's playing. It's a fanciful idea, but then, afterwards, as I browse some articles on the hall's early years, my eyes are drawn to the word 'Stradivarius'. Corrie translates for me. Apparently, Cortot had declared that the acoustic of his new hall was so good that he described it as sounding 'like a Stradivarius'.[59] If the twin concepts of a cello and twentieth-century modernity are woven into the building itself, then why not the vestiges of Pál Hermann's performance, the living embodiment of both?

INTERLUDE

Gazing at the Cello II

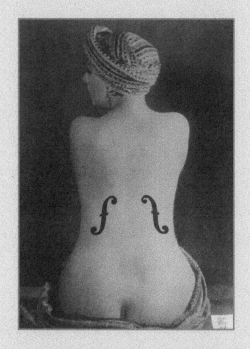

Man Ray's *Le Violon d'Ingres*.

In Paris in 1924, the American photographer Man Ray created an image that he entitled *Le Violon d'Ingres*. It was a tribute to Jean-Auguste-Dominique Ingres, a nineteenth-century painter of nudes, but this image is a classical nude with a twist. Ray's model, known as Kiki, is photographed from behind, seated so only her torso, head and neck are visible, the curves of her buttocks shadowed so that the gap between them implies the place where a cello's spike ought to be. She is a human stringed instrument, ostensibly a violin, as Ray entitles the image, but the choice of the word *violon* rather than *violoncelle* is to play with words. 'Le Violon d'Ingres' (Ingres's violin) implies a hobby, a plaything, a woman who is a human toy and pastime for the man who beholds and controls her. Ray printed the photograph of her nude body, and then painted F holes on the image, just above her hip bones. He then re-photographed the whole, including the painted additions. In only a few strokes of a brush, she is turned from woman into human cello, one indistinguishable from the other.

Man Ray doesn't seem to want to decide whether he is objectifying or appreciating the female violin/cello. Kiki's hair is bound up in a circular turban suggesting the carved lines of the scroll through layers of cloth, as well as removing one more identifying aspect of the individual woman. She is not herself but a visual pun: an object on which to gaze, or to be played, depending on our whim.

Augustus John created two strikingly different portraits of very different twentieth-century cellists – his unacknowledged daughter Amaryllis Fleming, and Guilhermina Suggia. Amaryllis is, rather fancifully, my cello grandmother, having taught my own teacher, Nick Roberts (whom I left in Oxford Violins at the beginning of my journey). He often refers to verbal images she used, and has inherited her knack of condensing the most complex elements of technique into easily memorable kernels of wisdom. He speaks of her with such warmth that I feel I knew her. In 2019, around the twentieth anniversary of her death, Nick and I took ourselves down to Kent to 'raise a glass to Amo', with the great and venerable luthier Charles Beare. In the study of his immaculately converted oast house hangs Augustus John's charcoal sketch of Amaryllis. It is more of a caress than a picture, drawn in red chalk; Amaryllis's portrait appears to have been spun out of her fiery auburn hair. The single line that suggests her merges her body seamlessly with her cello. Charles claims he could identify Amo's Stradivari from John's scantiest chalk suggestion of a scroll. He gazes up at the portrait with a reverential expression, and we raise a toast.

Augustus John's other portrait of a cellist is altogether more famous. Captured by John's paint brush, Guilhermina Suggia is sharply defined, a finished portrait in oils, not a casual sketch like John's impression of Amaryllis. It is a full-length study, taking in every proudly defiant aspect of her, from her Stradivari's spike to the top of her hair. Her pose suggests a player who is haughty, impassioned and clearly a handful.

Augustus John's portraits of Guilhermina Suggia
and Amaryllis Fleming.

Suggia's portrait did a great deal to shape her reputation. The voluptuous scarlet skirts, the dominatrix-like, dangerous attitude conveyed in the portrait practically became her brand. For Augustus John, a famed devourer of women, she was an object of desire in a way that his own daughter was not. And so he paints one as sheer sex, riding her cello through red waves of silk, and the other as tenderly feminine. We assume that an artist captures both their subject and something of how they perceive their subject's personality. But how much of these two is John and how much the women themselves?

In a sense, there is a certain honesty about Ray's photograph. It is clearly absurd, constructed. This is a woman, not a wooden instrument. It is a metaphor. And it is not about her, but about her being perceived by Ray. John's two cellists are both highly feminine, but at opposite ends of the scale.

Gendered meanings are constructed within relationships between humans and instruments, above and beyond our own individual relationships with 'Monseigneur' (to use Lise Cristiani's term of address for her cello) or indeed 'Madame'. But it's not just gender being constructed here. To play an instrument is to wield power – power to make people listen to you, to enchant them, to hold them under your spell. Power even to control time – to render a piece at your own speed, leaving an audience no choice but to listen to your interpretation unfold in real time, *your* time.[60] The player breathes life into their cello, imbues it with sound and, to various degrees, personality. But there is also another source of power – that of the performer over their audience, and that of the observer: listening to, perceiving, painting what they see, shaping the power dynamic by adding their own interpretation.

It seems ridiculous to ask what we think we are looking at when we gaze at a cello, but the curvaceous, low-toned instrument before us is, in fact, variously a fiddle, bass fiddle, base-violin, church bass, buck fiddle, big fiddle, bass, bass violin, violincello or violoncello. Or just a 'cello', amongst friends. Over its 400-year life, the cello and its antecedents have been many things to many people. A cello's identity is not static, and it has a far longer memory than we do. Ben Jonson, in his 1601 play *Poëtaster*, makes what might be the first mention of a cello in English: 'Come, we must have you turn fiddler again, slave, get a bass violin at your back, and march in a tawny coat, with one sleeve, to Goose Fair'. Even within the twentieth century, almost in living memory, a cello still held multiple identities: Thomas Hardy refers to a cello as both bass viol and a violoncello, within the same paragraph.[61]

The names by which a cello is known are a tangle. It depends whether you are talking about an English cello or an Italian one. It matters whether you like the player or not – a musician with gravitas would play a violoncello; an irritating and minor figure might be fiddling (while Rome burns, perhaps). The violin family originated in Italy, so we might trace the development of the violoncello back to Stradivari or Amati. But cellos smaller than the great Italian instruments were being made in England at least fifty years before Stradivari opened his workshop in Cremona. And, as Ben Jonson's lines show, they weren't known by the anglicized version of an Italian term.

The difference in nomenclature was only a part of the difference in attitude to the instrument. Players of fiddles didn't develop the intense, singular relationships we associate with cellos and their players now. A fiddler, in the Scottish tradition, would have started off learning to play a cello-like instrument, then shifted up the stave to the violin. Instrument historian Brenda Neece believes that this was because the bass parts were usually the simplest, so children could be trained to play in chamber groups from an early age and quite literally work their way up to the trickier tunes. They would then have been expected to be able to turn their hand to any one of the string family when required.[62] A string player wouldn't necessarily have identified themself as a cellist. But generations of players would have grown up with a sense that the bass violin was the original point of comparison, their earliest physical memory of the violin family. All viols are played vertically, so playing an instrument under your chin was a new-fangled development, moving away from the fundamental truth that a stringed instrument ought to be embraced between one's legs.

The very earliest cello treatises show us that cello fingering was once the same as that of the violin, not using the fourth finger, probably so players could easily swap between the different-sized instruments.[63] When the great Italian cellists began coming to give concerts in Britain in the 1600s, they brought their Italian violoncellos with them. The British started to rename their bass violins accordingly, although a number misremembered the spelling, and the erroneous 'violincello' began a brief life. In the late eighteenth century, the cellist Robert Crome tried to teach us how to play this new instrument, which seemed to be taking over in popularity from the viol. He wrote one of the first books of instruction, telling his eager pupils which way up the new instrument went, but without plumping for one singular name for it.

Instructions for the Violoncello or Bass Violin.

The Violoncello is an Excellent Instrument, not only in Concert, but for playing in Lessons &c. This Instrument may be consider'd as a Large Fiddle only held the contrary way, and the fourth String is next the Bow-Hand, as the Body is turn'd downward, the lower part is to rest on the Calves of the Leggs supported with the Knees.

As the Bass Violin is in great Esteem I have here given some useful and plain Instructions for the Learner, as this Instrument appears to be Built on the Ruins of another; I mean the Viol or fix'd string'd Bass, which in the last Century was held in great Esteem, and of general use in Concerts. [...] The Violin in those Days was look'd on as a contemptible Instrument; it was harsh and too loud, they could not bear to have their Viols overpower'd, however as the Violin became more general it was Judged necessary to use Bass Violins or Violoncello's, (that is, four-string'd basses), as being much more powerful and suitable to the Fiddle.[64]

Whatever we call it, most can agree with Man Ray's suggestion that a cello is strikingly human. But it also resists our fanciful anthropomorphism. A cello is as much set screw, plug, tail gut, saddle nut, peg box, pegs, bridge, endpin and tailpiece, as it is a body. Peeking through the serpentine holes in the body of the cello, we find, not a liminal space between earth and heaven, but a matter of rough carpentry. A master luthier once described himself to me, jokingly, as a 'wood butcher'. The phrase does scant justice to his skills and craftsmanship, but in this tongue-in-cheek description he was acknowledging the material element of his craft. When we take a cello apart, we learn that the magic takes place in the space between the bass bar (a length of wood glued onto the inside of the front) and the soundpost wedged between front and back like the central pole of a circus tent. We find prosaic wooden blocks bookending the top and bottom of the instrument, and a wooden frame lining the join between front, back and ribs. These are usually made from pine, and in its unvarnished state a cello is more redolent of the cheap furniture we got tired of in the 1990s than one of the Western world's greatest creations. While the wood on the inside is rather unglamorous, the various types of wood used for the outside are far more poetic. Their names are suggestive of scented forests, or rare and precious gifts: ebony for the nut and tailpiece; rosewood or boxwood for the pegs, tailpiece and endpin; maple or poplar for the back and sides; spruce for the top.

In short, the inside of a cello is a most disappointing place of pilgrimage (except, perhaps, for any interesting maker's label we might happen upon). We hope to visit the site where the miracle takes place, to learn something of it, just as we might visit the museum house of a great composer and lean on the silk ropes that cordon us off, to gaze in awe at their possessions. But just as the absence of the famous composer is the most distinct feature of their carefully preserved home, so the absence of visible sound within a cello is palpable. When we are invited by a luthier to take a tour inside the inner sanctum of a cello, we prepare to learn some of its mysteries. But the warning signs are there before they lift the top off the instrument – it's called the 'belly', or sometimes the 'table'. This alone should be enough to indicate that, whatever we expect, the instrument isn't likely to deliver any great wisdom when it is so unsure of its own identity, being positioned somewhere between a body and a desk.

Being able to see is a useful tool, but it is only one tool, and far from the whole story.[65] How can such a rough piece of mere cabinetry presume to hold us under such a spell? And then refuse, not only to reflect its sonic elegance, but to divulge any of its secrets? Put the lid back on, however, and the cello glows once more with its magic.

2nd Movement – Journeys

Musician, hand to bow grafted in equal mastery,
Goes like an angel where no mortal dare.

(from Ursula Wood, 'To a 'Cellist')

Monguilhem – Pál Hermann

November 2021

Pál Hermann's appearance at the Salle Cortot was to be his last concert in Paris. He remained in the city until the spring of 1940, but life was rapidly becoming as impossible as it had been in Berlin. Without concerts he could not earn a living, and it was clear that the Nazi invasion was imminent. Exactly 100 years after Lise Cristiani had left Paris with a one-way ticket and a cello case, Pál departed for a remote village west of Toulouse with nothing but his Gagliano. Only their cellos were to return to the capital.

❧

Four hours after leaving Montparnasse station, I walk out into the wintry sunshine at Pau, in the Pyrénées-Atlantiques. After some stumbling negotiation with the hire car administrator and a lot of hopeful gesticulating, I load my cello into the passenger seat of a shiny black Volkswagen. Together we head south through neat little villages with large rectangles of fine grey gravel at their centre, each flanked by plane trees that merge in canopies overhead. After an hour or so, I arrive in the tiny village of Estang, near Monguilhem, and park in the Place du 4 Septembre, opposite my destination, the Hotel de Commerce. This village is close to the isolated houses where Pál Hermann stayed after leaving Paris, and there is little he would not have recognized in its appearance today.

The hotel's side door is open, and I walk in to find a waitress, who gestures recalcitrantly towards reception. Up in my room I put my suitcase down, kick off my shoes and open the tall, brown-painted shutters, swinging them back on their ornate hinges, flat against the external walls. Outside, a vegetable stall is set up between khaki-trunked trees. Above are shuttered windows and ancient-looking terracotta roofs. Somewhere in the distance a wood pigeon calls.

I have an hour before I'm due to meet up again with Corrie. This time, she will introduce me to her son Paul van Gastel and her now very frail and elderly cousin Tik (like Corrie, she was christened Cornelia, but has retained her family nickname of Tik throughout her long life). I sit in my little lino-floored beige and pink room, and begin to engage in all the pointless nesting routines required to make a hotel feel like a home. I take my cello out of its case and settle it on the bed. It looks like it's taking a nap. I change my shoes, then my clothes, then my shoes again. I arrange my phone charger, and even empty my handbag of rubbish, as if I'm expecting some kind of inspection. In doing so I find a little pair of dressing-up sunglasses with lenses shaped like stars that belong to my little boy; I feel a stab of longing for the tiny, upturned face that wears them. I return to looking out into the square. Car doors slam, people shout. The post van comes and goes, the hairdresser opens her door to sweep. A small dog passes, then returns. I wonder how the hours must have passed for Pál, alone and watching a world go by in which he had no part.

At midday the bells ring. I can see one on a roof a couple of streets away from my window, curlicue iron suspending it, and a metal pendant flag, cut as if to pretend it were flapping in a permanent breeze. I absent-mindedly check the pitch of the bell opposite my window against my cello strings. It's an F. My correct guess gives me a pointless but undeniable buzz of pleasure.

Below in the square, a small grey car draws up. Minutes later, the hotel receptionist knocks on my door. 'Vos cousins sont ici.' I take a breath, pick up the recording equipment that accompanies me to every interview, give my cello a last glance to make sure it's comfortable, and follow her down the stairs. There, on a heated terrace, under an L-shaped structure made of oak beams and terracotta tiles, a tall, slender man helps a tiny, bent-over lady with her jacket. Corrie takes her place at the other side of the table. I am struck by how much Paul seems to have inherited from his grandfather. His long limbs, charmingly gangly, and his gently boisterous, easy manner seem to be a direct recreation of his namesake. Corrie, Paul and I embrace, and I gently hold the hands of the fragile, bird-like little Tik. I hardly dare hug her for fear of doing damage, her spine is so contorted with osteoporosis. When she looks up, her face is delicate, with great, searching brown eyes. We bend down, turning our ears to her, to catch her voice. I am praying my recording device is sensitive enough to pick up her whisper.

The waiter reads out the menu to us, and I'm none the wiser. I take a quietly anarchic pleasure in not knowing what I have just ordered. To my right is the persistent trickle of a water feature, a construction of white bricks topped with red tiles that looks like a huge barbeque, the water hidden deep inside. The conversation flows interchangeably between French, Dutch and English. Sometimes I'm not sure which language I'm listening to, and at those moments the pure, uninterpreted sounds of voices and flowing water transform into something like music. Tik explains that, during the war, her family were too conspicuous out here in suspicious rural France, being foreign. The Weevers spoke Dutch but it sounded dangerously like German, so they switched to French, and Tik grew up bilingual, the intimate, family conversations in Dutch, the more formal reserved for French.

❧

After lunch, Tik takes me to the mill that was her childhood home, and in whose grounds she still lives. She and
her family came to live in this remote spot because her great-
aunt and great-uncle Louise Bachiene and Jaap de Graaff
had moved here from London in the 1930s. They bought a
magnificent white house known as Beaussiet, which sat at
the centre of its own ample farmland, between the villages of
Monguilhem and Estang. Once they were established there,
Jaap and Louise suggested that Tik's parents, Jan and Hinke
Weevers, join them and help them set up a business distilling
Armagnac, the distinctive local variety of brandy. They built
them a house in the forest where a watermill had stood and
called it Le Moulin Neuf (the New Mill); it was here that Tik
and her siblings grew up.

Today, the most striking aspect of Le Moulin Neuf is the
resounding silence that surrounds it like low-lying cloud. In
the midst of dense woodland, with disused farmyard machin-
ery littering the grass, and goats that stare balefully at you
from their perches on upturned logs, it is a rather forlorn
place. Next to the house is a curious but charming building,
like a Swiss chalet, with a high protruding balcony, sloping
roof with geometric decoration in white and red painted
bricks, and shutters above it that give the impression a cuckoo
might pop out of a window on the hour.

Tik has a fragile old family photograph album with
marbled hardback red covers and crisp tracing-paper pages.
As we look through the photographs, Tik and I perch on
plastic chairs in her kitchen, amongst an extraordinary array
of bottles, packages and paint tins, all piled up along the
walls. She makes me tea, heating water in a plastic pot in
the microwave ('What would I want with a kettle? It's just
me here,' she says). As she shuffles between the debris of her
makeshift kitchen to find a second cup, dusty from disuse in

a box at the back of a shelf, she adds, 'One can manage on very little, you know.'

I gingerly turn the pages of her album, to find an image of Jaap de Graaff's chauffeur – who is about to leave them to join the French army – standing proudly with Jaap and Louise by his car, in his new military uniform. It is one of many 'parting' photographs, Tik tells me. On the next page is a photograph of Pál at Beaussiet, wearing his distinctive long winter coat, next to Jaap (hands in pockets, in the centre) and Louise. Around them stand the players of the Hungarian Quartet, including Zoltán Székely, and the cellist Vilmos Palotai. It is February 1939, and the quartet may have been performing in Toulouse, visiting Beaussiet in passing. Pál and the quartet returned to Paris, to rehearse in his flat for a week at the end of February. Pál's last letter from his Paris apartment was sent on 16 January 1940. By mid-June, the capital was under Nazi control.

The Hungarian Quartet, Jaap de Graaff and Pál Hermann (centre) at Beaussiet.

The quartet did not forget him after the war, nor the kindness of his in-laws. In the 1950s they returned to the de Graaffs' house, and even performed outside on the grass at Le Moulin Neuf, but Pál was not there to enjoy their performance.

～

When France was carved up between the Vichy government and the Nazis in 1940, the Weevers and de Graaffs found themselves within the designated 'free zone', which was governed from Vichy and not directly occupied by the Nazis until November 1942. At some point between January and March 1940, Pál left Paris, for the comparative safety of Monguilhem and Estang, alternating between the family's two homes.

I am not reliant solely on photographs to reconstruct this stage of Pál Hermann's life. The family has also entrusted me with his diary from this time – a record that has been seen by only a handful of people. As I sit studying it in Tik's ramshackle kitchen, I'm very conscious of the trust that has been placed in me by Corrie and Paul. It is a precious document – its timeframe being the only period of Pál's life for which we have his thoughts, recorded day by day, an invitation to perceive events as he saw them.

Pál stayed at Beaussiet and Le Moulin Neuf for a short while before he registered on 4 March as a member of one of the temporary units of the French Foreign Legion known as the Régiments de Marche de Volontaires Étrangers or RMVE (Regiments of Marching Overseas Volunteers), a varied assortment of men of every nationality who had volunteered to bolster the French war effort. He was one of around 15,000 internationals living in France, many of whom were Jews, who had emigrated from central and eastern Europe across the French border. He could not take his cello with him to army camp, so the Gagliano remained safely at Beaussiet, under the care of Jaap and Louise, while he, along with many other equally unsuited civilians, learnt how to be a soldier.

The RMVE trained in a military academy established for the purpose at Le Barcarès, a tiny seaside town on the Mediterranean coast near Perpignan. Despite the physical rigours of his new regime, which for any musician used to spending hours sitting practising would have been a shock, the whole experience of training on the beach felt like a vacation to Pál. When he was not training, he swam in the Mediterranean or relaxed on the sand. In his diary he recorded his observations and thoughts. He wrote how the other men around him, when at rest on the beach, would squint in the sunshine at the photographs of loved ones they kept in buttoned-up tunic pockets. We do not know whether he did the same, or whether the pictures of Corrie and her mother would have raised too many painful questions from his fellow volunteers. Pál Hermann the Jewish father, husband and internationally renowned cellist no longer existed. To the men around him he was simply a quiet and enigmatic Hungarian, with an intriguingly high level of musicianship for the hastily assembled army band in which he played.

Pál was careful not to write about his past life in his war-time diary, aware of the danger it might pose both to him and his relatives if it fell into the wrong hands. Instead, he confined himself to wistful observations on an uncertain present, with no mention of his daughter, or of Ada's loss. I wonder how Corrie feels about her absence in his journal. Later however, in amongst the concert programmes and letters that were saved, Corrie and I find a 'certificate of presence in the army corps', including, handwritten at the top, a note that he has a refugee daughter in Holland. When I show her, Corrie smiles to see this little mention of herself, a small token that she was present and part of his identity, even when they were separated.

Pál's days in training were spent in the knowledge that at any moment an order might come, instructing his regiment to march north. He spent his time peeling potatoes, rehearsing the band and trying to get to grips with complicated equipment and backpacks (the latter apparently defeated them all, even with an instructive diagram). There was a sense that the routines of camp life were nothing more than a temporary moment out of time, and that soon the Mediterranean coast would be left behind. Pál did not know when that might be, or what might replace it. Yet, however superficially genteel Le Barcarès seemed, he was surrounded by evidence of the brutality of war. Makeshift camps had been set up all along the beach, in which thousands of refugees from Franco's Spain were corralled. On 10 May 1940, after eight months of what became known as the 'phoney war', Germany launched a major offensive in the west. Their astonishingly successful 'blitzkrieg' invasion of the Low Countries and northern France was followed on 5 June by the beginning of the German army's operation to complete the conquest of France. It was named *Fall Rot* – 'Case Red'.

Pál's regiment received orders to travel north by train, towards the invading army; he was to fight men who might, until recently, have been his fellow citizens in Berlin, even perhaps his friends and colleagues. Now his comrades were men who knew nothing about him. His experiences set him apart from the other men, many of whom were much younger. He could sing their regimental song as lustily as them, but it appears from his diaries that he could not bring himself to be raucous and take part in drunken debauchery when the opportunity presented itself. On one occasion he describes in his diary how his platoon came upon an abandoned wine cellar. While the other men shouted and paddled ecstatically about, ankle deep in red wine, Pál hung back, appalled. Even when he tried to join in, by filling a flask he'd picked up by the roadside, he found that it leaked.

Over the next few weeks, Pál kept track of his regiment's movements as they travelled from village to village to try to take their place in the defence against the German army. The platoon had a violin and harmonica with them, the only evidence that they were originally intended to be a marching band, and Pál took great pleasure in the musical expression of the different nationalities that made up his regiment. The Spanish soldiers passed the time during lengthy train stops or quiet moments in the evenings by forming a ring around one man, and dancing around him, clapping and stamping. Pál enjoyed listening to the men singing in their native languages, and was captivated in particular by the peculiarly distinctive timbre of the high tenor voices of the Russian soldiers.

As with many war diaries, the physicality of the writer's existence looms large, from the many discomforts to the all-too-brief moments of respite. Pál writes repeatedly of coffee: the perpetual search for it, and his delight in obtaining any after a long night of marching. He notes the comfort of fresh straw to sleep on, in railway carriages and on the floors of deserted houses. The objects that he carries with him through the changing landscapes take on a particular, talismanic significance: flasks, cumbersome backpacks and the restrictive, heavy overcoat that weighed him down.

He observes and records detail with the delicate brush strokes of a painter, or indeed a composer with a deep sensitivity to texture and colour. Motifs appear and reappear in his writing: moments of solidity amongst the uncertainty of contradictory orders and shambolic retreats. He is struck in particular by a house he notices in one of the villages his regiment passes through on its way to the front, recognizing it when they return the same way in confused retreat a few days later.

Here, in a little square, a house appeared which was literally torn into two pieces by a bomb; we could see the rooms and the furniture in a cross-section. A bed was in its right place, a mirror hung above it diagonally which reflected the street with us marching on it.[1]

He does not speculate that the house and his fascination with it might serve as a metaphor for his sense of himself, torn between two personae and two lives, seemingly ordinary and functional yet disrupted and displaced.

Pál's narrative enacts in its very structure both the barrier between him and the men around him, and a sense of chronic dislocation within himself. He often steps out of his own identity and observes himself in the third person. Calling himself 'the Hungarian soldier', he becomes an unanchored presence, a shadow that flickers through the narrative, as if he were haunting his own story.

> Finally our platoon had to stop and wait. It was a special moment. We were waiting in the dark and watching all the figures of our marching regiment; masses of soldiers, sometimes a car of an officer, horses, cars and 8 or 9 tanks.
>
> Beside the road there was a soldier half lying looking at the marching, quickly he fell into deep sleep.
>
> Perhaps he was dreaming back to the better times when he did not have to march in the mud. For this soldier the journey was very oppressive, with 60 drinking − and seemingly immature − soldiers in one wagon. He could not imagine how life would be as a soldier. But this negative feeling went away when he arrived. He has made friends and found a place in this society that is so different from normal life. He was no longer alone and he always had something to do: the bad feelings were gone.

As it turned out, the French soldiers already engaged on the front line were unable to hold out long enough for the volunteer reinforcements to arrive. Pál's regiment was instructed to retreat almost as soon as it reached the fighting. Constantly on guard for ambushes and braced to engage in hand-to-hand fighting at any moment, the greatest danger the men actually faced was from the air.

> Three or four beautiful silver lit planes flew south, they then disappeared in the distance. New ones came (or the same? –) back to north. Then again from the other side; again and again.
>
> There were about six of them right above us again when suddenly they started firing their machine guns: prrr-prrr-rrrrrrr-prr and so on. They were approximately 1000 metres above us – obviously they were not shooting at us disorganized handful of marching soldiers; they were shooting at the other planes.
>
> We dropped ourselves to the ground, helter-skelter; searching for a 'good place' in the grass on the side of the road. We could hear our own deranged breathing even louder than the sound of the machine guns – our half-opened mouths less than a few centimetres away from the ground.

The air attacks became more and more frequent, and the men had no defence other than to dive into grass and woodland for cover. They dug ditches for themselves with their steel helmets (like shallow graves, Pál thought), and covered themselves with leaves. Listening to the sounds of the bombardment and the sirens as the planes circled like vast, screeching birds of prey, Pál noticed that the horses nearby whinnied in terror every time a plane shrieked past and a bomb exploded. Face down in his ditch, the animals and men around him became one, emitting a visceral, primal music of despair: 'it sounded like a desperate moan. – Aren't these <u>men</u> who are moaning ?!'

The chaos and hopelessness of it all were as demoralizing as the constant air attacks. The men were instructed to march to particular destinations, got lost, scattered, retreated, then retraced their steps once more. Pál craved community and family – everything that he had lost at that moment when the tide had swept Ada out into the sea. He knew that if, as now seemed inevitable, the Nazis continued to march through France unstopped, then as both a soldier and a Jew he would have, as he put it, 'pas d'chance...'. But even in the depths of his misery he took comfort in the camaraderie of the regiment, grieving amongst men who understood and shared his despair without needing to articulate or explain it.

∼

By 14 June 1940, Pál's fears were realized: the German army outflanked the Maginot Line and pushed deep into France, occupying Paris unopposed. The French government fled and, three days later, on 17 June, France surrendered. Shortly

Pál Hermann at La Barcarès, June 1940.

after, the French army was disbanded and Pál found himself unemployed. In Tik's photo album there is a picture of him in uniform, standing on a sandy beach by army huts. It was taken on 23 June 1940, just before he was demobilized. His hands are clasped unmilitarily together, his weight on one leg like a slightly awkward civilian. The photo may have been taken by Jaap de Graaff, who had come to collect him and take him back to Monguilhem to begin long months in semi-hiding. He had little to return to, apart from his cello.

For the next few months, Pál lived at Le Moulin Neuf with Tik's father Jan Weevers. Jan was a keen amateur violinist and they played duets while Tik and her siblings were out at school. At other times, Pál would walk out along the river that runs behind the house and provided the power to the mill back in the days when it was still in use. It was a good fifteen-minute walk to any other habitation, and the family had no transport. Pál did not even have a bicycle. His existence had, overnight, become one of extreme isolation.

∽

Back in Paris, I hadn't been sure what Corrie and I were looking for when we stood outside the addresses her father had chosen temporarily to call home. I wonder if, in this remotest of places, I now know. With the image of those modern apartments in mind, I can appreciate just how much of an exile his life at Beaussiet and Le Moulin Neuf must have seemed. All his life he had lived at the centre of Europe's cultural capitals: Budapest, Berlin, Brussels, Paris. Now he had been forced from one extreme to another. I picture him, displaced from his successful career, wandering aimlessly through the dark grasses and huge ferns that merge within the shadows of the trees.

Later that afternoon, Tik accompanies me to Beaussiet. We drive along straight, empty roads, past square fields in which maize will be planted in the spring. The spiky brown

Beaussiet today.

seed heads of teasel stand high along the borders in the dry, sand-coloured soil. Elsewhere, wobbling ancient vines hang leafless from their supporting wires in rows. The great white house stands alone amid overgrown grasses between Estang and Monguilhem. It is now accessible by a narrow tarmac road, which has been given the name 'Route de Beaussiet' but which was previously simply a track across the de Graaffs' land. On the other side of the road are a series of houses and farms, divided up by privet hedges. Before the family sold the property in the 1970s, all the land and its buildings belonged to the house, including the four farms that we can see in the distance.

Tik used to stay at Beaussiet during the holidays, then lived here for two years in the early 1950s when she attended a nearby school that was too far to reach by bicycle from Le Moulin Neuf. The elegant house she shows me is dominated by a tower on one side, topped by a pointed square roof. Below are the cracked remnants of a wide patio, where sparrows hop over the uneven paving slabs. This was the veranda,

Tik tells me. I imagine the meals served there, the wine and conversation, and Pál bringing his cello outside to play under its shade. By the side gate is a well, with slabs over it. I ask Tik if she remembers it open. Yes, she says – during the war, this was how they drew water for the garden. And for the house? There is a little lake nearby.

The garden is full of great palms. The bare stems of roses and Virginia creeper climb the white walls of the house, and at the back a vast magnolia tree elicits a murmur of recognition from Tik. Its huge leaves, crunchy and brown, litter the ground beneath it. A many-paned wooden greenhouse stands behind, looking very much as it would have done when Pál stayed here, with the remnants of what were once neat beds of radishes and lettuces in front of it. Hydrangea bushes obscure the ground-floor windows. We try every window and door. All are locked, and the shutters closed.

All in all, Beaussiet has the appearance of an abandoned and desolate building. However, there are three men in green polo shirts with industrial-sized strimmers noisily attacking corners of the wilderness. This is a house in the process of being claimed once more. But the new owners will never be able to look at it with Tik's quiet, proprietorial familiarity. She points to the single-storey annexe at the back. That was the kitchen, she says, and there, on one side, the living room for the staff, and their bedrooms on the other side. There used to be more staff than inhabitants (although visitors were plentiful), with a chauffeur, cook, gardener and housekeeper. Tik points to her bedroom, a shuttered window above and to the right of the front door. And there, further to the right, is an elegant, floor-length window opening out onto a stone balcony topped with a wooden balustrade. That, she says, was Pál's room, when he had had enough of the chaos of Le Moulin Neuf and all its children. That's where he escaped to practise.

He could play at Beaussiet undisturbed, the windows of his room thrown open, curtains billowing. Today, unlike the ground floor, the shutters above are open. Tik and I stand looking up at the balcony from the new road outside the garden gate, and it doesn't take much to imagine the sound of the cello, above the strimmers' hum.

Back at Le Moulin Neuf, Tik and I return to the leather-bound photograph albums, and she shows me pages of neatly aligned images of Beaussiet in its glory days. There is invariably a dog outside it in the photographs. The palms that are now an unwieldy height, towering out of wild grasses, were then all diminutive and well tended, protruding neatly from flowering borders that line the gravel paths.

Beaussiet was dangerously close to the border of the Free Zone, itself a concept that offered at best a fragile protection. Notwithstanding, from the summer of 1940 onwards, Jaap and Louise offered refuge to a steady stream of musicians and artists heading south in the hope of being smuggled out of the country. Many of them were contacts of people the de Graaffs had known in London, when, during the First World War, they had supported Dutch and Belgian artist refugees by buying their work and befriending them.[2] Now a succession of dancers, sculptors and pianists arrived at the white house, having fled south from Paris and Brussels in the hope of making it across the Pyrenees to Spain, and from there to America. When the time came for them to move on, they assembled on the now vanished veranda for their 'leaving' photographs, like the chauffeur before them.

By 1941 the French police were rounding up thousands of Jews in the Free Zone, enthusiastically complying with Nazi occupation policy across Europe. The Vichy government went far beyond what the Germans demanded, handing over more Jews than the Nazis had asked for, rounding them up, murdering them outright or sending them to concentration camps where hundreds of thousands would die of disease and malnutrition. Pál Hermann's safety was precarious both as a foreigner and as someone who had served in the army, but

Refugees at Beaussiet, including sculptor Frederic Minne
(standing, right) with Jaap and Louise.

had he been discovered to be a Jew, he would have been at
risk both from the Germans and from the local citizens he
had enlisted to protect.

In November 1942, in response to the Allied landings in
North Africa, the Germans invaded the Free Zone. At once,
the slippery distinction between the occupied and unoccupied areas dissolved, with all of northern and southern France
becoming subject to Nazi control. Houses were burnt, and the
members of the Resistance – who until then had found the
woods and homes around Estang and Monguilhem a good
hiding place just beyond the zone boundary – were hunted
down. On 3 July 1944 nine local men were taken into the

woods around Le Moulin Neuf and murdered as a reprisal for Nazis who had been killed by the Resistance. The local archives preserve the serious faces of those nine men, some little more than boys, staring out from a newspaper article reporting their deaths.

Tik remembers this period vividly. On one occasion, she had been staying at the house of family friends when the Gestapo burst in, with the intention of arresting the father, having been informed that he was involved with the Resistance. She watched as the Gestapo ransacked the house, overturning wardrobes and searching under beds, until they had satisfied themselves that he was not there. The grandfather was cowering in a corner of the room, so they arrested him instead.

Despite the increasing dangers, Beaussiet and Le Moulin Neuf were probably amongst the safest options for Pál, since none of the locals knew he was Jewish. Most did not even know he was there. A rule had been introduced, making it obligatory for anyone crossing in and out of the boundary that marked the end of the Free Zone to have a permit, a *laissez-passer de ligne de démarcation*. It was a rule the Weevers deliberately ignored. Tik and her family never registered with the Gestapo, meaning that there was no paperwork to declare how many people lived in their house, or who they were.

While it isn't clear exactly how long Pál lived between the households, there are two surviving letters, written by him from Beaussiet and sent via his nephew in neutral Zürich, in April and May 1941. Staying hidden at Le Moulin Neuf and Beaussiet might have been the safest option, but Pál simply did not have the financial means to remain in isolation indefinitely. Doubtless the de Graaffs would have continued to support him, but he was young and full of energy, and driven to perform, as well as proud enough to want to fend for himself. He was also a man who craved company and stimulation. So, at some point in the latter half of 1941, he left Jaap and Louise, and moved

One of the last photographs of Pál Hermann,
· taken in Toulouse in 1942.

150 kilometres away to Toulouse. There he rented a room and
acquired some cello pupils.

At this point, the trail goes cold, as Pál was deliberately not
in direct contact with anyone in the family in case it might
endanger them. Tik's father Jan sent him money to help him
survive, but even that was done through a third party. There
are three photographs of Pál in Tik's family album, marked
'Toulouse'. Her father had on occasion cycled the long
distance to visit him, and it is likely that Jan took these
images on one of their rare days out in the countryside
together. Jan was the last of the family ever to see Pál, and
these photographs are the final images of him that we have.
Wearing his distinctive long woollen coat, he smiles wanly at
the camera. By this point, Corrie had not seen her father for

three years. It would be many more years before she would see these pictures.

Pál Hermann could barely scratch a living with just a handful of cello pupils. He needed to be performing again, for the income, but perhaps also for his own sanity. One of Corrie's programmes shows that he took the substantial risk of performing in public under his own name on 8 March 1942. He played Haydn, Chopin, Paganini and Schubert in the Schola Caecilia, 10 Rue St-Anne. This was when Toulouse was still in the Free Zone. Soon after, the small freedoms that had been allowed in anti-Semitic Vichy France became even fewer, and the risks associated with public appearance increased. This was his last known performance.

Against the odds, Pál managed to live quietly in Toulouse for a further two years. Corrie has four letters from this time, which her father sent via Switzerland to her and her aunt Loes in Amersfoort. From these we can find his addresses, as he moves around the city, staying first with a family named Cassanova at 25 Rue des Velotiers, then moving to 93 Rue des Trente-Six-Ponts. Finally, in his last correspondence, he is staying at 19 Rue de Gorp.

In the final postcard the family received from him, written in August 1943, Pál mentions that he sometimes plays in a church to supplement his loss of earnings while his pupils are on holiday.[3] Toulouse was heavily policed by the Gestapo, and by making himself visible he was taking a huge risk, so at some point around this time, he obtained false papers and adopted an alias. As far as the authorities were concerned, he was a Frenchman called de Cotigny. Pál Hermann, one of the greatest cellists of his generation, had ceased to exist.

∽

One afternoon in April 1944, Pál left his cello in his apartment in the Rue de Gorp and walked to the elegant square known as Place Wilson, in the centre of town. According to documents now in the Shoah Archive in Paris, no. 5 Place Wilson was a large red brick building that had belonged to a Jewish couple, Isidore and Georges Manasse-Manuel, and which had been requisitioned by the Nazis as an office on 28 March 1942.[4] Pál might well have been heading there to have his false passport extended. It is not clear what happened next. One account suggests that he had decided to take the risk of asking the authorities if he might be given special authorization to perform, but his enquiry had aroused suspicion. Corrie believes he was caught in a street round-up. The square would have been sealed off, and everyone in it would have had their papers closely examined. Perhaps his forged de Cotigny papers were not convincing enough.[5] Whatever happened, he was placed under arrest. He never returned to the Rue de Gorp. Instead, he was put in a truck destined for Toulouse station.

While many of those arrested that day were forced to leave children, partners and other relatives, Pál was leaving behind his beloved cello. Had he put it in the case after his last practice, or was it lying on its side, waiting for his return? The intimate relationship of years, the only connection he still possessed to his former life, had been ended abruptly. His Gagliano was to be added to the meticulously kept Gestapo lists of paintings, furniture and instruments stolen from Jewish households. The cello was designated Nazi property, but its new 'owners' would have had no idea of the value of their new acquisition.

∼

As I travel back up through the French countryside to Paris, my mind returns to a list I had seen while doing research in the archives of the Vienna City Library, where I came across an alphabetical register listing composers who were prominent in the 1940s. The register is rather like a phone book or 'Who's Who' of the time. However, what my eyes were drawn to were the neat purple lines that are ruled through approximately a quarter of the names (for instance, only one out of five composers with a surname beginning with H remains). These were the Jewish composers, systematically erased from the register.[6]

Western classical music is a history of harmonies and sounds that speak to each other across the centuries. But it is also a history of absences, and of gaps, of composers, instrumentalists and instruments that have fallen silent. Yet these musicians, too, wove their threads into the fabric of musical influence, and something of them remains, although we must look and listen hard to find them. What we have of music now is moulded by and contingent on those gaps. Pál Hermann and his cello were to become one of the many silences that shape musical history.

Drancy, Paris – Pál Hermann

Just before Pál was transported from Toulouse at the end of April 1944, he somehow obtained a slip of paper and scribbled a note on it, with no idea whether it might ever reach its destination. In as few words as possible, he told Tik's father Jan that he had been caught, and that his destination was Drancy, the transit camp in the north-eastern suburbs of Paris. It was a collection point for Jews and other victims of persecution, who were herded together there to await deportation, almost invariably to Auschwitz. Pál knew that he might never have another opportunity of letting the family know what had happened to him, and that his chances of returning alive were extremely slim. If he could not contact them, it would be months before they even noticed his absence.

No one knows how the note reached Le Moulin Neuf or who risked their life to take it, but long after, Tik remembered seeing it. Her father had kept it for many years – the last example of Pál's handwriting, that someone had taken the trouble (and risked considerable danger) to hand-deliver to the family home. This little slip of paper could not change Pál's fate, but it could save his cello. His Gagliano was left in his boarded-up apartment until it could be taken to Germany. On receiving the note, Jan determined it would not remain there, whatever the risks of stealing it back.

~

In the Memorial de la Shoah Archive, in the Marais in Paris, there are over seven thousand photographs of Drancy internment camp. Looking through them, the same scenes appear and reappear. The mess of barbed wire fence around the perimeter, and the diagonal stripes of the guard's sentry box just within the fence. The men, wearing scarves, flat caps and berets, wandering around the rectangle of mud at the centre of the horseshoe-shaped complex. At the glassless windows overlooking the yard, faces of families are pressed, spectral presences, staring out at... what? Some prisoners are scrubbing their clothes, outside in wooden troughs with what looks like only a dribble of water running down the centre, as they pummel and squeeze undergarments. Most of them would soon be forced to exchange their own clothes for the striped uniform of Auschwitz. In every image, photograph after photograph, the faces of the men share a particular haunted look, whether they are wide-eyed, challenging the camera, or captured with faces downcast. And these are the images taken by the Nazis, for propaganda, the archivist tells me. They are not to be trusted and make the camp look much more sanitary and hospitable than it really was.

I had accompanied Corrie to the archive during our time in Paris so we could find her father's name on the rows of marble walls that are arranged outside its entrance. These great walls are a monument to the French Jews killed in the Shoah. The archivist shows us out into the courtyard, and we locate wall 17. There we find hundreds upon hundreds of people whose name

Corrie Hermann at The Wall of Names in Paris.

began with H, who had nothing in common other than the misfortune to be Jewish in the wrong place at the wrong time.

Column 6, row 2. Corrie raises her hand and traces her finger over her father's name. We stand silently together, surrounded by the thousands of engraved names.

Corrie is still resting her hand on the wall by her father's name. Finally, she lowers her arm and turns slowly away. 'So many. Well.'

ᔐ

For most, Drancy was not a destination but a holding space, and the inhabitants had no idea where or for what they were destined. In camp slang, they were 'living on *pitchipoi* time', as one survivor described it. *Pitchipoi* is Yiddish for nowhere, and was as good a way as any to quantify what they could hardly grasp. It was commonly held that those deported were travelling to *pitchipoi*. Few in Drancy knew the full extent of what was really happening in the camps in the east, but they did know that no one returned.

Pál Hermann arrived here only a few months before the camps were disbanded and France was liberated. In the Paris archives I found his admission records for Drancy. When prisoners arrived at the admissions hut, the SS guards systematically and with their trademark efficiency stole everything of value that they had brought with them, and then recorded its existence. So we learn that Pál had nothing on him, apart from a little money. He would have arrived in the clothes in which he had gone to Place Wilson, hardly imagining that he would never return to his apartment.

The only other record of his arrival in the camp is a little slip of paper that neither Corrie nor I had seen before. Jewish internees were made to do the administration of the camp, so the handwriting on the form would have been that of a fellow prisoner. The administrators were usually internees whose complicated status made it likely that they would be resident in the camp for longer than most. They might have a passport from a protected country, or a spouse who was not Jewish, which would mean they would be classed as not immediately transportable. In a long, squat wooden hut between the horseshoe of high-rise flats, this particular prisoner recorded on Pál's form that his address was 19 Rue de Gorp, and that his profession was 'violoncell'. But it is the writing in another hand, added in coloured crayon, that catches my eye. Firstly, there are the initials 'V.1.E.' written under the address. This, I learn, stands for 'veuf. 1. enfant' (widower, one child). Corrie sucks in her breath as I point this out to her. Even there, in that bleakest of moments, she was present and remembered.

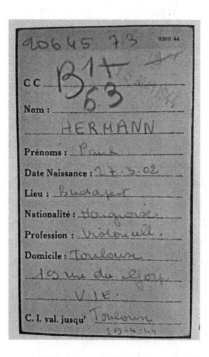

When camp commandant Alois Brunner had taken over the running of Drancy in June 1943, he had simplified the twenty-three categories of prisoner to just six. This meant that there were fewer reasons for someone to be spared, and less administration. Prisoners who were not instantly deportable would have C.1 written on their forms. Those who had no reason to be kept alive, were given the letter B. On the top of Pál's admission form, written diagonally in blue, is B1+. Pál was marked for death on his arrival.

∿

This was not a part of the trip on which Corrie wanted to accompany me, so I take the Métro and then the bus to Drancy alone, to see what I can find of the camp that was the gathering point for so many Jews from all over France. The town itself is as irredeemably dreary as its name implies. It's somewhere I hope never to have to revisit. As I circle it in a packed bus, heading in I don't know which direction, I watch an interminable parade of concrete high-rise blocks in varying states of disrepair jolt past the window. The bus stops in traffic alongside one block that is still being built. I inspect the computer-generated images on the hoardings: there is a picture of a young woman in an incongruous little black cocktail dress engaging a good-looking man in conversation on an imagined balcony. I look at the actual street in front of the building site. A tramp sits slumped in a sleeping bag at the bus stop. A young mother shouts at a crying toddler.

There is nothing lovely to see anywhere. This is the suburb of Drancy where, in the 1920s, the architects Eugène Beaudouin and Marcel Lods created a modernist community and named their vision La Cité de la Muette, the Silent City, anticipating a peaceful, quiet environment for its modern families. It was a dream for the future: for sanitary, aspirational social housing; the first high-rise residential tower blocks in France. And it was as unrealistic as the utopian visions pasted on the hoardings of today's new developments. Before building work was even completed, the Silent City had been requisitioned by the Nazis. Initially, it became a police barracks, but was then converted into the largest detention

Drancy camp.

centre in France for Jews and other political prisoners await-
ing deportation.

When I get to the apartment blocks that were once the
camp, I find to my surprise that an elementary school has
been built in an equally unlovely and dilapidated building
so close that it is practically touching the left side of the
complex. A gaggle of parents cluster round, waiting for their
children to emerge. To their right stands a wooden cattle
truck. It is out of context, not least as it is a short bus ride
from here to the train tracks at Bobigny station, but the link
is clear – for 90 per cent of the 67,500 French, Polish and
German Jews held here, the only way out of Drancy was by
truck. Fewer than 2,000 of those held here survived the war.

Between fifty and eighty-five people were crammed into
each seven-by-twenty-metre room. In the first few years there
was no furniture at all, but by 1944 a few bunk beds and a
wooden table had been added. However, the rooms were so

cold that some of this furniture was burnt by the prisoners, choosing temporary warmth above comfort. Most slept on fetid straw on the floor, which was alive with lice and bugs, and the beds themselves had straw matting which was just as heavily populated. According to one witness, you could see the creatures crawling across the ceiling. Hygiene was hopeless, as untreated raw concrete was impossible to clean. There were only two shower rooms for the whole camp, and the buildings built to house 700 ended up imprisoning around 7,000 at a time.

There were no activities, nothing to occupy the prisoners' time or thoughts, although there were occasional attempts to entertain the many children in the camp with a clandestine concert. Sometimes some poetry recitations or readings of Mallarmé or Baudelaire took place amongst the prisoners, but any official entertainment was strictly forbidden.

The barbed wire that surrounded the camp marked the division between two worlds. The windows that were outward-facing were boarded up, turning the camp's collective gaze in on itself. The rules were rigorously enforced by French gendarmes until 1943, after which the Gestapo guarded the camp themselves.

Any contact with civilians was punished by a stint in the basement prison cells. Internees were also put in the cells for stealing potato peelings, which was a particular temptation for those on peeling duty, as hunger was an obsession in the camp. They were allowed 300 grams of bread each day, with a watery broth for lunch. Meat or pasta was given once every eight days.

On my right, as I stand surrounded on three sides by rows of blank windows, are staircases 1–6. This is where prisoners were taken on the morning they were to be deported. Anyone who had been in the camp for more than a week or two would know the procedure, as in lieu of any other distraction, prisoners spent hours staring out of the windows, observing every movement in the courtyard. Those on the list were usually only told the night before, or early on the morning that they were to be deported. Such an announcement was what everyone in the camp feared most, the shadow that hung over them. Seventy-nine trains, long snakes of cattle trucks, packed with hundreds of Jewish children and adults, left Drancy concentration camp between 1942 and 1944. Pál had arrived just after a convoy had left. On 15 May 1944, after only two weeks in the camp, he was told he was to be on the next transport. Early on the morning of the 16th he was taken from the Silent City and put on a bus to the station at Bobigny. From there he was to be part of the train that was to become known as 'Convoy 73'.

Convoys were usually sent to Auschwitz, but the convoy on which Pál was to travel was different. He was to be one of 878 men who were crowded into the trucks for three days, most of whom were destined for Kaunas in Lithuania, the others for Tallinn in Estonia. Why this one convoy went there remains a mystery. When Drancy was abandoned by the Nazis in mid-August 1944, most of the documents were burnt, but prisoners managed to salvage a register of the names of those deported. This is the only record we have of Pál Hermann's convoy, and we can only assume that any further details were destroyed in the Nazis' hurried bonfire in the camp's final days. One account, by French politician Simone Veil, sheds a little light. She was being held in the camp with her family at the same time as Pál, and wrote in her memoir that Commandant Brunner told the young men of sixteen and over that, if they agreed to join the convoy, they would be given engineering work in France. Simone, her mother and sister all implored her brother Jean to volunteer for the group of men the commandant was assembling, in the belief that it would save him from being deported east, or ending up in Germany. The men, including Simone's brother and father, signed up voluntarily, and waited for their orders. 'Of course the whole thing was a blind; the commanders had never had any intention of employing Jews in the Todt business [a Nazi engineering organization].'[7]

It is not clear whether Pál Hermann volunteered for the convoy, or if his name was added to the list by the authorities. One theory is that the convoy was a ruse to get the strongest, most able-bodied men out of the camp, without any dangerous uprising. If so, then Pál would have been a prime candidate for the convoy, being young and fit, and not yet imprisoned long enough for his health to suffer. If he was signed up without his knowledge, it would have been the duty of his staircase supervisor, another non-deportable Jewish prisoner, to break the news to him. In some cases, internees pleaded to be allowed to swap places on account of their personal circumstances. Some of the lists reveal crossings-out and changes as last-minute reprieves were negotiated – lives saved and extinguished by the stroke of a pen. There is no line through Pál Hermann's name.

Faces would have watched from the windows all around as he was brought down to the yard at first light and lined up with the others to have his head shaved by one of the detainee barbers. He was then sent back to his room to have the morning cup of lukewarm coffee (which apparently resembled dishwater), and made to wash in the trickle of water from the hose in the corner of the room. There was a roll call, and prisoners designated for deportation were then herded together behind barbed wire in the front six staircases, divided from the rest, and watched closely by the gendarmes or SS to ensure there was no possibility of their melting back into the body of the camp. Men and women were separated, and some committed suicide at this point, throwing themselves down the steep concrete staircases or from the empty window frames. They did not know what they would face after Drancy, but assumed, often correctly, that instant death was preferable.

At dawn, the buses would arrive. There are very few photographic images of Drancy that are not staged propaganda. However, sketches drawn by internees do survive, and form a particularly important record of camp life. Looking through them, I find one sketch which puzzles me at first, depicting a hail of what look like large pieces of confetti raining down from windows, with men leaning out towards the yard. I later find in a survivor's testimony that this scene depicted internees left in the rooms above throwing morsels of saved bread down to a departing convoy. It is like a benediction, literal manna from heaven, reaching those below in a human-made hell.

Sketched by internee Georges Horan, 1945.

Sometimes the departing prisoners would sing 'Auld Lang Syne' or the 'Marseillaise', but mostly an eerie stillness prevailed, broken only by the low throb of the bus engines. Silence or music; nothing in between.[8] By July 1943, a year before Pál's internment, the camp commandant had taken over the nearby disued station at Bobigny as an ideal transfer point for the Drancy buses and their passengers. There were no disruptive civilians to witness what took place: just an isolated, nineteenth-century building that had once housed the railway workers. Long snakes of dark wooden cattle trucks lined up to meet the buses, and Nazi guards were ready to push the prisoners in. There were only two buckets in each truck: one of dirty water, the other a latrine. The stench would quickly become appalling. Simone Veil was herself transported from Drancy on 13 April 1944, and described the experience:

> There was a lot of jostling as everyone tried to make room for himself. We took turns to sit or lie down for a while. The SS only checked the transport at every station-stop. They walked up and down the train, issuing the warning that if anyone tried to escape, the whole truckload would be shot. Our submission was proof of the ignorance we were in. If we had had any idea of what awaited us, we would have begged the young people to risk jumping out of the train.

୬

I have been standing, staring at the windows of staircases 1–6 for some time. After a while I become aware of an elderly man, sitting on a bench under the young trees that now provide shade in the large rectangular yard. He is watching me.

'Qu'est-ce que vous faites?' he asks. I wonder how to explain. 'C'est un violon?' He points in the direction of my cello.

'Non,' I begin, 'it's a cello.'

I'd been resting my chin on the top of the case, lost in thought. It's now almost dark.

'Pouvez-vous le jouer?' he asks. A strange question.

'Well, yes…' I say. I feel some more explanation is needed, so I tell him I'm finding out what happened to a cellist called Pál Hermann, who was here. And my cello comes with me on my journey.

The man shakes his head in thought. I assume he thinks I'm quite mad. 'Jouez donc!' he says. 'Jouez pour votre Pál Hermann!'

I hadn't expected that. I hesitate, but the school run has finished, and there's no one else around. I get my cello out, sit on the iron steps of the cattle truck, and play several bars of Hermann's cello concerto. It echoes around the concrete buildings. I don't think my cello has ever sounded so mournful, or so alone.

Cattle truck, and staircases 1–6.

The man listens solemnly, nodding as if in agreement with the music. Then, with a crinkled suggestion of a smile: 'La Cité de la muette ne sera plus silencieuse.' And he nods to me, and ambles away.

INTERLUDE

Understanding the Cello: Stradivari I

Steven Isserlis is in the fortunate position of being able to pick and choose between two cellos. 'They have different souls, different voices, very distinct individualities and characteristics,' he told me when we chatted back in London. 'It's amazing when I play two Strads side by side: it's me playing, my voice, but they're so utterly different. It's almost funny!' He is a veteran Stradivari-owner, having played for many years on the 'De Munck' (also known as the 'Feuermann') Stradivari, made in 1730. He now plays on the 'Marquis de Corberon' Stradivari of 1726.

I ask him how he would characterize the 'Marquis de Corberon''s voice.

'Aah.' He smiles, seeming almost physically to relish talking about it. It is a real love affair – his eyes become misty when contemplating the voice of his beloved. 'It's aristocratic and poetic. A dream cello.' He has had it for over ten years, a loan from the Royal Academy of Music. They explained at the time that it was a loan for five years. 'But the cello and I were already in love. I simply looked at them and said "No, it's for life. You don't understand. If you take it away from me I'll kill myself, therefore it *is* for life." I was only semi-joking. I'd be utterly devastated if they took it.'

He describes his Stradivari as an 'old soul'. It's an idea I love. If a cello is an old soul, then its players, over the centuries, add their own contributions to that soul. If so, then perhaps Pál Hermann was never truly separated from his cello.

Anita Lasker-Wallfisch's son Raphael grew up in awe of his teachers' Stradivari cellos. First, he learnt from Amedeo Baldovino, playing the 'Mara' Stradivari, then the flame-haired and gloriously eccentric Amaryllis Fleming, with her Stradivari of 1717, which still carries her name. Like so many of Amaryllis's pupils, his face lights up when I mention her name. After she died, Raphael played her Stradivari for a long while. It was as if he were keeping her voice alive, long after she had become unable to draw the bow across the strings herself. He had hoped to buy it, until one fateful evening during a concert at Chester Town Hall he made up his mind never to be the owner of a Stradivari.

As he walked on stage for the second half of the concert, he walked too fast. He tripped, caught the spike on the step, and fell hard on his knees. The 300-year-old cello pole-vaulted across the stage and landed on its bridge. 'I felt sick. I was in total shock. I was supposed to play! I just picked up what was left of it, and staggered dizzily to my chair.' The audience sat in complete silence. After what felt like minutes he forced himself to look down at the cello, to assess the damage.

Splitting the front of a cello is, in Raphael's words, like 'irreparable brain damage. There is no way back from it, and I had watched it come crashing down onto its bridge. It was near impossible for the feet not to have pushed through the wood and splintered it. But I was amazed to find that the front was intact. I could see that the bridge itself looked a little wonky, so I tried then and there to adjust it, praying that on closer inspection I wouldn't see the soundpost poking out through the wood like a badly fractured bone. But no – it seemed nothing short of a miracle.'

Only then did he notice that the whole front was hanging off the ribs, almost completely severed from the rest of the body of the instrument. 'And still nobody said a word. I started to panic. There it was in my hands, Amo's precious Stradivari, unique and a part of her, entrusted to me temporarily by Charles Beare, one of the most respected cello dealers, and it was just hanging together with a bit of glue here, a bit of glue there.'

'What did you do?' I ask him.

'I tuned it. I couldn't think what else to do. It didn't occur to me to walk back off the stage – people had come for a concert, to hear this cello played, and I held in my hands the wreck of something that resembled a cello. Not surprisingly it sounded terrible when I played it. Somehow I staggered through the whole of the Rachmaninov Sonata with the front banging against the body like two dustbin lids.

'Afterwards, I wrapped it up so carefully and placed it in its case like a dead loved one. I couldn't believe what I had done to it. On the way home from the concert I wept as I drove. At 8 the next morning I was knocking at the nearest cello maker's door for help. He reassured me that while it looked desperate, it was in fact quite simple to fix, and glued it back together in a day. As soon as I could, I handed the Stradivari back, heart pounding, to Charles, saying "Thank you, but no thanks." It wasn't that I didn't love it – I really did. It was simply that I felt I couldn't handle the responsibility.'

I am reminded of a comment by Piatigorsky:

My cello has been transported on mules, camels, trucks, rowboats, droshkies, bicycles, gondolas, jeeps, a submarine off Italy, subways, trams, sleds, junks – and on a stretcher in Amalfi. But by far the most nerve-racking experience of all is when, in full dress, I must transport the cello in my own hands across the stage each time I have to play.[9]

I asked Raphael whether he ever saw the cello again.

'Indeed,' he replied, 'but years later. It was owned by an American cellist. I was delighted to see it again – it felt like finding a lost and precious friend after many years. She let me hold it, and play a few notes – it all felt so familiar. But I was very happy to hand it back. A Stradivari is too much of a liability. And I've learnt to walk much slower whilst holding a cello.'

Does a Stradivari really sound so much better than any other instrument? Julian Lloyd Webber has owned a Stradivari for many years. I went to meet him in Birmingham, where he was Principal of the Birmingham Conservatoire, to ask whether he believed we can tell a Stradivari from a less distinguished cello.

'The most extraordinary thing about Stradivari is that he had no idea of the kind of places that his instruments would end up being played in, such as the Royal Albert Hall,' Julian told me. 'And yet his are still the instruments with the biggest sound. Despite all the technology, modern manufacturers have still not been able to create an instrument that sounds like that. They get close, but I think a Stradivari is still 10 per cent better. I just don't think they can get the same quality of wood – Stradivari's is tough and takes the strain.'

When I put this idea to luthier Bruno Guastalla in Oxford, he jumps up and turns on an Anglepoise lamp. 'Aha,' he says. 'I have a theory about this.' After rummaging around under the workbench, he produces a tiger-striped back of a violin. It is clearly centuries old, battered and time-worn. 'Look at this, as I hold it under the light. You see?'

I look. It looks like a back of a violin, in close proximity to a lamp. I feel I am missing something.

He fishes out a modern back, recently varnished in a russet orange, and holds it up. 'Good. And now look.'

This time, the light shines through it, in streaks, illuminating the wood as if it were glowing embers.

He explains that, as the wood ages, so its natural resin dries, gradually, over many years, until the oldest instruments become solid, the fibres bound together so closely that no light can penetrate. It is a process that takes hundreds of years, and results in something that Stradivari and the early makers in Cremona could not have anticipated – an instrument that, like a good wine, has improved immeasurably with age. The fibres of the wood, knitted together over time, resonate in a way that can never be replicated by a younger piece of wood. In effect, the instrument is continuing to improve itself, long after the hand that shaped it has gone.[10]

It's not proven, but Bruno thinks this might help to explain why the oldest instruments, which tend to be the most valuable and prized, have the capacity to resonate in a way that has never been replicated. Some instrument makers and players go further still, maintaining that Stradivari had a certain magic which even Guarneri and Grancino didn't quite manage to achieve.

Violinist Joshua Bell was in London for a concert at the Royal Albert Hall when he stopped at Charles Beare's violin shop in Marylebone to buy some new strings. Charles happened to have a great Stradivari violin on the premises at the time, which was about to be sent to Germany: the 'Gibson ex Huberman' Stradivari of 1713. When Joshua picked it up and started to play he found himself shaking after he'd played only a few notes. It was his voice, his violin. He knew he had to have it.

> It is an amazing chemistry that one has with your instrument. And it's an amazing thing when you play a note and feel the overtones ringing. It's also a piece of history, and a beautiful work of art. It's so many things. And there are moments when I connect on stage, in front of an audience, and I'm playing great music, a Beethoven concerto, one of the greatest human achievements, on one of the greatest instruments ever made by a human being. These things, put together, make you feel elevated and incredibly privileged.[11]

As Joshua indicates, Huberman's Stradivari, with its unquestionably glorious, gutsy sound, is more than the sum of its parts. It is a story: an artefact resonant with emotion, meaning and history. The violin had been purchased for the prodigy Bronisław Huberman, who was born in 1882 in the poor Jewish quarters of Częstochowa in Poland, only about ninety miles from Anita Lasker-Wallfisch's hometown of Wrocław. In 1936 Huberman had taken his double violin case to the Carnegie Hall, and was playing his violin by Guarneri 'del Gesù' on stage, leaving his Stradivari in the dressing room. Julian Altman, a twenty-year-old American boy, well known at the hall as he played there in youth orchestras, had persuaded the backstage security to let him watch the concert from the wings. He later claimed that he had bribed them with cigars. As they went out to smoke, he walked into Huberman's dressing room, put the Stradivari under his coat and left.[12] In the interval, Huberman's assistant realized the case was empty, and there was general pandemonium. Huberman expected it might not be lost for long – it had previously been stolen from his hotel room in Vienna in 1919 but had been recovered very shortly after. Any instrument maker would recognize it, and it would be impossible to sell. But Altman didn't intend to sell it. He simply wanted to play it, so covered its priceless varnish with black shoe polish as a rough disguise and played it in cafés in Washington, DC and New York for the next fifty years. Only in the 1980s, when about to die in his prison cell (his adult career did not get any more moral), did he tell his wife to look between the outer leather cover of his violin case and the hard lid. There she found papers and newspaper clips relating to the theft, and realized what her husband had done.

By that time it was too late to return it to Huberman, who had died in 1947. And so, after Charles Beare had undertaken nine months of painstaking varnish restoration, the violin became Joshua Bell's. Would the violin have had anything like the visceral impact it had on Joshua when he first played it, if it were a modern instrument, or indeed, if he had played the same instrument, with no awareness of its history?

We cannot deny that there is an aura of legend wreathed around the extraordinary sound of great Italian instruments. There are so many theories as to why the sound of a Stradivari carries to the back of a concert hall, and why the wood or the varnish have a particular quality. Every luthier and every player has their favourite hypothesis. But, so far, none of them have been proved. I'd like to believe in a special race of Stradivari instruments, set apart, gods dwelling discreetly amongst mortals. But after my experiences of listening to (or not listening to) Nick's Grancino cello in Oxford, I can't be so sure.

For a start, there is no single 'Stradivari' sound. Antonio Stradivari spent his career experimenting, and not all those experiments paid off. While we think we hear something distinctive and extraordinary when we believe we're in the presence of a Stradivari, a 2012 study known as the Paris Double-Blind Experiment suggests otherwise. Soloists were given a valuable old Italian violin, and a modern instrument of similar quality, and asked to say which they preferred.[13] Without knowing which instrument was which, most came down on the side of the modern instrument. Later, the same experiment was conducted with an audience of luthiers, performers and the general public. Which instrument was being played – the old master or the modern violin? Which 'projected' or, in other words, had a sound that could be heard well at the back of the hall, and which sound did they prefer? Again, players and audience opted for the modern instruments. The researchers concluded not only that no one can tell the difference between the sound of a Stradivari and a modern violin, but that often the Stradivari was less favoured. At one point, a sextet from the Berlin Philharmonic all played on Stradivari instruments. The viola player was obliged to have some repairs on his and swapped his instrument for a modern viola at the last minute. He was singled out for praise in reviews of their performance, the beauty of his Stradivari viola being particularly commented on.

I asked the German cellist Maria Kleigel, who played the 'Gendron' Stradivari of 1693 for many years, whether she thought that – let's whisper it – the magic of the Stradivari is all in the mind. She thought for a moment, and then laughed. 'Let me tell you something that until now I have kept secret,' she said.

The 'Gendron' was a source of endless fascination, for audiences and the press alike. Maria did countless interviews about the instrument, and it was always commented on in reviews of her concerts. Being loaned the 'Gendron' was testament to her mastery of the cello; in turn it lent her playing an extra layer of glamour, mystique and excitement. She played up to her demanding celebrity partner, raising her game to meet its expectations, but taking care of the instrument was a great responsibility, as well as a privilege. She could not risk using such a spectacular cello for teaching, so she had a copy of it made: a body-double to take on the daily hard labour and grind. The 'Gendron' was reserved for the intimacy of the practice room and for shining in public.

One day she noticed that the left foot of the 'Gendron''s bridge was beginning to sag. The convex curve of the front of the instrument had started to become concave, as the bridge slowly began to push a hole into its front. The wood of a Stradivari is perilously thin, and any damage of this magnitude would be hard for the instrument to recover from. It was, in effect, fighting for its life. Maria was advised that she must have the cello 'operated' upon. There had been a weakness in its front for a century or so, but now it had become critical. With great reservations she handed her precious cello over to a luthier, for what might be up to a year-long convalescence. The 'Gendron''s front needed to be removed and the instrument put into a plaster cast to preserve its fragile shape. It was major surgery and came with a great deal of risk. No one could predict what the instrument's sound would be like when the operation was over, or what even the tiniest of changes would do to its personality.

Maria had to decide how to continue to play while her cello was in pieces. She might be able to borrow another valuable instrument, but it would not be the same. She would have to get to know it, learn its vocabulary, learn how to coax out the colours she required from it, and build up trust. She had become so used to the 'Gendron' and its quirks and oddities that it seemed too big a task to learn the secret language of another instrument. And it felt disloyal.

Instead, she began to use her modern teaching copy as a temporary replacement for the 'Gendron'. It was worth a fraction of the original, created as a homage to it, rather than a personality in its own right; but it was the nearest thing to the 'Gendron''s voice (and, by extension, her own) while the Stradivari was out of action. The touch was the same, the handsome appearance of the copy cello was identical. The only difference was the sound, which was palpably changed, lacking the quality of the original. The 'Gendron' had the advantage of hundreds of years of having every resonance, every harmonic coaxed and polished from it by the world's best players. There could be no comparison.

Maria did not tell anyone of the substitution. At first it felt too intimate a piece of news to share; the future of the 'Gendron' was too uncertain, and she felt that her own playing was inseparable from it. They always appeared in public together, and

Maria alone, without her glittering star of a cello, felt like a different proposition after so many years of their partnership. She was not ready to go solo, so she did not mention that the cello she now appeared with was, effectively, a fake.

She took the copy cello to Asia, playing it on tour in Japan in recitals and with orchestras. All the reviews commented on the unique, golden sound of her Stradivari, just as they would have done the year before. She was confused and a little amused. After concerts she held her instrument out to star-struck musicians, students and audience members who pleaded with her to see it, and touched it gingerly as if it were a holy relic. They believed they were, through their contact with the instrument, in communion with the greatest instrument maker the world had ever known. No one guessed. Would they have thought they heard the same honeyed sound had Maria told them that she had just played to them on a modern instrument 'knocked up' by an unknown German luthier a couple of years before?

Maria learnt that, in the hands of the same player, there was far less difference than she expected between one of the world's greatest instruments and its inferior copy. She found that it was *her* sound she was creating, *her* vision, the colours that *she* conjured in her imagination. The cello, far from leading her, as she had believed the 'Gendron' did, was in fact her servant, not her master. This realization reshaped her understanding of where she stood in relation to her instrument for the rest of her career.

When she was reunited with the 'Gendron', newly patched up, she found to her immeasurable relief that it was just as good as she had remembered. But for her, something fundamental had shifted. She now understood that this iconic piece of history, prized at millions, was not the star of the show. It was there to serve her.

From Paris to Cremona – Lise Cristiani

December 2021

As my cello and I travel, our partnership is creating around us a network of new friendships, chance meetings and companions dead and alive. And as I trace the stories of other players and their instruments, I find I am learning to delight in our reacquaintance, step by slow step.

Lise Cristiani travelled with her cello for company from Paris in 1848, right across Russia from west to east. Today, rumblings of unrest in Russia are preventing me from doing the same, so instead I am heading to Cremona to find her travelling companion, the 'Cristiani' Stradivari. But first I have to get myself from Drancy in the suburbs, over to the Gare de Lyon.

My cello and I wait in a taxi queue next to a woman trimmed from shoes to hat in luxuriously puffy real fur. She looks more lupine than human. The snow starts to fall around us. I imagine my cello shivering in its case and think of Lise Cristiani wrapping hers up in wolf furs to keep it from the Russian cold. Eventually a taxi arrives, and we leave Drancy and its dreary tower blocks behind. Soon we are back in the more familiar Parisian landscape of boulevards lined with cafés and restaurants, whose plastic awnings cover the wide pavements. We crawl slowly down Rue de Lafayette and Boulevard Beaumarchais, then eventually past the Opéra Bastille, all glass and curves. The taxi driver is singing along to U2, tapping his hand vigorously in time. Police vans, nasal sirens blaring, push past us in the heavy traffic, nosing us in and out of our lane. I feel a stab of anxiety at our creeping progress: the train to Cremona is due to leave quite soon now, and it's the last one today. Joggers pass us, their unhindered advance mocking our slowness. A man walks along with a Christmas tree, children with knitted mittens kick at the snow. 'C'est loin?' I ask nervously, at intervals. The taxi driver either ignores me or gives me an answer I can't understand, so I give up.

Running for a train with a cello on your back is no joke. The train to Cremona is at the far end of the Gare de Lyon. And not this bit of the station, a coffee seller tells me. I need Salle 2, right over there in the distance. I plod at what speed I can muster down a vast marble corridor with enticing-looking patisseries and perfumes, only to find that my train is on the very last platform, and my carriage turns out to be at the far end of the second of two trains standing at the same platform. (I have one foot on the metal step into a carriage on the first train, before I realize it is destined for the Alps.) I fling myself at the second train as the whistle blows, and the train is moving before I've taken my arms out of my cello case straps. Still panting from the exertion, I settle down for the eight-hour journey and pray I'm not heading for Grenoble.

As the hours pass and the sky darkens, the train makes its way south-east through a snowstorm of increasing intensity, until the stations we stop at along the way are interchangeable: their silent white buildings ghostly in the halos of neon, snow falling steadily in the beams thrown by the lights of the engine. It's the most perfect weather for imagining Lise's journey across the snowy steppes of Russia.

∽

Lise Cristiani was as much a travel writer and explorer as she was a cellist, a woman for whom boundaries, between genders, between civilization and the unknown, were not obstacles but challenges. Living with her story, and puzzling over her strange choices, I have come to believe that she was impelled by a deep curiosity and a sense of adventure. Whether or not she chose to play the cello of her own free will, the relationship she subsequently developed with it set her on a very particular path that was marked by the breaking of barriers. Her success on her unusual choice of instrument allowed her to travel to Denmark, Sweden, Austria, Poland and Germany, and, as was reasonably standard for musicians of the time, Russia. It was a well-established stop on the international concert circuit – Clara and Robert Schumann were just two of the star musicians of the day who played in St Petersburg – but Lise Cristiani's Russian adventures would take her far beyond the concert halls of the major cities. 'I let myself be heard in places where no artist had ever gone,' she wrote.

Part of the motivation for her trip into the eastern parts of the Russian empire may have been financial. After her initial concerts in St Petersburg and Kazan were less of a success than she'd hoped for, she postponed her intended journey back to Paris via London, and instead, pressed on through Russia. She may not have had sufficient money to travel home, or she may have been reluctant to return a failure. Plausibly, she might simply have wanted to take the opportunity to go off grid and explore. Whatever the reason for her change of plan, she found that the further she ventured, the less her gender and status as a genteel European lady seemed to matter, either to her or to her audiences. Was this an intended by-product of her decision to turn from ornament of the stage to explorer, or an added incentive? Perhaps she had intuited that there was little left for her in Europe once her audiences' interest in her as a young prodigy started to fade. Before arriving in Russia she had already acquired the title of 'principal cellist' from the King of Denmark, and earned the nickname 'Saint Cécile of France' in Sweden. But once the initial excitement had worn off, there was only so much curiosity the public could feel for a woman playing a man's instrument.

Between 1849 and 1853 she was to take her cello to regions further from Europe than most Western musicians had yet travelled, and with very different assumptions as to what women could or could not do. Her adventures were posthumously recorded (with some artistic licence and embellishment) in two articles, for the Parisian journals *Le Tour du monde* and *Journal des débats,* and facsimile copies of both are accompanying me as I travel.

❧

I crossed more than 400 rivers, small, medium and large, including the Urals, the Irtysh, the Yenisei, the Lena, the Aldan, the Amur and its mouths. I made all this way in the brishka, in the sledge, in the cart, in the carriage, sometimes pulled by horses, sometimes by reindeer, sometimes by dogs; sometimes

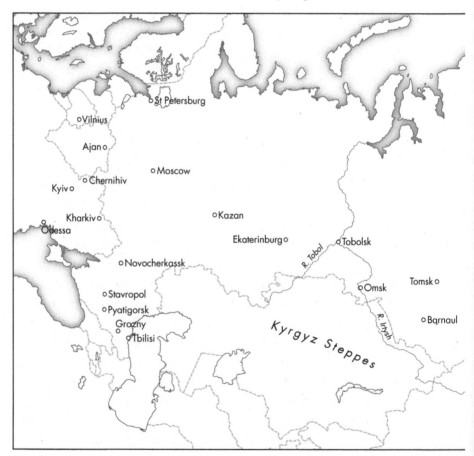

we had to go on by foot, and most of the time on horseback. I also travelled several hundred miles by ship on the rivers, and more than fifty days on the Pacific Ocean. I was received by the Kalmyks, the Kyrgyz, the Cossacks, the East Yaks, the Chinese, the Tungus, the people from Yakutsk, the Buryats, the Peuts from the island of Kamchatka, the savages from Sakhalin...[14]

In December 1848 Lise Cristiani set off from St Petersburg for Ekaterinburg in the Urals. Her travelling companions comprised her cello ('Monseigneur Stradivarius, my noble spouse!'), 'a fat Russian chambermaid and an old German pianist'. The concerts in Ekaterinburg proved to be a financial

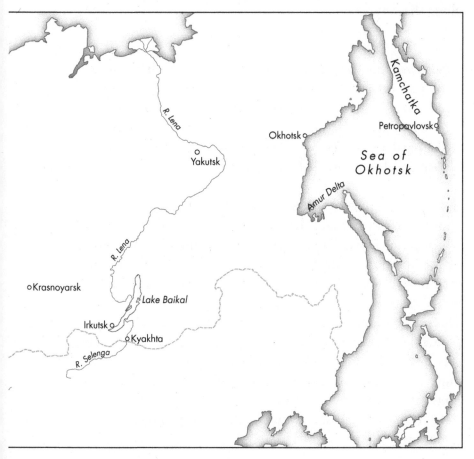

success, but instead of using the money to return home, she pressed on, ever further eastward, to Tobolsk, where her performances met with similar acclaim. When she left the city, on 15 January, it was 'with great pomp, with an escort of 25 or 30 Cossacks and numerous dog sleds, loaded with everything of the finest in the city'.

Over the next five years, with her Stradivari in tow, she would cover more than twenty thousand kilometres, experiencing the most inhospitable climates and landscapes. She trekked north-east across Russia, crossing Siberia from Tobolsk, where the rivers Tobol and Irtysh meet, to the Pacific coast in Russia's far east, performing at least forty concerts along the way.

～

So, here I am once again embarked on a crazy undertaking. I confess that I set out with pleasure on a journey that will be the crowning glory of my eccentric artist's life! However, it is not without a twinge of regret that I contemplate the two thousand leagues that I am about to add to the three thousand that already separate me from my home.

By the beginning of 1849, Lise had managed to travel to Omsk, Tomsk, Barnaul, Krasnoyarsk and finally Irkutsk, at which point travel conditions and the unpredictable nature of the weather made further progress too difficult for her little party. Irkutsk, the capital of eastern Siberia, is situated where three rivers merge and is 'at the edge of the world'. There Lise found an eclectic mix of artisans, merchants and political exiles. It was the last staging post of Europeanism, even of Christianity, with a small German community and a number of churches. It even had a theatre, although there was no theatre company to perform in it.

In Irkutsk Lise stayed with the governor-general, an important figure named Count Nikolay Nikolayevich

Count Muravyov-Amursky, painted by
Konstantin Makovsky in 1863.

Muravyov-Amursky, and his French wife, both of whom
struck up a friendship with her. Muravyov is remembered now
for extending the Russian empire as far as the Sea of Japan
in the east. At this point, he was planning an expedition east
across Siberia to Kamchatka, and then on to Petropavlovsk,
a port city which was half-Russian, half-Chinese, on the
border of the two empires. From there he intended to survey
the Amur delta and the far reaches of the provinces he controlled. His wife always accompanied him on his expeditions,
and the couple invited Lise to continue her travels with their
party to this area of political turbulence, under the much-
needed protection of the military. The summer season was
beginning in Irkutsk, so the upper-class concertgoers who

would most enjoy her performances would be absent, spending the warmer months of this decidedly chilly region in the countryside. Muravyov had instructions from the tsar to conquer the Amur delta – a military operation hardly compatible with a concert tour. But Lise apparently suggested to General Muravyov that 'in order to shorten the boredom of travelling, she should take her lovely Stradivarius with her'. 'Very well!' he responded. 'Go and conquer the estuary of the Amur, it will be quite a novelty to see a young Parisian woman playing the cello on the expedition, especially if they start firing cannon.'

At this point in her travels, Lise Cristiani seems to have been driven by a genuine sense of adventure. On 15 May 1849 she wrote: 'Now I have once again embarked on a mad venture. I admit that it is with pleasure that I begin this journey, which will complete the originality of my artistic life.' She lists with some delight the adventuring garb in which she and her cello set out:

Large riding boots with spurs; trousers of English knit up to the feet, a waistcoat of English flannel, chequered in black and white, a pocket paletot of black cotton, high-collared waistcoat, cravat neckerchief, a hat of grey felt, military gloves, the rod on the wrist, a coat of rubber fastened to the saddle, large, high-collared boots to cross rivers hanging on the horse's flanks, a mosquito net encircling my hat; the look of a cavalier, the face browned, a wild mount, always galloping, and there you have Lise in all her glory. As for Monseigneur Stradivarius, my noble spouse, from whom I did not wish to part, this was his travelling outfit: a wrought-iron box, soldered with lead, warmly quilted and padded inside; a paletot of wolf-skin, the pelt tied underneath, proper and fastened to the flanks of an exhausted bucephalo, which rumbled the instrument with importance, while I, mothering it with an anxious and

jealous look, followed it triumphantly seated on a Cossack
saddle, the coat closed up to the neck, the mosquito net
folded down, the rain on my back and the river under my
feet. Never has a violoncello of such noble lineage found
itself in such an adventure.

Since her Paris debut in virginal white she had mostly performed in 'a black, lacklustre dress, which must have been
the idea of a painter, because the brown violoncello and
the little lilies on the dark background look quite pictur-
esque'.[15] Now, she swapped the skirts for trousers, relishing
the freedom of her new androgynous identity. Her relationship with her instrument was a dynamic part of this
exhilarating, new-found agency – she was at once married
to her cello 'spouse' and mother to it; they were a pair of
adventurers in it together.

An impression of Lise's travels with the Muravyov party,
from *Le Tour du monde*.

Lise Cristiani spent eighteen days on a ship, travelling the 700 miles along Lake Baikal and then up the River Lena to Yakutsk, but did not feel on arrival that it would be a suitable place for a concert. For 'such ruffians it was impossible to even think of unpacking Stradivarius'. After a week or so in Yakutsk, she travelled on with the Muravyovs and their entourage, first 'in a cart, over broken roads', then in a small open ship, and finally for 260 miles on horseback. At the beginning of July 1849 she reached Okhotsk on the shores of the Pacific Ocean, where a government ship was waiting to carry her and her party 350 miles over the Sea of Okhotsk to Kamchatka – the furthest limit of Asia.

> in the Sea of Okhotsk, which we had tackled slowly, due to adverse winds, we had no other distraction than to watch the joyful frolicking of the whales. One of these enormous cetaceans tried to join us on our boat, much to the dismay of our passengers, who had an awful shock, not to mention great emotion, and were terribly scared. It was night-time; gasping, we ran onto the bridge. 'Who is it? What is it?' … 'Look!'. And we see the monster calmly making itself at home beneath our keel. Each of us, overwhelmed by a common sense of caution, began to talk quietly, out of fear of frightening the impressionable animal carrying us. Eventually, after having caught its breath, the whale thrust itself into the abyss, leaving a large whirlpool behind itself. We only saw it again once more, with its back to the sun, a mile away from us. Since, during the previous evening, Stradivari had offered the most touching melodies to the wind and waves, we guessed that the cetacean had been attracted by these unusual sounds; a naturalist accompanying us did not dismiss this idea, and from this moment it was decided on board that whales, like tortoises, were top-notch dilettanti.

On 10 or 11 August 1849, Lise arrived in Petropavlovsk, a port and the main settlement of the Kamchatka Peninsula.

In this unique country during winter it is not at all unusual to go and watch sleds being pulled by dogs who have been trained well in advance for the exercise. They have taken to their roles so well that even horses would struggle to match their speed. During the summer these animals are shackled and strewn together with five or six thousand other dogs close to the city at the edge of a stream with hundreds of branches which tend to wind around a hill. Here, each dog digs itself a shelter in the ground. They are brought sundried fish twice a day and have no other food throughout the whole of winter.

At Countess Muravyov's instigation, she gave a concert in Petropavlovsk, which had had little or no exposure to Western European music. She played solo, presumably because there was neither a piano nor anyone to play it. The concert was well received, and the local dignitaries treated her to a feast that included bears' paws, which she seemed not to baulk at. The audience had included the crew of a French merchant ship docked at the port, who had apparently enjoyed her recital immensely: the 'wonder and amazement of the French sailors was beyond description'.

Lise set sail from Petropavlovsk; while there is no record of the date of her departure, she records that she was at sea for twenty days, sailing back across the Pacific before arriving in Ajan, south of Okhotsk. Here, her style of music-making was not such a novelty, and she was able to play chamber music with local players. It was a relief 'to make real music with real musicians'. On the onward journey, however, she decided not to give a concert in Okhotsk as planned because her cello was in poor condition, hardly surprising given the travel conditions and climatic extremes. It is hard to imagine how she maintained such a delicate instrument under such circumstances, with no luthiers to attend to it. A month in Yakutsk followed, as 'we had to stop and wait for the sledge, whether we liked it or not'. She was at least able to give concerts, before setting off to travel the vast distance west, back across the country to Lake Baikal once more. It is one of the largest lakes in the world, covering 2,500 square miles, and is bordered by rocks. More than eighty rivers flow into it, making it not only one of the widest but also one of the deepest. Navigating it is dangerous since the winds are highly variable and its banks offer no shelter. But Lise was lucky: 'The crossing was remarkably quick, though the wind was so violent that the waves were rising as if in the middle of the sea and we had the embarrassment of suffering from seasickness on calm waters.'

With the great bulk of Russia now at her back, Lise travelled south over the mountains to Kyakhta, south of Irkutsk, and the last Russian trading post at the eastern end of the Russian frontier. She was now five times nearer Beijing than St Petersburg, as she noted with much satisfaction: the wilder the better for her. She had already travelled 4,000 miles since leaving Moscow and was keen to visit the Chinese capital, but to her great disappointment the authorities would not allow such a high-profile young female European access to China. They were nevertheless the soul of hospitality, offering their European visitors gifts and entertainment. Tea was sipped and pleasantries exchanged, while the Chinese cross-questioned them as to their motives for being there. The reason Lise gave was 'pure curiosity'.

After dinner one evening, she was invited to visit the theatre. She noted that the female roles were played by fifteen-year-old girls with 'good figures'. As a young woman herself, conscious of her appearance on stage, she took a particular interest in these teenage performers. The performance itself, however, left her cold; worse still, it seems that, for all her musical sophistication, Lise Cristiani was not particularly interested in cultural exchange. The interval between each scene was filled by a salvo of instruments. 'It was necessary to listen to this dreadful music to get an idea of the hullabaloo which all these tambourines, these gongs, these cymbals, and particularly a type of tambourine with two rings (which could be heard from a mile away) can produce.'

Nevertheless, with a Parisian eye for couture, she was won over by the remarkably beautiful costumes made from old, rare Chinese fabrics, even if she was unimpressed by the actors wearing them. Lise's response to the people of Kyakhta vacillated between a repugnance that to a modern reader smacks of racism, and an attraction or curiosity that is compelling. She sneered at the 'puny' men, with 'pale and sickly white faces, dark black, oily hair and small but expressive and intellectual eyes'. She was irritated by their ignorance and lack of imagination, but was equally aware of and sympathetic to the oppression and lack of education of which these were the result.

The next day Lise recorded a visit to the Buryat people of the mountains near Lake Baikal. She was escorted to them by an extravagantly exotic entourage consisting of 300 cavaliers wearing pointed fur hats and beautiful satin robes in different colours. They carried bows and arrows with shoulder straps and were mounted upon richly caparisoned horses. The Buryats were unimpressed with Lise's horses – they belonged to the local peasantry – and were not keen on allowing them to cross the Selinga river. They harnessed their own horses for her and her companions to ride instead, and galloped away with Lise and her cello into the steppe, while the cavaliers who surrounded them performed back-breaking flips to honour her and her party. It was a hair-raising ride: the Buryat horses were rarely called on to pull carriages, and she didn't believe they would reach their destination alive.

As she discovered more about the Buryat people, Lise's opinion moved quickly from romantic curiosity to disgust – they were followers of shamanism, a religious practice common amongst the people of eastern Siberia. She learnt that their supreme god lived in the sun and had a multitude of inferior deities under his command. His wife, amongst the 'less advanced' of these people, was 'an unsavoury object which hardly has a soul'. She continued dismissively, 'Fortunately, the members of this profane cult are on the decrease each day.'

She visited a Buddhist temple, where her relief at encountering what to her was a more acceptable form of religion was vitiated by her extreme distaste for non-Western music. If music is a universal language, then Lise Cristiani certainly didn't think it survived translation. She heard singing lamas,

> crouched like tailors in the temple, alternately chant sacred hymns (with rhythms surprisingly resembling our own church hymns) or perform diabolical symphonies on impossible instruments which unfortunately, for the ears of listeners, have a surprising resemblance to those of the Chinese; this horrible music awaited us upon our arrival and accompanied us on our way out for several metres.

~

The return journey to Irkutsk proved perilous. Separated from the rest of the group at one point, Lise was left to the mercy of a stumbling horse and an unsympathetic soldier.

> My man disappears before me, trotting away on his horse. We travel through a swamp which becomes more and more impossible to cross; I hope that he will slow down a bit; not at all, he remains at the same pace. Our horses fall, roll, do a thousand leaps and bounds, sometimes right, sometimes left, to avoid burying themselves in the sludge or to avoid the hailstones raining on their bodies. Nothing stops my companion, nothing stops me.
>
> A mountain replaces the swamp; a rapid descent hindered by rocks follows the mountain. Our exhausted horses refuse the speed of our course; we encourage them with nagaïka

whips: my companion keeps going and I closely follow him. Night falls and dangerous paths multiply beneath our feet; our exhausted horses struggle at each rock, at each root; my terrible guide maintains his hellish trot; I ask for a moment of grace; the darkness prevents me from being able to distinguish my path. 'Impossible,' he replied to me from afar. And I see it ahead of me in the pitch black. 'All is well, God is taking care of everything,' I shout back. I tighten my stirrups, pass the bridle twice over my hands, force out a wild scream, spur my miserable steed's flanks and let the hailstones from my whip fall onto his back; with all of this done, I left it in God's hands to take me where he pleased and in the horse's to get me there.

Lise arrived in Irkutsk during the winter of 1849, where she performed a 'farewell concert' that was, by all accounts, magnificent. There she left the Muravyovs and their military protection. She employed two Cossack soldiers to accompany her and her chambermaid, continuing her journey west from Irkutsk by sleigh, and stopping to give impromptu concerts whenever the opportunity presented itself. Performances in Krasnoyarsk apparently met with enthusiasm 'to the point of delirium'; encouraged by her success, she continued 'scattering melodies and concerts along the way wherever one could find even the shadow of an audience'.

The area was remote but not entirely devoid of organized music, and in Tomsk she found to her delight that the town had a large orchestra, 'which even played cleanly'. From there she made the long journey west to Tobolsk, near Ekaterinburg, for two months of concerts in the early spring of 1850. Audience member Franzeva Istoricheskiy Vestnik recalled that:

In the governor's beautiful house there were balls and often musical soirées were organised, at which sometimes artists from Moscow and St Petersburg took part: singers, pianists and violinists. I well remember Mahler giving a wonderful concert on the pianoforte; but better than all the others was Mlle Khristiani [*sic*] who had given concerts in France and Germany with great success. She decided to come to us at Tobolsk, probably out of a desire for new experiences. She captivated us at Tobolsk not only by her delightful playing on the violoncello, but also with her amiability and playfulness of mind.[16]

Lise was clearly in good spirits, and Vestnik remembered how she 'spoke cheerfully and playfully about her journey'.

Many members of Lise's audiences in Siberia were political exiles, including supporters of the liberal 'Decembrist' revolt of December 1825, who had been forced to leave Russia's major cultural centres because of their political stance, but who craved music and the arts. One of these was a cellist named Petr Svistunov, the eldest son of Mariya Svistunova, a musically accomplished lady-in-waiting to the Russian court. He had been sent into exile with hard labour in 1826 for being involved in a secret organization called the Southern League which was associated with the Decembrist's attempted coup; his mother had emigrated to Paris. Lise Cristiani's visit was a memorable experience for Svistunov: a tangential connection to his absent mother and a rare moment of brightness in a dreary and isolated existence.

Svistunov tried to make music in Tobolsk, organizing tours and concerts for young musicians, and quartet evenings in which he played. He hosted Lise, and performed with her as a duet partner in one of the concerts he organized for her. When she left Tobolsk, he wrote to his sister complaining of the difficulty in obtaining sheet music, but mentioning in particular his desire to obtain the music for Mendelssohn's 'Song without Words' (which was not yet published). He could only have heard it played by Lise, its dedicatee. Once she was gone, he missed the excitement and the touch of celebrity that her visit had brought to the quiet backwater in which he was obliged to remain. 'For Tobolsk it was the best concert heard since we have lived here. Since Cristiani has been gone, the humdrum of everyday life has begun again.'

For Lise, life also grew darker, as she set off in February to cross the Kyrgyz steppes of Kazakhstan, wreathed in snow. Her letters home begin to register a note of despair and depression that is a long way from the adventurous spirit of the girl who had eagerly accompanied the Muravyovs a year before.

> This eternal shroud of snow has brought a chill to my heart. I have just crossed 3000 versts of plains; nothing, nothing but snow! Snow that has fallen, snow that is falling, snow that will fall. An endless steppe where one gets lost, where one gets buried! My soul has finally let itself be wrapped in this funereal winding sheet: it seems to me that it lies frozen in front of my body – my body that contemplates it but does not have the strength to warm it up.

She survived the journey across the steppe, returning to Moscow in March 1850 to give more concerts. All that is known about them is that, for whatever reason, they were not a financial success; after more concerts in April she was obliged to take to the road once more. Here there is a gap in the narrative for two years, as she struggled to support herself, condemned now to travel in search of income rather than exploring for the sake of adventure. There was nothing at all romantic about her state of mind when, faced with poverty, and without the money even to return home, she was obliged to consider selling the only asset she had: her cello.

If only I could get a good price for it, I would return to Paris, of course not without the terrible pain that this sad separation would cause me, I love my faithful companion more than anything! But what of it, if I have to part with him, then I will bow, what are a few tears more or less?

Between January and March 1852 she travelled west across Ukraine, playing in Kharkiv, Chernihiv and Kyiv. She met the celebrated French cellist Adrien-François Servais, with whom she had been compared (largely unfavourably) in her European reviews, and crossed what are now the borders between Poland, Lithuania and Ukraine to play in Vilnius and Odessa. At the end of 1852, Lise travelled to the Caucasus, journeying via Stavropol to Grozny in Chechnya, where Russia was fighting a war of conquest against the peoples of the North Caucasus. It was a volatile and dangerous region, with high levels of kidnappings and murders, and Lise appears to have been in no condition to withstand either the climate or the dangers of the place. She was by now, her grandfather would later write, 'already suffering from a kind of fever and emaciation'.

Lise had organized to stay with a Prince Bariatinski, whom she had never met, and was pleasantly surprised to find an unexpectedly 'handsome young man', not the 'old, unintelligent head of grumpy appearance' she had expected.[17] Once in the safety of the prince's home, she became a kind of forces' sweetheart *avant la lettre*, spending most of January 1853 playing for the soldiers stationed there. It was clearly a relief to her to find some purpose in what had become a life of aimless travel, and she delighted in providing a glamorous, feminine distraction for the men, many of whom would lose their lives in the fighting with the indigenous inhabitants of the region. 'How many of them, to whom I had promised a romance in the evening, which had been particularly dear to them, I never saw again, only as nocturnal ghosts.' She both played and sang for them, and swapped her leather boots and explorer's garb for her most beautiful concert dresses to distract the 'poor devils who could fall victim to a Chechen bullet from one moment to the next'.

However much she enjoyed offering comfort to her admiring audience of young men, Lise knew she could not impose on the prince's hospitality forever. She was condemned to go on, although by now she had had enough. There is no record of when she left, or what her destination was, but by early September the tone of her correspondence had become alarming.

> I have death in my soul, my pains rise, my strength wanes; what is to become of me now? I have tried everything, even in this damned country where a gun lurks behind every bush, but I have no luck, instead of the bullet I was looking for I got nothing but sweets snatched from Shamil in some scuffle. Isn't that a great misfortune?

The next concerts of which there is any record were in Tbilisi on 21 March and Pyatigorsk on 18 July 1853. Leo Tolstoy attended in Pyatigorsk, and made the following peremptory and typically grumpy note of the event in his diary: 'Got up late. Nikólenka interrupted me. Had scarcely begun to write when we went to Masha's and I stopped there all day. I went to Christiani's [sic] concert. Poor stuff. Why does nobody love me? I am not a fool, not deformed, not a bad man, not an ignoramus. It is incomprehensible.'[18] It is difficult to know how to read his cursory dismissal of Lise's performance. Is it simply in keeping with the grumpy mood of the rest of Tolstoy's diary entry, or was she really struggling, her mental health and lack of physical strength preventing her from playing well? There are no reviews with which to compare this note, and she does not mention the quality of her playing. But her instrument certainly suffered. The 'Cristiani' Stradivari still today bears the marks of the extreme temperatures that both player and instrument had endured. There are cracks in the wood of its front, despite the protection of wolf fur and lead case.

~

Towards the end of September 1853, Lise arrived in Novocherkassk, near Rostov in the Caucasus. Looking back on her journey, tired, depressed and ill, she wrote:

> I played in places where no artist had hitherto set foot, I gave around forty public concerts, not counting the private soirées and the times I was able to find to play music for my own pleasure. Such is the sum of my bold adventure. 'A rolling stone gathers no moss' says an old proverb; I have proved the veracity of this saying myself. I feel dead inside...

Her arrival in Novocherkassk coincided with an outbreak of cholera. Weakened from her years of wandering, she quickly succumbed. After only a day's illness, Lise Cristiani died on 24 October, the day before she was scheduled to give a concert. She was twenty-six years old. No one knows where her body was buried. There are no accounts of her funeral, no letters written to her relatives that have survived.

Lise had been travelling all of her adult life. Since her debut in the Salle Herz, she had spent more time abroad than in Paris, and uprootedness was more a way of life for her than an exceptional circumstance. Now, she was displaced even in death, since there was no question of her body returning to France. Her cello, however, could not remain in the depths of the Caucasus, so the French ambassador arranged to have 'Monseigneur Stradivarius' return home, alone. A year later, the Parisian music journal *Le Ménestrel* reported that the famous Stradivari 'ex-Cristiani' was being sold by the luthier Montel.

The design for Lise Cristiani's tomb.

According to *Le Tour du monde*, the townspeople of Novocherkassk designed a magnificent tomb for Cristiani, into which is carved a representation of her faithful travelling companion – her Stradivari – as if husband and wife were buried together in the same grave. The only picture of the tomb I can find is at the end of the journal's article. However, when I talked to Marie-Thérèse Grisenti, a Parisian cellist and one of very few players who know Lise Cristiani's story, she told me that she didn't believe this tomb existed. The engraving is the architect's impression of the tomb, but the money for this extravagant tribute was never raised. It was never built, she said. Lise was forgotten in the confusion of a virulent cholera epidemic in which people were losing their loved ones every day. What was the death of a French girl who had been in the city for only a day, compared to the death of a husband, wife or child?

After her death, Lise's grandfather and brother set about commemorating her, both in verse and in the Parisian journals. They were the men who had given her the cello, the object that had been both her liberation and her destruction. They had not seen her for five years and could have had no idea of the woman she had become during her expedition. But their words must stand as her memorial, nonetheless. Lise Cristiani's disappearance is a double vanishing: erased both physically, her body lost in deepest Russia, and metaphorically, from musical history. Her beloved Monseigneur Stradivari, however, would enjoy a rather different fate.[19]

Cremona – Lise Cristiani

Cremona station is more palazzo than railway terminus. Its pastel stucco walls set off an ornately carved wooden ticket office, and its graceful decorated halls are the perfect preparation for the city itself. Painted in glowing shades of peach and ochre, most of the buildings have a gentle, understated elegance. The ancient cobbled streets are so narrow that the wintry gloom is broken by pools of light from lanterns slung on central overhead wires, as there is no room on the little pavements for lampposts.

I settle my cello in my new Airbnb and set off to visit the Museo del Violino and one of its most prized possessions, Cristiani's Stradivari. As I leave the building, I can hear an accordion player. The streets of Cremona are full of music. A short while later a saxophonist walks by, playing a funky version of 'Jingle Bells'. I pass a luthier's shop window in which a cello is displayed with reindeer antlers perched rakishly over its scroll. Inside the colonnades of the museum I am greeted by a huge metal statue of a man completely made of musical staves and notes. The statue, by Jaume Plensa, is entitled 'L'anima della musica' – 'The Soul of Music'. The phrase would come to take on a significance for me that I could not have guessed as I stood in front of it that wintry morning.

I head up the steps, past 'The Soul of Music', into the museum. This is not, in fact, my first visit. A couple of years earlier, I had managed to obtain the torturously complicated paperwork to allow me to play the 'Cristiani'. It took months of negotiation between the BBC and the museum, but permission had eventually been given. The museum had closed the public galleries, and an armed guard had stood by as the museum's director, Fausto Cacciatori, produced a key attached to his belt like a gaoler, and carefully and with much ceremony unlocked the glass box that held the 'Cristiani'. Gingerly, reverently, he unhooked the instrument from the wire that suspended it by its scroll and handed it to me. Together we examined the front and back, the gentle curve of its ribs, the texture of the varnish. Fausto produced a chair, and motioned for me to sit. With much trepidation I began to play, never with him more than a few centimetres from the scroll of the instrument.

When I drew the bow across the strings, it felt as if the whole cello shuddered with vibrations of pleasure, almost wriggling in its wooden skin. And *what* a sound it made. Rich, resonant, like all the most exquisite sounds distilled into one note. The response between hair and string was so immediate, I hardly needed to move the bow to elicit a sound, and to play felt like releasing a bird from captivity. I couldn't help thinking that things that are made to move *want* to move. This was a cello that wanted to fly and take me soaring up with it.

As I played (Mendelssohn's 'Song without Words', inevitably), I was keenly aware of Lise Cristiani herself. My hands and fingers were touching the instrument she had handled, making the same shapes that were necessary to produce the sounds she had made. Playing her cello brought me as near as it is possible to get to hearing Lise's own voice.

At the same time, I knew it was not quite that simple. The strings were not the original strings, of course, and they bore little relation to the ones Lise would have played on. Instead of the gut strings that she would have used in the 1800s these were modern and harsher, and the bow I used was not her bow, so inevitably made a different contact with the instrument. Even if I'd had identical strings, and the bow had been kept with the instrument all these years, I could not hope to coax the voice of some past cellist into being, like the summoning up of a spirit. The pressure I used was not likely to be the way Lise would have drawn sound out of her cello. My physical build is different from hers. She might have played with more or less tension, more or less attack at the beginning of the note. She might have played with more commitment to the end of the bow, a faster, or more relaxed vibrato.

I knew I could not hear the voice she heard, but only an echo of something she might have recognized, resonating faintly under a more modern, alien sound. A cello is not a medium, and playing is not a séance for communing with past masters. But there was, all the same, some thread of connection to the past. As I listened, not to the note I was playing, but to the whisper under it, I was conscious of a desire to make the cello give up its ghosts. I was searching for a shadow behind the sound, a memory shaped by centuries of movement.

✧

The permissions process has changed since my first visit, and I know that I will not be permitted to play the cello today. Now I will only be able to look at it through a layer of thick, protective glass. While I am eager to see it again, a part of me is dreading its silence. The 'Cristiani' without a player will remain mute and secret.

There are sleeping beauties like this all over the world. Waiting in vaults and glass cases to be heard. When Guillermina Suggia died, her will stipulated that her Stradivari should be left to the town of Oporto in Portugal, to be kept in a museum there. She decreed that it could only be played if cellists came to the town to play it – it was not to be taken out of the city. Occasionally cellists come, but for the rest of the time it waits silently.

Not everyone can bear the idea of their instrument being silent. When Julian Lloyd Webber was forced to sell his beloved 'Barjanksy' Stradivari, he felt very strongly that he could not countenance giving it to anyone who would keep it locked in a vault. 'There is nothing sadder than a cello that is not played,' he says. 'The most criminal thing would be if it just ended up in a museum.'[20]

Human nature drives us to want to hear our dead. We listen back through generations, across graves. 'What would the late "so and so" have said?' we ask ourselves repeatedly. A cello in this sense represents a kind of resurrection – the body that survives beyond the lifetime of its player. How tempting, then, to want to put my ear to the F holes of the 'Cristiani', to listen for its heartbeat.

∾

The silence of the cellos in the museum in Cremona is not just the silence of extraordinary instruments kept in glass cases. The museum is full of parts of instruments, objects that speak of a cello's journey from tree to concert platform. They gesture towards a different silence, the silence before a cello's birth – 'before life and after', as Thomas Hardy has it.

As I wander around the collections, I move from room to

room, pulling open drawers full of wooden and card templates delineating the various shapes that go to make up a cello. They are the dismembered constituent parts of the greatest instruments ever to be made. Cello by numbers. A rib here, a fingerboard there. There are recipes for instruments, pieces, moulds, shapes suggesting cellos and violins.

But there's something missing, surely – a magical ingredient. It's like constructing a person bit by bit, a collar bone shaped like this, this many ribs, shin bones, thigh bones. But what is their sense of humour like? How easily do they cry? Assembled with animal glue, chiselled away, pared and shaped, these fragments and parts will create a space in which a personality, unique and unpredictable, with its own unimagined voice, can have life breathed into it.

Objects draw us together, connecting those who have made and used them across time. When Stradivari and the luthiers in his workshop were creating these patterns, they were also creating the blueprint for centuries of communities. An international network of luthiers and performers through the ages, copying, studying and mastering the art of making and performing.

~

I am aware that I am delaying the moment of my re-encounter with the 'Cristiani'. I walk at a deliberately slow pace, working my way through the development of stringed instruments from the 1400s to the present. I watch the short videos of a luthier making a violin from a mould, shaping the thin wood around the sides, carving the neck and scroll, until some unpromising pieces of tree are coaxed into becoming a miracle of engineering. I stop to read the history of Stradivari. Then, finally, when there is nothing left for me to look at, I climb the stairs to the central room known as il Tesoro Trovato – the Treasure Trove. It is the 'soul' of the museum's collection, and at its very heart is the 'Cristiani'.

I know where I'm going. But even prior experience doesn't lessen the disconcerting, otherworldly experience of standing in the Treasure Trove. This is the room in which some of the most precious instruments in the world are displayed. In the half-lit gloom of the dark red velvet walls, the violins and cellos hang in their glass cases. I find myself thinking of meat in a butcher's shop, or foetuses in jars of liquid. There is a cacophony of dissonant string playing piped continually through speakers on both sides. Perhaps one clear and coherent sound would be too specific and distracting, but the effect is eerie, almost unbearable. The room is a womb-like mausoleum, with a swirling, pre-natal mash-up of sound.

Yet at the centre of it all is silence. When I came here on my previous visit, I invited the Korean violinist Min Kym to accompany me. A child prodigy (with all the loneliness and insecurities that entails), she had built her career around

The Treasure Trove, with the 'Cristiani' centre stage.

her Stradivari violin. It was 'The One' for her, her 'soulmate'. And then it was stolen. She waited for three years before the police were able to recover it, but by that time she could not afford to buy it back from the insurers. She held it and played it once, before it was taken away by the investor who had just bought it. Her voice, held in that violin, is now somewhere in a bank vault, a part of her she will never hear again. It's a loss she experiences as the deepest grief.[21] When on that previous visit we walked together into the Treasure Trove, the silenced instruments as inaccessible as her incarcerated violin, she went to the glass cases and put her ear to them. She told me she was trying to hear them whisper to her, to catch a flicker of a breath.

ꜱ

When visiting Charles Beare's home in Kent, I had relayed to him that Min Kym and I had felt a sense of mourning for the silence of the 'Cristiani' cello. As a practical man, and an instrument dealer, he was having none of it. 'These instruments must and should be kept in glass cases,' he insisted. 'They are great works of craftsmanship, and they need to be preserved as a template and something to aspire to for makers.' And of course on one level he was right. He had in fact worked to acquire the Stradivari instruments for the city of Cremona between 1961 and 2000, including securing the 'Cristiani' for the museum, and in recognition of his achievements the city had made him an honorary citizen. When he looks at the 'Cristiani' he sees the product of a craftsman, whereas Min and I see something mute and untouched, something that could sing in our hands.

When I returned from this first trip I had told cellist Natalie Clein about Min's loss of her Stradivari, and her despair and depression as she tried to retrieve it from the men who stole it.

'What would it feel like to lose your cello?' I asked her.

Natalie was horrified at the very idea. She clutched her throat. 'Here. I'd feel it here,' she said, instinctively. Then she reflected for a moment. 'I'd feel as though my voice had been taken from me.'

Silence is not only a verb, it is also a noun, a place of possibilities and freedom. Plato talks about words needing to be read aloud so they are not just left standing in silence. I feel that Min's and my perception of what an instrument is and what it means, of the very life within it, is something similar. Ivan Gaskell, an expert in material culture, describes how collaborations between museums and indigenous populations have resulted in museum curators realizing that some objects have a life they have not acknowledged. To imprison such objects in a case is like keeping animals in too small a cage. Gaskell believes that museums have sometimes failed to perceive the religious or medicinal significance of some objects in their collections, particularly those that belong to other cultures. Recently, curators have been more attentive to the power that these objects have, the voices they haven't been listening for, and treat them differently. Objects such as the contents of Plains Indians' medicine bundles or the dangerous medicinal designs on warriors' shields are now respectfully hidden from view. Other objects that might require appeasing are now stored and displayed with 'small offerings of tobacco, sweetgrass or sage'.[22] This feels more like it to me. Perhaps a cello, when incarcerated in a museum, ought to be stored with its own voice. A recording of it, playing constantly.

Today, wandering between the violins and violas, I find myself thinking that the antiquity of the instruments, whether whole or in pieces in their display cases, brings home their otherness, their difference. We can't listen back through the centuries with pure ears; we are contaminated by the music we have heard that the past player would never have dreamt of. Nothing played in E minor on a cello can be free of the chocolatey, dark stirrings of Brahms's E minor Cello Sonata, and, of course, Elgar's Cello Concerto. And then there's the fact that our pitch is different; what we think of as the note A is set at 440 Hertz, whereas a cellist from, say, the 1740s would have heard an A as a semitone lower than the one we're used to. If even notes and keys sound different to us than they would have to a player such as Lise Cristiani, then trying to hear what her cello might have to tell us is a hopeless cause.

To make matters more complicated, even if we are allowed to take a precious cello from its glass prison, it can take time to master a great instrument, and to learn its language. Cellos have their own idiosyncratic behaviours and their own dialect and attitudes. Some strings need to be coaxed, drawn reluctantly out of themselves. Other strings or particular registers are bright and not at all camera-shy. A skilled player will map out their movements around the cello to avoid or showcase its different aspects, able to predict how it will behave. Often these tics are learnt the hard way, in rehearsal and in concert. Some notes are always reliable, others might let you down. How close to the bridge will the cello let you play before it squeaks? How slowly can you draw the bow across the strings before they refuse to resonate? Where exactly between fingerboard and bridge do you play to achieve the colours you want? The external result is the music: ordered sound, played as dictated on the page. But underneath there is a tacit conversation: a loving, coaxing, often frustrating negotiation going on between player and instrument. A private, intimate meta-text to the music itself.

꩜

I have made my way through the gloom and plush velvet of the Tesoro Trovato, along the rows of instruments hanging as if in formaldehyde, until there is nothing else to look at but the one centrepiece of this collection. Right in front of me, right here, is… a big, empty glass case. The label is there – 'Stradivari, "ex-Cristiani"' – but no instrument. Nothing. This is a kind of silence I was not expecting.

I stand there for a full minute. I feel rather daft, as if I have been stood up. After all, I have come a very long way to see this cello, and had all kinds of grand plans, most of which included pleading with Fausto Cacciatori to let me play it, even without the paperwork. Instead, not only can I not touch it, I cannot even see it. I have now stood in front of the empty case for longer than is reasonable and, feeling rather self-conscious and at a loss, I move off into a side room to revisit some of the hanging violins. When I return, the glass case is open, and Fausto and another man are putting the 'Cristiani' carefully back in its place. I don't know whether to be relieved or frustrated – I've missed it being unlocked and out, but at least it's back, still in Cremona and on show. As it turns out, luck is on my side: the dark, curly-haired young man with Fausto is the cellist Andrea Nocerino. He is one of the very few who are allowed to play the instrument, and had been practising on the 'Cristiani' ready to perform in the museum's auditorium tomorrow at noon. I may not be able to play the cello myself, but I've unwittingly timed my visit for one of the few times in the last couple of years that the 'Cristiani' is to be played.

⌣

Andrea's relationship with the 'Cristiani' began two years previously, when he was engaged to spend six weeks recording every possible sound the 'Cristiani' could make, at every conceivable dynamic, an in-depth mapping of all the possibilities of the instrument. Should the 'Cristiani' ever be destroyed, or become too fragile to play, its voice would live on, as digital data. The sound engineers were trying to capture the soul of the instrument, note by note, and the operation was enormous. During the recording sessions the surrounding streets were closed to cars, for absolute silence, and all traffic was rerouted – as if saving the sounds of the cello was akin to an extended royal visit.

I wonder about the grammar of any sentence recorded note by note like this. The virtual 'Cristiani' sounds good, Andrea tells me, but suspiciously good. It's too perfect to be true, with none of the squeaks and hisses of mortal, fallible performance. His experience puts me in mind of a quote by the musicologist Murray Schafer, who coined the enticingly resonant term 'soundscape'.[23] Schafer understood the transience of sound, noting that 'all sounds of the present will soon become sounds of the past'.[24] And so, in a project rather similar to the 'Cristiani' recording, he began to collect soundscapes, capturing the whistles of factories, the patterns of nature, the bells of a village church, in order to create his own museum of sounds.

Few people have had the opportunity even to touch the 'Cristiani'. How did Andrea feel about being thrown together with the greatest cello in the world, to explore every possibility, every element? 'I was scared at first', he tells me, 'and couldn't do the right thing to start with, as I was so anxious not to push the instrument and damage it.' So he began to get to know the cello from just one sound, one simple note, gradually feeling his way until he had understood what the cello required of him. As we talked, I realized he'd had the same experience as I had: of the 'Cristiani' wanting to race away under my fingers.

'On each note there is an exact moment of vibration, a golden point,' Andrea says. 'When the note is exactly in tune, then it suddenly leaps and sings. It doesn't do this when pushed. It's like a light turning on. It isn't even something you can hear – it's a vibration, a purr in the instrument. The fingers and your body feel it first, then it reaches the ear. This vibration is really beautiful, but it can be too much for the instrument. It's almost transgressively beautiful. The instrument shudders, there is a buzz – the purfling, edging around the front of the instrument, vibrates, slightly loose in its setting. It's too much for it.'

There is another curious phenomenon associated with the 'Cristiani'. When a player's body touches the wood of the cello for a length of time, a white cloud appears on the instrument: a fog at the point of contact, which disappears after a few hours. No one has any idea why. 'The first time it happened, I screamed!' says Andrea. No one at the museum had ever seen this before, as no one had been allowed to play it for this length of time. 'They're running some tests, but no one knows why this happens. It's like it's haunted.'

I explain to Andrea that I'm interested in what stories a cello can tell us: in this case that Lise Cristiani's cello was her body-double, and I'm convinced that something of her is retained in it after thousands of hours of playing. Even if it's as prosaic as damage to the varnish. Andrea nods enthusiastically. 'Yes, that's *exactly* how I feel it is,' he says.

He tells me about the celebrations to commemorate the eighteenth-century composer and violinist Giuseppe Tartini in Trieste, coincidentally the city to which I'll be travelling after I leave Cremona. As part of the celebrations, Tartini's own violin was played at the music school there. 'What was it like?' Andrea had asked the violinist. 'Horrible!' she'd said. It was badly kept, with terrible strings on it. 'But the instrument's quality was not the point. The amazing thing was, we could all hear the third sound when she played.'

'What', I ask him, 'is the third sound?'

'It's something Tartini discovered. He wrote about it. The Tartini tone. He derived a whole theory, and there are scientific reasons why this happens. But the point is, that with his beaten-up old violin, we can hear what *he* heard. We can retrace his steps, see how he reached the conclusions and theories about music that he did, as we hear what his violin was telling him. Together they had explored these possibilities, man and violin, and now only the violin survives to tell us.'

In Andrea's company, I begin to feel more confident about my own conviction that we can look for someone in their instrument. Even if the bonds that link player and cello together are as basic and practical as physical damage to the instrument, they still open a door for us into a previous player's world. Lise Cristiani saw those temperature cracks appear. She knew how to navigate the quirks of the instrument, just as Andrea now does.

'To play the "Cristiani",' he continues, 'there are vibrations you feel. Following them becomes more important than the piece itself. You're following a different map, and it isn't the notes on the stave.' Andrea is convinced these vibratory patterns come from the work of other cellists who have played the instrument repeatedly before him. 'They're like the traces of an archaeological building. They are the footsteps in which we follow. Someone has done the work already, and I'm map-reading their musical personality, shaping my playing to their pattern.' And because there have been so few serious players of the instrument since her, he feels he has a direct line back to Lise herself. The notes on the 'Cristiani' are in slightly different places than on other cellos, as the fingerboard is enormously long. So to play it we must place our fingers in the very particular places Lise would have done. Even if the fingerboard has been changed, the experience of the stretches between the notes remains the same.

'When I play my own cello I have to direct everything: dynamics, tone quality. It's a double job. Whereas when I play the "Cristiani" I find it has its own musical opinions. And if I don't follow what it brings to me, it just won't be the same. It will crack or lack resonance. There's no point straying off the path. There are three people in the relationship when you play a cello like this: the composer, the cellist and the "Cristiani". So even if it isn't Lise's voice we're hearing and tapping into, it's the voice of her instrument, the map she would have learnt, and followed herself.'

I am reminded of the conversation I had had back in England with Julian Lloyd Webber. He told me he used to feel that if he was playing a piece on his 'Barjansky' Stradivari for the first time, he often had a sense as to whether the cello had played it before. Something about the way the instrument resonated would gently steer his performance. He felt this with the Dvořák Cello Concerto. 'It was as if it was saying "Okay, you do it *this* way."' Conversely, there were other pieces he would play that he felt certain the cello had not played before.

I asked Julian whether he thought he could feel the ghosts of its previous players. To my surprise, he nodded. 'Particularly when I first played the Delius concerto. My cello sang, it felt so free. It really was as if it knew it. It was only after some time that I remembered that the "Barjansky" Stradivari had actually been the instrument to premiere that concerto, decades before.

ॐ

Andrea and I have wandered around most of the glass cases, and the bits of instrument moulds, and find ourselves drawn back to the 'Cristiani', hanging in the half-light. I have made my peace with not being able to play it. I know that, between us, Andrea and I have touched something that was Lise Cristiani's, that she would recognize. To play a historic instrument is to hold hands across the past with those who have gone before. But what kind of hand-holding is it when we play instruments whose previous owners are unknown? Perhaps it is our knowledge of Lise that shapes our experience of playing her cello, rather than the other way round.

There are no answers to these questions, only the undeniable sense that we feel closer to Lise when we play her instrument. And that is enough for now.

⌇

The next morning, before Andrea's lunchtime performance, I meet some of the students at the instrument-making college nearby. One of the students has created a cello by copying an old instrument, faithfully recreating every bump and scratch from the original. The varnish is curious, so dark it is almost black. That, he tells me, is because the original had been badly revarnished at some point, so he has meticulously recreated the mistake. I play it in the garden of the institute, and it sounds lovely, despite looking strikingly gothic.

Playing the blackened copy cello.

As I play, I try to tease out what it is I find so odd about this recreation of an old master, so oddly over-faithful that it is almost sabotage. As biographers we follow in the footsteps of our subjects, trying to see the views from the same windows they looked out of, and imagining their silhouette framed there, even sleeping in the bed they slept in, trying to capture the sound of their breath, the rustle of the bedsheets. Similarly, we read the markings on the body of an instrument, the scratches and bumps, the ravages of time, the careful repair work, in order to learn of the player who owned it. Some cellos, like the 'Cristiani', are testament to those lives – the body of the instrument inscribed with its players' experiences. During the First World War, cellist-soldiers cobbled together instruments out of boxes and wire, to play in the trenches and behind the lines. More conventional veteran instruments were also in the line of duty, some with Ypres, Somme or Passchendaele carved into their varnish like tattoos, or with wound stripes painted onto their sides. To recreate such an instrument, to fake its history, would be somehow wrong.

Although the ageing process the eager student in Cremona was trying to fake is not one with a specifically traumatic history, I feel that, in some odd way, his patchy black varnish has crossed a line. With his heavy antiquing, inscribing the marks and discolorations of an old instrument onto the body of his newly created cello, he has made an instrument that is trying to lay claim to a longer history of bumps, bruises and adventures than it is entitled to.

A cello's cracks and scratches tell stories. Napoleon once watched Jean-Louis Duport give a recital on his Stradivari in the Tuileries Palace. The cello was later to be known as the 'Duport' and would be owned by Rostropovich. Once Duport had finished playing, Napoleon congratulated him and demanded to have a go himself. 'How do you hold the damned thing?' he asked. As he manhandled the instrument, squeezing it roughly between his legs, his spurs scratched the wood. The scratches are visible to this day.[25]

Instruments like the 'Duport', and indeed the 'Cristiani', have always been mistreated. Niccolò Paganini owned a 1717 Rogeri cello (he didn't limit himself to the violin, but also played every other instrument in the string family) which garnered many stories. On a tour in Ireland, he was travelling across the countryside in deep snow, when his cello slipped from the back of his carriage. No one noticed the loss until the carriage reached its destination. When Paganini retraced his steps, he eventually found the cello 'lying in a snow-heap with its case burst open, and surrounded by a group of small boys, who labouring under the delusion that they beheld a coffin, were trying to catch a glimpse of the corpse'.[26] Paganini also carved his initials NP on the back button, supposedly when forced to sell it to pay a gambling debt.[27] In Berlin, I had seen a quartet of instruments in the Philharmonie instrument museum that had belonged to Beethoven. It had long been proven that they were not made by the great makers their labels claimed, but their value lay instead in the huge scratches on their backs: Beethoven had used a compass point to etch a large, swirling B onto the back of each of them, and finished it off with a wax seal pressed onto the varnish for good effect. The damage and the story they tell has increased the value of the instruments tenfold.

Today, we can barely breathe on the 'Cristiani'. Back in the 1850s, Lise submerged it in a river, and dragged it on sledges through the most extreme cold. Now its scars testify to their adventures on behalf of both of them.

᠅

I am in a state of some excitement by lunchtime, as I walk into the auditorium of the Museo del Violino. The 'Cristiani' is alone on the stage. Unlike its debut in Berlin, it is not propped 'melancholically' against a chair, but has been placed on its back on top of a closed grand piano on a padded cover to await Andrea's arrival.

Andrea walks swiftly onto the stage, picks up the cello and gives a short speech to the audience, to explain why this will be a solo cello recital, even though he's playing sonatas by Brahms and Hindemith, both of which are intended as duos for piano and cello. Not today. The music isn't the point. 'We will hear the sound of Stradivari, not Brahms. We are here for this beautiful cello.' Andrea raises the bow. The Hindemith takes me straight to Pál Hermann, imagining his Gagliano playing those same notes, but the modernity and aggression of the piece feel out of place to me when emanating from the graceful 'Cristiani'.

Then Andrea begins to play the slow movement of the Brahms F minor Sonata. Without the piano accompaniment it feels disembodied, lost even. The 'Cristiani', too, seems like it is navigating unknown territory. There is a searching quality in the sound of the unaccompanied cello, as if the instrument is missing someone. I find myself trying to articulate what I'm hearing. It is a gentle, intimate sound, resonant and rounded, a sound that draws you in. It's generous, full and dark – but that's where I stop. None of these adjectives gets close to the actual experience of the sound in the room around us. Language simply doesn't begin to reach, let alone encapsulate it.

INTERLUDE

Understanding the Cello:
Stradivari II

Cremona is a place of pilgrimage for those wanting to deepen their knowledge of stringed instruments, and in particular for anyone fascinated by Antonio Stradivari. I wanted to find out all this city dedicated to worship of the master luthier could tell me. What makes an instrument by Stradivari so remarkable? In the Museo del Violino's shop, I pick up an enormous poster of the 'Cristiani' and a few books on violin makers. A young man with scruffy curly hair stands chatting to a woman behind the till. I ask her where I should go to find places in the town relevant to Stradivari, and where to find the best luthiers' workshops. She points to the man. 'Abraham here has his own workshop – he's a luthier. And what's more,' she adds unexpectedly, 'he has made this perfume.' She picks up a tester bottle from the counter by her till. He doesn't look much like a perfumier to me, more like a backpacking gap student. Amused by my surprise, he talks me through it. He had been stranded in Cremona during the Covid pandemic, separated from his home workshop in Barcelona. The instrument research project he had been working on had not been able to continue, so instead, he spent the time developing perfume from, of all things, his instrument varnish. 'The recipe's exactly the same!' he tells me, as if that might sell it. I immediately think of boiling hooves and squashed beetles. 'Really?' I say, half impressed, half suspicious. He sprays some on my wrist and I have to admit it smells fantastic. I immediately buy some, as it's impossible to resist the opportunity to smell like a Stradivari.

Abraham Díaz Romero has some free time, and offers to accompany me around the streets of Cremona. He tells me about the perfume I'm now wearing. Called '704', it takes its ingredients from what we know of Stradivari's 1704 varnish recipe. There's oil of lavender, which helps the varnish to be applied smoothly (without it, the resin in the varnish makes it stick like glue), eucalyptus, lemon flower, oil of bergamot and amber, and for elasticity we have benzoian, a kind of sap from a tree that grows in Java and Sumatra. It falls, he tells me, in tear drops. In fact, in Abraham's poetic translation, it weeps white tears, and sometimes red, enclosing a white droplet.

Abraham takes me to his master's workshop, to see for myself the ingredients I'm wearing. The magic of Stradivari, presented in dusty jam jars. Walking through the cobbled streets, he tells me about Stradivari, with whom he is happy to admit he is obsessed, like many another luthier in this extraordinary city. Stradivari was born in 1644, probably in exile from Cremona, which had been hit by plague in 1630.[28] He married twice and had eleven children, one of whom died in infancy. Two of his sons by his first wife, Francesco and Omobono, went on to take over their father's workshop.

We stop outside Stradivari's childhood home, a four-storey, mustard-coloured building, with ancient wooden shutters covering the large windows above a marble-fronted shop. I look suitably impressed. Abraham leans conspiratorially towards me. 'But what you have to know', he whispers, as if giving away trade secrets, 'is that legend has it that it isn't *this* house here with the huge marble plaque and life-size statue of Stradivari outside; it's this one, the bread shop next door. An architect read the plans of the city wrongly when they were trying to identify it. Not many normal people know that,' he adds with a grin. By normal, he means 'not a Cremonese luthier'. I'm not sure what pleases me more – being privileged with this secret, or being included in the abnormal world of the luthier. Just beyond the tall, terraced house, further along the cobbled shopping street lit tastefully with Christmas lights, is the church of St Agata. 'This is where Stradivari married his first wife,' Abraham tells me. It's a huge Palladian edifice, proud and striking. I imagine the short walk from his home with his new bride, already four months pregnant with their daughter, the air thick with bells, on the morning of 4 July 1667. Francesca Ferraboschi was to bear him six children, who played and fought in the rooms on the ground and first floors, while Stradivari created his own family of instruments in the rooms above.

Sixty-three of Stradivari's cellos still exist, all made between 1680 and 1736, the year before his death. Almost all now have their own names. There's the 'Castelbarco' (1697), the 'Servais' (1701), the 'Duport' (1711), the 'Batta' (1714), the 'Piatti' (1720), to name just a few of this wooden family of celebrity siblings. Their names are associated with the identities and secrets of their past owners, like a family tree, a cast of personalities. They have a pan-historic, quasi-mythical status, directing our attention not only to their beauty and value but also to the stories they hold. Their names are their biographies, portals into their hidden lives and the lives of their players.

We arrive at Piazza Roma, where Stradivari's second home and workshop were located alongside the greatest violin makers of his day: Niccolò Amati, with whom Stradivari studied, Guarneri 'del Gesù' and Francesco Rugeri. In the twentieth century, Mussolini pulled down all the workshops to make way for an austere marble shopping arcade, simultaneously destroying the monastery of San Domenico opposite and its graveyard, where Stradivari was buried. At the time, there was hardly any interest in the old makers. Now, the garden features a replica of Stradivari's tomb but his body has gone. A bone collector took his skeleton at the time of the demolition. Another absence. History is littered, even made, of gaps: bodies that are lost, homes that have vanished.

Stradivari's workshop exists now only in the imagination, and in a handful of artistic impressions, such as the darkly lit, cave-like recreation by Cremonese painter Alessandro Rinaldi that hangs in the museum. But its destruction is also its saving grace. In his continuing elusiveness, Stradivari resolutely avoids being pickled and preserved for the gaze of the adoring visitor.

Our next stop is a small blue door with 'Massimo Ardoli, 'Luthier' carved onto a plaque. An unvarnished violin hangs in the window. 'Here is where my teacher works,' Abraham says, the bell above the door ringing as we enter. In the wood-filled gloom of the workshop, I could easily believe that Ardoli, small and ageless in a great leather apron, has been making violins for three hundred years. He doesn't seem the least bit fazed to find an academic from Oxford in an enormous sheepskin coat, cello on back, clattering through his door. He begins to show me some of his instruments, as if this has been a long-planned guided tour. One of these is the most beautiful viola I've ever seen: a copy of the viola from a quartet of instruments by Stradivari, known as the 'Spanish' quartet, with intricately inlaid and painted patterns on the ribs. I run my finger over the inlay. What is this made of? He and Abraham explain that some believe Stradivari used mammoth bones for the white powder to mix with glue for his inlay. I have to get them to retranslate a number of times before I can believe I've understood correctly. Apparently, there is a graveyard of mammoths in Siberia, and their 10,000-year-old tusks and bones are available to purchase for surprisingly little.[29]

But it's the varnish I really want to know about. Varnish doesn't just contain the sound of a naked instrument, it gathers it. Without it, the sound of the resonating wood is too alive, too present. Back in London, one of the luthiers at W. E. Hill & Sons had told me that, of all the great instruments he'd known, the 'Cristiani' was his favourite instrument of all time, chiefly on account of its varnish. 'I knew it from books, but when I saw it the first time, I was speechless. The structure of the varnish is incredible. It's not over-polished, but perfectly unspoilt.' What was he seeing that I was not? When I look at the 'Cristiani', my fingers are itching to play it. But when a luthier looks at the same cello – he beholds a translucent miracle.

Massimo Ardoli, Abraham Díaz Romero and Massimo's assistant, in front of the shelves of varnish ingredients.

Massimo and Abraham are only too keen to induct me into the secrets of the sticky goo. Massimo tells me about his favoured varnish, a yellow, amber, orange colour, not too dark, but with a little reflection of red. Typically Cremonese. I follow as he and Abraham lead me through an archway in the ancient workshop into what might almost be a pantry, with rows upon rows of jam jars stacked on shelves. Everything I see looks exactly as if it could have been Stradivari's own workshop, with dim electric light being the only difference.

Abraham, Massimo and an apprentice who has appeared from the depths of the workshop take the jars down one after another for me to inspect and sniff. I'm still reeling from the mammoths, but now I'm introduced to some kind of little root or vegetable known as *sangue di drago*, and some dark amber fragments a little like shards of glass, which, I'm told are *gommalacca* (in English, gum lac). Massimo hands me a sprinkling of what he describes as 'the clean one'. Then he shows me the dirty one. It's made up of tiny dark brown pellets or crumbs. It is heated until it becomes liquid, and then mixed with 99.9 per cent white alcohol. 'And what exactly is *gommalacca*?' 'The shit of a worm of India', Massimo unceremoniously announces.[30] A goodly supply of it is currently in my palm. I swiftly deposit it back in its jam jar. More jars are opened and held out for me to sniff. I'm handed some roots of robbia, which make a beautiful red colour when chopped up or pickled in alcohol, then some cochineal, with its beetly provenance. In another jar there is a yellow substance which I'm told is cow's urine. I start to have a sneaking suspicion that this is an elaborate hoax, but the men lovingly handling these jam jars are in absolute earnest.

As I'm handed a jar of turmeric it strikes me that the process of varnish making is remarkably close to cooking. The ingredients are all natural, and the techniques for combining them have evolved very little from their (often quite literal) roots. Abraham shows me a jam jar full of the 704 varnish perfume. It looks absolutely disgusting. He picks up a piece of wood destined to be a violin rib and gently paints some coloured 704 varnish on. A good finish requires fifteen days of painting and twenty-three or so layers, he tells me. Under his brush, the varnish spreads like magic, creating a reddish-brown glow. 'Look – *bellissimo!*'

I've always been struck by the lyrical descriptions of varnish on instrument certificates in the W. E. Hill & Sons archives. They often sound like ideas for a heritage paint company. In the case of the 'Cristiani', the varnish is described as 'plum-red in colour, of exceptional beauty'. The names of the ingredients, too, hold their own particular kind of appeal. Juniper, for instance, which gives the varnish structure, and elemi, a sort of lemon flower, which makes the varnish elastic. But there's a finer line than we might care to admit between poetry and incantations for a witches' brew. I'm handed another jar, and we're firmly back into the territory of spells as I am instructed to sniff a bottle of horse's urine, which, I'm told, is useful for bow hair. Apparently, the hair of a female horse is better quality but breaks more easily. The repeated peeing of the horse on her own tail makes the hair grow more brittle, splitting it into smaller hairs, which offer more resistance against the string. A better bite; a better sound. This information is vividly communicated to me in a mixture of Italian and broken English, with much energetic miming to convey the meaning.

Only a few years after Stradivari died in 1737, his sons Omobono and Francesco, as well as Guarneri 'del Gesù' and Carlo Bergonzi, also died. A whole violin-making school – which at its height had dominated European instrument making – ended almost overnight. Their traditions were temporarily lost, along with the old recipes for the varnish, which each maker had created. Through hypothesis and experimentation, luthier Simone Sacconi attempted to resurrect them;

since his findings were published in 1972, each maker has adapted them to make them their own.[31]

Somewhere in the town, closely guarded, are the only three copies of an ancient leather-bound volume known as the *Pharmacopoeia*. It is, in effect, a recipe (or potion) book. Few people are given permission to read it. But the Cremonese know the power of its secrets. It tells us about the supplies available to artists in the city at the time of Stradivari, which in turn reveals much about the pigments and ingredients that might have been used by the luthiers. The colouring of linseed oil, for example, was a complicated and intricate procedure, and yet the *Pharmacopoeia* tells us that it was highly advanced as a practice in Cremona, and the result was commercially available to the city's artists and instrument makers. There was a culture of art in the Renaissance, a science of colour, that drove advances in the process. Each colour had its own physical attributes, as well as its own spiritual dimensions. Some were extremely expensive: cochineal and lapis lazuli would arrive relatively pure and cheap at the port in Venice, then become more and more cut down and costly as the pigments made their way further inland. In a sinister parallel with the opium trade, they often came at a deadly price. Stradivari bought vermilion to colour his varnish. Used in a very low concentration, it is safe when suspended in a liquid like a glaze but if it isn't neutralized it can be lethal: its chemical component is mercury sulphide. 'Deadly to work with,' Massimo tells me. 'The life expectancy of a miner in a vermilion mine was around two years.' The opaque pigment floating within a transparent liquid creates a pointillist effect, giving the varnish a sense of depth. 'It's a complex effect on the eye, a dance. It's a deadly dance, but it is a dance.'

From the 1680s on, Stradivari began to use a specific deep red colour formed from anthraquinone and carminic acid. The latter comes from a number of sources, such as kermes, a Mediterranean parasite, and Mexican cochineal, who produce the acid in order to deter predators.[32] The cochineal bugs were plucked off the prickly pear cacti that were their natural habitat, crushed and turned into pigment. When Stradivari purchased the colour, 1 gram of pure silver would have bought him roughly thirty-five dead insects, weighing 1.8 grams. To make even a small batch of instrument varnish required 250 grams of cochineal. This precious, vibrant red swept across Europe like a craze, and the tiny beetles became a most prized commodity. Queen Elizabeth dressed her ladies-in-waiting solely in red, in order to be able to enjoy looking at this new colour that symbolized wealth and opulence. Renaissance painters also used the pigment. In Caravaggio's *The Musicians* (1595), the focal point of the painting is the rich, deep red cloth luxuriantly draped over the arm of the lutenist at its centre.

There is no varnish as strongly contested or as mythologized as Stradivari's. It gestures beyond the practical and craftsmanly into the world of alchemy. But is there really *still* such mystery surrounding it? Advances in organic chemistry have allowed us to identify most of the basic ingredients: linseed oil, a type of pine resin, possibly larch resins, possibly amber (although there's little evidence for it), and bone ash used for fillers.

But there's more to explore, more questions to ask. We know the ingredients, but what were the quantities? How many layers were applied, and in what sequence? How many times did he run the brush over the instrument? Was the base layer egg-white glue, or something else to create a protein emulsion? Was it applied straight onto the wood, or just after the first layer, as an *impregnatura*?

'Think of it as Neapolitan cooking,' I am told by Abraham. 'The ingredients are few and basic: peppers, garlic, tomatoes, and olive oil. And with those four ingredients, a Neapolitan chef can make something fabulous. Others can make a mess. It is all about the hands these ingredients find themselves in. The ingredients are no mystery, but the skill, and the results, are delightfully mysterious. And these varnishes needed to be cooked with enormous skill. And once cooked to perfection, as much skill was required in the application.'

'Now *here's* a colour!' Massimo holds up a piece of wood painted in *style de gram*, often called 'holy yellow' – an inexpensive pigment made from a Mediterranean weed. This was often used by Milanese makers such as Grancino, who did not have access to the same pigments as the makers in Cremona. Indeed, I recognize the golden tint from Nick Roberts's Grancino cello.

'Why *holy* yellow?' I ask.

'It is a wonderful gold, used to paint the halos of the saints. How do you increase the spiritual value of a work of art, of an instrument? You anoint it with the same gold as the saints! A holy cello.'

Massimo puts the jars back on the dusty shelves and begins the evening's job of shutting up the workshop. As Abraham and I roam the streets once more, now so late into the evening that they are ours alone, our footsteps resonate on the same cobbles the luthiers walked to reach their workshops on the Via Garibaldi, past the pharmacy, with its many glass jars, inviting them to experiment and to combine the worlds of chemistry and craft. Renaissance architecture pays a debt to Roman architect Vitruvius, who in turn pays a debt to Euclid. The symmetry of Cremona's great cathedral, and of Stradivari's own parish church of St Agata, is informed by principles which are in the city's air, in its water. Caravaggio's red, Euclid's geometrical principles, and the pigments drawn from the most eccentric of sources were everywhere in Renaissance Cremona, and all came together in Stradivari's workshop to create instruments that can never exactly be replicated. They are intrinsically of their time, culture and landscape, with a touch of the ineffable thrown in for good measure.

Trieste – Amedeo Baldovino

January 2022

Six hours or so and three changes of train later, and I am about to arrive in Trieste to learn about the 'Mara' Stradivari – the world's most famous shipwrecked cello. Amedeo Baldovino, the cellist of the Trieste Piano Trio and former owner of the 'Mara', is long dead, but I am going to visit the trio's violinist, Renato Zanettovich. He is 100 years old. After nearly two years of Covid lockdowns, this is a journey I never thought I would be able to make. Before, he might have been able to tell me about what it was like to play in the Trieste Trio for many years, blending his violin's sound with that of one of the world's greatest cellos. He might have been able to give me an account of the night the trio were shipwrecked and the cello was lost. Now, I am told, he will barely be able to talk to me at all. It seems, on the surface of things, a very long way to go to meet a man who may not even know I'm there. However, musicians understand better than most that speech is only one way to communicate.

ᔆ

Perky little recorded chimes announce the train's guard, who informs us that we will arrive early. Early?! To anyone brought up on the UK train network, such a concept is inconceivable. Soon the train slows. The line into Trieste runs high above a wooded valley, then enters a stone tunnel blasted through a rock face, before emerging into a vertiginous blue wash of ocean. The passengers turn their heads, magnetized, to the windows on our right. Sky, mottled with cloud, answered by water, light catching the tops of a myriad tiny waves like wrinkled skin. The train is so close to the water, yet so high above it, that it feels as if we are on a pier. And then the gentle descent, and we nose our way into Trieste Centrale.

Waiting for me by the exit is Marco Zanettovich, the son of the great violinist Renato, his legs encased in blue jeans, his hair curly at the back but thinning on top. His eyes are a piercing light blue, and I briefly wonder whether they've been coloured by years of looking out to sea from his home town. Marco recognizes me and opens his arms in a gesture of delight.

I am hoping that, with his help, I can start to piece together some of the fragments of information I have gleaned from archives about the fate of the irreplaceable 'Mara', and the experiences of the trio. We find ourselves a café and set to work. 'Now. To start at the beginning,' says Marco, enthusiastically rubbing his hands. One by one I show him all the manuscripts I've collected: interviews with survivors, press coverage documenting the confusion of the day after, and later, more measured reports. Passing the story between us, a detail here, a question there, we shape the narrative together. It feels pleasingly like playing chamber music, developing motifs and melodies, adding to and supporting another player's music. I show him the photographs I've tracked down, including Pathé newsreel of haggard-looking survivors being led to shore, blankets draped over their shoulders. But no report or witness statement quite agrees with any other. The impression this assembled clamour of contradictory voices leaves me with is a melange of half-glimpsed moments, the confusion of that dreadful night. I want to hear what anecdotes Marco has inherited from his father, fully expecting that they, too, will be at odds with some of the official accounts. One question, above all, preoccupies me. What happened to the 'Mara'?

꩜

In the 1960s, Jeannette Arata de Erize, the glamorous founder of the largest music society in Buenos Aires (the Mozarteum Argentino) invited many internationally famous ensembles and soloists to play there. The Trio Trieste were amongst her regulars. In 1963 she organized a tour for the trio across South America for what in Europe were the summer months, but over there was winter. On the evening of 9 July, Renato Zanettovich, Amedeo Baldovino and the pianist Dario de Rosa performed a programme of Haydn, Shostakovich and Beethoven's 'Archduke' Trio in Montevideo, Uruguay. Marco shows me the yellowing programme from that evening. Rather than biographies of the individual players, it is the cello that is mentioned as the distinguishing feature of the group. Amedeo Baldovino, we are told, 'has one of the most famous Stradivarius named "Mara" made by the Luthier in 1711'.

The Trieste Piano Trio, with the 'Mara' Stradivari.

The day after the concert they intended to take a flight from Montevideo, over the 250-kilometre-wide estuary of the Río de la Plata (or River Plate) to Buenos Aires, from where they would travel to Rosario for their next concert. They waited all day to leave, but thick fog had settled around the airport and river, submerging the landscape and grounding all the planes. By evening it became clear the fog was not going to lift. It would have been easy enough to get a message to Elize, to tell her of the problem, but Renato Zanettovich, Marco tells me, was not someone to be deterred by such a trivial detail as the total lack of transport. The idea of cancelling their concert at the Mozarteum was simply unthinkable. They would get there, by whatever means. Back in Trieste they lived practically on the water, and travelling by sea was second nature to the trio, so Renato made enquiries at the dock. He was told that there were no boats prepared to travel in such conditions. For most mortals, such a situation would have been enough of a justification to postpone, spend a few more days in Montevideo, and travel when the weather improved. Not so for Renato. He persisted, until he found one ferry captain, 'mad enough', in his son's words, to set sail. He was (and Marco gesticulates wildly as he describes it) racing around on deck, proclaiming, 'We can sail! No problem! All aboard!' I picture a Uruguayan Ahab in a captain's cap, wild-eyed in the fog.

The trio's agent booked them three single cabins on the *Ciudad de Asunción*, which was now preparing to depart at 8 p.m. that evening, for a twelve-hour journey across the Plate. Later, when Amedeo recounted the events of that night to the luthier Charles Beare, he recalled 'The ship looked to me like a ghost ship, almost like a spectre. I chanced to mention smilingly to my friends "Shipwreck tonight".'[33]

Whatever reservations Amedeo Baldovino and Dario de Rosa might have had, Zanettovich's determination not to cancel prevailed, and they boarded the *Ciudad de Asunción* on the night of 10 July. The boat was a 2,330-ton wooden steamer, which had sailed from Montevideo to Buenos Aires and back again every night for over thirty years, ferrying passengers and cargo. This night, the ferry was to take the most valuable cargo that had ever been entrusted to it: a Guadagnini violin and the 'Mara' Stradivari. The musicians were just three amongst 419 passengers and crew – far more people than the boat could comfortably accommodate, but with no other transport available, they had all poured on board to cross the great expanse of the Plate.

Dinner was served as soon as they set sail. Amedeo recalled the dining room being crowded and lively. 'Before retiring to our cabins we took a turn around the deck. A strange voyage. Had it not been for the sound of the engines one would not have realised one was moving on the calm waters. One could see nothing.' The trio settled themselves and their instruments in cabins below deck for the night. Amedeo placed the 'Mara' in its case on the other bed in his cabin. Renato Zanettovich had with him a larger than usual violin case, as he had acquired a second violin from distant relatives in Montevideo. In one half of the case his spectacular Guadagnini lay nestled in the plush velvet, next to his music for the tour. In the other half was a cheap German violin that relatives no longer had a use for, and which he planned to sell on their behalf or give to a student. The three men settled down to sleep, confident they would reach Buenos Aires by breakfast.

⤳

Just before dawn on 12 July 1963, Amedeo awoke to the sound of men shouting. He assumed that the clamour was a 'boisterous South American party'. As he listened, he was struck by the absence of any other sound. The great engine had stopped. His first thought was that they were in the harbour. Then he realized it was far too soon for them to have arrived. He heard a loud knocking on his cabin door.

And on the next cabin, and the next. The stillness was broken by screams of women and more shouting. The cabin floor was listing unnaturally to one side. And all the time, the low rumbling of the engine was eerily absent.

He opened the door of his cabin, still half asleep. He could make out one word repeated amid the general clamour – 'Salvavidas! Salvavidas!' Lifejackets. Amedeo reached for his cello case with the instinct of a parent for a child, and dragged the 'Mara' up on deck, meeting Dario and Renato in the narrow corridor to the stairs, the latter with his violin case held securely under his arm. Through the fog, which now seemed to be lit by some unearthly glow, they saw hundreds of people illuminated. Limbs, luggage, glimpses of faces with eyes fixed in fear, as people scrambled up from below, more or less clothed, often hand in hand. 'Some optimists came with a suitcase,' Amedeo recalled. He had not given a thought to his other belongings, but clutched his cello case tightly. Crew members were circulating, organizing people, trying to calm them with some comforting information. It was only a temporary problem, nothing to worry about.

Acrid wisps of smoke were creeping in tendrils through the still thick fog. The crowd began to panic, pushing each other out of the way, frantic to reach the lifeboats. 'All of a sudden I saw a flame under the bridge. Suddenly, everyone was aware that their lives were hanging in the balance.' Children cried, men shouted indistinct commands, adding to the panic and general confusion – 'Jump! Don't jump! Get to the boats – salvavidas! Where are the crew?! Salvavidas!'

Those at the front were fighting over the few places in the lifeboats, clinging to the sides of the wooden hulls and prising others' fingers off the edge, increasing the screams of those left on deck. As the ship began to lurch unevenly, men pushed women and children out of the way to get to the boats. The trio, by instinct as much as by design, clung close together. Amedeo hugged his precious Stradivari as he watched the figures flailing in front of him in the darkness. Just then, a flickering of light made them turn. A huge fire was spreading towards them. All around was the darkness of the water, black and freezing. They were thirty miles away from the port at Buenos Aires, but they could have been at the end of the earth. It was at this point, Marco remembers his father telling him, that they realized neither they nor their instruments were likely to survive.

Then the shouting changed. The passengers who had fought their way to the lifeboats had begun to realize that the vessels were jammed, and could not be moved from their positions on deck. Only one of the lifeboats seemed to have a working mechanism. The trio watched in horrified silence, the light from the approaching flames growing ever brighter, as passengers tore one another from the only functioning boat and tried to scramble into it themselves. Even through the fog they could see it was dangerously overloaded. They watched as it was lowered, too quickly, into the darkness below, heard the screams and splash as it immediately capsized.

The smoke and flames were by now engulfing the ship, and the choice was between being burnt alive or drowned. Amedeo suddenly remembered that, in their walk around the deck earlier that evening, he had seen some single life rafts towards the boat's stern. The three men somehow managed to identify them through the smoky gloom, and dragged them to the side of the ship. Each one was the size of an elongated oil drum and opened from a hinge in the middle. Despite being short, Amedeo was the strongest of the three. He dragged three rafts to the edge of the leaning deck, braced himself so as not to slip over, and hurled them into the blackness lapping metres beneath them, past burning debris and away from the other struggling passengers. The other two men scrambled their way to the brink, and together all three of them jumped.

After a moment of weightless falling in the choking blackness, they felt the shock of contact, the icy water rapidly filling their mouths, ears and nostrils. As they sank, the sound of shouting above transmogrified into a strangely distant memory. Eventually they resurfaced in a thrashing of limbs, gasping and coughing as their lungs expanded, grateful for the night air with its acrid tang of smoke.

Amedeo started to panic. He didn't think he could make it to the raft. But after long seconds of believing he was about to die, his grasping fingers closed around the rope at its edges before he even realized he had found it. Later, in his account of the night, he remembered how he had struggled to get close to Renato, who was already on his raft. 'Dario had also succeeded, but was further away. We didn't manage to join up with him, and he disappeared into the fog. Only the ship in flames, and the screams and cries of the passengers made us realise how close we were to death.'

They searched what they could see of the horizon for any lights or chance of rescue. Bodies floated past them, and burning pieces of wood. Suitcases. The odd shoe. As the hours passed they watched the shadows of others quietly slipping under the water, too cold and exhausted to hold on to whatever flotsam they had found. 'I don't remember how we passed the hours that followed. I know that we ended up by finding ourselves alone; everything had been absorbed into the fog and darkness; the shouts and cries from Dario became more indistinct.'

Amedeo and Renato talked for hours to keep their spirits up, but eventually they fell silent, concentrating all their energy on waiting. 'The first thing that happened was the beginning of first light. I saw a vague dark form appear through the fog. It looked like a sail, and then it revealed itself as a man sitting on a raft like our own. It was as if our hopes had been realised.' Was it Dario de Rosa, floating back towards them, against innumerable odds? Amedeo's account is unclear, shrouded in fog, images and memories moving in and out of focus. Later they would learn that rescue helicopters had been sent out but were defeated by the fog. Other rescue ships, and an American research ship, the *Oxford*, were sent to try to pick up survivors, but the visibility was so poor it was hard to identify any objects in the water beyond a short distance from the boat. After an eternity of silence, the floating men were surprised by the sound of the siren of a ship which cut suddenly through the fog. 'It was close enough for us to see that it was a small ship of the Argentine Navy. But after a few unbelievable seconds the object disappeared into the fog as rapidly as it had appeared. It was a terrible moment. We stopped shouting, and tried to recover our composure. I don't know how much time passed in this new situation. It was no longer a struggle to save oneself from death, but the desperation of losing one's life. We understood the meaning of fear.'

Eventually, a searchlight appeared, mounted on the prow of a large naval vessel. As it bore down on them, they must have considered the possibility that they could be pulled into its undertow. A crane high above them on deck lowered lifeboats, which could approach the floating duo. They could hardly feel their legs, let alone use them to haul themselves out. Renato and Amedeo were pulled out of the water by

The *Ciudad de Asunción*, semi-submerged.

ropes and lay gasping on deck. There were others already rescued on board. Blankets were found, and wrapped around their shaking shoulders. Amedeo did not remember getting into the lifeboat, but he remembered that, when he realized he was safe, he 'felt as well and aware of life as never before'. Others were not so lucky. The lifeboat circled amongst the floating debris, looking for more survivors. 'I remember precisely a boy who was staring silently out of the water. We pulled over towards him, the sailors left him alone. There would be time to pick up the dead later.'

But where was Dario? Had he been the figure on a raft that they'd sighted, drifting like a human ghost ship through the darkness? It is not clear, but Amedeo did recall catching sight of a second lifeboat; looking across, he remembered his 'great joy and relief' as he recognized the pianist amongst the figures on deck.

Reunited on board the naval ship, the trio were helped into dry clothes. Baldovino, normally distinguished by his perfectly groomed and dapper appearance, was given a 'military jacket of the lowest grade, and plastic sandals'. Such details he remembered perfectly. He also remembered, with some satisfaction, that he 'managed to obtain a bottle of brandy, on my own initiative, which I drained before arriving on dry land'.[34]

As the trio were in relatively good condition in comparison to those who hadn't been fortunate enough to find rafts, they were left alone with their brandy, while the naval crew busied themselves with those who urgently needed assistance. Abbé Pierre, a French Catholic priest and founder of the charity Emmaus, had been one of the passengers on the *Ciudad de Asunción* and was rescued by the same vessel as the trio. He had saved his own life by cutting free a wooden part of the boat with a penknife he happened to have in his pocket, and clinging to it. Amedeo remembered how the abbé 'and almost all the others were to a greater or lesser degree traumatised by shock'.[35]

Although Amedeo was prepared to recount his own actions that night, when he was asked to describe what he had witnessed, he declined. Some silences are better left unfilled. 'I prefer to avoid giving details of some of the things I still remember. The main drama was that of those who were trying to find all kinds of loved ones and who were waiting with feelings alternating between hope and desperation.' Inevitably, once their own safety was guaranteed, the trio's thoughts turned to those that they loved. It was only then, Marco remembers his father saying, that they realized that they had lost their instruments.

ᔆ

On my second evening in Trieste, the moon hangs above one of the many great churches, with cloud formations like black espaliered branches. Marco and I are walking along the seafront. On our left, the old 1920s art deco hydro port jutting out into the water, to welcome passengers from their hydroplanes. On our right, the old docks, where merchants would have left their boats, piling their sacks of coffee or cloth onto their backs, to take them directly to the shops lining the ground floors of the tall buildings in Trieste's neat gridwork of streets. A sudden wind begins to buffet us, coming from no particular direction. It feels as though it has been artificially generated by a film crew for special effect. 'That is the Bora,' Marco tells me. It rolls down from the hills of Slovenia and roars suddenly and unpredictably through the streets of Trieste. Tomorrow, the night wind will clear the air to a crystalline brilliance, and we will be able to glimpse the towers of Venice on the far horizon. Tonight, we remain on our surreal, blustery film set. We stop at the water's edge, gazing into the dark, listening to the hypnotic rhythm of the water lapping quietly against the great stones of the harbour. 'Tell me what you've found out about the River Plate,' Marco says.

I tell him how the fog that night had been so dense that the captain could not see the buoys that had been placed to guide ships between the hulks and sandbanks on the river bed. He had strayed out of the narrow course that he had followed every other night for years. Within minutes, the boat struck a submerged wreck, the remains of a freighter called the *Marionga J Cairns*, and water began to flood the lower part of the ship. This was the point at which the crew raised the alarm, trying to assemble passengers on deck to head to the lifeboats. Unlike on the *Titanic*, despite overcrowding, there were enough lifeboats for everyone. But at that point the boiler room flooded and the *Ciudad* caught fire. In the ensuing panic, the frantic passengers (rather than crew) tried to operate the lifeboats themselves, causing them to become stuck.

In the end, just one lifeboat reached the water, and none were usable. The passengers were forced to jump as the *Ciudad* sank almost completely below the water's surface. Only part of the deck remained visible, which might have provided some protection, had it not been rapidly consumed by fire. The captain and his crew were later convicted of gross negligence. Their navigation error had killed at least fifty-three people, and badly injured many more.

We are silent for a moment. Marco throws a pebble into the black water in front of us. I tell him about a treasure hunter I have managed to contact, a colourful character called Ruben Collado who knows the River Plate better than anyone. He told me how the shallow muddy waters of the river 'with the colour of the lion' (as he puts it) hide over two thousand sunken ships from all eras. In fact the Río de la Plata, with its frequent storms, hidden rocks and sandbanks, is known across the world as 'the hell of sailors' or 'naval cemetery'. It is unlikely that the trio knew this when they stepped on board the boat that night. Collado maintains that 'there are countless treasures in gold and silver bars still waiting to be brought up to surface. It is known that galleons full of gold headed for Spain and loaded with hundreds of cannons and very important documents for those days would run aground in the rocky beds of the Uruguayan shores on dark nights, sinking with their treasures still on board.'

Marco smiles. 'My father would love that! "But", he'd say, "what treasure could be worth more than a violin and a cello?"'

⁓

Amedeo Baldovino later wrote that 'We reached land in great confusion, with a mixture of joy and grief, and were sent off – those who were in good enough condition – into the City in a Navy bus.' He was still fifty kilometres from Buenos Aires, and now desperate to get to the city to try to find news of his cello. He knew that the hunt for survivors and bodies was continuing, and must have hoped that there was some chance that his instrument could be found.

As the bus rumbled along, with frustrating slowness, they passed a railway station, outside which was a queue of taxis. Amedeo thought that they might be able to cover the distance more quickly in one, so asked to be let off the bus. The driver of the first free taxi looked at him suspiciously, and shook his head. As Amedeo was still wearing the old navy jacket and sandals, he must have presented an uncharacteristically alarming spectacle. Beyond exhausted, and still in some state of shock, he did not know what to do. Turning, he saw he was standing beside a newsstand, with the evening's papers lined up on it. In huge headlines he read about the shipwreck on the Plate, and saw for the first time the wreckage of the *Ciudad*. It had been at best only semi-visible to him in the foggy darkness, but now the full horror of the familiar and yet alien image struck him: the ship sticking out of the water with its upper decks almost completely burnt out. He gesticulated to the driver who had refused to take him, pointing first to the photographs and then to himself. Finally the man understood and helped him into the car, showering him with questions.

When they reached the hotel, Amedeo was relieved to see the consul general, who had come to help the trio. The consul was a similar height to Amedeo, so was able to lend him some more respectable and better-fitting clothes. He was deeply anxious about his cello, but still in too much of a daze to comprehend its loss. While he, Renato and Dario fell into exhausted sleep in their hotel beds, divers continued their search for any last survivors amongst the bodies, washed kilometres apart on the vast stretch of water. Faced with such a task, would they have even considered looking for a violin and a cello?

∾

Amedeo Baldovino's account of the whole ordeal is remarkably precise and detailed, but it is striking that he did not mention anything about those long hours in the darkness, when they had all but given up hope of rescue. I am hoping Marco can give me more information.

'Well,' Marco says, 'this is what my father was always particularly proud of. He never talked to me about the bodies, or how he felt, surviving when so many others didn't. He never spoke of the children who died around him that night. Instead, he told me how the two of them had discussed the details of their concert, still advertised for the next night. They worked out the best fingering patterns, talked about the repertoire, discussed different speeds for particular moments. At no point did they entertain the idea that they might not be alive by the evening, or that Dario might already be drowned. Music was the only thing they spoke about.'

I think back to the times when I had plagued my grandfather with questions about his time in the RAF during the

Second World War. He would only tell me about the episode when he lured a camel into the mess tent in Egypt and couldn't get it out again. He never mentioned being shot at, or the deaths of almost all the friends with whom he had enlisted. We shape our stories for our audience, and this was the version Renato chose to tell his son as a young boy.

I am sceptical. 'Fingering patterns? Really?'

'But no!' Marco says. 'You don't understand. Talking about music was exactly what those three men would have done. It was *all* they did. Anything else would have been bizarre.' He pauses. 'Tomorrow, I will help you understand. And in order to know these three *particular* men, who lived for music, you must know this city. They were shaped by Trieste. And it is like nowhere else.'

৵

Mid-morning and bright sunshine, the blue of the sky melting into the sea. We are careering around in Marco's little Fiat. Whenever he becomes overexcited about our conversation, raking back through the past, he lifts both hands from the steering wheel. 'And this is HISTORY, dear Kate! Real HISTORY!' I grin, and grip the dashboard.

Trieste is a city of wrought-iron balconies, carved stone figurines, and cafés in which people settle down for the day to read the papers and entertain a succession of friends. This was the world into which Renato Zanettovich and Dario de Rosa were born. Neither Renato nor Dario was particularly well off, although the building in which Renato grew up is impressive. Marco takes me to his father's first house. Carducci Street is wide and busy, full of shoppers, with the typical grand façades of Trieste above the shopfronts. The land available to build on in Trieste is limited by sea on one side and the mountainous landscape of the Carso on the other, so the buildings pile high, floor upon floor. The Zanettoviches lived on the fourth floor. Renato's family was not musical, but the floor below was being used as a music school at the time. Renato would accost the older children coming and going from their lessons, pleading with them to show him their instruments, until he was given his own little violin. Dario and Renato grew up playing chamber music together, and were already famous in Trieste before their teens.

Amedeo moved to Trieste in young adulthood, having spent his childhood in Egypt and then Bologna. He too had been a child prodigy but, unlike the other two members of the trio, he was from an extremely wealthy family, which enabled him to purchase his extraordinary Stradivari.

~

Marco's memories of Amedeo Baldovino are less than flattering. He met him many times, when he was growing up. 'He was a man *non simpatico*,' he says, shaking his head. *Simpatico* – a concept that appeals to me, and one for which I've never found a satisfactory translation into English – is more than just sympathetic or nice, friendly. It is closer to amiable, generous-spirited. Either way, these are all qualities that Amedeo did *not* display, at least in the eyes of the young boy whose home he came to rehearse in. 'He was more like this,' says Marco, making a gesture that is even less translatable, involving raising his head haughtily and flicking the end of his nose up and down with his finger.

In London, before my visit to Trieste, I had had coffee with cellist Raphael Wallfisch, who had asked me where I planned to travel with my cello as I wrote this book. I mentioned that I'd be taking the train up to Venice, and on to Trieste, to find out about the 'Mara' and its shipwreck. Raphael put down his cup. 'I know that cello!' he exclaimed. When he was only sixteen, his teacher had sent him to Italy to study with Amedeo. At the time, Amedeo had temporarily left Trieste for Perugia, in Tuscany, and Raphael had camped out in his larder, like a Victorian apprentice. 'Elisa the housekeeper had a bed in the kitchen in case she needed to stay over. I simply moved into it.'

What was Amedeo like? Raphael laughed. 'Oh, he was tough! Very strong and fiery. He was a genius, a little man, he could sit down and play Paganini *Caprices*. Because he was quite small, he often used five fingers, playing on his thumb to get round the cello with his narrow hands. His playing was very clean, but he never practised. He couldn't understand why I was bothering practising!' His pupils had always to call him Maestro, and to dress properly for their lessons (Amedeo himself was never without gelled hair and a cravat). He expected total commitment, but would not tolerate being bombarded with questions.

Raphael's friend, the quietly thoughtful cellist Sebastian Comberti, had also made the journey out to Italy to study with Amedeo. He remembers him as a tiny, dapper man, and very aristocratic. At the time, Amedeo was obliged to teach in order to qualify for his Italian pension. His heart wasn't in his obligatory class of ten-year-olds, so he delegated his teaching to the teenage Sebastian on arrival, leaving him to muddle through with a classroom of children only eight years younger than he was, and the promise of lessons at the weekend as his payment. When he had moments off between his children's classes, Sebastian would practise in the empty rooms in the music school. If the Maestro happened to walk past and didn't like what he overheard, he would burst through the door and shout instructions: 'No, *no*! Do it slower! No, not like *that*!'

⁓

The next morning, Marco takes me up to the Temple of Monte Grisa: a monumental late-1960s construction of vast concrete triangles, a cross between Coventry Cathedral and a Toblerone. It stands on the edge of the rocky hilltop high above Trieste, and he has brought me here for the panoramic views of the bay and the distinctive landscape of the region, which is called the Carso. The countryside, only a few kilometres from the Slovenian border, is a rough mixture of carbonite rock, sandy scrub and thin pines. It is only here that you find this combination of limestone, dolomite and gypsum. Marco reaches down and picks up two glittering white lumps of it for me to keep.

The landscape has a strange power. There is nothing tranquil about it; rather it exudes a raw energy. In fact, one of the Carso's special features is its tendency to disappear into sink holes with no notice, craters opening up amongst the rocks, pathways to the underworld – or to hell, depending on whose view you take. These voids reach down into vast networks of caves and underground rivers that run many metres beneath the woodlands.[36] One of these caves is allegedly big enough to accommodate the whole of Venice's Basilica of St Mark. Only when pressed will Marco tell me about the darker side of this place. During the Second World War, some of these sink holes (known as *foibe*) became sites for killing and disposing of bodies. Both before and after the German invasion in 1943, many residents of Trieste were arrested, usually during the night, and dragged up here into the wooded darkness, often bound with barbed wire. They were either shot at the side of the holes or thrown in alive.

'My mother was a teacher, in a good school,' Marco tells me. 'One morning a pupil of hers, a big boy, big – *Come si dice?* – like a wardrobe, seemed distracted in class. When she called him over at the end of the lesson, he told her that he and his family had been taken by two soldiers during the night. "But how are you here?" she asked him. "Well," the boy said, "I realised when we were marched up through the Carso that they were planning to throw us into a hole. So I threw them in first."' Marco shrugs. 'So it was,' he adds.

And for the Trieste Trio? What was it like for them during the war? Dario and Renato were born in 1919 and 1921, and were already famous as a trio with their first cellist, Libero Lana, when the German army invaded Trieste in 1943. They took their instruments into the cellars of nearby buildings at night, when the town sheltered in basements or in the long tunnel hewn through the rock that joins one side of the city with the other. In the countryside around Trieste, as well as the *foibe*, the mountains became a beautiful but deadly war zone. They were hollowed out, the exteriors pockmarked with machine gun emplacements, and inside were tunnels in which soldiers and members of the Resistance hid.

Between the bombings, the trio carried on their studies and concerts. To one side of the city the Germans established a concentration camp.

'Did your father know about it?' I asked Marco.

'Oh yes, everyone knew.'

The SS had taken over a disused rice-husking factory, where they held Jews before deporting them to Auschwitz, and tortured and killed political prisoners. Today, the camp buildings remain, industrial red brick, their black window frames overlooking the site where the crematoria were.

'Renato and Dario played for the German army, many times. They knew that the secret to life was… music. If these men come, with their machine guns, and kill everyone, they will have no music. And the German soldiers loved music. So if they played, they were safe. They would not be taken to the camp.'

And so they played for the Nazis. But after Trieste was liberated, they played for the Americans, and for the people of Trieste.

At the heart of Trieste's music-making is the Conservatoire Giuseppe Tartini, which is known as one of the best in Europe.[37] The trio studied there between 1928 and 1938, and later taught the students themselves. It was their base, their spiritual home. Marco takes me to see the building that has housed it since shortly after the war, where the trio also studied and taught. It is a great white and cream stucco building, known as the Palazzo Rittmeyer. Inside, an impressive open staircase, punctuated by marble pillars, snakes around a central hall the height of the building. Leading from it are forty-eight practice and teaching rooms, one orchestral music hall and one chamber music hall.

I walk along the pavement towards the entrance and my shoulder brushes against the first of three dried-up garlands nailed to the wall, decorated with faded *tricolore* ribbon and little silver balls that catch the midday sunlight. These balls are the equivalent of cloth poppies for Remembrance Day in the UK, and would once have been surrounded with laurel leaves. I ask Marco what the garlands commemorate. He looks sombre. In 1944, when the trio were in their early twenties and Renato was living in his family apartment nearby, the Palazzo Rittmeyer was a base for Nazi soldiers. The fighting in the Carso around the city was intense, but the Germans were confident about their hold on Trieste; there were so many of them that the streets positively crawled with German soldiers. On 22 April a former Azerbaijani soldier known as Mihajlo and his accomplice, Ivan Ruskj, entered the Palazzo Rittmeyer disguised in Nazi uniform. They walked past a group of soldiers and made their way up the central staircase. They found the upstairs dining room and sat down at a free table. After a few minutes two waiters asked them to leave. This was an officers' mess, and Ruskj was of the wrong rank, according to his stolen uniform. The two men dutifully left, but not before they had carefully placed the bag they had been carrying under the table. It contained a time bomb. The explosion tore apart the palazzo's façade and destroyed several rooms inside. Five soldiers and a cook were killed.[39]

Rather than wait to find out who was responsible, the Nazis rounded up fifty-one young Italians, Slovenes and Croatians – men, women and boys who had either failed to show correct papers that day or were being held as political prisoners. The morning after the bombing they drove them in trucks to the damaged palazzo, tied their hands behind their backs and hanged them, five at a time. Within an hour, there were bodies swinging from every available space in the majestic hallway, tied by the neck to the pillars and banisters, and thrown over the side into the void. The feet of the dead above brushed the heads of those below. When there was no more space on the two floors of staircase, they began to hang their victims from the windows of the building, turning the palazzo into a grotesque morgue, festooned with suspended corpses. Standing outside the building, Marco and I count thirty-five large sash windows on the front façade alone. Inside, bodies hung from the chandeliers and from the furniture. And just in case any of the citizens of Trieste failed to be suitably horrified, the Nazis gave orders for the tram that regularly passed the palazzo to slow down, so everyone was forced to take in the full extent of the massacre.

The bodies were left there for five days. It was to be one of the most brutal reprisal attacks on civilians in Italy during the war.

At that moment, the swinging doors to the main entrance open, and two girls exit, laughing, violin cases on their shoulders. I don't know what to say.

Shortly after the war ended, the trio moved with the music school into this site of massacre. Against a background of fascism, bombing and mass murder, they continued to create a world for themselves that was as far removed from the Nazi occupation as it was possible to be. They took the beauty of their surroundings, the culture, the value placed on art and music, and used them to exclude all that was barbaric and distasteful. They had grown up with examples of the very worst of man's brutality, in a community that was under threat and living permanently in fear. They had found a way to survive through their music. Perhaps the only thing most of the people of Trieste had in common with their persecutors was a deeply held belief that music should be valued above all else.

The trio's celebrity status, even as children, kept them safe. As adults, the men lived only for their art, and were selective about what else they engaged with. They were products of their city, but they had also developed a strategy for psychic survival, the same strategy they would use when they later found themselves in the freezing water of the River Plate. Floating there in the darkness, with nothing to suggest that they would be rescued, they talked about fingering patterns and bow speeds. It wasn't shock or denial. Nor was it a lack of empathy, or great bravery. It was a long-practised method of resisting darkness and terror, woven into the fabric of their being from early childhood. The Scuola Tartini had replaced death with music. And so did they, on the night of 10 July 1963.

Marco nods. 'Come with me,' he says. 'You need to meet my father.'

In a genteel suburb of Trieste, horse chestnut trees spill out above the railings of gardens, glimpses of azure sea between their fingertips. As ever, Marco speeds his little Fiat into a spot that is not a parking space, brakes dramatically and gaily abandons it diagonally across a corner of pavement. We walk to a small building, divided up into flats. Marco gestures to the tiny lift and I squash myself in, the little double doors like a Wild West saloon only just shutting as they scrape across the front of my cello case. Three floors up, and we are at the door of his father's flat. I step into a world of music, fixed in time somewhere around the 1960s.

My eyes are drawn to the huge, brown and golden leaf patterns on the textured wallpaper and, in front of them, a striking cartoon. Marco follows the direction of my gaze. It is a caricature of the trio – drawn by an architect friend of the group. In it, Renato's bow merges into the line of the open

piano lid, violinist and pianist barely distinguishable in their comically dramatic gestures. At the centre, a demonic version of Amedeo frowns, his trademark perfect hair greased fiercely into a side parting. It is a sketch positively bursting with personality and life.

In the living room, on either side of the mirror, are stacks of cloth-bound music scores. Next to the scores hang two sepia photographs. The first is of an enchanting little boy, no more than four years old. He is wearing pin-striped shorts, his hair swept neatly to the side. He is looking straight at the camera with a most earnest expression, and is posing with a tiny violin. He holds it awkwardly, with the scroll pointing straight ahead, and a bow that is almost as long as he is. In the second, the little boy is now in his early teens, and already becoming established as a chamber music performer, with the Trio that would define his career. Here, they are posed on stage in the old music school, below Renato's family apartment on Via Carducci.

Young Renato, with the Trio's first cellist Libero Lana.

Marco tells me that his father had been given a tin of sweets at the age of three. The tin was shaped like a little guitar, and he had put it straight onto his shoulder as a violin. From that moment, Renato had thought about little else. 'His world became the same shape as that tin.' He saw, thought and talked about nothing other than violins. As Marco puts it, 'Musicians, with a capital M, do not live in the same world as everyone else. Music is a world bigger than this one.' So it was for the trio. Whatever was happening politically as these boys grew, the music that they made together became their entire focus. And so when the Trio changed cellists, it didn't matter to Renato whether Amedeo Baldovino was *simpatico* or not; what he saw in someone was their musicianship. No matter that you were a delightful person, with an average ability on your instrument – you were nothing to him. He barely saw you. His world was one only of music, and music of the highest possible standard. Nothing else mattered, and no obstacles were too great. Even shipwreck. 'And so, Kate,' Marco says with a smile, 'you can begin to close your circle. These men, drifting down the River Plate in the fog, did not talk about music as a distraction, they talked about music because that was what they did. The ship-wreck was the distraction!'

∽

It was only when Amedeo had woken up in his hotel in Buenos Aires, after fourteen hours of rest, that he was ready to comprehend the full scale of his loss of the 'Mara'. But almost as soon as he had begun to panic, there was a knock at his door. It was Renato with a morning paper, pointing at a headline: 'The Stradivari has been rescued!'

Amedeo did not respond with the flood of joy and relief Renato had expected as he had hurried along the corridor with his news. He could not shake the conviction that the instrument was lost. He later recalled the moment in an interview:

From the photographs which continued to appear in the papers, one could clearly see how the fire had devastated the still visible part of the *Ciudad d'Asunción*. The cello case had stayed there in some place which I could not remember. I was certain that I had not thrown it into the water. How could it possibly have been rescued? Surely, they had found the case of some guitar which, in turn, had given the journalists an opportunity to use their imaginations.

Then there was a telephone call from the local television network. They wanted an interview with Amedeo to capture him enthusing on camera about the miraculous rescue of his instrument. It was too much for him. 'I lost patience with them and said that nothing had been found. I affirmed, in pretty bad language, that I was certain it had been lost.'

It was only after several hours that the trio's concert agent telephoned to tell him that he must return to the naval base at La Plata, where he would be reunited with the object which everyone was sure was the Stradivari, saved from the waters of the immense river.

Still Amedeo refused to believe it. A car arrived to take him to the officials at the base, where he was to identify the 'body' of what was believed to be his cello. At the naval club, the three men were received 'very elegantly'. A captain appeared bearing aperitifs and speaking excitedly of the 'recovery'. Amedeo sipped his drink, not knowing what to think. Then, a sailor appeared carrying a distinctive W. E. Hill & Sons cello case. 'I could not believe my eyes. There could not be another one like it in the whole of South America.'

With great trepidation he watched as the case was opened. For a moment there was silence. Then Renato, standing next to him, let out a desperate 'Oh my God!'

It was not the sight of an instrument that greeted him, but a quantity of small pieces of wood. For a moment Amedeo tried his best to identify, and to reassemble them into the cello

The 'Mara'.

he knew. 'In a short time I realised that it could not be done. It was impossible to distinguish between all the fragments.'

~

To my right, at the end of the L-shaped room, past the two pianos and the music stand, I hear a low moan. Marco gestures for me to step round, and there is his father, one wasted hand tightly clasping the arm of the helper who sits next to him. He is half recumbent in a raised metal hospital bed-chair, thin legs in shorts. I find myself momentarily layering one image on another, a palimpsest of the serious little boy in his shorts and this fragile, old man, once again in the clothes of his boyhood.

As Marco touches his arm, he slowly turns his head.

'Papa!' Marco says. 'I've brought someone to see you! She's from Oxford, and she's writing about you!'

Renato's hand flutters, and he lifts it shakily. 'Violiniste?' he whispers.

'No, Papa, she's a cellist,' Marco says. Renato makes a tiny gesture that appears to be a nod of approval.

'Play to him,' urges Marco quietly. Feeling as nervous as if this were a major audition, I unclick the metal buckles on my case, and pull the piano stool over until I am within his line of vision, his head lying sideways on the headrest of his chair. 'Schubert!' Marco says suddenly, and starts singing in a hearty baritone. To my surprise, Renato joins in almost immediately, a quavering, but identifiable melody. The Quintet in C major. I begin to play the great melody from the first movement, in which the two cellos (oh, the luxury of two cellos together!) weave in and out of each other in thirds, with the three upper strings accompanying them, a feather bed of *pizzicati* outlining just enough harmony. The two violins then take the tune from them, and the roles are reversed. It is one of my favourite moments in the chamber music repertoire. Renato murmurs as I play, a vocalizing that is between singing and audible recollection, if remembering had a sound.

Kate and Renato.

For a long while afterwards he is silent. He appears tired, asleep with his eyes open. Marco had warned me as we drove here that now, aged 100, his father is present, but absent. Only five or so years ago he was a force of nature, still giving masterclasses at the Conservatoire, demanding the very best standards from the awed students. Now, surrounded by the mementos of his great career, his hands hold not a violin but the reassuring arm of the lady who feeds him and chats quietly to him. What music is passing through his mind, as he lies there, silent? Which fingering patterns is he discussing with Amedeo when he is absent from those of us in the room? Perhaps, in his extreme old age, he is slipping ever more permanently towards living on his great planet, the world that only Musicians with a capital M can inhabit.

∽

I ask Marco whether his father ever showed any signs of trauma after the shipwreck. 'No!' Marco says, definitely. 'My father was someone who thought life was an adventure. Whatever the problem, he found the answer.'

Silence.

I picture the men again, cello and violin cases drifting off into the infinite blackness around them, their hands clinging to the cylinders of the life rafts, resolutely discussing Schubert. Marco thinks for a minute. Then he adds, 'Now though, lying in that bed with its raised sides, he sometimes reaches up his hands for help, like he's trapped. I think he feels he is drowning.'

3rd Movement – Silence

To comprehend beyond experience...

(from Ursula Wood, 'To a 'Cellist')

Berlin – Anita Lasker-Wallfisch

January 2022

When I was in Berlin back in October, I had told my companion and guide Verena Alves about Anita Lasker-Wallfisch, who had grown up in Breslau (now Wrocław, in Poland), lived in Berlin for a while and eventually found her way to London after the war. She was too young to have given public performances here like Lise Cristiani, Amedeo Baldovino and Pál Hermann, but the parallels with Pál's experience of the city are striking. Both young Jewish cellists made their home here at a time of great promise for their careers, only for their lives to be interrupted by the rise of Nazism. Leaving Berlin marked the end of security for them both. From then on they had to rely on their cellos for survival. Now I am returning to Berlin to meet up with Verena once more, and to visit the places that had been important to Anita during her all-too-brief time in the capital.

$\backsim$

Anita Lasker-Wallfisch's experience of the cello had always been tinged with the awareness of struggle. Her first teacher in Breslau had been shot through the left hand during the First World War, and had stiff fingers as a result. He had learnt how to play holding his bow in the 'wrong' hand. It must have made it hard for his young pupil to copy what he demonstrated. In the late 1930s, he and all the other Jewish teachers fled Breslau, leaving the eleven-year-old Anita with her beautiful Ventapane cello, her fierce ambition and no one to teach her.

Anita is in her nineties when we meet for the first time. She is fed up with being interviewed, yet she welcomed me into her house in north London with good grace, and a certain degree of curiosity about my cello-focused project. She was wreathed in cigarette smoke, and smiled wryly when I pointed out that the health warning on the packet seems ironic considering the many times she had cheated death. Her face is strikingly young despite her great age, and her dark eyes are coupled with a smile that is radiant. She walks slowly and with difficulty, but this doesn't occlude her formidable energy and drive.

'I always wanted to study with Pablo Casals,' she says. 'I adored him. As a girl I had a beautiful picture of him hanging over my bed. He was my hero. I wrote him a letter, asking to learn with him in Paris. He wrote back with lovely handwriting. I wish I still had that letter. Of course it never happened.'

Finding any teacher at all in the 1930s was difficult. No one in Breslau was allowed to take on a Jewish girl. The best non-Jewish cellist in the area came to her family home and heard her play. 'He told my mother that he would have loved to teach me, but did not dare.'

One day Leo Rostal came to Breslau to play a cello concerto with the city's Kulturbund Orchestra. The Jüdische Kulturbund (Jewish League of Culture) had been set up several years previously to provide employment for Jewish actors, singers and musicians who had lost their jobs under the Nazi regime. Leo, brother of Max Rostal (the violinist in Casals's trio), was the leader of the cello section of the Kulturbund Orchestra in Berlin.

Had Pál Hermann not fled Berlin in 1933 he would most likely have found himself playing with Leo Rostal, as all the most distinguished Jewish cellists were corralled together in this one orchestra. Perhaps he would even have been invited to Breslau in Leo's place and have met Anita. But in the late 1930s, Leo, not Pál, was the orchestra's principal cellist, and it was Leo who was invited to travel from Berlin to play the Saint-Saëns concerto. Anita's mother was a talented violinist and played in the same concert. Afterwards the family hosted Leo in their large apartment. Anita still remembers it vividly.

'Leo stayed with us on that occasion. He was a bloody good cellist! Whilst he was with us he heard me play. "In four years' time," he told my proud mother, "your daughter will be a famous cellist!"'

Leo was so impressed with Anita's playing that he invited her to study with him in Berlin, and in 1938 she moved to the capital, leaving her family behind in Breslau.

'My parents found me a room in a flat of a retired schoolteacher. They hoped she would take care of my academic lessons. She was supposed to teach me for two hours each morning, but she was completely nuts, and only two pages ahead of me – I learnt nothing from her.'

Anita's host fed her largely on Brussel sprouts. Anita almost physically shudders at the memory of this 'deeply weird' woman. 'Whenever she walked into the room she would pick up and kiss all the cushions, and a walking stick that belonged to her dead mother!'

Despite the sprouts, Anita looks back on her months in Berlin as one of the golden periods of her life. She had cello lessons on alternate days, and the quality of this intensive study with Leo set her up as a cellist. He gave her a solid technique and the confidence that she could be a good player; less helpfully, he taught her how to smoke.

Besides Leo Rostal and her landlady, Anita knew no one in Berlin other than one boy, six years older than her, who always took the lesson before hers. She would arrive at Leo's house and sit waiting with her cello outside the room as

Anita aged twelve or thirteen in Berlin, with her Ventapane.

Fritz Lustig played. She told me how in awe she was of him, as she listened to his superb playing through the door. Fritz died only a few years ago, and I was proud to be able to tell his son, BBC journalist Robin Lustig, how highly Anita had rated his father's playing.

Like Anita, Fritz Lustig had always wanted to be a cellist, but when it became clear that music college would be closed to Jewish students, his parents realized he would have to emigrate to continue his studies. At the time Anita met him, he was waiting for the opportunity to leave the country and was working intensively with Leo to polish up his technique.

When Anita was not studying, she made the most of her unusual freedom, with no constraints other than her morning's tuition. 'I had the most fantastic time pretending to be an adult, and probably not doing enough practice.' She browsed the nearby department store KaDeWe (Berliners' shorthand for Kaufhaus des Westens) and became fiercely addicted to the nougat they sold there.

While Anita was munching and smoking her way round Berlin, revelling in her new-found freedom, life for the Jewish families around her was increasingly inhibited. New and restrictive laws were continually being introduced at this time, making life more and more difficult and creating an atmosphere of constant fear. Gatherings were prohibited in Jewish homes. As Fritz later recalled,

> We were always very conscious of the fact that if we were caught, we would be arrested by the Gestapo, and almost certainly despatched to a concentration camp. Even then, that was considered to be equivalent to a death sentence. Rumours were rife of Jewish women who had been sent a cardboard box said to contain the ashes of their husbands, who had been 'shot while trying to escape' – the universal reason given for otherwise unexplained deaths.[1]

Anita, while not oblivious to the increasing hostility around her, existed in her own bubble of early adolescence. When I asked her if she had been lonely in Berlin, she retorted: 'Absolutely not! It was the happiest time of my life! And my companion was my lovely cello.'

∾

Anita's companion was made by Lorenzo Ventapane, one of the most renowned Neapolitan cello makers, in the early nineteenth century. His instruments are easy to spot, as they have particularly long F holes, snaking either side of the bridge. I later learnt that Ventapane probably studied with the Gagliano family. It is a link, however tenuous, to Pál Hermann's cello, both instruments crafted using the same techniques, their varnish drying in the blazing southern Italian sunshine.

Ventapane cellos can vary in quality, but Anita was not of an age or a level of experience to be critical. To the promising young girl who played it, this Ventapane was a fantastic instrument, and it accompanied her on her journey from precocious child to young professional. But this golden time of music-making and chocolate consumption inevitably could not last.

༄

On the night of 9 November 1938, the Gestapo gave orders just before midnight for Jewish shops and synagogues to be ransacked. Fritz remembered that

> there was a Jewish-owned off-licence on the ground floor of the house next to ours, and as I approached it I could see a noisy crowd in front of the shop. The window had been broken, and people were helping themselves to the contents. Earlier in the evening, they had tried to set fire to it, and my father had phoned the fire brigade. Of course, there had been no response as instructions had been issued from on high that these so-called 'spontaneous', but in fact highly organised, demonstrations of the German people's 'revulsion and anger' were not to be curbed in any way.

Anita's abiding memory of the morning after Kristallnacht was her shock and confusion at seeing alcohol flowing in the streets, amid the broken glass. It's a very particular image and, given that Fritz lived close to Anita, just behind KaDeWe, there is a chance it might be the same street that they both remember. Over the following two days, at least ninety-one Jews were killed, and 30,000 Jewish men aged between sixteen and sixty were arrested and sent to concentration camps, about a quarter of all male Jews in Germany at the time.[2] In those forty-eight hours, 7,500 Jewish shops and 1,000 synagogues were attacked. Ku'damm was at the centre of the violence in Berlin on 9 November 1938. One horrified eye-witness said that it 'looked like a battle-field'.[3] Even Hermann Goering commented after that night: 'I would not wish to be a Jew in Germany.' SS officers had been stationed every few shops up and down the street, to supervise the destruction of everything Jewish. Crowds looted freely, grabbing whatever they could from the windows and shelves.

At the time it was impossible to get any sense of the scale of events, even in the centre of Berlin. Fritz recalled his amazement at finding 'a copy of the *London Times* and reading a report from its Berlin correspondent relating in detail the events of what was later to become known as Kristallnacht – "the night of broken glass"'.

The events of Kristallnacht were just as terrifying in Breslau as in Berlin, but Anita's parents thought she would be safer at home, with the protection of adults. So she was summoned back to Breslau. Without having the chance to say goodbye either to Fritz or to her cello teacher, she packed up her things and picked her way through the debris with her cello and suitcase to the train station.

Fritz and his father went into hiding, moving between friends' houses to avoid detection. So many Jews were in the same situation that they became known as 'U-Boot – or U-Boat – Juden'; they surfaced only when necessary. By the spring of 1939 Fritz's parents had managed to arrange for him to leave Germany for the UK; they followed a year later.[4] By that time, Leo Rostal had emigrated to America. It was to be years before anyone would teach Anita again.

༄

Having tried a variety of the nougat on offer at KaDeWe as a tribute to Anita, I am about to leave Berlin and take my cello on the same train journey made by Anita and her Ventapane. But before I go, Verena and I walk along Unter den Linden and through Alexanderplatz. The wind is fierce. Bicycles, hoardings and scooters are all blown flat, and the tower cranes are weaving dangerously above our heads. Just before we reach the Spree, we pass the Staatsoper Unter den Linden, one of Berlin's three opera houses, which provides one side of an open square, opposite one of the main buildings of Humboldt University. This imposing old building is known as the 'Kermode' – a drawer – as its undulating front resembles a bureau. In 1933, the Nazis looted hundreds of 'degenerate' books from inside the 'drawer', took them from the building, piled them up at the centre of the square and set fire to them.

Verena shows me something I might not have noticed had I been here alone; at the centre of Alexanderplatz a flagstone has been removed and replaced with thick glass. Looking through it, down beneath our feet, I see a white-painted library with row upon row of empty shelves. This is an art installation by Michel Ullman, created to commemorate the book burning of 10 May 1933.

We are looking through the present into the absence of the past. Beside the monumental stuccoed buildings, this looking down, below the ground, is particularly poignant. Its understated, undemanding quality is its strength. You can either walk over it and miss it completely, or suddenly become aware of the absences that pave every inch of this city. Missing books, gaps in culture, an artwork that takes up a negative space under the ground, all whisper of past destruction. 'You start with burning books, by the end, you're burning people', the Jewish poet Heinrich Heine had written more than a hundred years earlier. Here, at the heart of musical Berlin, culture and its destruction exist side by side.

Pál Hermann never returned to Berlin. When Fritz Lustig and Anita made the return journeys many years later, there was little left for them to recognize. The streets lined with 1950s apartment blocks held no memories for them. But under the ground, the infrastructure was still there, even after the bombing; as a result, the layout of the city remains largely the same. Like this sunken library, the surface buildings may be erased, but the earth holds the memory of their presence.

～

As my train destined for Poland slowly makes its way out of Berlin Hauptbahnhof, I look out at the building sites and huge apartment blocks as they slip by, tracked by the path of the Spree. The glass dome of the Bundestag disappears behind the ramshackle temporary buildings that have sprung up in the gaps between warehouses along the river. A colourful handmade wooden building, assembled from crates, by the look of it, bears the word Musikschule across its door in wonky wooden letters. How different this landscape would have looked to Anita, when she made this journey eighty-three years before. But a little of the egalitarian spirit of the music school run by Pál Hermann, Ernst-Lothar von Knorr and Paul Hindemith lives on.

INTERLUDE

Listening to the Cello I

Vibrato, combined with the movement of a bow pulled across a string, sets the air inside a cello vibrating in particular ways. This series of interrelated movements is the essence of the process of music-making, from vibration into sound. But we take this for granted, so much so that even setting it out like this seems unnecessarily dry and arid, compared to the unthinkingly natural gesture of picking up a bow and strok-ing a string.

As part of my quest to examine the cello from all angles, I want to find a way to notice this process differently, to bypass the inevitably automatic connection between bow movement and sound that I can never un-learn. So, rather eccentrically perhaps, I'm turning to the bee community to teach me. Honeybees communicate through vibrato. When a bee vibrates, it is speaking through movement in subtle, nuanced ways. When we play with vibrato, we're polishing the sound by rocking our fingers backwards and forwards, mirroring a bee's movements. I'm interested in what happens when we take ourselves out of the equation, and leave a cello to vibrate in dialogue with bees, instead of humans. And so, I am driving up to Nottingham to meet physicist Martin Bencsik, his cello and its 400,000 buzzing inhabitants.

One rhythmic pattern of bee behaviour is so famous that even I have heard of it. This is (delightfully) known as the 'waggle dance', and is an alert to tell the other bees of a good food resource. A foraging bee might happen upon a bush of fantastic flowers, and it will then return to the hive to tell the others through vibration. The dance was discovered in the 1930s by an Austrian scientist called Karl von Frisch, who placed artificial sources of food on little plates at different distances and in different places around a hive, and manually labelled his bees with a brush as they visited the feeding station, before watching them dancing in the observation hive. He sat there for years, with a notebook on his lap ready to write down the bees' responses. Eventually he deduced from the bee's waggling vibrations that they could not only tell each other about the food sources when they discovered them, but could also communicate how good they were, how far the sources were from the hive, and in which direction to find them. All through rhythm. But Frisch's discovery was simply too much for the scientific community at the time. Many scientists refused to believe him. They couldn't countenance that it could be possible for such a small insect to give such specific instructions.

Frisch had discovered one of the most sophisticated communication mechanisms in the biological world. Its significance can't be overestimated, says Martin Bencsik, nearly jumping from his chair in his eagerness to communicate the importance of this discovery to me. Martin was born in Lyon, and his lilting hint of a French accent and Gallic arm-waving lends a compelling drama to everything he says. Frisch's finding shocked the world; but, although he announced it in 1940, it took until 1971 for him to be given the Nobel Prize in Physiology or Medicine for his work. Martin becomes even more emphatic. 'The Nobel Prize is *the* highest, most prestigious award for a scientist. There is nothing higher! Yet there was no visible change following Frisch's discovery – bee-keeping husbandry continued as before, mankind did not appear to benefit, no business opportunities were created, and our health hasn't changed. There are no repercussions *whatsoever* of the kind that science is presently seeking. Frisch's discovery was knowledge, purely for the sake of knowledge. And it won the highest award. Why? Because the repercussions of his research are profound, even though no one would fund his research now. His discovery has shifted our view of where we stand in the animal kingdom, a bit like discovering that it is the Sun that is the centre of our planetary system, not the Earth.'

We order coffees and settle on hard felt-covered chairs in the glass-surrounded café at the heart of Nottingham Trent University's campus. Martin is a slightly built man, with an intensely penetrating stare and the habit of asking almost uncomfortably searching questions. 'You're writing a book about the cello? Why? What do you hope to achieve?' He is a scientist to the core – the idea of a research project without a quantifiable goal is clearly worrying him. But he has decided to humour me and is generous with his time. And something of my quest appeals to him: seeking knowledge simply for the sake of it, a more modest version of Frisch's endeavour, perhaps. Much of our time together will be spent investigating the most extraordinary cello I have ever played, but Martin says that it is important that I understand the significance of it first. And that means learning to listen to and understand the bees that inhabit it.

Martin is deeply unimpressed with humans, and profoundly in awe of bees. His world view is unorthodox, but compelling. It just happens that his wife Deirdre is a professional cellist, and so, in despair at humankind's toxic combination of assumed superiority and environmental destruction, together they had the idea of giving Martin's bees a cello. The first question he is usually asked, not unreasonably, is… why?

'Because I think it's a *shocking sacrifice!* A cello feels like an amazing achievement of mankind. It is so beautiful. It is the result of so many years of improvement tweaking this and that. It's so valuable – a symbol of sophistication. But it's a cavity of the correct volume for a hive, and it would be so shocking to give it to my bees. Here, my bees – have a cello! The ultimate sacrifice. What? A *cello?* It's such a precious thing! But the honeybee deserves it! So let's put bees in cellos to *show* people they deserve it.'

Martin's gesticulations are more and more flamboyant, and people are starting to glance at us – this is a quiet café. But I'm gripped; his passion is infectious.

When Martin had first introduced the bees to their cello he had hoped that the instrument might be induced to sing by the activity of the bees inside it.

'If you stimulate a string, a cello will provide a loud sound. I looked into the reversibility of this – if you provide a sound inside, would the strings resonate? It works for piano strings. But cello strings are extremely thick, and they need the bow to stimulate them. If you project a sound into a cello, the body will resonate, but the strings will not.'

Martin and I drive past the outskirts of Nottingham onto country roads, and follow a pot-holed track to a small stately home. I'm surprised to see the house is made of crumbly red bricks; it is the earliest great home ever built in brick, he explains. The gardens are lined with manicured hedges and beds of well-positioned flowers, a feast for bees. We pass under some ancient oaks, around the topiary and into a walled orchard, with a row of hives on one side, which, Martin tells me, are his. And there, in the centre of the orchard, a wooden pergola stands. At its centre is The Cello, held upright by a subtle wooden stand unobtrusively attached to its neck. It is a lone centrepiece, sculptural and isolated. It's captivating.

The very oddness of seeing a standing, solitary cello in such an incongruous setting is fascinating, and makes me question, momentarily, what it is. Is it an instrument, an art installation or a hive? It is alone, but teeming with lives: silent, but continually making music. It seems to resist definition.

After a lifetime of living with and around cellos, to encounter an instrument that can offer me something I've never seen or heard before is an extraordinary experience. This cello does not belong to us. It is a home, and we can visit it only by prevailing upon the goodwill and hospitality of its thousands of inhabitants. As we make our way through the long grass to the centre of the orchard, we instinctively start to talk in a whisper. This cello, I feel, is owned by its bees, just as Martin had intended. 'Here, my bees! Have a cello – you deserve it!' he had said. And here, in the pale autumnal sunlight, I start to understand that he was right.

We put down our bags a little way off from the cello pergola, and Martin offers me a white suit complete with protective hat and veil. But I feel that it would be impertinent to wear them. These are not philistine wasps but meticulous, sophisticated artisans. I would be positively embarrassed at approaching them clad neurotically in white armour. No – any bees that love a cello are bees with whom I have enough affinity to establish some degree of trust. These are bees after my own heart.

We are about fifteen feet away when suddenly the cello seems to darken. A thundercloud of bodies, miniature swallows swirling and dipping, emerge from the front of the instrument in a dark mass. It is as if black notes have emigrated off the stave and are visible, emanating from the instrument in some glorious cluster chord, thousands upon thousands of tiny black dots.

Every day this bee exodus takes place, usually in the afternoon. It lasts for twenty minutes. Almost everyone in the hive flies out in a matter of seconds, circles around and eventually re-enters. Are they stretching their legs, or having a toilet break *en masse*? It's a mystery. One theory is that it is the first flight of the baby bees. It only happens in summer, when the babies are born, and it takes a baby bee a few days to be strong enough to fly. Perhaps the adults are crowding round them, protecting them in an intimidating cloud as they struggle along, trying out their wings for the first time. I'm reminded of my first proud, wobbly trips out to the shops with a newborn.

The cello's F holes are the bees' two front doors. They are easy to fly out of, but harder to navigate back into. As the bees

The bee cello's Perspex back.

begin to return from their excursion they land badly, and so begins a delightful medley of pinging, thumping and twanging as they crash land on the strings or on the wooden front of the cello. The bees are playing the cello themselves.

Now, most of the bees are back inside, and what looks like the blackness within the F holes, usually signalling the cavity within, has in fact become a darkness of solid bodies. It's like a packed train in rush hour. Or a party with too many guests in an unrealistically small room: the bees are spilling out of their own doors. I realize that I have never seen, and probably never will again, a cello that is solidly full. The space that resonates – its voice box, in effect – is not there. Every square centimetre is taken up, either with long strips of honeycomb or with tiny bodies.

Now the inhabitants are home, I can start to inspect the front of their house. We circle the cello at a respectful distance, and Martin shows me that he has replaced the wooden back with translucent Perspex. It is a stroke of genius: what from the front appears to be a standard instrument (if you overlook the seething insects), from behind is an amber and black mass of honeycomb structures, and constant movement. We are peering through a window into the centre of their home.

These bees are uncharacteristically keen on home improvements, Martin tells me. Bees do not normally demonstrate any interest in the external appearance of their hives. In the bee cello, however, they behave in ways that have never been seen before. These bees understand that their home is special, and have taken it upon themselves to improve upon its design.

Martin shows me how, to his delight and mystification, they have propolized (a strangely satisfying word for 'glued') the soundpost onto the front and back of the cello with plant resin. The soundpost is normally held in place inside the instrument by sheer pressure, the equivalent of a stone pillar holding up a cathedral roof. When a soundpost collapses, there is the most almighty crack, like a pistol shot. It's terrifying. Why leave things to chance? Glue it on.

The bees' two F-shaped front doors snake on either side of the bridge. The F was a shape that was perfectly acceptable to Stradivari, but is apparently not good enough for the bees. They take issue with the little carved notches at the top and bottom of each F, and with the notch in the centre. These decorative gaps are too small for them to squeeze through, and so represent an unnecessary loss of heat (this is Martin's theory, at any rate). Perhaps they simply find a more rounded decoration aesthetically pleasing. Either way, they've meticulously glued up all the narrow gaps, but always with respect for the varnish, and with perfect symmetry.

They are clearly not impressed by all the loose ends in the design of a cello. Once they'd dealt with the threat of the unattached soundpost and sorted the messy F-hole design, they turned their attention to the bridge. Like the sound post, a cello's bridge is held to the front of the instrument by nothing other than the tension of the strings. This system has served humans well, but as far as bees are concerned, it is too slapdash and temporary. So they have glued the feet of the bridge to the woodwork with resin that they've neatly deposited around the joins between bridge and front.

Why have they bothered? No one knows, although Martin thinks there might be a clue in their odd behaviour during that summer's heat wave. When it is extremely hot the bees cannot cool down. Normally they stay inside the cello, but on a few occasions during their first summer in their new home the temperature reached around thirty-five degrees. The whole hive poured out of the F holes to congregate around the bridge, arranging themselves in a dark, swinging bundle beneath it. They had decided to use the bridge as a hammock. Had they already identified this feature of the cello as a pleasantly airy ledge that they might need for cooling themselves, and gone to the trouble of securing it in advance? No bees have ever maintained or improved the front of their hive before – it's completely unheard of, Martin tells me.

Whatever the reasons for their unprecedented DIY, there is something intrinsically different about the bees' relationship to their cello that has made the colony behave in new ways. The cello *means* something to them. They see and understand it, and have invested their time and energy to shape it into something new.

The relationship between cello and bees is reciprocal. They offer it a tweaked, improved design, but the cello can also give them something, or so Martin believes. When it is warm, they sit on the front of the instrument, on the varnished wood. Martin has observed that a bee sitting on this shiny surface will begin to sweep it with her front legs, while gently stroking the cello with her head. He's seen hundreds of them do it, but it is only here, on the front of the bee cello, that such behaviour has ever been observed. There is no explanation for it as yet, but one possibility might be that it is the first time they have seen themselves reflected – they would never be on a shiny surface in other circumstances, so the cello bees are the only bees to have seen themselves, and are trying to communicate with their own reflections. It's fascinating to watch them; they look utterly engrossed – backwards and forwards, backwards and forwards, the same obsessive motion, for hours at a time, stroking the cello's smooth front with their mandibles, calm and focused. They are in thrall to their own reflections. The cello has offered the bees back to themselves for the first time in the creatures' history.

We observe all this in silence. The only sound is the wind, whipping through the branches and grasses of the orchard around us. The cello appears unplayed: a home, not a source of sound. Martin grins. He fishes a little microphone called an accelerometer out of his pocket, pokes it into one of the round holes on the bridge, and hands me a pair of head-phones. As soon as I put them on I am aware I've entered another world. The bees' vibrations can be heard: rattling, rustling and droning. This cello, so static and silent, is in fact full of movement and rhythm.

As Martin and I listen, tuning our ears to the bees' differ-ent patterns, we both involuntarily hold our breath, as our ears start to discern an eerie, unlooked-for music. We listen intently, staring at each other. The cello has only recently been placed here, in this orchard. Previously, it was in a sheltered corner of the university campus. Here, exposed, this is the first day the wind has blown so forcefully through the cello's wooden pagoda. As it does so, we find we can hear it stroking the strings, creating music that is imperceptible to the naked ear. Wind and cello together are making an invisible, spectral music. The effect is a little like a wind chime, and hauntingly beautiful, rising and falling above the bees' own rhythms. We are eavesdropping on a secret duet between the cello and its inhabitants. It feels almost impertinent.

Reluctant as I am to impose myself on this perfect musical relationship, I can't countenance leaving without having seen what happens when the bees' home is played with a bow. Will they respond? Will they swarm? Or will certain pitches make them behave differently?

I still feel that it would be impolite to dress up in layers of protective clothing. So I approach the cello calmly, respect-fully, as if trying to win the trust of an unpredictable horse or snarling dog. I have brought a bow with me, and now I tighten the hair, ready to play. What would bees like to listen to? Only unaccompanied Bach will sound complete without a piano accompaniment, and I want them to have as satisfying a musical experience as possible.

It's not a great cello to play – the strings are a preposterous distance from the fingerboard – big enough for a bee to pass under, in fact. Most awkward is the bending over to play, while standing; and the wooden prop that holds its neck has to be negotiated. It was never going to be a performance of recital quality, but tentatively I begin to play Bach's First Cello Suite. The familiar rocking pattern of the bow across the strings is perennially soothing to play, and I hope that the bees might be lulled by it too.

With every note I play I'm aware that I could be about to put my finger on a bee. Around ten to twenty fly nonchalantly around my fingers and bow, while others carry on with their business calmly, seemingly disregarding my music. I listen to their responses through the headphones as I play, and notice that there is no frenzied increase in activity in response to what might have been considered a threat. In fact, they have slowed down, quietening themselves, an audibly perceptible lull in conversation as they listen.

Martin later tells me that in theory it would be possible to immobilize bees with vibration, if we vibrated the cello for long enough, or strongly enough, and at the right frequency. My Bach has a less dramatic but still discernible effect. When the immobilizing vibration ceases, the bees don't get aggressive, Martin explains – they just go back to whatever they were doing before. It's as if they've been temporarily hypnotized. It is not known why this phenomenon takes place, but Martin believes it is because bees listen through their legs, apprehending the vibrations. Their listening is of a particular quality, their whole body engaged in the activity of hearing. They pay attention, just as a concert audience might settle to listen as the baton is raised.

Sure enough, when I finish playing, the bees go quietly on with their business. I have the distinct feeling I am being humoured by them, and can almost swear I hear a polite, lukewarm smattering of applause coming from thousands of tiny legs.

Never could I imagine a situation in which Bach would feel too clumsy, too obvious. But here, butting in on a duet so fragile it might have been woven in a spider's silk thread rather than steel strings and stretched horsehair, I feel my music to be inopportune, an interruption. The ethereal conversation between cello and bee is not something in which I can join. I step back from the instrument, brush a bee or two out of my hair, and Martin quietly puts the headphones away. The cello, once more, appears to be standing in silent isolation. I find myself remembering the old question 'If a tree falls in a forest and no one is around to hear it, does it make a sound?' If a cello plays alone in an orchard, who hears it? Not us. But perhaps there is some music that is not for human ears. I have eavesdropped long enough.

Martin reaches into his rucksack and produces, incongruously, some crystal shot glasses and a flask. He pours a thick, amber-coloured liquid into the glasses, and hands me one. We stand around the cello, raising our glasses in a respectful toast to it and its inhabitants, as we taste the sweet warmth of his homemade honey mead.

Wrocław – Anita Lasker-Wallfisch

February 2022

I had once been the proud owner of a beautiful cello made by Ventapane. God knows who plays on it now.

(Anita Lasker-Wallfisch, in conversation with the author, September 2021)

Travelling through Poland I pass great silver birch forests, the occasional level crossing with a little village behind it, storks in a field, vast rivers sprawling suddenly like glittering miracles, the odd tractor following the progress of the train along the woodland track next to the rails. From time to time a small town appears, its imminent arrival announced by large metal warehouses, piles of sand, soil and broken tarmac divided by graffitied concrete walls like vast compost heaps, and, in the distance, a skyline of church towers and identical high-rise blocks in surprising shades of green, yellow and peach, arranged in a line like the teeth of some almighty comb. In front of them, formations of geese fly against the direction of the train, in fully formed Vs.

⌁

At Wrocław station I am met by jazz pianist Kuba Stankiewicz, a great bear of a man with a gentle expression, and his friend the harpsichordist Ola Rupocińska, a petite woman with waves of blonde hair tucked under a knitted hat. Both have lived and performed in Wrocław all their lives.

First they take me to the Music Academy where they teach. I had decided that for this leg of the journey it would simply be too much to take my cello on every train with me, so I have left it in the Philharmonie Hall in Berlin under Verena's watchful eye, until I return in a couple of weeks. Kuba and Ola have found a cello student who has a spare instrument I can borrow while I am in Wrocław, and we locate her in the cello room of the academy. Małgosia is apologetic – 'It's my second instrument, not very good.' I hold it up to look for a label through the F hole – Guadagnini! *Really?* No, not really. On closer inspection the label appears to have been dipped in tea to make it seem aged. This cello is a little dog that thinks it's a big dog, but I have to admire its ambition and swagger.

Wrocław is a city where identities and very often the buildings themselves fail to remain static. Everything here was renamed, including the city itself, which changed from the pre-war German Breslau to the post-war Polish Wrocław, and the vast majority of the pre-war population never returned after 1945. In this context, this odd hybrid of student instrument and fake old master seems curiously fitting. Almost nothing in this city is what it was. But the girl from whom I'm borrowing this 'Guadagnini' is as close to an equivalent of Anita Lasker-Wallfisch, seventy-five years on, as it is possible to be.

Anita was born and lived here until she was sixteen. There was no music conservatoire in those days, although she would have known the prominent old building that houses it. Even if there had been the possibility of her studying in her home town, such an institution certainly would not have been allowed to take a Jewish student. Nineteen-year-old Małgosia is Jewish, but when I remark on this, she looks guarded, suspicious even. In that hesitation, enquiring politely why I am interested in her Jewishness, I glimpse a whole history of trans-generational pain and mistrust. When I explain about my interest in Anita her expression relaxes, and she tells me readily about her life as a Jewish girl in Wrocław. She attends the newly reconstructed Synagogue of the White Stork, at the heart of what was the Jewish community in Anita's day, and she has Jewish friends amongst the students and people of the town, with whom she meets regularly and celebrates festivals.

In the rows of cello cases, with the large, shuttered windows opening out onto a vista of the river outside, I find my worlds coming together. Not only in this modern reincarnation of Anita, but in the cello room itself. Behind Małgosia is the famous picture of the Portuguese cellist Guilhermina Suggia, with her foaming flounces of scarlet silk. And next to Suggia hangs a photograph of Pablo Casals, Anita's hero and intended teacher. Serious and not remotely flamboyant, he gazes down on the Wrocław students' cellos lined up below his portrait. Had the events of Anita's life been different, her Ventapane cello might have stood here with the other cases.

This sense of the direct lineage of generations of Wrocław cellists is something of which the conservatoire is consciously proud. Kuba, Ola and Małgosia show me a large board in the foyer devoted to a 'family tree' of cellists who passed through the academy, from its post-war opening to the present day. At the top is the name of the first cello teacher and the students whom he taught, then the students they taught, and so on, until we get to the space where Małgosia's name will be written. She is only three or so generations away from the students of the 1940s. I touch my finger on the space where Anita's name might have been.

The Breslau that Anita knew as a girl was a cultured, thriving city, the capital of the Prussian province of Lower Silesia. It prospered by being in the centre of the trade between western Europe, Poland and Russia. It had factories making railway engines and carriages, and a strong woollen industry. There was the Stadttheater, which put on operas, and there were singing festivals, in true German style. For recreation there was (and still is) a famous zoo, and a cinema.

(From left to right) Anita with her sisters Renate and Marianne, and her parents Edith and Alfons, in the late 1930s.

The city was full of parks. There was even a circus. On Sundays Breslau's inhabitants would stroll along the riverside promenades, stopping at the many beer gardens and restaurants that overlooked the water. The pre-war Jewish community made up 5 per cent of the population, second in size only to the community in Berlin. For generations they had lived peacefully as integrated – and frequently important – members of the city, represented across the arts, medicine and the law, and owning many of the shops. Anita's father, Alfons Lasker, was a prominent lawyer, with an office in the centre of town, behind the police headquarters and prison.

Hyper-inflation in the 1920s had hit Breslau hard, and many of the unemployed and poverty-stricken welcomed the National Socialists, with their promises of employment, as the answer to their prayers. During Anita's early life, the city's cosmopolitan, tolerant society transformed itself into one where, as in Berlin, books were burnt and the swastika worshipped like a religious icon. From the mid-1930s, many of the teenagers of Anita's generation joined the Hitler Youth and marched through the streets of Breslau, proudly displaying their guns. Anita got used to hearing their shouts: 'Verbrennt die Synagogen! Boykottieren Sie jüdische Geschäfte!' ('Burn the synagogues! Boycott Jewish shops!'). People who had included Jews in their circle of friends started to cut them out, and the Jewish community found itself shunned and isolated. Anita remembers that the process was both rapid and insidious. An atmosphere of fear seemed to grow from nowhere, subtly enveloping the family as they became increasingly ostracized. She was spat at on the street and victimized at school. As her family only went to the synagogue on special occasions, Anita had barely noticed her own Jewishness before, and was bewildered by this sudden stigma that she had apparently carried without knowing it.

❧

Today, there is political unrest brewing, but from a different source. As I travel, increasingly troubling reports are beginning to circulate of Vladimir Putin lining up troops to threaten Ukraine. I had hoped to travel on to Estonia and Ukraine after Lithuania, but troops are being sent to their Russian borders. No one is sure whether Putin will back down, or whether there will be all-out war in the region. When Lise Cristiani was travelling with her cello through a region on the brink of war, she was told 'It will be funny to hear a cello play when they fire the cannons.' The present-day situation strikes me as distinctly less than amusing. Kuba and Ola are concerned, but sanguine. 'There's a joke here in Poland', Kuba tells me. 'Someone is travelling from Russia, and gets to the Polish border. "Name?" demands the border guard. "Pavel." "Address?" "14 Ekaterin Street, Moscow." "Occupation?" "No, not this time – I'm just visiting."'

❧

Anita's Breslau has over the centuries been Vretslav, Presslaw, Wrotizla, and now Wrocław. Wrocław today is an elegant town, the 'flower of Europe', as it has been called. The River Oder winds through its centre, past a twin-towered medieval cathedral, near to the city hall or Rathaus, a gothic fantasy of red brick gables and pinnacles. It even has an astronomical clock, Ola tells me with evident pride. It has always been a university town, a centre for intellectuals, for theatre and music. Now, says Kuba, one in six members of the population come here to study at the university, and remain to make their lives here. Małgosia is exactly the kind of musician who will stay, as part of the still tiny Jewish community that is rebuilding itself here.

Until the final year of the war, the city remained much as Anita would have known it. When the Soviet army advanced towards Germany, however, it became an important centre for communication for the Nazi regime, and in September 1944 Hitler designated the whole town a fortress. Some refugees managed to get out in time, but most of the inhabitants were trapped, as the city was surrounded. Some of those who did escape found a false safety in Dresden, only to be caught in the firestorm that consumed the city in the Anglo-American bombing raid of February 1945. Others starved and froze as they attempted to flee in the depths of winter. Those who remained faced a siege that was to be the longest of any German city. By the time Breslau fell to the Soviet troops in May 1945, seven out of ten houses were uninhabitable.[5]

෴

On the way from the station, Ola and Kuba had driven me up the main road leading into the city. Today it is called Powstańców Śląskich, but under the Nazis in the mid-1930s it had been given the unlovely title 'Strasse der SA' (the SA being the *Sturmabteilung* ('stormtroopers'), the original paramilitary wing of the Nazi Party, which aided Hitler in his rise to power). This is the street on which Anita's family apartment had stood. Known then as Kaiser Wilhelm Strasse, it was once the most desirable area of town, lined with grand, ornate apartment blocks. Many of the residents were Jewish bankers, lawyers and owners of businesses, so culturally German that they didn't believe for a moment that the state would turn on them. There is no trace of them now, or of their houses. Today, Powstańców Śląskich is a wide thoroughfare with several lanes of traffic, lined with faceless modern buildings. The road was so heavily bombed during the Soviet siege of the city that it was reduced to rubble. The piles of bricks and beams were taken to Warsaw to help rebuild the devastated Polish capital. All that remained was piled up into a vast, tiered hill like a Neolithic earthwork amongst the buildings on the edge of the city. On the top of this mound, high up overlooking the new city, stands a single forlorn climbing frame, its orange-painted poles gripping the stones that once formed the homes of children like Anita and her sisters.

Strasse der SA, as Anita would have known it.

I was worried that the streets I wanted to find would be hard to trace. 'Not a problem', Kuba and Ola assure me. 'Everyone knows the old names.' Even though the renaming took place before most of the city's present-day inhabitants were born, the population still see a shadow of the past behind the new identities.

I wonder how much is left in Wrocław of the world Anita knew. It seems at first that everything has gone, but Wrocław is a palimpsest of a city. The German names lie like a reflection in water, under the Polish identities. Here and there, amid peeling paint, there are glimpses of German signs inscribed on the few buildings that were left standing, revealed once more by the decay of the last few decades. But for me, trying to find traces of what had been, and of the German-Jewish lives that were lived here before the name of Hitler changed anything, was a little like trying to find the voice of a player in their cello. There are some clues, some remnants, but ultimately it is a ghost hunt.

⁓

The Laskers were a cultured, highly educated family. The parents were strict, but not more so than any other parents, according to Anita. She and her sisters, Renate and Marianne, were not allowed to sit in armchairs in case they slouched. Her father, who sang Schubert lieder beautifully, was a gifted linguist and insisted on the girls learning to speak French, believing that a person 'has as many souls as they have languages'. As a child Anita thought this ridiculous, but now, in old age, she knows it to be true. When I suggested to her that music could be another soul, she smiles. 'Father also used to say "It doesn't matter what they take away from you, they can never take the culture that you have in your head."'

String quartets were played at least once a week in the Laskers' spacious family home. Three-year-old Anita had first turned a broom handle into the neck of an imaginary cello

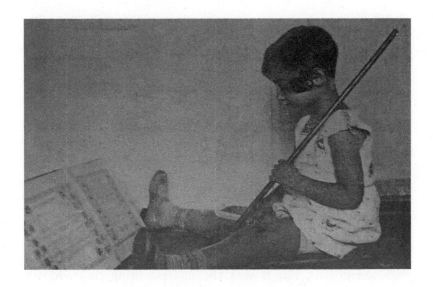

Anita and her pretend cello.

and pretended to play it with a comb for a bow, alerting her parents to her passion for the instrument. Once she had a real instrument, and her sightreading was proficient enough, she was allowed to join the chamber music sessions, playing Beethoven duets with her mother. Her proud parents made Anita perform on her Ventapane cello for distinguished visitors. Thus she first met and impressed Leo Rostal, and was invited to Berlin.

On Saturday afternoons, Anita's whole family would sit together, with coffee and wonderful cakes that she still remembers with much nostalgia, and her father would tell the girls stories from his experiences of the First World War, teach them about opera and read to them from the classics. By the time she was eight, in 1933, Jews had been banned from the beautiful baroque opera house. But before that, trips to the opera were a regular occurrence, with the sisters having to learn the plots before every production. As late as 1942, Anita remembers reading the libretto of Verdi's *Don Carlos* with her father, while the world around them fell apart. As a little girl, she knew that Hitler was an evil man, and she understood that something bad had happened, but she did not know exactly what it was. She recalls hearing her parents mentioning his name after the election of January 1933, but they stopped talking as she came into the room.

On 15 September 1939, just after war had been declared, the Laskers were ordered to leave their luxurious flat, their grand piano and most of their possessions. Gradually, this policy of enforced evacuation from homes became more systematic. By 1941, all the Jews in Breslau had been corralled together in one area near the centre, around the Jewish orphanage and the Synagogue of the White Stork. It wasn't a closed ghetto, but it was the nearest thing to it. Many Jews were forced to live in cramped conditions with people they might never previously have met. Anita, Renate and her parents moved into a four-room flat nearer the centre of town. The flat belonged to Anita's aunt Kate and her (in Anita's words) 'most disagreeable' husband; they shared the cramped space with Anita's grandmother, a friend of Renate's, and other elderly lodgers.

The flat was at 1 Höfchenstrasse, on a crossroads that still exists, but, as with Strasse der SA, there is nothing to see now of the buildings themselves. Instead, on one side there is a huge construction site where men are still working to fill in the bomb damage. On the other sides of the crossroads are typical concrete flats, built hastily by the Soviets to house the thousands of homeless after the war, and now covered with graffiti.

As I get to know the city under Kuba and Ola's guidance, I find everywhere the most eclectic mix of buildings – grey, drab communist buildings sit side by side with medieval architecture, nestled against gleaming constructions from the 1990s. Almost every street has a large space with a digger busy next to buildings that end too abruptly. They tell me that, if I'd come here twenty years ago, it would have been a completely different story. These sites of construction were until recently sites of absence, of memory. This is a place whose spectacular transition is still in progress, delayed by decades of Soviet neglect. But a few buildings down from her aunt's street corner, I at last find a building Anita would certainly have recognized – a solitary, turn-of-the-century apartment block, ornately carved, which would have been visible from her aunt's windows.

~

Anita was desperate to continue her studies after her enforced return home from Berlin in 1939. She even tried to persuade her parents to let her go back to the German capital. But when it became obvious, even to her, that it would never be safe for her to do so under a Nazi leader, she renewed her plans to travel to Paris to learn with Pablo Casals. But it was not to be. Over the course of the next few months, the family made a succession of attempts to escape, all of them unsuccessful.

Her father Alfons's correspondence from the time charts his efforts to rescue his family.[6] He first appealed to the American authorities, on the grounds that his brother, a celebrated chess champion, lived in the USA, but was told that the Polish immigrant quota had already been used up. He tried to emigrate to England, but in order to enter the country the family had to prove they were only in transit. He even attempted to get to Chile, but again with no success.

Alfons then managed to find an address at which they could stay in Italy, which was the first step towards emigrating there. This looked like the most achievable route of escape, and, even as late as 1940, gave them some hope of leaving. After much negotiation and form filling, the whole family went to the Italian embassy in a state of great excitement, to get the final stamps on their passports. Anita watched as the administrator was about to bring his stamp down on their papers. She saw him pause, put the stamp down on the desk, and turn away. Anita never found out what it was that had stopped him. The family returned home without their emigration papers.

At the time, Anita had no idea of the extent of her parents' efforts to escape, or of the series of disappointments they were suffering. They tried to maintain a sense of 'ordinary' life for their daughters, against increasingly overwhelming odds. When her parents realized they could not leave as a family, they concentrated their efforts on trying to get their daughters to safety. Anita's elder sister Marianne was already safe in England, and they managed to find a British school that agreed to take Renate. They had bought her uniform, and a Reverend Fisher was prepared to act as a guardian for her. She was due to travel on 28 September 1940, but just days before that date, all foreign borders were closed. Renate remained in Breslau and Anita was forced to give up all hope of Paris. The family had to acknowledge that they were trapped.

⌒

Soon after the Laskers had moved in with Aunt Kate, Anita and Renate were required by law to work. School had already become an impossibility and it was now replaced with slave labour. Renate was forced to sort putrid detritus on a rubbish tip; she quickly became extremely ill. Anita had to get up at 4 a.m. every morning to travel out of Breslau to work in a paper factory. When Renate recovered her health, she joined Anita at the factory. The pay was just enough to cover their travel, but no more. On Saturday afternoons the family still sat together, trying to pretend life was normal, playing chamber music and reading together. The girls' work was demeaning and dirty, but it at least meant that they were considered 'useful' by the Gestapo, and their employment kept their names from appearing on the lists of those to be deported. Their parents were not so lucky.

On 9 April 1942, Alfons and Edith received a deportation order, giving them twenty-four hours to report to an assembly point at Scheisswerder, a large area which was normally used for a fun fair. Today it is a vast power station, with looming chimneys painted in wide red and white stripes. That night, Alfons made Anita stay up late, teaching her how to pay the bills and manage the household finances. Overnight she had to become an adult. When morning came, Renate and Anita wanted to go with their parents. Rather than deny his daughters outright, Alfons pretended to 'ask' the Gestapo whether they could come too. Returning to the house, he told Anita his request had been refused. Looking back, Anita thinks he must have known the fate that awaited them. This little lie was her father's way of sparing her from the truth.

Once her parents had been taken, Anita and Renate had little choice but to get on with the business of surviving day by day, with no thought for the future. Their uncle and aunt had already been deported, and the elderly lodgers and their grandmother, a formidable, distant woman, waited impotently for their turn, while Anita and Renate did their best to take care of them.

The girls' work cut across the few hours Jews were permitted to shop for food, so, in order to feed their dependent household, they were obliged to steal non-Jewish coupons from the factory. Renate didn't look Jewish, so she took the huge risk of removing her star to enable her to buy food in Aryan shops. Soon the order came for their grandmother's deportation. Anita had to take her to a school yard to be registered. Even at the time, Anita knew that an ill, eighty-two-year-old woman stood no chance of survival. She accompanied the old lady to the table where a Gestapo officer was calling out names from a long list. 'Lasker!' he barked. Anita's grandmother pulled herself up to her full height, and walked slowly up to him. '*Frau* Lasker to you,' she said, in a loud voice. There was a sudden silence. Anita held her breath, expecting her grandmother to be kicked, hit with a rifle butt or worse. The officer looked at this elderly woman, her medicine bottle swinging round her neck. '*Frau* Lasker,' he said.

Over the coming months, Alfons managed to send his daughters two postcards from Izbica camp, near Lublin. Anita never knew how he managed to get them out of the camp. The first implored the girls to send food and said that their mother could not write because she was unwell. Many years later, Anita went to the Holocaust archive in London, where she found some documentation on Izbica camp.[7] There she learnt that, after a time in captivity, the convoy that included her parents had been forced to undress, dig their own graves and stand naked, before being shot. The last words Alfons wrote to his daughters were simply: 'I lift my eyes up to the heavens from whence cometh my help.'

ও

Before her parents were deported, they were obliged to itemize and record everything that they left behind in the flat. In the Wrocław city archives, in Alfons's neatly sloping handwriting, is the list that he had spent his final evening compiling. It was officially sanctioned theft but, as Anita remembers, it was accepted as normal at the time. The sixteen-page form is an itinerary of a life: all the familiar, homely 'stuff' a family acquires to surround, comfort and define them. But set out with boxes next to each item for quantity and value, the list represents a home dissected, its itemized objects shorn of their memories and associations. 'It was pathetic. Everything you ever owned, listed,' Anita practically spits, her fury still palpable seventy years on.

Standing outside the space where 1 Höfchenstrasse once stood, I read Alfons's document, aloud. As I recite, I am reminded of Thomas Aquinas's words: 'The things that we love tell us what we are.' Spoken aloud, the objects shift from a list to a spell-like incantation. One bedstead. Two armchairs. One bedside rug. One desk lamp. One wall clock.

Three pillows. Perhaps, by naming these quotidian absences, I can disturb the air of this windy concrete street that appears to have forgotten what once took place here.

On page nine, I come upon the section for instruments. It is left blank, with only some sheet music declared. The Ventapane cello is not listed. Just as her parents would now vanish from official records, so too does Anita's cello. But, Anita says, 'of the three, only the cello stood a chance of surviving'.

꙳

When I first heard Anita tell her story, I had been struck by the idea that I might be able to track down her Ventapane. There are individuals in France and America who have built up a network to help trace looted Nazi instruments, and many have been returned to the families of those who had owned them. How extraordinary it would be to be able to find this precious object from her lost childhood, this one surviving member of her family, with whom she could share her memories of the vanished world of her youth. What symmetry there would be, presenting it to her in her old age, after so many decades of absence.

Some months before I met Anita, I had begun to work with Carla Shapreau, a San Francisco-based academic, to track the cello down. As we began work, I realized that Carla, an expert on tracing instruments stolen during the war, needed to construct a biography of the cello in order to have any chance of finding it. One Ventapane might look like any other Ventapane but, with a detailed life story, it could be identified by its alterations and repairs: like recognizing a long-lost child by a scar or secret mole. Only by matching up the cello's life story with the story its physical body could tell, could it be returned to Anita.

Carla asked me a stream of questions: 'To the extent Anita can recall, please send on all possibly relevant names of prior owners/possessors of the cello as well as the cities they may have lived in when the instrument was purchased and/

or maintained. Did Anita's mother or father purchase this cello for her? How did this cello come into Anita's hands? What was its history before she owned it, and might Anita recall which violin dealer she or her parents used for its maintenance?'

Only Anita could know such detail about her instrument. The cello could be saved through its relationship to its owner alone; her intimate knowledge of its story was the key to its return. But the more time I spent with Anita, the more I began to suspect that, even by entertaining the fantasy of finding her cello, I was trespassing on a relationship that was as close as that of two family members. It wasn't for me to know the instrument's secrets. Drinking coffee in her smoke-filled kitchen in north London back in the autumn, I hadn't intended to mention anything about the possibility of finding her Ventapane. But as we were talking about the instrument, and the moment seemed to present itself, I tentatively asked how she would feel if she could be reunited with her cello once again.

'I've seen a few Ventapanes being played but none of them were mine. God knows where that instrument went in the end.' She was silent for a moment, as she lit another cigarette.

'Would you like to see it again?' I ventured.

She paused.

'No. It was a different life.'

A door, firmly shut. I was almost ashamed to have imagined that I might be able to meddle in her story, to arrange a reunion for her, as a biographer might shuffle and filter the facts of a life to suit their authorial purpose. Her cello belonged to a life that had ended: brutally, and with finality. My desire to round off her story with a manufactured happy ending held no appeal for her. Forced to curate her memories in order to make it possible to live with them, the boundaries she had constructed around them must remain immutable.

'Now has got nothing to do with then', Anita told me, and I must take her at her word.

I may not be able to restore the cello to her, but I can, without fear of trespass, learn a little more of its story. Anita is keen to tell me about another inhabitant of Breslau, a non-Jewish violin maker by the name of (Walter) Matthias Mehne who was a great family friend. He lived and worked with his father Eugen near the centre of town, on the first floor of a building on the corner of the great square then called Tauentzienplatz. The Mehne family were the last people to see Anita's cello, or at least to know that it was hers. Anita cannot recall exactly what happened to her Ventapane but believes it was given to Mehne for safe-keeping. 'Every Jewish person who had anything would give it to Mehne,' she says.

Anita's aunt Kate and her husband were both amateur cellists, so there was already a cello in their flat when the Lasker family were obliged to move in with them. There was so little space that another cello would have been difficult to accommodate. If Anita ever had the energy after her long hours in the factory to practise, it would have been on the instrument that was already there. Her uncle and aunt were deported before her parents, and the fate of their cello, and indeed of the relatives themselves, is unknown. All Anita remembers is that, when the apartment was finally claimed by the Gestapo, the new inhabitant had the audacity to complain about the absence of a cello. The canvas cello case, lying empty in the hall, told them they had been cheated of a valuable possession.

Matthias Mehne's shop was the central meeting point for Breslau's string players, home to an informal community that represented culture and the nearest thing to normality in the midst of an impossibly bleak world. Matthias himself was something of an attraction. Born in 1908, he was a good-looking young man, who later proudly told his daughter that there used to be a steady flow of young Jewish girls who would appear in the shop to buy new E strings for their violins, having deliberately frayed their perfectly serviceable ones with their nail files. They were rarely in a hurry to leave. In fact, every musician who was anyone came to the shop. The great Polish violinist Bronisław Huberman brought his Stradivari to the Mehnes. And when the cellist Gregor Piatigorsky played his first concert in Breslau and his luggage got lost, he performed in Eugen's tails and Matthias's white dress shirt.

Matthias had known Anita's teacher Leo Rostal well, and had even come to Berlin at one point to meet up with her and bring her the Ventapane, presumably after some repairs. When the prohibitions against Jews entering Aryan shops became stricter, Anita was forbidden to use his violin shop. But Matthias Mehne represented the last link to the musical

Tauentzienplatz with Mehne's instrument shop on the left, with three little violin silhouettes visible in the first-floor windows.

life Anita had lost almost as soon as it had begun. She knew she would have been arrested, and most likely deported, had she been caught, but she continued visiting him, with her yellow star covered.

Anita remembers the distinctive red violin-shaped signs in the first-floor windows. From the photographs I have found, they appear to be white, but it is impossible to tell on sepia images. Anita's memory is in full technicolour. However, I can't help wondering whether she remembers a feeling, rather than an accurate detail. As Anita puts it, Mehne was 'so anti-Nazi it was dangerous'. The shop was in an extremely prominent position in the city, but Eugen and Matthias refused to hang out fascist banners or display a picture of Hitler, both of which were obligatory. Such obvious disobedience must have attracted the attention of the authorities. At a time when the city was loaded with the symbolism of violence, the Mehnes' cut-out violins insisted on the shape of stringed instruments in defiance of the blazing red swastikas draped from every other window in Tauentzienplatz.

I track down Matthias's daughter in London, where she is a classical music agent. Bettina Mehne has grown up with stories of her father's fondness for the Lasker family. One anecdote in particular stands out in her memory. On Kristallnacht, while Anita was asleep alone in Berlin, her father Alfons was taken from their family home in Breslau, not by an anti-Semitic mob, but by Matthias Mehne. From his shop's central position, Matthias could see the lootings and burning as soon as they began, and he quickly realized that Alfons would be in danger. He could not bring Alfons back to the shop without endangering his own parents, so he put him in his car and drove around the city with him all night. This came with considerable risks. Matthias was a well-known figure in Breslau. He was a socialite, well recognized at the riding stables, and he drove a very distinctive convertible Mercedes (his flashy car is a detail that both

Anita and Bettina particularly recall). Driving around in it during the night was a dangerous gambit, but he was relying on the mob being too occupied to notice, or simply assuming he was out partying, as was often the case. At any point the car could have been stopped, and both men would certainly have been arrested. The streets were littered with the wreckage of Jewish shops, and the vast domed synagogue opposite Alfons's office by the police station was burning to the ground. As in Berlin, firemen were standing by, stopping the flames reaching non-Jewish houses, but doing nothing to stop the destruction of the synagogue.

$\backsim$

In 2013, seventy-five years after Kristallnacht, Bettina Mehne organized a weekend of Jewish music in Vienna to commemorate the events of that terrible night, and invited Anita to take part. As Anita's memory turned to that nocturnal car journey, and her own friendship with Bettina's father, her thoughts had also turned to the loss of her cello.

She told Bettina that she thought she might perhaps have encountered her cello again, a few months earlier. Anita described the 'bizarre' feeling she had had when the owner of a Ventapane had shown her their instrument. It could have been hers, but she wasn't sure. She wanted to know whether she had indeed seen a ghost. I ask Bettina, who is a cellist herself, whether she believes it might have been Anita's own cello. She is not convinced. 'There is such a bond with your instrument,' she says, 'a muscle memory that remembers the feel of it. If an instrument connects with you, you know instantly. There is so much soul in an instrument, and everyone who plays it leaves something of themselves in it. If Anita had touched her Ventapane again, the cello would have made itself known to her.' It's a strong, beguiling claim. But – really? It puts me in mind of Julian Lloyd Webber's theory that his cello already knew the Delius concerto, and almost played it itself, like a player piano. Even from my unashamedly romantic stand-point, I must admit to raising a sceptical eyebrow.

෴

On 16 May 1942, officials from the Chief Financial Praesidium came to Anita's aunt's flat to register its contents for confiscation. Sixteen-year-old Anita was trying to run the household, looking after her sister, lodgers and grandmother. It was up to her to go to the Gestapo Office to appeal to the customs inspectors to change their minds. When a person was deported, the Gestapo would seal their rooms so their possessions could not be taken by friends or relatives. They even sealed drawers. Left with no instrument, no possessions and no responsible adults to take care of her, Anita's plea was simply that they might remove the seal on one drawer, in order for her to access a change of bedclothes. 'It was absolutely ludicrous,' Anita remembers.

There is no mention of the instruments in the surviving list of the flat's contents, but in a letter to Anita from the Chief Financial President he refuses to return her other confiscated possessions. There is a more enigmatic instruction: 'To NN to find out where the musical instruments (the grand piano and cello) from the Lasker flat have gone.' Is this an order to Anita, to tell him where she has hidden the instruments, or is it a refusal in reply to her demands to know what the Nazis have done with them? And who is NN?

On 3 June, Anita visited the customs office for a second time. She made a declaration about the instruments:

As far as I know, the musical instruments in question (the grand piano and cello) were the property of my uncle Ernst Israel Schreiber who was expelled on 21st November 1941 and in whose flat my family lived as sub-tenants. The grand piano was taken away from the flat with the rest of the furniture. I do not know what happened to the cello. The empty case is still standing in the hall and has not so far been collected. It is possible that the cello belonged to my uncle's brother, Hans Israel Schreiber, Telegraphenstrasse 3, and that he collected it.

I find it hard to forget the image of the sixteen-year-old girl, alone, telling some man in Nazi uniform about the empty cello case standing in the hall, delineating the space where an instrument should have been. It was not her Ventapane, but the case still stands in her memory to this day, as a monument to both her loss and her defiance.

∽

As Anita and Renate could not pay the rent, they were eventually sent to the Jewish orphanage, the Waisenhaus, in the centre of town at Wallstrasse 9. They fought the move, thinking it would limit their chances of escape, but as soon as they were there, they couldn't believe they'd resisted for so long. Rather than having to fend for themselves, they were provided with food by other people. It felt like luxury.

The Waisenhaus is still standing today, part of a complex of buildings that back on to the Synagogue of the White Stork. On my second morning in Wrocław, I go to meet Bente Kahan, an actor-singer who is a prominent member of the synagogue's community, and famous for her performances of Yiddish folk songs and songs written by victims of the Holocaust. Bente has spent much of her time in Wrocław trying to restore what she can of the Jewish life here that Anita would have known. She tells me all about the synagogue. While the 'New' Synagogue was completely destroyed during Kristallnacht, the 'White Stork' was surrounded by other buildings, so the SS did not set fire to it, contenting themselves with smashing the windows instead. During Soviet rule it became more and more dilapidated, until it was left with no floor or windows, and a huge hole in the wall where the Torah should have been stored. Bente spent many years obtaining grants to restore it, and it is now a luminous building, freshly painted in cream and peach, with delicate art deco patterns of lilies around its curved balconies.

Bente shows me a film she made during lockdown, a concert of her singing Jewish music written by composers who were killed by the Nazis. Around her and the string players from Wrocław's chamber orchestra appear to be the walls of what was known as the 'New' Synagogue, impossibly recreated with virtual technology. The camera takes us around the building as they perform, filling a virtual space with their music. In reality, the site where the 'New' synagogue stood is now a clump of bushes, marked by a small monument, overshadowed by the looming prison and police station. The effect of the camera's movement around the stonework that is not there is surreal. Interspersed are photographs of the Jewish community from around the time Anita lived nearby: a little girl with a bow in her hair holding hands in the street with her mother; a wedding couple, smiling outside on the steps that are nowhere now.

At Bente's invitation, we bring some music to the only surviving synagogue. I sit on the stage and play *Kol Nidrei*, Bruch's plaintive Jewish lament, to the 'White Stork'. The acoustic is excellent – alive, resonant. The building echoes with the music. Bente sings to me in her deep, haunting mezzo. First a well-known Yiddish song called 'Oyfen Pripetchik', about children sitting around a fire learning their letters.[8] The tune is simple, and I play with her after a verse or two. It is a children's song, encouraging them to learn the Torah, but the fourth stanza reads like a premonition:

When, children, you will grow older
You will understand
How many tears lie in these letters
And how much crying.

Bente then sings me some songs her father had collected in a notebook just after the war, songs so rare hardly anyone knows them now. She sings with great passion, moving hypnotically from a whisper to great sobs of sorrow. One song is about a little child in the Shtetl, whose mother has died.[9] The chorus is the child's voice, at her mother's grave, asking to join her. There is a stepmother, cruel, uncaring, who beats the child. And again the chorus returns, 'Please, mother, let me join you. I don't want to be alone.'

∿

From the Waisenhaus next door to the synagogue, Anita and Renate continued their daily commute to work in the paper factory. They worked alongside French prisoners of war and non-Jewish French and Polish civilians. The foreign enforced workers were occasionally allowed to go home on leave. Anita has always been someone who will inevitably do whatever she is forbidden from doing. Told not to speak to the French prisoners, she went out of her way to do so. The French which Anita had learnt from her parents now proved invaluable. When the prisoners gave them forged papers, the girls would fill in the gaps with the Gothic-script German they'd learnt at school, providing civilian identities for the prisoners of war, and thereby securing them 'home leave', from which they would never return. They enjoyed their clandestine work, Anita remembers. It was better to feel that they were damaging the Nazi system in their own small way, not just waiting passively to be caught. If they were to be arrested, it would be for doing something rebellious, rather than the accident of being born Jewish.

In the factory there was a toilet with a hole in the wall. It was a little opening on to the refectory used by the prisoners, through which Anita could whisper, pushing messages and papers through the gap – 'a little bit like *A Midsummer Night's Dream*', she says. One day she found the hole blocked and knew they had been found out. At that point, the girls decided they needed to organize their own escape. They quickly produced papers for themselves, Anita renaming herself Marlene de Montaigne, and reinventing herself as a worker in an upholstery factory. She memorized her new birthplace and her mother's maiden name, 'like a character in an adventure story'. The girls had some addresses they could go to in Paris, and if they managed to get there they then planned to go south to the Unoccupied Zone, unknowingly intending to following Pál Hermann's own route through France. Anita filled a rucksack, donated by Matthias Mehne, with everything that could be obtained for her new life.

On the day of their escape, Anita and Renate didn't go to the factory but spent the day with a married couple they trusted, one of whom was Jewish. The couple insisted on taking the girls to Breslau Central Station, from where they were to catch their train.

༄

Renate had gone ahead with a suitcase, and was inside the train carriage as Anita stood on the platform with the rucksack, saying goodbye to their two friends. Looking back, Anita believes that their movements must have been observed for some time. Just as Renate stepped out of the carriage to see what was detaining her sister, the four were surrounded by plain clothes Gestapo, quickly followed by uniformed men with dogs. Only the suitcase left for Paris.

Anita has lived with her remorse and regret at her friends' arrest ever since.[10] But at that moment she had to manage her fear, and think as clearly as she could. She and Renate were marched to the Railway Police Station nearby, where they were held in a cell for several hours. The sisters agreed that suicide would be better than whatever the Gestapo had in store for them. Hidden in her stocking, Anita had a little bottle of cyanide. It had been given to her by a Jewish boy called Konrad, in case of just such an eventuality. Now Anita and Renate managed to divide the white powder into two portions under the table at which they had been made to sit. They both had enough to end their lives as soon as they swallowed it. But when to take it? They were waiting for the car to transport them to the centre of town for their interrogation, but it never arrived, so they were ordered to march, escorted by policemen and dogs, through the blacked-out streets to the Gestapo headquarters by the side of the river. Now was their moment.

On the corner of Gartenstrasse and Schweidnitzer Strasse they began their count of three. They intended to die at the same time. Anita slipped the powder into her mouth, but the poison failed to take hold. She and Renate were still marching along as it dawned on her that she had tasted sweetness instead of the expected bitter almond tang of cyanide. Konrad had reclaimed his bottle temporarily some weeks ago, and given it back to her the day before her escape attempt. Instead of the poison, he had substituted icing sugar. After the war she and Konrad were reunited – she a cellist and he a professional conductor. 'And do you know what I said to him? Thanks for the sugar!'

⌣

I try to picture Anita choosing this place to end her life. She had hardly begun the march to the Gestapo headquarters. The station is less than a minute's walk behind us and, as she turned the corner, waiting for the cyanide's effects to begin, she would have seen the trees and bushes of Tauentzienplatz, and the violin shapes in the Mehnes' shop windows. I realize with a start that, if her Ventapane had indeed been in Mehne's care, she would have been within sight of her cello when she decided to kill herself.

Ola and Kuba help me find the street corner on which Anita and Renate committed their sugar suicide. Walking

The corner of Gartenstrasse today.

round the corner, we are confronted with an enormous and powerfully horrible mural. Three aggressive rifle-toting figures in pseudo-military uniform bristle above us, along with three giant red-eyed wolves: a strange echo of the guard dogs that had surrounded Anita. Ola explains that these grim-looking men and women are celebrated figures who had fought against communist rule in the years leading up to 1989. The mural has been painted by the local football team, who align themselves with these revered figures, but the team's supporters are extremely right wing, so this mural and its associations are synonymous with racism, and anti-Semitism in particular. Its complicated message of aggression, and the ripples of unrest and oppression, seem to pass like ground tremors through this spot.

〜

Matthias Mehne was informed on the Friday that he had to report to the Gestapo for questioning on the following Monday. It was a deliberate tactic to induce fear, leaving the victim with a weekend of uncertainty. Was his summons in relation to his refusal to display a picture of the Führer, or for something far more serious? He had no idea that Anita had been arrested, but by the beginning of the week he too was imprisoned. The Gestapo had identified the rucksack Anita had been carrying. It is most likely that Matthias was held in the cells under the Gestapo building, where there is now a plaque commemorating the many civilians of Breslau who were tortured and murdered there. It is one of the bleakest, most forbidding buildings in the city. Anita was being held in the prison next door.

Matthias fully expected to die, and with good reason − the Gestapo were perfectly clear that they intended to shoot him for his part in Anita's escape attempt. When his case came to trial, however, the judge commuted the sentence; he realized he knew Matthias from the riding stables where they both kept horses. It was an incredible stroke of luck. The judge convinced the Gestapo that it would be better for Matthias to be sent into the army, with the likelihood that the enemy would probably shoot him anyway, and save them the trouble.

In Matthias's absence, his family fled Breslau on foot. His father and sister walked to the town of Geisenkirchen with whatever they could carry, knowing they could not go back. Bettina believes her grandparents hid most of their possessions − including a dinner set for twenty-five, golden spoons and several instruments − in a cave outside Breslau, although she mistrusts her memory on this. There is no way of knowing now whether one of these instruments was Anita's Ventapane, having been entrusted to the Mehnes' care, but if they had taken everything of value, it would have been high on the list of objects to save. Matthias managed to survive the war and set up shop in Berlin in the late 1940s. He later told his daughter how he had hoped to return to Breslau after the war to recover the family's belongings, but once the city had fallen into Soviet hands it was impossible.

∾

Next door to the Gestapo headquarters stands a red brick, turreted prison of pseudo-medieval construction. After her interrogation and a cursory trial, Anita was held here for a year. The prison is very close to the centre of the town, but inside its walls she was cut off completely. Renate was being held elsewhere. 'Prison was horrible,' Anita tells me. There were three and sometimes four people in a one-bed cell, a bucket with a lid for a toilet, and a little metal bowl to wash in. They had to polish it with brick dust until it shone. She was never allowed out of her cell, other than for half an hour of walking in the yard in circles, with her hands behind her back.

Breslau prison.

During the winter of 1943, Anita was moved, for the first time, to a different cell, where she was to wait to be transferred.

'You learn the routine of a prison. Monday and Tuesday, you're about to be transported to another prison. On Thursday, prisoners were deported to Auschwitz.'

When her cell door was unlocked and she was ordered out, it was a Thursday.

Oświęcim –
Anita Lasker-Wallfisch

Auschwitz was a camp of absurd contradictions and insane inventions. One of its ironies was the music.

*(from Margarita Schwalbovà, 'A Doctor Gives
Her Account of Auschwitz-Birkenau')*

In London I had sat in Anita's kitchen, cutting the chocolate cake I had brought her, as she prepared coffee. Her son, Raphael Wallfisch, had told me she had a particular fondness for chocolate cake. She took a modest slice, explaining that she was being 'schmoozed up' by the Austrian embassy that afternoon. She was hoping for Sachertorte there, but would save another slice of my chocolate cake for later, in case the Austrians had disappointed her. She carefully pushed a plate with her reserve piece to the side of the table.

In her memoir, she wrote of how violently she loathed the taste of the interminable turnip soup in Auschwitz, slopped into tin bowls day after day. A concentration camp was no place to be picky over the menu, and she was on the edge of starvation, but she simply could not stomach any more of the putrid liquid. Some of the other women in her hut saved the precious lumps of potato that occasionally turned up in their

266

soup, and kept her alive with their scraps. It was a gesture of kindness she has never forgotten.

Those women, like Anita, were members of the Auschwitz-Birkenau women's orchestra, a motley band assembled from all over Europe, who survived Auschwitz for no other reason than the fact of their musical training. Anita was their cellist.

∽

When Anita arrived at the camp in December 1943, she was herded with hundreds of other prisoners from the cattle trucks to the nearest huts.

'I arrived with a group of criminals, which was advantageous,' she told me. 'To be a criminal was better than to be a Jew. Many Jews were sent straight from the train into the gas chambers.'

On arrival, all prisoners were marked with a triangle sewn onto their clothes to show what category they fell into. Jews were identified by a red triangle with a yellow stripe, sewn to overlap with a yellow triangle to form the star of David. Homosexuals (almost exclusively German) wore a pink triangle, black triangles for Roma, red for political prisoners and green for criminals. Very few Jews were marked green. It was one of the many small miracles that conspired to save Anita's life: 90 per cent of those marked as Jewish were murdered.

Her clothes were taken, along with her few other possessions, and she was made to stand naked in the middle of the 'processing' hut, her head shaved and her brown curls in coils around her feet. She glanced up and saw the shower-like contraptions fixed to the ceiling. She remembers everyone else leaving the hut and the door shutting. She did not scream, or try to run. She simply stood there alone, shivering, her eyes closed, waiting for the hiss of the gas. Nothing happened. After a while the hair shavers and tattooists returned. Later she learnt that this was the de-lousing room, and these were genuine showers.

The processing hut and shower block today.

The girl prisoner whose job it was to tattoo numbers on the prisoners' arms questioned Anita earnestly for any information from the outside world as she branded 69388 onto her arm. Anita told her all she knew, but for reasons she has never fathomed, it felt important to tell the girl that she played the cello. What does one talk about when expecting to die? She had come into contact with prisoners in Breslau who knew exactly what took place in the extermination camps, and she was under no illusions about her chances of survival. The camp was dominated by tall chimneys billowing out the black smoke of the burning bodies, day and night. Ash covered everything, and could be tasted in the wind. Anita repeatedly told me, with the ring of a phrase that had become well worn for her during those years, 'The only way anyone expected to leave was through those chimneys.' But this brief moment of conversation with the tattooist was to change her fate. 'A cellist? My God! You're saved!' exclaimed the girl. The camp orchestra had a cello but no one to play it. In the space of a few seconds, Anita's status in the camp went from dispensable to essential, making hers one of the few lives considered worth saving.

Before Anita could audition for the orchestra, she was kept in the Quarantine Block. Conditions there were abominable. The sleeping quarters consisted of a type of shelf – or *kojen*, as they were called – on which everyone lay squashed together. 'Most of one's time was spent on roll call,' she remembered, standing outside five deep in the freezing cold, inadequately dressed, in order to be counted. 'I never understood the German mania for counting people. Since they were so preoccupied with destroying as many of us as possible, why was it so important to count everybody? However, there it was, and enduring *Appell* was a sort of torture itself. You were strictly forbidden to move, and because the procedure lasted an eternity, it will be clear what that meant for the prisoners who, almost without exception, suffered from dysentery. In plain language, many of us just stood there with shit running down our legs, in complete agony. How easy it was to call us "dirty smelling pigs". It is impossible to convey how extreme our misery was.'

Finally the order came; the cellist should report to the Music Block. Anita opened the wooden door to find an orchestra sitting in uniformed rows. Its conductor, Alma Rosé, incongruously glamorous in her own clothes, stood out against the striped uniforms and drab grey of the others. Alma handed Anita a cello. It was the first touch of something familiar and beautiful since she had been put into prison a year before. She had not played a cello for two years. For this strangest of 'auditions', she played the slow movement of the Boccherini Cello Concerto. Alma was delighted. Her orchestral trial complete, Anita was made an official member of the camp orchestra on the spot, and joined them for their rehearsal of one of Schubert's *Marches Militaires*.

∽

From that moment, her cello gave Anita a means of defining herself. This meant more to her than just physical survival. On that first day she had been transformed into an anonymous prisoner, her clothes and her hair removed, her brutalized arm throbbing. Now, her ability to play the cello enabled her to claim back her identity. She was no longer one of thousands of indistinguishable prisoners but the Cellist.

> 'Of course I had always loved the cello. But it saved my life and my sister's. There had been a cellist there before me, but they had died. I know nothing about them. It was simply coincidence that they were dead, and I arrived at that moment. Somebody, God knows who, brought a cello to Auschwitz. You didn't even think of asking. You never asked who.'

Anita stops to light another cigarette, and her last sentence is left hanging, a reminder of the camp etiquette, unspoken and universal. Never ask, never question. Survival required tunnel vision, and survival did not end in 1945. When Primo Levi tried to ask why a guard had behaved as he did, he was told, now famously, 'Here there is no why.'[11] As far as Anita is concerned, such questions are not a part of her story.

Anita's voice, a low, Marlene Dietrich mezzo with a gentle German accent, becomes emphatic, at times almost fierce when there is the implication that we have ventured onto territory on which she will not, or cannot, tread. I am acutely aware of the privilege that she is granting me in talking of these events. I can be permitted to glimpse only the aspects of her narrative that she chooses to share. Her account is accurate and dispassionate, shaped through many repetitions, for the benefit of politicians and schoolchildren. As I listen, I find that her silences and omissions become loud absences, almost as powerful as her extraordinary story itself. Increasingly, I have the sense that she is leading me, very much in control, down a narrow corridor. To left and to right are many doors, but should I so much as push at them, I will find them firmly locked. It is my privilege to be there, with her, to hear what she wishes me to know, and to listen. I have no part in shaping her narrative, and that is as it should be.

But I find it hard to erase from my mind the image of that previous cellist, about whom no one must ask. Anita was saved by her ability to play a recently dead woman's cello. She sat in that woman's place around the instrument, and drew a sound from it that this already forgotten woman had heard, many thousands of times. Anita was animating a voice that was the only physical vestige of a woman who had disappeared, erased even from the memory of the camp. Had the previous cellist lived, Anita's own survival would have been far less assured. There was only one instrument available to the orchestra.[12] As one survivor wrote, 'everyone dies and lives in place of another, without reason or meaning; the camp is the place in which no one can truly die or survive in his own place.'[13]

Later on, I learn from the archives at Auschwitz that the cello Anita was given had previously been played by a German Jew called Maria Kroner, who had died in August 1943. Restoring Maria's name to the narrative, and allowing her to take her place, however slight, in the history of the orchestra is a small act of restitution. Maria's life could not be saved, but her cello had saved Anita's.

But where had the cello that they had both played come from? Had it been brought into the camp by Maria herself? Back in 1940, in the early days of the camp, and before its extension – Auschwitz II-Birkenau – had been built, there were many Polish musicians and actors being held in Auschwitz I. They sought permission from the commandant, Rudolf Höss,

The men's orchestra of Auschwitz I in the early 1940s.

to ask their families to send them their instruments. When he realized he could organize an orchestra for the entertainment of the officers and their families living there, and to make the men march more efficiently in order, he agreed. For the prisoners, playing in the orchestra meant exemption from hard labour outside the camp, and occasional extra meals of potato soup. The first concert of the men's orchestra in Auschwitz was held on 6 January 1941.

Many of the instruments had not yet arrived by the new year, however, and assistant bandmaster Henryk Król later recalled that the concert took place using instruments that had been seized from street musicians in the nearby town of Oświęcim (Auschwitz is its Germanicized name).[14] An abandoned piano was fished out of the River Soła and repaired in the music block. Other instruments were taken from the storehouses of confiscated prisoners' belongings.[15] As the Jewish genocide progressed, more and more prisoners arrived, bringing their most precious possessions with them. While the majority of Jewish prisoners were gassed on arrival, their instruments were then stored in the camp, to be shipped to Germany or used by the camp orchestras.

⌇

Katarzyna Kuszaj-Jarnot is one of the team of guides and archivists who work at Auschwitz-Birkenau. On the day of my visit, she meets me in Auschwitz I, under the infamous gateway bearing the motto 'Arbeit macht frei', and we make our way to Birkenau, the part of the camp in which Anita was held, three kilometres away. In Birkenau we pick our way through the light clay mud of the central Lagerstrasse. Deep puddles reflect the barbed wire on either side of our path. As we walk, Katarzyna explains to me that 90 per cent of the camp documents were destroyed. Reconstructing what went on here is largely a matter of testimony, and inevitably, people remember different things, events happening in different places. Piecing together the orchestra's story is similarly a fluid process. So much has vanished. People, documentation, even buildings. All that remains of the hut where Anita lived with the orchestra is a rectangle of cracked concrete marked out on the ground, covered by clumps of purple-black moss, and large shards of broken glass that have lain there since 1945, when the hut was torn apart for firewood. There are a few instruments in the archive: but no cello.

Violinist Szymon Laks, who helped found Birkenau's men's orchestra, listed the instruments the musicians had at their disposal. Initially, there was a selection of brass, wind and percussion, but in 1944 they acquired a few violins, presumably from murdered Jewish arrivals, along with a trumpet and a cello that belonged to the sector of Birkenau which housed the families who had previously been held in the Theresienstadt ghetto. Continuing the music-making that had sustained them in Theresienstadt, they had formed a little orchestra. The cello's sudden availability was the result of one of the darkest moments of Auschwitz-Birkenau's bleak history. On the night of 8 March 1944, 4,000 Czech Jews from Theresienstadt – including many children, and the whole orchestra – were murdered in the gas chambers. The cello was one of the few survivors. Could any instrument hold such a desperate history as this? But to Laks, trying to sustain an ensemble that was continually depleted by suicide, illness and executions, a cello was a lifeline.[16]

When the camp was dismantled at the end of the war, the instruments in Auschwitz I were left in Block 24, which was the music room. After the evacuation in January 1945, the instruments and the sheet music that the prisoners had painstakingly copied out were destroyed, and the room was ransacked. Despite this, some instruments did survive until liberation, but there is no record of whether any of those destroyed or otherwise was a cello.[17]

∾

Existence in Auschwitz was not simply a matter of waiting for the inevitable. Survival, for however long it lasted, meant a struggle to find meaning and purpose to each day. The members of the women's orchestra, despite being half starved and frequently ill, were a little better placed than most other prisoners in the camp. Critically, for their hygiene and health, they had the use of a small toilet block outside the orchestra hut, in which they could shower twice a week. It had been built for the German political prisoners, who were treated much better than the rest of the camp inmates. The orchestra members were insistent about each other's cleanliness. Once a girl stopped bothering to try to clean herself, those around her knew she had given up, and despair was contagious.

Other prisoners had access only twice a day to the long rows of filthy toilet holes. Even this was a step up from the earlier days of the camp, when there had been no water, and no toilets at all. Now there were a few showers, which were allowed once a month. Walking round the camp with Katarzyna, and standing in the one remaining toilet block, which is grim but now sanitary, I find it impossible to imagine the squalor most prisoners were forced to endure.

The special conditions that Alma had secured for the orchestra inevitably resulted in jealousy and resentment from some prisoners. The orchestra lived and worked in Hut 12. There, Anita and the other players had access to water and their own individual wooden beds, instead of sleeping on fetid straw or three to a bunk. And whereas most other huts had mud or concrete with a gap between the floor and the walls, their hut had a wooden floor.

The orchestra was ordered to play at the main entrance to the camp, as the twelve thousand or so women condemned to ten hours a day of hard labour were marched in and out of the gates. Anita described the orchestra's routine in her memoir:

> Our main function was to go to the Main Gate every morning and every evening and play marches for the thousands of prisoners who worked outside the camp. It was imperative that these columns of prisoners should march neatly and in step, and we provided the music to achieve this. We sat out there in all weathers, sometimes in sub-zero temperatures, scantily dressed, and we played. In this uniquely strategic position we witnessed all sorts of things. For instance, prisoners unlucky enough to be caught with 'treasures' which they had managed to 'organize' [camp language for objects bartered for, or obtained], hoping they would not be frisked by the SS, would be made to kneel down and eat whatever they were caught with. I once saw a woman being forced to eat a packet of cigarettes.[18]

༄

For some, the music was an additional torment. One survivor's testimony in the archive recalls: 'The most infernal element of the camp orchestra's music making was the often jolly, upbeat marches they had to play, for hours at a time.' Trying to march in time to a jaunty rhythm was desperately difficult, and this prisoner was not alone in resenting the orchestra that drove them on. Another said: 'For me it was a curse. As we walked on command through the gate, in the winter, in the snow, the snow caked on our wooden clogs, we slipped and fell, we could not keep time with the marching rhythm. And we had to take off those clogs and walk barefoot through the snow [...] The overall role of the orchestra from day to day, for us prisoners, was terrible.'[19]

Many prisoners were near death, and many others returned as corpses, hung between their comrades' shoulders, on the march back into camp at the end of the day. 'For both, the

A sketch by prisoner Mieczysław Kościelniak of Alma conducting the orchestra, whilst the labourers return to the camp.

orchestra played. The parade march, at the end of the day, became a gruesomely incongruous funeral march.'[20] Witold Pilecki remembered how 'especially during the time of the march of the units returning from work, the entire macabre nature of the scene was evident [...] The beaten-up figures of prisoners wavering on their feet and exhausted by labour returned to the lively sound of marches of some sort, played at a fast tempo, that gave the impression of polkas or obereks, and not marches. [...] Columns of unbounded, physical human misery surrounded by a ring of men urging them on, exercising their clubs on the ranks and forcing them to walk to the tempo of a merry melody.'[21]

The idea of making music in such an environment was equally abhorrent to some of the musicians, who initially refused to join the orchestra. For those who did play, some felt that music was forever contaminated by the experience. 'After the war I would rather cut off my own fingers than pick up a saxophone or clarinet,' said Kazimierz Lewandowski, one of the members of the men's orchestra.

～

After the evening marches had been played, the women's orchestra began to rehearse, the sound carrying over the centre of the camp and across the barbed wire to the train line and the selection ramp at the heart of Birkenau. By the summer of 1944, when the Germans knew they were likely to lose the war, they decided to speed up the killing. Between ten and twelve thousand prisoners disembarked here every day, often within earshot of the orchestra.

The orchestra was not intentionally playing these prisoners to the gas chambers, although many survivor accounts assumed this was the case. Often it simply happened to be practising, as the trains arrived in the morning and evening or during one of the obligatory Sunday concerts. The same was true of the men's orchestra, on the other side of the tracks.

The selection ramp inside Birkenau, in 1944, and as it is today (looking away from the main gate). The orchestra played just behind the wire on the left, the crematoria are visible in the distance.

One musician recalled: 'From our podium the undulating column of the doomed, surrounded on both sides by densely deployed SS men, can be seen perfectly well [...] Attracted by the sounds of music, they turn their heads in our direction. Perhaps they think that, if there is music, they will not have it bad here.'[22]

∽

Within the orchestras themselves there were intense friendships and the most ferocious hatreds. They were a microcosm of society, made up of Jews and Aryans, Poles, Russians, Hungarians and Germans. It was, as Anita puts it, 'a tower of Babel'. Anita could only communicate with those who spoke German or French, so the Russians and Poles remained a mystery to her. In some respects the musicians were united against their common enemy, pulling together to help each other survive. However, even (or especially) in Auschwitz, there was also suspicion and hostility. The women with whom Anita could not communicate eyed her mistrustfully, and the automatic assumption, she remembers, was that you were a threat unless proven otherwise.

'So I don't talk to them. We don't think even to ask why the other person ended up in Auschwitz at all. Many years later I am in close contact with one of these other people, a Polish lady, a pure Aryan who played the violin in the orchestra. We never spoke to each other at the time. We came into contact again and met up in Krakow. She was nearly 100! We still had problems finding a common language, but we talked to each other, and wrote to each other in English. In short, we became friends, and found we had far more in common than that which divides us.'

Anita is describing Helena Dunicz-Niwińska, who had often led the orchestra. When decades later, the two women both returned to Auschwitz, the visit was much anticipated: a historic moment, captured by reporters and film crew. At one point, standing in the ruins of her old hut, Anita got out her cigarettes and lit up. The senior archivist, with much trepidation, approached her. 'Mrs Lasker-Wallfisch, I'm terribly sorry, but there is a no smoking policy here. Would you mind?' Anita took a step towards her and looked her straight in the eye. '*No one* tells me what to do in Auschwitz,' she said.

～

The women's orchestra was a great deal inferior to the orchestra of the men's camp, which consisted mostly of members of the Warsaw Philharmonic. 'They played proper music, we played light rubbish. Theirs was a much bigger orchestra, but because they hardly needed any rehearsal time, they were made to go out to work, digging in the fields. We were so bad we had to note-bash all day long. We played ridiculous repertoire – really amateur stuff. But it did mean that our work *was* playing – we didn't get sent out to labour.' Anita is thoroughly disparaging of the orchestra, but the fact that it achieved any standard at all was due to a figure for whom she has the highest respect: its director, the violinist Alma Rosé.

Alma boasted a formidable musical pedigree. Her mother was the sister of Gustav Mahler, and Alma herself had been a successful, glamorous soloist before the war, trained by her father, the great Arnold Rosé, principal violinist of the Vienna Philharmonic Orchestra. Alma adored him, and Anita believes it was his perfectionism that Alma had internalized and applied to her motley gaggle of starving girls. Drilling them was her personal tribute to Arnold. 'If ever we played anything even reasonably decently, her biggest accolade was "that was good enough for my father to hear".'

～

Despite being an extremely accomplished player, Alma had not achieved the career her father had hoped for her as an international soloist. Aware that she was a disappointment to

Alma and her *Walzermädeln*.

him, she turned to lighter music, and made her name training up a troupe of violin-playing girls in diaphanous, floaty blue dresses. In photographs of the troupe, violins appear to float above the pleats, frills and décolleté hems. These girls were all extremely attractive but they were also all excellent players. Alma trained these eight girls into choreographed performances of waltzes, every part memorized, every movement perfectly coordinated. Her *Wiener Walzermädeln* (Viennese waltz maidens) were a huge success with the press, who praised their 'intoxicating attraction' and their impressive range – 'from sweetness to a hurricane'. They were the finest ensemble of their kind, and Alma became a celebrity in her own right.

To this day, Anita is still bitterly angry that Alma's brilliant career was cut short by Auschwitz. 'She was only there because of a stupid mistake!' At the point at which the Nazis were rounding up Jews for the camps, Alma was in London with her father. 'She had a Czech passport because of her husband, so mistakenly she felt safe. She left London and went to Holland to do some really rather ordinary concerts, to be able to send some money to her father. She stayed too long, and was trapped. She need never have been there at all. They weren't even good concerts!' Anita thunders. 'What was she *thinking*?!'

Alma was arrested in 1942 as she attempted to escape to Switzerland. She was sent first to Drancy (a year before Pál Hermann had been held there), then to Auschwitz in 1943. She was supposed to have been gassed on arrival, but was saved by a confusion between her maiden and married names. Instead, she was taken first to the original camp, Auschwitz I, and put in the notorious Block 10. This was the province of Dr Josef Mengele, known as 'the angel of death', who used his inmates for depraved pseudo-medical experimentation. Alma may have been put there because she was married but still childless, and Mengele wanted her for an experiment that involved injecting hormones for enforced sterilization.

Before Mengele had time to inflict any of his horrific medical procedures on her, there was a call for a violinist to play on the occasion of the birthday of the SS doctor in charge of Block 10. Alma volunteered. Once her talent was discovered, she was transferred to Birkenau, to develop the orchestra.

The women's side of Birkenau camp was run by two women, Margot Dreschel and Maria Mandl, 'an absolutely ghastly person', says Anita. 'Dreschel hated us. There was a fight going on over us between them, apparently. But Mandl wanted an orchestra, and while she prevailed, we survived.' The beginnings of Mandl's orchestra had been assembled in April 1943, four months before Alma arrived. The Polish music teacher Zofia Trecofska had been running it, but it was a task beyond her abilities as a musician. When Alma took over, Zofia was moved into a position akin to orchestra manager, organizing clothes, food and music for the players who all lived together in Hut 12. The camp orchestra, or

'Lagerkapelle' as it was known, was made up at that time of girls who at best had only a couple of years' experience on their instruments.

In her memoir, Anita wrote:

If anybody has ever been faced with a challenge, it was Alma – in an unheard-of situation, and confronted with a most unusual collection of instruments that were played by an equally unusual collection of 'musicians'. One could have counted on the fingers of one hand the people whom one could really have called 'musicians'. With this material Alma set herself the task of creating a genuine orchestra, in which only the highest standards were acceptable. They were standards she herself had grown up to respect. In reality it meant that Alma had to drill practically everybody note by note, and she threw herself into the task with a fervour that seemed ridiculous in the circumstances. We must not forget that outside our little world the gas chambers were working non-stop.[23]

By Block 29, there is a long, thin flat mound, an outdoor stage effectively, just behind the two blocks by the main entrance. This is where the orchestra played in good weather from June 1943. There are some white stones set into the soil for a stage for the orchestra, with a harp painted on the stones in whitewash.[24] The main hospital hut, Block 20, known as the death block, was to the side of the stage on which Anita sat. Patients in the hospital barracks would have been able to hear the concerts from their beds behind the thin wooden walls.

Alma's Sunday concerts were a very serious business, and she put her whole soul into them: 'If it should chance to happen that an SS woman laughed or swore, Alma would stop conducting.' One prisoner recalled, 'She just breathed deeply and said: "I cannot play like this."'[25] When the orchestra rehearsed or played in their hut with the windows open, prisoners would gather to listen. For some, the concerts were a moment of respite. 'The Germans have wired everything in here and they watch that no one escapes, but I close my eyes and I'm outside the barbed wire. They don't know that we're all escapees.'[26]

The SS sometimes attended rehearsals of the orchestra for their own relaxation. Adam Kopycinski, from the men's orchestra in Auschwitz I, remembered how SS Hauptscharführer Gerhard Palitzsch, a particularly brutal man who was responsible for countless deaths in the camp, came to listen.

> He stood in the doorway, leaning against the door frame and slipping into a reverie. He sometimes stood there a long time – he clearly loved music. He knew in a strange way how to reconcile differing penchants. He was feared. People said that he came to pick out the next candidate to be shot.

Another player remembers seeing tears in Palitzsch's eyes as the orchestra played Schubert's Unfinished Symphony.[27]

Szymon Laks recalled,

> When an SS man listens to music, especially music that he really likes, he begins to strangely resemble a human being. His voice loses its characteristic gruffness, and he himself suddenly becomes kindly in his demeanour and one can talk to him almost like an equal. Sometimes one gets the impression that one melody or another brings to his mind people he loves, or the fiancée he has not seen for a long time, and his eyes grow foggy with the very image of human tears. [...] Can people who love music this much, who can cry while listening to it, be capable of inflicting such savagery on the rest of mankind? There exists a reality in which this cannot be believed. And yet...[28]

On Sunday afternoons, Anita and the orchestra would sit with their instruments, ready to play for whichever SS guard should happen to fancy hearing some music on their afternoon off. 'We were like a human jukebox. We would sit there and wait for the guards to come in during their spare time to request repertoire. They would ask for this and that. The system was unspeakable. These were educated, university people. Cultured, who appreciated art and music. Somehow they could appreciate beauty, and commit the atrocities that for them were normal.'

One day, Dr Mengele walked in. He was a particular classical music aficionado, and prisoners would be warned of his presence as he walked around the camp by his whistling of Romantic melodies. The women of the orchestra heard his whistling as he approached. Then, there he was, in the doorway of their hut. He looked at Anita, while they all held their breath. He fancied a spot of Schumann, apparently, and ordered her to play a cello solo for him. What if she froze? Or did not remember it? To disobey could mean death. Nobody wanted to be marked out by Dr Mengele.

'I simply wanted to get out of his presence. He wanted to hear the *Träumerei*.[29] I simply played it as fast as I could to get it over and done. All I could think about was getting out of there.'

∽

The women's orchestra depended on pleasing the SS for their continued survival, and Alma Rosé was the biggest asset the orchestra could have hoped for. She seemed to exert a magnetic power over both the performers and the guards who held her in the camp. The fact that she could be killed at any moment seemed scarcely to weigh with her, so great was her commitment to making music of the highest order possible in the circumstances. A Jewish doctor who survived the camp wrote about Alma in her memoir.

They did not put Alma in chains. She remained a free bird in her feelings and her faith like a naïve child. She always thought that she would survive the camp. [...] She did not see what was going on around her; her whole life was spent in a trance created by music. Her music.[30]

Was her insistence on music college standards when the orchestra could barely play a result of her own innate perfectionism, or was it about her own survival? Both, Anita believes. 'She refused to acknowledge where she was. It was a resistance to her environment.'

～

When Alma took over the orchestra, she expanded the repertoire beyond Zofia's remembered Polish folk tunes (amazingly, the SS didn't recognize them, so they unwittingly enjoyed listening to music by the enemy).[31] With the help of her copyists and music borrowed from the men's orchestra she managed to build up an impressive library of over two hundred pieces. Finding this repertoire and creating the parts was no small task, as Anita points out: 'If there was a score of something, it needed to be arranged for us. The copyists were the people who played so badly they couldn't be used, but Alma wanted to try to save as many as possible by drawing them into our so-called "safe place" as copyists. To put it bluntly, as long as the SS wanted music, they had to keep us! This was our bit of security. No point gassing the orchestra.'

None of the sheet music has survived, but Katarzyna Kuszaj-Jarnot has looked up every mention of repertoire in the archives, to piece together its eclectic programme of works. Although Jewish music was officially banned, the orchestra played Mendelssohn's Violin Concerto, without his name appearing in their makeshift programmes, Henryk Wieniawski's *Polonaises*, and arrangements of Chopin. There were also special arrangements of Beethoven's Fifth Symphony, the *Sonata Pathétique* and 'Für Elise', and Brahms's *Hungarian Dance No. 5*. Singers associated with the orchestra performed arias from Puccini's *Madame Butterfly* and from Bizet's *Carmen*. And there was plenty of Johann Strauss.

Sometimes, Alma would play privately, just for the members of the orchestra. However hideous the marches, a love of music endured amongst the players themselves. When it was not being appropriated as part of the Nazi 'death machine', music still had the power to transcend the wretched conditions of Auschwitz-Birkenau.

∾

At one point Anita, desperately ill with typhus, was admitted to the hospital hut. In her semi-conscious state she became aware of some guards passing by her bed, and heard them suggest her for the gas chambers. One of them recalled she was the camp cellist, and the guards walked on to the next bed. Once again, the cello had saved her life. Shortly after, although she could still barely see and it took all her energy to force herself upright enough to hold her instrument, she was back with her cello in Alma's rehearsals. When she inadvertently misread a note, Alma decided she would make an example of Anita. Her punishment for her mistake was to scrub the floor of the rehearsal block on her knees.

'I didn't like her of course! She was like the strictest headmistress! I can see the point now, but at the time I thought, bloody hell, this is ridiculous. I played a wrong note, but seriously! I'm in Auschwitz! But now I understand that she was making us concentrate so hard on stupid wrong notes that it stopped us looking at the smoke outside. I reproach her with nothing.'

Alma achieved a status that set her far apart from the other prisoners: suspiciously so, some prisoners thought. She was accused of being in league with the guards, and of favouritism: rejecting Polish players not because they were not good but because they were Aryan. It was a serious accusation.

Failing an audition for her orchestra was tantamount to having a death warrant signed.

On 3 April 1944, Alma herself fell ill. Despite the fact that she was teetotal, she had apparently drunk vodka at a gathering the night before, where she had been mingling with SS guards. Her friends believed she had been poisoned. The following day she lost consciousness, and her body was soon covered with blue spots. Her temperature plummeted and, even while unconscious, she convulsively gripped her head. Her hands cramped and she writhed from side to side. No one could decide whether it was a case of meningitis or typhus. The prisoner-doctors gave her a lumbar puncture and her stomach was flushed out, but it was too late to save her. Alma's hospital admission certificate, signed by Dr Mengele, is the only surviving official record of her presence in the camp.

Alma had always said to her players: 'If any of you survive, please tell my father what I've done here.' Years later, Anita met the aged Arnold Rosé in London. She told him about his daughter's work, and the circumstances of her death. 'He was a very old man, very ill. But he listened. I did my best to make him understand what she'd achieved. He said he was relieved that at least she hadn't suffocated in the gas chamber.'

༄

After Alma's death, another musician, Sonia Winogradowa, tried to continue the orchestra but couldn't manage much more than light music. Rehearsal time was cut, and the players were made to spend their time knitting and mending clothes. On 1 November 1944, Anita and the other Jewish members of the orchestra were ordered to stand apart at roll call. Anita was certain that they were to be murdered – the orchestra had served its purpose, and Alma was no longer there to protect them. The Jewish players were not allowed to fetch any possessions and were told to march immediately. Anita expected to turn left towards the crematoria at the back of the camp, as she had seen thousands do before. Instead, they were marched out of the main gate and put on a transport heading for Bergen-Belsen. Her cello was left behind in the empty hut.

༄

Once the women reached Belsen they tried to set up an orchestra but the commandant refused permission. The desire to play together was so strong that, deprived of actual instruments, they learnt to imitate their sounds, each becoming their violin, cello or flute, singing an orchestra together.[32] But not for long. Conditions in Belsen were even worse than Auschwitz and, in Anita's opinion, too appalling even for music.

When the liberating British and Canadian soldiers arrived on 15 April 1945, the camp was like an open grave. Anita was barely conscious when she heard the voices and loudspeakers announcing their arrival. As she began to realize she might have a future, she became consumed with the need to play, and her thoughts turned to the cello she had been forced to abandon in Auschwitz. While those around her concentrated on the basic elements of survival, she was desperate to get practising.

'I drove everyone crazy with my obsession for a cello. But being a decent person I insisted they mustn't take a cello away from a cellist. That would have been too terrible, to deprive someone of their instrument. After all, I knew what that was like.'

Almost as soon as the Allied troops had set up a displaced persons' camp on the edge of the Belsen compound, the survivors began asking for and organizing concerts, theatrical performances, dance and folk music. As Anita observes, it was an extraordinary testament to how essential the arts are, even to those who were ill and starving. By mid-May a music room had been established with the help of various aid organizations, and equipped with gramophones and musical instruments. Anita now had access to a radio, and the sound of familiar music played by professional orchestras was an integral part of her recovery. The realization that music could once again nourish her soul went hand in hand with rekindled hope for her future.

She could also resume contact with her sister Marianne in England. In a letter sent on 4 June 1945 she poured out her longing for a cello, hardly able to bring herself to write the sacred word. 'Perhaps, perhaps, perhaps, if the heavens are favourably disposed towards me I may in the not too distant future become the owner of a C-E-L-L-O. I can hardly wait.'

Eventually, Anita tells me, a cello was spotted languishing on top of a tall cupboard in the office of a local Bürgermeister. The liberating soldiers knew of the young girl who talked about nothing but cellos and brought it back to the camp for her. Anita becomes animated by the memory of it.

'Can you imagine suddenly having a cello in Belsen? It was incredible. But to start with I could hardly make any noise – I had no rosin, and the bow would hardly speak on the strings. Imagine the frustration, until I could get people to send me strings and some rosin. They were frayed old gut strings. But I was so desperate to practise. I had no muscle tone whatsoever – I had been at the point of starvation, and was desperate to play, without the strength to be able to.'

As she gained her strength, she began to perform for other ex-prisoners. One day, a few months after liberation, an Italian soldier, a former POW, appeared in the camp. His name was Giuseppe Selmi. Anita warmed to this kindly, shambolic man who had been conscripted into the army, and taken prisoner of war. Giuseppe was still dressed in the stained uniform in which he had been captured. His only possession besides the clothes he was wearing was a cello, even more beaten up and of poorer quality than the one found for Anita.

Their discovery of each other was one of the many extraordinary coincidences that mark Anita's life. Before the war he had been the principal cellist of the Rome Radio Orchestra. She was still only a teenager and had had no lessons for years. For the next few weeks they played together, practised together and performed duets and joint recitals. It was exactly what she needed. He was a fantastic player, and did what he could to help Anita develop her technique and strength.

'Later, I remember him coming to London to give a Wigmore Hall recital after the war. But he'd overslept! The audience was sitting there, waiting, and he came bounding in through the rows of seats, cello in a canvas bag. He got up onto the stage, sat down, took the cello out of his tattered old case and off he went!'

Many years after, Anita's son Raphael was asked to play the Schumann cello concerto with an orchestra in Rome. During the rehearsal, he was struck by the beauty of the playing of the man who was leading the cello section. Raphael made a point of introducing himself after the rehearsal, and complimented him on his playing. When the cellist told Raphael his name, he realized that this was the man with whom his mother had played, back in the camp, decades before.

✍

Soon there began a string of visits from military bands, musicians and revues coming from Britain to entertain the camp. The violinist Yehudi Menuhin was invited to give one of these recitals. A week before the trip, the young Benjamin Britten had been invited to a dinner party in London, at which Menuhin was also a guest. Britten learnt that the accompanist Gerald Moore had decided at the last minute not to go with Menuhin to Belsen, and Britten petitioned him to be allowed to take Moore's place. In Menuhin's words, 'Ben desperately wanted to go at all costs.'[33] Together they performed recitals for Anita and the other camp survivors, appalled at the state of the liberated prisoners. They 'could scarcely sit still & listen, and yet were thrilled to be played to'.[34] Menuhin later described the audience 'dressed in army blankets fashioned by clever tailors among them into skirts and suits. No doubt a few weeks since their rescue had put a little flesh on their bones, but to our unaccustomed eyes they seemed desperately haggard, and many were still in hospital.'[35]

Britten could hardly bear to describe what he'd seen. In a letter to his partner, the tenor Peter Pears, he wrote simply that: 'We stayed the night in Belsen, and saw over the hospital – and I needn't describe <u>that</u> to you […] I don't know why we should be so lucky, in all this misery.'[36] Journalists who visited the camp at the time felt they were still inarticulate with shock years after, and Pears believed that the experience influenced everything Britten subsequently wrote.

The recital that Anita witnessed has frequently been written about as a seminal moment for both performers. Like Alma Rosé, Anita made no allowances in her expectations. She had heard of Menuhin and, expecting to be deeply impressed, was surprised to find his playing underwhelming, with none of the emotion and sincerity of Casals. The young man accompanying him, whom nobody had heard of, was a different matter altogether. As Britten was later to remind her, she wouldn't have known him at that stage of his career even if she had recognized his name. As it happened, in the badly printed programmes, his name had been smudged and looked like Batten or Button. She was mesmerized by his playing, and wrote to her relatives in Britain about this pianist's extraordinarily sensitive and musical performance, particularly exceptional as the piano in the makeshift music room was about as inferior an instrument as her cello.

Menuhin does not emerge very well in Anita's memories of their encounter. 'I am very sceptical about his accounts of the event. In interviews he talked about what a great sacrifice it was for him to perform there, how terribly traumatic he had found it and what he'd suffered. And yet there were no bodies there by the time he visited – it was infinitely more sanitized than the Belsen we all knew. And yet he suffered, apparently.' In the 1950s, when Anita was already becoming a major figure in the London orchestral scene, she met Menuhin again. He was playing a concerto with the ensemble of which she was a founder member, the English Chamber Orchestra. Her desk partner urged her to speak to him and tell him that she'd been one of those displaced persons to whom he'd played back in 1945. 'I plucked up my courage and approached him. There he was, in the middle of a sea of people, this big, important man, with a huge queue waiting to speak to him. Eventually I got to him and said "That concert in Belsen, do you know, I was actually there?" He could not have been less interested. There was no reaction at all. "Oh really?" he said, half-heartedly, then looked straight over my shoulder to the next person. "Oh, Mrs so-and-so!" he said, gesturing past me. He couldn't get away fast enough.'

Britten was a different matter. 'Benjamin Britten was a very difficult guy, but I could communicate well with him.' Britten would speak to Anita in impeccable German when they rehearsed together. One day it struck her that he might be amused to read her account of his performance at the Belsen concert. After one rehearsal, she bashfully handed him the letter she had written to her sister just after the event, with the words, 'If you ever want to read an unbiased account of your piano playing...' His reaction could not have been further from Menuhin's indifference. 'My – oh! May I keep the letter?' She could see that he was terribly moved.

Britten did not talk to Anita about what he'd felt about the concert. But he was fascinated by her letter. In 1969 Britten's new concert hall in Snape Maltings, Suffolk, burnt down in an accidental fire just a day or so after Anita had performed there. When Anita saw Britten shortly afterwards, the first thing he said to her was 'Don't worry, I've still got your Belsen letter safe – it didn't get destroyed.'

～

I bring Anita back to her Belsen cello. Where is it now? Did it accompany her to London?

'The cello that had been found for me at Belsen was a dream come true for me. I adored it. But when I got to the UK I realized that it wasn't anything special – it was a terrible instrument, nothing more than a pathetic box. It is all relative. The interesting thing is, I have no recollection of what I did with it, whether I threw it in the dustbin.

'If you don't have a great instrument to build your technique around and develop a relationship with, you become more self-sufficient as a cellist. You don't have a cello that can help you. God knows how I managed to become a professional cellist without ever having had the chance to study properly.'

I ask her whether she thought of her cello as a partner, friend or child.

'No. I don't think in these terms. It was just important. Very important to me. Why? I don't know.'

～

Anita is silent. I feel as if we have just walked past another closed door. I am struck by how often she acknowledges that an experience is inexpressible, or that she chooses not to talk about some things, or sometimes not even to contemplate them. There are some subjects for which language is inadequate. Was music, for her, another kind of language, allowing her to express some of those things that simply could not be put into words? She thinks for a moment, then says: 'But nobody would understand it, if they heard it.' After a moment, she continues: 'I'm often asked, particularly in Germany, how I can play now, when it was what I did in the camps. But now has got *nothing* to do with then. Music is indestructible. Hitler destroyed so much, but music you can't destroy – that's the important thing of it. It is like language: one speaks in terrible circumstances and continues to speak afterwards. You don't hold it against language, so you don't hold these evils against music.

'If music had been poisoned for me by having to play for Mengele and the others, it would have been the greatest loss. Was the cello the thing that kept me going? Certainly. But we are all driven to survive. Everybody wants to live. I was just very lucky that it was the cello that made it possible.'

Kaunas – Pál Hermann

The past is never dead. It is not even past.

(William Faulkner, *Requiem for a Nun*)

After a long coach journey through thick forests and small towns with box-shaped houses in pastel-painted concrete, I am finally on the train at Trzebinia. I am making my way at speed in the direction of the border between Poland and Belarus. But it is February 2022, Russian troops are massing on the border of Ukraine and the threat of invasion is becoming increasingly real. Everyone I speak to is now extremely concerned. A Russian invasion of eastern Europe is more than a hypothetical scenario – many people here are still scarred by the last one.

My intercity train is playing a Chopin nocturne through its tinny speakers as I find my seat. I sit, warm, comfortable, sipping a cup of tea. Kaunas is an eleven-hour journey from Auschwitz and will take me two days. Pál Hermann, coming from Paris in a cramped cattle truck at a fraction of the speed, would have been travelling in conditions so intolerable that not everyone on the train would be alive by the end of the trip.

Despite some websites that confidently tell me otherwise, there are currently no trains at all that will take you from Poland to Lithuania. The one train line has been temporarily dug up. So I have devised a complicated route requiring changes at Krakow and Warsaw, and an overnight stay in Bialystok, forty-five minutes from the border with Belarus. From there I can catch a train to Suwalki, which is the nearest I can get to Lithuania before the railway runs out. The taxi driver who takes me from my hotel to Bialystok station tells me that he intends to leave the town as soon as he can arrange it. 'Putin's tanks will come rolling!' he exclaims, waving his arms to indicate their movement. 'And I will NOT be here!'

I am early for the train, so shelter from the snow in a small café opposite the station. For breakfast the options are meat dumplings, sauerkraut and something white that looks like a parcel. I opt for the parcel. Along with the strongest instant coffee I have ever tried to drink, I tuck into what turns out to be a surprising and tasty pancake with ricotta inside and a faintly lemon-flavoured watery custard poured on top. Elderly women sit at the plastic tables around me, shaking snow from their headscarves. Every other word they say seems to be 'Putin' or 'Russki'.

Leaving it as long as I dare, I reluctantly relinquish the warmth of the café and slither through the snow to the station. The display board had been saying that the Suwalki train was delayed for ten minutes, but has now decided it isn't. I can see the train pulling in in the distance. It's the only train that day. I hurl myself around the station like a bird trapped in a room, almost banging on the glass to try to find a way out. The exits to the platforms are all blocked off because the tracks have been dug up outside. I'm frantic. To get to my train I have to walk out of the entrance, round a large complex of buildings, cross the train tracks, go up a slippery metal staircase and over a bridge to reach the furthest platform. I leave the way I came, pick a path through the diggers and hoardings, which I can barely see in what is fast turning into a blizzard, and eventually make it to what I hope is the correct train as the guard is blowing the whistle. I throw myself on board, gasping for breath. I have never been so glad not to be encumbered with a cello.

I run out of track altogether at Suwalki, and I've been assured by Kuba that at this point his friend Krystoph Dostępnya, a truck-driver, will come and collect me and drive me over the Lithuanian border to Kaunas. I am the only passenger to disembark at Suwalki. Crossing the white mounds that conceal the tracks, I see three men at the far end of the platform. As I approach them I see that one of them is an elderly man with an impressively large handlebar moustache. Another, who I later learn to be Krystoph, is a well-built man in his fifties, dressed in a tight black bomber jacket, and with a ponytail streaked with grey. The third is surrounded by police in balaclavas, with truncheons. It turns out that this is Max, a friend of Krystoph, who is in fact British but has lived in Poland for most of his life. He has committed the faux pas of walking across the tracks at a point that is not a designated crossing. When the policemen have finished with him, he joins us looking entirely unrepentant. Max, I find out, is used to being arrested. He is a veteran anti-apartheid and anti-Iraq War campaigner, and seems to thrive on his encounters with the police.

When the policemen have left, Krystoph tells me that this morning their friend Emilia, a local choir director, had gone to Warsaw station with the intention of meeting me and handing over a new cello for me to borrow while I'm in Lithuania. It would have been a great plan, had I not been in Bialystok, three hours away. Not to be deterred, she has apparently put the cello on a bus, bound cross-country for Suwalki. My heart misses a beat. We are to meet it off the bus, apparently. 'I like to do only the impossible!' Emilia tells me, via WhatsApp. 'Let us have faith in good people!' Putting aside all boringly practical questions (Is it insured? Am I liable if it doesn't turn up? How do we even know which bus it is on or what time it will arrive? Whose cello actually is it?), I try to focus on the cello's adventure, imagine this instrument I have not yet met, sitting in its seat alone, travelling its parallel journey to my own, and try to share Emilia's faith that it will all work out.

While we wait for a few hours for the cello to catch up with us, the men take me for lunch in the only restaurant in town. As we order, I ask Max about life here. 'Suwalki is always the measure of the worst place to be', he tells me, cheerfully. 'Weather forecasts might say Warsaw five degrees, Krakow eight, Suwalki minus ten. It's the Siberia of Poland.' Soon, my food arrives: a wild mushroom soup in a huge tureen with a lid, and two slices of thick black bread. Max has taken a strangely perverse delight in ordering me typically Polish things that he personally wouldn't touch. 'People don't come here for the food,' he says. My soup is actually delicious. The broth is strongly flavoured, with chopped herbs floating in it alongside strangely shaped fungi and lumps of meat. The mushrooms are harvested from the forests around Suwalki,

Max explains. Not more than seventy or so people die from eating the wrong ones each year. His eyes are so twinkly with subversive mischief I can't actually tell if he's joking. He is too scared to eat them, he admits, as I take my first bite. 'But Piotr here is very good at picking the safe ones.' He elbows Piotr, the owner of the handlebar moustache. He is a carpenter from Ukraine with as little English as I possess Ukrainian. We grin amiably at each other.

After the soup, an enormous plate arrives for me. The men laugh, delighted at my disbelief at its size. There is a mountain of sauerkraut, with two vast suet dumplings. I think of a photograph Kuba had shown me back in Wrocław of a huge white zeppelin hovering over the music school in the 1940s. The resemblance is uncanny. 'There's meat inside,' says Max, encouragingly. 'They may be swimming in grease, but they're good if you're working in the fields, or going out to dig a trench.' I'm intending to do neither, so I share a good proportion of the dish with the very slender Piotr, who hasn't ordered any food as he's apparently watching his figure. He slaps his imperceptible belly and shakes his head theatrically.

Krystoph is Polish, but spends two weeks of every four driving his lorry in Norway because the pay is better over there. Max came from the UK to study in a film school during communism and fell in love with Poland. Now in his sixties, he has moved from London to retire here. 'Summers are beautiful here,' he tells me. 'People measure quality of life by money, material goods. For me it's fresh air; here the forest is still beating the cars, not the other way round. We all meet every weekend in the sauna, then we jump into the lake. Change your travel plans and come and join us. We want you to stay for longer,' he explains. 'That way, we'll get a bigger chapter in your book!'

After I've eaten what I can of the dumplings, Krystoph announces it's time to set off for Kaunas. But first we need to intercept the cello. We sit in the car outside the coach station, snow falling around us, our breath steaming up the windows, straining for a glimpse of a coach turning into the coach park. After all these weeks searching for missing cellos, what if I've just added another to my list? The irony is not lost on me. Half an hour after it was expected, the coach lumbers slowly round the corner. Krystoph jumps out of the car, and to my relief returns a short while later with a large black instrument case in his hands. The cello has arrived, despite a change of driver mid-route, and much general confusion as to what on earth it was doing in the bus. We manoeuvre it into the boot, Krystoph turns the radio to Rock FM and we're off.

On either side of the road the flat white expanses of fields are broken by little clusters of hand-built wooden dwellings, just visible beyond the high banks of snow. At the border, two men with guns stand guard outside a huge 1930s building that looks completely deserted, with paint peeling off it. The narrow approach road is used almost exclusively by lorries. We're one of the only cars, but the soldiers don't stop us. I am struck by the difference between here and Berlin, where, to buy a coffee, I have to show my Covid pass, a certificate for a negative test done within the last twenty-four hours, and my passport. Here, nobody wears a mask, or even stops us to check our paperwork as we cross over from one country to another.

∽

The radio is now off and there is silence, or quiet conversation in Polish in the front of the car. As we drive on, and night starts to fall, I put my headphones on to listen to Pál Hermann's cello concerto.[37] It feels like the most immediate way to have his voice with me as I look out of the window at mile after mile of snow-heavy forest. The manuscript of the concerto is a recent find, and an extraordinary story in itself. In 2016 Paul van Gastel unearthed a box full of his grandfather's manuscripts, which included the first movement of a cello concerto and its piano accompaniment. After much searching, he also found the orchestral parts. Paul then worked with Italian composer Fabio Conti to create a full concerto by using music from other chamber music and song manuscripts. Most remarkably, whilst creating the other movements of the concerto, Paul and Fabio made the decision to represent Pál Hermann's absence within the work itself. For one entire movement the cellist sits on stage, silent, while the orchestra plays Pál's music around him.

As the music begins I am instantly immersed in the familiar darkness of the strings, the sinuous cello line winding like tendrils around the orchestra in the first few phrases. Outside I can just make out the scenery changing as we move deeper into Lithuania: little clusters of grey suburban villas or wooden huts, a level crossing, flat marshland with bullrushes punctuating the horizontal, and we are submerged in the forest once more.

On my recording the cello soloist falls silent and the orchestra continues without him. The absence of cello sound is almost audible. I close my eyes, picturing the performer sitting motionless, silent on stage. I see the line of 878 men back in Drancy camp, Convoy 73, standing in single file, surrounded on three sides by the concrete courtyard of the Silent City, just as the orchestra seems to embrace the motionless cellist.

The first time I listened to the concerto, back in Oxford, I understood the cello's silence as a dramatization of Pál Hermann's silencing. A framing of his absence from musical history. Travelling through the dark to Kaunas, I hear it a little differently. I hear the silence of the men of Convoy 73. A space that stands for the thoughts that they left unspoken on this journey, the landscape they half-glimpsed through the slatted wood of a cattle truck, the fears that were inarticulable, even to themselves.

We never come to a musical work with pure ears; there is

no zero. But the more we know about a work, the more we moderate what we hear, and shift our understanding of it. Back-shadowing is, simply put, the process of judging the past through the lens of our present. It's a simple enough concept, but I am intrigued by it. As the fir trees all around us become silhouetted against the headlights, I find myself thinking of the shadow cast over Pál Hermann and his cello, the sounds of the Nazi commands, and the quiet Hungarian man, tall and elegant, whose soul was so full of music, rhythm, laughter, language, silenced by those orders.

∽

Kaunas is a city of majestic churches, cobbled streets and handsome squares, divided by the rivers Nemis and Nemunas, which join together at the centre of the city. Everywhere there are fairy lights, as if it is perpetually Christmas. I leave Krystoph in a bar in need of refreshment before his long journey home, and head for my apartment and bed. I am awoken in the early hours by the fabric of the building shaking, vibrated by a flotilla of chinook helicopters passing low overhead. The next morning, 24 February, my taxi drives me out of the town centre and up pot-holed roads by the side of the motorway to an area of what looks like wooded parkland. We pull up alongside a rather dated visitor centre, which has not changed since it was built in the early 1960s. Out of its glass door emerges Vytautas Petrikenas, the head of history here at Kaunas's Ninth Fort. He has recognized me by the cello case, and stretches out a hand. 'They've invaded Ukraine,' he says, almost before we have greeted each other. It is as if by saying it aloud he can help himself make sense of it. There's nothing I can say. I nod, and we briefly grasp each other's hands.

Vytautas is passionately committed to his role as custodian of the past. For the next six hours he tells me the history of his beloved country, from the Middle Ages to the news this morning. He speaks with urgency, hardly pausing for breath. He grew up in the old part of Kaunas, where his mother illegally traded wool for the odd banana or satsuma for her children. On one occasion she was arrested, but managed to bribe her way out of a prison sentence. Under Soviet rule, the shabby apartment blocks I passed on the way through the suburbs had been terrifying places to live, with walls so thin that neighbours were each other's worst enemy, reporting overheard conversations to the authorities. When the country was liberated in 1988, a traumatized generation emerged who are obsessively private, wanting to live away from the eyes and ears of the city. Kaunas, he tells me, is a beautiful, prosperous place, but its scars have only recently started to heal.

As Vytautas talks, I get the sense that he feels driven to share his city's history, and he is doing more than providing me with background information for my research. Buffeted between Germany and Russia for many centuries, Kaunas has been the scene of repeated genocides, and he wants this to be incorporated into the narrative that it is his job to tell. Again and again, he urges me: 'Write in your book – we have *not* learnt from history. We have tried to teach people, tried to show them, but they have *not* learnt.'

Lithuania has a population of around two million, less than that of many large cities, but size is not to be confused with significance. It was once a great power, at a time when Moscow was only a minor city. Hundreds of years ago, Lithuanians missed their chance to quell the Russian dictators as they grew in power, and they have been paying the price ever since. Lithuania was to be betrayed in secret protocols of the Nazi–Soviet Pact of 23 August 1939, which divided eastern Europe into spheres of German and Soviet interest. The pact marked the end of Lithuanian independence. By the summer of 1940, the country was a constituent republic of the USSR, part of the defence line built pre-emptively by the Soviets against their (temporary) German ally of convenience, a line which they hadn't even finished building, from Estonia to the Black Sea, when the Germans invaded and took over the country in 1941. Many initially welcomed Nazi rule, thinking it might be better than being under Russian control.

In the Middle Ages, Jews were invited to settle in Lithuania, and in the nineteenth and twentieth centuries they had migrated there from all over eastern Europe and Russia for safety. The nearby city of Vilnius had been known as the Jewish Capital of Europe. Kaunas wasn't far behind: a third of its population were Jewish. In the 1930s, the Nazis began to bombard the non-Jewish population with propaganda, telling them how they were being subordinated to the Jewish overlords who hogged all the money, then suggesting to the Jewish community that they would be safer all living together, with promises to protect them. Many Jews voluntarily sold their homes to buy houses in what would later become the Kaunas ghetto, walking into a trap that was soon to close. During the war, the whole of the population of one of the two ghettos in Kaunas would be murdered, the ghetto was repopulated, then burnt to the ground. Then the round-ups began.

The Ninth Fort, known as the Fort of Death, is one of eleven forts that had been planned as a defence of the city in the 1880s, although this was the last to be finished, in 1913. It was used by the Soviets during 1941 as a prison for Lithuanians. When the Nazis invaded in October 1941, it became an extermination centre for Jewish families, both from the ghetto and from all over Europe. On their return, the Soviets were to reclaim the fort as a prison from 1945 to 1948.

Vytautas and I leave the offices of the visitor centre and walk up the hill. As we round the hill, the fort emerges, a squat, joyless building, shielded by mounds of grassy earth. Around the outside it is surrounded by a brick wall broken

The Ninth Fort today.

up by observation posts. The building stands three storeys high, now painted incongruously in pink, although in 1944 it would have been grey. Inside, the fort is streaming with damp, and the domed roofs of the corridors that link its cells are reflected in sheets of water.

༄

No one knows why Convoy 73 was the only one of the many transports from Drancy that was destined for the Baltic states and not Auschwitz, although Vytautas believes it may have been a matter of railway congestion. At the time, huge numbers of Hungarian Jews were being deported to Auschwitz. This was at the height of the Nazi 'final solution', and train lines were jammed by the number of convoys heading into Poland, as well as supplies and troops going to the front line. Sending Convoy 73 on a long route north meant it did not add to the congestion. Had Pál's convoy not been the one exception, he might have arrived at Auschwitz to hear the orchestra playing, as so many other convoys did during that spring. As an able-bodied man with the possibility both of working and of playing in the men's orchestra, he might, like Anita, have been saved. Instead, Convoy 73 went to Kaunas, where around 600 of the convoy's 878 men were murdered after what was believed to be a stay of only three days. Those not taken to the fort were to continue on the train to Reval (now Tallinn) in Estonia, where all but twenty-two were killed.[38]

～

Vytautas takes me into the cells. The stone walls are two metres thick and the cold chills to the bone. There are bars, metal gates and huge locks everywhere. It is a ghastly place – dripping, cold and dark. He tells me that at one point after the war these cells had been used to store food products, and the walls were whitewashed as a result. But as the damp paint had flaked or been scraped away, a multitude of names and dates appeared, scratched into the soft stone. He gestures to me to look, and they are clearly visible. Names of prisoners, trying to leave some sign for their relatives, for posterity. Proof that they were here, a final act of resistance in the face of their erasure.

Two particular phrases, scratched into the paint, catch my eye.

'Drancy, Paris, 1944'.

And, next to it, in bold capitals: 'Nous sommes 900 Français'.

These are the last words of Convoy 73, waiting for whatever it was that was to befall them. 'None of these inscriptions say goodbye,' Vytautas quietly points out. And he's right. These are records of fact. 'We were here', in the hope that

'Nous sommes 900 Français, 18 – V – 44'.

they might be transferred to other camps and this scratched inscription might help them to be traced. They may even have thought that they were about to be sent to work in the suburbs of Kaunas.

Vytautas wants to film me playing Pál Hermann's concerto in the cell, so it can be used as an installation and visitors can hear his music. My hands are so cold I can't imagine how I can actually move my fingers, but this isn't about the quality of the performance. He finds me a chair, and I sit in the last place we know that Convoy 73 were definitely alive, with the graffiti on the wall just behind me. By the light of the barred window, my feet in the shallow puddles on the floor, I play. Pál Hermann, but also Bach's mournful prelude from the Second Cello Suite in D minor. The acoustic is better than any concert hall, and the sound flies out of the cello.

A concerto is a story, the testimony of its solo instrument, a presentation of itself against the backdrop of the orchestra. But Pál Hermann's concerto embodies both his testimony and

his silence, just as Pál himself is present yet absent within his own story. We can trace his final days only so far, before the records run out. The last documented trace of him is his name on the convoy register back in Drancy. Once he boarded the train, his final destination either Kaunas or Tallinn, he ceased officially to exist.

While the Germans prided themselves on keeping meticulous records, they were just as meticulous in destroying them. Auschwitz and Drancy have the little information that they do because of prisoners working in administration who smuggled it out, or because of the small quantity of documents left behind by the Germans in their hurry to evacuate the camp as the Soviets approached. But deaths in the east were a different story. Here, Jews were murdered in what has been called the 'Holocaust by bullets', not in the gas chambers. It may very well be that no records at all were kept of who was being shot. And even if the deaths were recorded at the time, those records have long since been destroyed.

Pál Hermann's story and that of the other men of Convoy 73 represents a contested space; shifting, uncertain ground. Relatives who campaigned for death certificates for their fathers, brothers and husbands were given papers with 'died in Auschwitz' written on them: a matter of expediency rather than truth. In the confusion after the Holocaust, time and again official memory was falsified, and individual memories were obliterated. In Auschwitz, an entire room is dedicated to housing the enormous lists compiled after the war to record the fates of deported Jews. Pál Hermann's name is there, with Tallinn listed as his place of death. But both the archivists there and Vytautas agree that this information is based on nothing more than the final destination of his convoy, few of whom made it further than Kaunas.

Even amongst Holocaust survivors, memory does not remain static, or even reliable. Survivor Aleks Faitelson later wrote:

> There is truth, and there is truth (emes), and each individual also has his own truth, hence the contradictions between what one person who was in the Kaunas ghetto writes or tells, and the story of his friend who was also there. Each one has a different version. Everyone who has the opportunity to do so, immortalizes, as it were, his version – but not forever.[39]

Primo Levi said that 'Testimony contains a lacuna. The survivors agree about this. [...] witnesses are by definition survivors and so all, to some degree, enjoyed a privilege [...] No one has told the destiny of the common prisoner, since it was not materially possible for him to survive.'[40]

Perhaps only in the silence of the central movement of Pál's concerto, in the absence of notes, of facts, is there something indisputable. One of the things of which we can be entirely certain in Pál Hermann's story is his premature and abrupt silence.

༄

Survivors speak in the place of those who died, 'by proxy, as pseudo-witnesses; they bear witness to a missing testimony'. But as the Italian philosopher Giorgio Agamben points out, the dead have nothing to say, no instructions or memories to be transmitted. 'Whoever assumes the charge of bearing witness in their name knows that he or she must bear witness in the name of the impossibility of bearing witness. No one can bear witness from the inside of death, and there is no voice for the disappearance of voice.'[41]

But I go back to Anita's words: 'Music is indestructible. Hitler destroyed so much, but music you can't destroy – that's the important thing of it.' In Pál Hermann's case, we have his compositions, his voice on manuscript paper.

Memory, as the poet Carmen Bugan puts it, is like the river of Heraclitus. You can step into it multiple times, but it will never be the same twice. And so the language of memory is fluid, mirroring the endlessly changing nature of memory itself. In a story like Pál Hermann's, where the gaps are as resonant as the known facts, it seems fitting to frame his narrative not through words but through the combination of music and silence that his concerto offers us. Music holds what falls between the cracks of human experience, and can provide a framework, a space in which to contemplate it. It holds silence before and after its notes. Silence as memorial, or as resistance. As a space in which to place a man who has no known grave, no place to be remembered.

༄

If we are to assume that Pál did indeed disembark from the train at Kaunas, as is most likely, then what can we know about his time there? Convoy 73 believed they were being sent to work but, unlike Auschwitz, Kaunas was not a labour camp. This means that there were very few survivors, as its purpose was extermination. One theory was that

> the convoy were sent to the Baltic countries to dig up the corpses so that they would never be found or the events reconstructed. It has indeed now been proved that the few survivors from that transport were assigned to this grisly task. Rather than using Baltic nationals, who might have spread the word of the massacres, the Nazi authorities had chosen to import French men to do it, afterwards murdering them in their turn.[42]

Around the Ninth Fort fourteen huge pits were dug on the side of the hill and were filled with bodies covered with quick-lime. As the tide of war began to turn against them, the Nazis became concerned that such an obvious mass grave would be proof of the thousands of murders that had been committed here. Prisoners were made to exhume the bodies from the pits in order to burn them with wood and petrol – alongside the fresh corpses as the executions continued. The corpse burners were then killed and added to the pyres. However, a handful of them escaped on Christmas night 1943. One of these men, twenty-one-year-old Aleks Faitelson, recorded his experiences at the fort, five months before Pál arrived there.

> Those who had not been shot dead still had their mouths open, suffocated under the weight of the earth piled over them [...] To this day I see their clenched fists, as if they summon me to avenge them! My parents were amongst them. And I had to carry them to the pyre, to commit them to the flames. Clouds of smoke rose to cleave the heavens. But on earth, nothing changed [...] An officer of the Gestapo in uniform stood by, and on the buckle of his wide belt we could read the words 'Gott ist mit uns!' All night long the fire burned, its flames licking the dead victims. To ensure that no traces remained,

those bones that had not been completely roasted, were chopped up, and together with the ashes were scattered by the wind over the fields.[43]

There is no way to know for certain if Pál was forced to endure this kind of work at Kaunas, or even if he had been one of the minority of men taken on to Tallinn, where his tasks might have been the same as Faitelson's. But Vytautas has some information that offers the thinnest thread of consolation. He knows from what little documentation the fort has on the convoy that the men from Drancy were there for only a matter of days, not long enough to work. At the time of the convoy's arrival at the fort, there were plenty of local Lithuanian criminals employed to dig the graves and burn bodies, so there would have been no need of foreign labour for such a short time. The men of Convoy 73 were to be killed, but they were spared the horrors of digging up and burning bodies before their own deaths.

∾

On the third day of their imprisonment in the fort, the men were led out into the courtyard, one cell at a time. There, overlooked by a high brick watchtower, was another reinforced metal door, leading out of the compound. When it was opened, Pál would have seen high grass banks on either side. Had he been able to climb one, he would have been able to look over Kaunas's rooftops on his left, to the river flowing through the centre of the city. But from his perspective between the mounds of grassy earth all he would have been able to see was sky, and a small cluster of trees nearby. He would have been led down the straight, deep trench, away from the fort for fifty metres, to a wall with a bricked-up door. To his right he would have seen another trench, with piles of petrol cans and firewood. Perhaps there would already have been bodies burning. He might have waited as the men in front of him were lined up by the corner

The wall in 1944, and today (*below*).

of this wall in pairs and shot; or, to speed matters up, he might have been grouped together with the other forty or so men of his cell, and ordered to stand in front of the machine gun and rifles positioned on top of the mounds overlooking them.

I cannot look any longer at this wall, pockmarked with hundreds of bullet holes, or at the field beyond it, where his ashes would have been distributed. Instead, I turn my head to the copse of spruce trees Pál had passed on his short walk to this evil place. Vytautas breaks the silence. 'I often look at those trees. They are the only living witnesses to all this. If only their wood could tell us what it saw.'

I think of the tree from which Pál's Gagliano was made. It strikes me, with a jolt, that that too was a spruce.

INTERLUDE

Listening to the Cello II

One summer afternoon, before I set off for the Continent, I made the long trudge up Prince Consort Road from South Kensington tube in London, cello case dragging on its rucksack straps. I was on my way to meet the experimental, 'avant-garde' cellist Anton Lukoszevieze. I'd seen footage of him playing on YouTube, and the uncompromisingly strange and unfamiliar sound he coaxed from his instrument had captivated me.

Walking along, the barely conscious irritation of the cello case banging at my heels was strangely nostalgic. I had made this journey countless times when I was a student at the Royal College of Music, becoming expert at getting the angle of the case on my back just right as I slipped through the snapping barriers on the underground, before the long, plodding walk past the great Victorian museums.

Outside the Royal College, on the stone steps under the glass and iron portico, I see a man in a shabby tweed jacket, sitting with a cello case in front of him. Awkward and dour, Anton acknowledges me with the briefest of handshakes. He is very serious, shy and intense. I like him immediately. There is no small talk, no coffee and chat. We find our room and we're straight to it, cellos out.

'What do you want to know?' he asks, almost suspicious. Good question. I want to know whatever he wants to tell me. I want to understand what the cello means to him, and why he pushes its voice further than anyone has before. And I hope, by listening to him, to find a little more of what it means to me.

Many years ago, my teacher tried to help me understand exactly the angle of my left elbow. It should, I learnt, be supporting my fingers, not too flat against the body, not uncomfortably high in the air. I was little, and I couldn't quite understand how it should feel, so tried to memorize what my teacher's arm looked like. I wasn't understanding the sensation for myself, so inevitably it didn't work. In order to help me work out how I wanted to feel, my teacher told me to try pushing my arm to extremes – to put my elbow so high it was ridiculous, and play. Clearly wrong. Then to flatten it against my ribs. Impossible; my fingers slid off the strings. Gradually, from these points of extremity, I began to see how I could find my balance, somewhere in the middle.

Now, the more time I spend thinking about the cello, the more I am learning to question everything: sound, movement, speed. Taking every aspect of cello playing apart, I can put it back together to form my own patterns, my own dance with my cello as partner. It is a process that is never complete and can be taken further than I had previously dreamt of. This was what I wanted Anton to tell me about. I wanted to hear from a man whose cello playing was so extreme that nothing was taken for granted or beyond being interrogated. He was to be the equivalent of my elbow pressed firmly into my side.

We start by dispensing with normal notes, and listening to what the cello is saying above and beneath them. When you only touch a string lightly, you can create a fluty, otherworldly note called a harmonic. If you want a 'proper' note, you press the string down to the fingerboard to change the string's length and make a pitch. The composer John Lely had written a piece for Anton in 2006 that is constructed only of harmonics in very slow glissandi up and down the cello.[44]

John Lely had been having trouble sleeping at around the time the idea for *Harmonics for Real Strings* occurred to him. Lying awake, listening to short-wave radio, he would scan through the frequency spectrum, turning the dial in one direction, slowly and consistently. After a while he found himself listening to the process, appreciating the variety of sounds that emerged from the loudspeaker – sounds of gradual transition, sounds as by-products.

'It's the most simple piece', Anton tells me, 'but an ingenious idea.' It explores the natural Pythagorean phenomenon of each string: its natural harmonics. Under his guidance, I pick up my cello and try it. I start with an open string, and then gradually introduce my finger at the very top of the string where the fingerboard begins, pressing too lightly to play a note, but strongly enough to elicit a harmonic, and begin an extraordinarily slow and measured sliding glissando to the bridge that continues for minutes. After a while the muscle ache of forcing the bow and arm to travel so artificially slowly is excruciating. But the journey is worth it. I watch in a kind of painful trance as my slowly travelling finger uncovers all the nodal points of the string – its partials and the harmonic series. The whistling, hollow-sounding notes lack the solidity of a note played with the finger firmly pressed down. They are suggestions of notes, flickers of pitch, and they jump from high to low in what appears to be no order at all. I can't help thinking that this is more séance than performance. I had summoned the cello's ghosts.

There is something very odd about watching a finger move gradually and resolutely in one direction, while listening to the pitch leap all over the place, from high to low. The mismatch between eye and ear is disconcerting. We must question what we see, what we hear, how we connect sounds. When we witness a performance, what are we looking at? What does a performer's movement, and the mechanics of drawing a sound from an instrument, add to our understanding of what we're hearing? This performance is intensely still. It is meditative, but not intentionally. It is phenomenological, drawing attention to the cello's physicality in a different way. The beauty of it for Anton is that it 'just happens'. The bow starts moving, the slowly travelling finger begins its long journey towards the bridge, and the piece plays itself.

Cellists know where most notes are on the cello, just as we know how to read or walk. But we have nothing like this intrinsic sense for the harmonics hovering underneath our conventional language of A, Bb, B, C. Press your finger down only lightly, and it's like a deep-sea exploration. What ought to be familiar is in fact rich and strange; odd creatures with weird features glide past us in the depths.

I'm still playing slowly, travelling up the fingerboard. A shifting kaleidoscope of squeals and pure, meditative sounds. My hand continues to move inexorably from the scroll towards the bridge in one direction, but the notes jump, octaves at a time, backwards and forwards. As I experiment, I start to realize that playing only harmonics demands a different quality of attention. We need to listen between the gaps. Years of training teach us to analyse every sound that we draw from our instruments. We are directed, without even noticing it, towards making beautiful sounds, and these squeaks and growls coming from under my fingers are not always lovely. Our hierarchy of sounds, privileging the elegant and attractive, is called into question.

What appeals most to Anton is that, in revealing these hidden notes, he is making concrete sound. These notes are themselves, not signifying anything other. 'We don't analyse the wind, or the sound of the sea; we just take them as they are,' he says.

There's a pleasingly tidal wash about the hazy harmonics ebbing and flowing. Just as the tide is shaped by the moon, so the physical structure of the cello shapes the form of *Harmonics on Real Strings*. Its range is determined by the length of the string; on a double bass or a violin it becomes a different work. It is in fact a cello-shaped piece, singing the form and dimensions of the instrument that plays it.

Anton and I fall to talking about bows, as the cello is only part of the story. The bow, when your technique is good enough, feels like an extension of your arm: a limb, half wood and half flesh, that connects your cello body to your actual torso.

I tell Anton that I've been reading some of the earliest cello tutors. In *The Compleat Tutor for the Violoncello* (1765), Robert Crome informs the eager amateur cellist that 'The Bow may be consider'd as the Tongue of the Instrument as all the Expression is from the bow; the Bow in playing is always in action, but the fingers are often of no use.' He warns his reader not to underestimate how tricky bowing is: ''tho' some may think the Bow is of no great consequence they may be assur'd tis much more difficult than the Fingering, after the Fingers have rightly found their places, for the Fingers ripen much sooner than the Bow'.[45]

Jean-Baptiste Bréval's 1804 *Traité du violoncelle* tells us that 'The bow is without argument the lynchpin of all that goes into the mechanism of the art of playing stringed instruments. It is the bow that obeys the impulse it receives; expresses the thought; forms the sound.'[46]

Anton listens intently, then suddenly puts down his instrument and reaches into his cello case. I notice he has a secret compartment, hidden in the dark velvet plush of the interior. Opening the cloth flap, he produces the oddest bow I've ever seen, possibly the weirdest ever created. It looks like a large wooden hacksaw. This, he says, with the flicker of a smile, is a bow that plays four strings simultaneously. It was designed by German cellist Michael Bach in the 1990s. He hands it to me, and I'm surprised by its weight. Instead of the stick being essentially straight, with a gentle concave dip in the centre like the curve of our lower spine, it has an extreme convex bend, making it almost semicircular.

It is only in comparatively recent times that we've played with straight bows. Baroque bows have a very gradual convex shape, and the notes that they coax from a cello have a wafting, soft–strong–soft shape, quite different from the more continuous pressure of their modern, straighter successors. The Frankenstein's monster of a bow that Anton hands me feels like a descendant of its gentle baroque forbear, with its dramatically curved, rainbow-shaped stick. Its hair is remarkably loose, practically flapping between the two ends of the wood. We normally tighten the hair with a small metal device at the square end of the bow (the pleasingly named 'frog'), until the tension is enough for the strings and hair to engage in a visceral, bouncing rela-tionship. The hairs of *this* bow mould themselves over all four strings spinelessly, embracing the whole curve of the cello's bridge. There is something disconcerting, unpleasant even, about this. But the bow's flaccidity is essential to its purpose: the hair's floppy caress creates a four-note sound like a drone. Anton shows me a little lever built into the frog, which he can use to control the angle of the hair with his thumb.

I ask Anton whether this is the most bizarre implement he's used to make a sound from a cello. 'No,' he says, without hesitation. 'Not by half!' I suspected as much. This bow is in fact really conservative by Anton's standards. He tells me in the most matter-of-fact tones that he was once asked to play with a meat cleaver for a bow. I raise an eyebrow. It was fairly blunt, he assured me, and as long as he was careful, he found he could play without accidentally sawing through either the strings or his own fingers. He has experimented with a number of other possibilities: sticks, tools and so forth. I wonder how it changes the relationship to the instrument. If a bow is an extension of our arm, then how does a cleaver alter the experience of playing? 'It's about control,' Anton says. 'If you only have a short length to bow with, you go with it.' After a moment of intense consideration: 'And if it's a meat cleaver then you think "Shit, I mustn't drop it."'

He often improvises with clothes pegs. He showed me how the sound changes when he puts a peg on the string in the space normally reserved for the bow, splitting the length of the string in two unequal parts. Playing the longer part of the string above the peg creates eerie, multiple sounds like a gamelan or wind chime. It sounds less mellow when you bow *between* clothes peg and bridge, which makes a rasping screech. The sound creates a sense of anxiety, for me at any rate, and I comment on this to Anton. Surely this is noise, not music? He disagrees. In the 1950s, as composers experimented with sound for sound's sake, or *musique concrète*, people quickly became used to taped sound, noises that were experimented with. Our peg-induced screeching is part of the process of embracing every sound a cello can make. Cello as noise. There are no aesthetic boundaries or barriers for Anton. 'An amplifier's feedback in a rock group is seen to be a cool thing. Why not with a cello? It's about different aesthetics. Music is not supposed to be exclusively beautiful, smooth and soothing, any more than we privilege Merchant Ivory costume drama over horror films. It is about expression.'

When I ask him about his relationship to his cello he jumps at the question with unexpected enthusiasm – 'Oh, I *really* love my cello!' he exclaims, giving it an involuntary hug. He never lets anyone play it. But at the same time, he's quite clear that it's a tool for a job. It's just there. 'The word "instrument" means something like a tool, doesn't it?' he says, almost apologetically.

He takes pleasure in his cello's lack of a pedigree. 'This cello is a mongrel,' he explains. It looks Neapolitan but has been repaired and altered in English workshops many years ago. It's betwixt and between, like its player. Anton is half-Lithuanian, and his surname, Lukoszevieze, was in fact a mistake, as a baffled immigration officer once wrote down an approximation of the family name, thereby changing his family's identity for future generations. Somehow it suits him perfectly to have a name that is all but unpronounceable, and makes one listen, pay attention differently.

Anton is a musician who has spent his career playing and listening in a different way from others. He has never been interested in the conventional paths for a cellist: of orchestral playing, chamber music or teaching. He survived the hot-house intensity of music college, but found the whole experience traumatic. It taught him that he and his cello had to find their own path.

So he spent a long time learning very difficult repertoire alone, becoming attentive to new sounds and new ways of approaching his instrument. He was an inventor, working in isolation, rethinking sound, experimenting with technique, questioning everything he had learnt. Without the daily routine of rehearsals and session work, he had the opportunity to reassess how to play his cello.

His view of his instrument is an interesting antidote to the more romantic perceptions of the cello as lover, child, alter ego. Our assumption that a cello is a body that only makes beautiful expressive sounds is culturally ingrained. But for Anton, the cello is a sound-making box capable of a far wider range than we ordinarily ask of it. I ask him what the most physically gruelling piece in his repertoire is. He thinks it is probably a work written by Xenakis, with 156 consecutive down bows (a gesture a little like repeatedly stroking a cat, but more energetic). Written for a cello competition in the 1960s, it's ferociously taxing. He has to prepare for a month to play it. 'Does it feel like a battle against your cello?' He thinks about this. 'No, we're in it together. But absent yourself from the cello for any length of time, and the callouses go. It's hard to pull it back.' Anton's relationship with his cello is about what demands will be made on their two bodies. They have to pull each performance off together, like a racehorse and jockey.

For many years, I played almost exclusively on a baroque cello, living in a world of Bach, Handel and Vivaldi. It was easier to work around injury on a softer instrument. The coaxing of sound out of gut strings is less demanding on your arms than attacking metal ones that are tuned to a higher pitch than an early instrument, so are under higher tension. As a result, it is more natural for me now to play with a still, non-vibrating left hand than to use vibrato, a feature which really took off as musicians started to emulate post-classical vocal style, when singers began to sing with more of a 'wobble'. Every aspiring young cellist wants to be allowed to learn vibrato – it's a rite of passage, like being allowed to wear high heels or make-up, marking the transition from a rudimentary sound to a more sophisticated, adult timbre. But I notice with some curiosity that Anton seems instinctively to use hardly any vibrato. I ask him why. He is surprisingly passionate on the subject.

'Why *do* we do it?' he demands. I'm not sure what to answer. He plays me a passage from Messiaen's *Quartet for the End of Time* with no vibrato. It sounds ethereal. He's recorded the whole work like this: a vibrato-less performance of a twentieth-century masterpiece. Wind players used to use vibrato, and there are glorious recordings of clarinettists from the 1950s with a lovely, plummy wobbling tone, but it's not fashionable now, designated to the same moment in history as the BBC accent, or the cut-glass vowels of singers such as Kathleen Ferrier. 'String players are still vibrating away, but why aren't brass or wind doing it?' Anton asks, indignantly. 'Why just the strings?'

He tells me about a masterclass he gave, in which he asked a technically brilliant young cellist to play a high phrase without vibrato, as, although her playing was virtuosic and impressive, it was not quite in tune. He was trying to get her to listen attentively to the intonation, to unmask it. She tried, but simply could not make herself do it. The habit of vibrato was so deeply learnt that it was physically impossible for her to play without it.

I started to wonder whether there is some aspect of our relationship to our cellos that we miss out on as young students if we pile on vibrato as soon as we have the coordination to be able to do it. If we've never really listened hard to the pure, naked note, never pared our playing down to the bone, can we connect fully with our instrument? Vibrato can be amazing, says Anton, but he believes the ideal is to try to learn in a parallel way – with vibrato, and also without. Only then do you learn to sustain the sound, to hold it without allowing it to die away. You learn that it is the *bow* that keeps the sound present, not the vibrato. Your playing at the tip of the bow should be as strong as at your hand. Without vibrato there's an honesty: anything other than absolute clarity of intonation is immediately noticeable. Anton is passionate about stripping it all back to what the cello itself has to offer us.

Playing with Anton has made me question the ways in which I have been trained to listen, and I have started to realize that the cello has so much more to say to me if I change some of the variables. The freedom of experimentation, and of listening in a different way is exhilarating. Critic Jacques Attali said: 'For twenty five centuries, Western knowledge has tried to look upon the world. It has failed to comprehend that the world is not for the beholding, it is for hearing. It is not legible but audible.'[47] I am starting to understand what he meant.

4th Movement – Sound

Silence and sound in measured harmony

(from Ursula Wood, 'To a 'Cellist')

Suwalki – An Unexpected Detour

Late February 2022

I am sitting in my rented flat in Kaunas, the shadows gathering, when the phone rings. It is Krystoph calling from Suwalki. He says the motorways are already congested with Ukrainian refugees. 'I'm coming to get you in two hours. We don't know if you'll be able to get out if we leave it until tomorrow,' I thank him. 'I'm not frightened,' he adds, to reassure me. Neither was I, until he mentioned it.

After his call, I take a last walk through the streets. It is impossible to imagine this place could be under threat, although the constant helicopters flying overhead towards the Russian border are ominous enough. I had planned to go to Vilnius tomorrow, where Lise Cristiani had performed in the Presidential Palace in 1852, but that is out of the question now, as it is the headquarters of the government, and Lithuania has declared a state of emergency.

I try to absorb the sight of the buildings around me, and wonder if this will be the last chance I ever have to visit Kaunas, this lovely European city of culture, when Krystoph pulls up in his car. The roads are crowded as we leave, and there are queues stretching off the forecourt on every petrol station. Some have run out of fuel altogether. 'In Suwalki, the bancomats are already empty,' Krystoph tells me. 'Everyone is ready – but for what?' We approach the border. Unlike when we entered Lithuania, which seems a year ago now, the border is lit up with blue flashing lights. There are military trucks, soldiers, police everywhere. NATO helicopters are whirring overhead. A policeman signals us to pull over. Krystoph swears in Polish, and I can see his fingers tighten on the steering wheel. He doesn't have a passport on him, or a Covid pass or certificate – and nor is he vaccinated. But as we begin to slow down at the side of the road, the policeman turns away. Krystoph sees his moment, stamps on the accelerator, and we speed off.

～

After a while, the roads turn from new motorway into bumpy single-lane tracks. We're back in Poland. Sometime after, tracks peter out into farmland. We are surrounded by deeply furrowed earth, the shapes of black forest on the edges of the fields, and darkness. Krystoph stops, and squints out of the window in the hope of seeing something he recognizes in the profound darkness. We start off again, tyres spinning in the mud. It is impossible to tell if we are driving along a tractor track or a furrow. Eventually, lights appear in the distance and Krystoph picks his way across the vast expanse of soil towards them. We are heading for the conductor Emilia's house. Hidden off road on the edge of the forest, it is a large white building, which used to be the village school. Although I have yet to meet her, she has offered to let me stay, before I can get back to Berlin to continue my journey.

As soon as the light from the opening door envelops us it is clear this is a place of laughter and warmth. Emilia and her husband Sebastian greet me warmly, and behind them is a crowd of their friends, who have all assembled to welcome me back on my unexpected second visit to Suwalki. There is a flurry of hugs and handshakes. Everyone is talking excitedly in Polish, and making a fuss of Emilia's handsome white collie dog Mishka, whose job apparently is to keep the forest wolves away, but, as Emilia tells me, is a sensitive soul like she is and feels things very deeply. Mishka looks adoringly up at her. Sebastian brings out plates of goat's cheese, moulded into the shape of hearts, and some hard-boiled chickens' eggs, laid that morning. The cheese has been freshly made, from the milk of the goats outside.

Emilia's home is tastefully decorated, with stripped wood floors, and flickering candles illuminating plants and colourful fabrics. We sit on sofa beds draped with throws, while everyone pours black tea and wine, and helps themselves to slices of cheese. Emilia is radiant. With a willowy figure, high cheek bones and short brown hair swept to one side, she seems to exude happiness. I ask her about the choir she has started here in Suwalki. 'There are some really good voices,' she says proudly. Amongst them are a man who is a pig farmer and another who has cows. 'Neither have sung before, but I teach them to read music, and they sing very well. Here people are very far apart, in the forest. It can be lonely, and when we sing together, there is no loneliness.' She also teaches little children, introducing them to the violin, and the piano. 'There is no music here for them', she explains, 'and the families are not rich. They will not travel to a music school unless their child is very talented, perhaps. I try to show them what their child can do, and help the child find music.'

Emilia had been responsible for trying to unite me with the borrowed cello before I went to Kaunas. Now I have the chance to thank her in person for her efforts. She recounts, with much laughter, how she had turned up in Warsaw with the cello for me to borrow, not realizing I was nowhere near the city. She got onto the train she supposed I was on, and dragged the cello through every carriage, sliding open the compartment doors and inquiring of everyone, asleep or awake, whether they were wanting a cello. When they answered in Polish, she knew they were not me, and moved on. Everyone laughs, but it is evident that underneath the evening's merriment there is an atmosphere of deep anxiety. A friend in Kyiv is sending updates to Sebastian every now and then. He checks his phone constantly, reading the messages out to us. There are explosions in the city, the metro is closed. Another friend texts to say that the railway stations on the border are crammed with women and children trying to get on trains out of Ukraine.

In the morning when I wake, the house is quiet. Emilia and Sebastian are still sleeping, with Mishka patiently guarding their door. I go to the window to see what I'd missed in the dark. Chickens and a tabby cat are strolling on the grass outside. Everywhere there are the wintry skeletons of trees, and rolling fields in brown and khaki map out low hills; there are no buildings to be seen in any direction.

After breakfast, Krystoph comes to pick me up. He takes me to spend the day with Max. Piotr is staying with him, unable to get back to his family across the Ukrainian border. In order to get to Max's house on the good roads, which are less pot-holed than the tracks on the Polish side, we cross back over into Lithuania briefly. Krystoph tells me that, when he was younger, if he and his friends fancied a hot dog – which weren't available in Poland at that time – they used to make this journey into Lithuania. Once, they were stopped by the guards and spent all night in custody (he points out a grim-looking detention block, now with small saplings growing through its smashed windows), in the end mending the guard's computers in exchange for their release. 'Did you get the hot dog?' I ask. 'No, I wasn't hungry after that,' he replies.

Rather than retire in the UK, Max bought a little log cabin comprising three rooms, which stands alone on the side of a hill, overlooking one of the many lakes that punctuate the miles of dense forest all around. From there he can sit on his balcony and watch the water, the changing seasons, the birds. The lake outside is still frozen but, because the house is so tiny, the heat from the log-burning stove in the centre is almost oppressive. In one corner stands a huge wooden rocking chair, its rockers fashioned from old cartwheels. It was made for him by Piotr, who now proudly shows me photos on his iPad of similar creations back in Ukraine: tables made of wheels, great wooden chairs and, intriguingly, a shrine made of ice. We go for a walk along the lake, splashing from sinking wooden jetties into the water and bullrushes, and back onto the bank again. Max's terrifying dog (the result of an unhappy union between an Alsatian and a wolf, as far as I can tell) comes with us. I am keen to keep him at a distance. 'He's mad,' says Max. 'He attacks everyone. He is a wolf, but he's *my* wolf,' he adds fondly. Piotr eyes the slavering beast suspiciously, and I have the melodies from Prokofiev's *Peter and the Wolf*, a favourite of my little son's, in my head for the rest of the day.

Later, we all go to their friend Teresa's house, the 'god-mother' of the social group, as she is known. I had met Teresa, an elegant, petite woman with stylishly arranged dark hair, the night before at Emilia's impromptu party. Her house, deep in another part of the forest, has been in her husband's family since 1830, when they became forest-ers. As traditionally Polish as it is possible to be, it has a large wooden balcony, sloping triangular roof and wooden painted walls. Inside, the furniture is heavy and dark, with effigies of the Madonna on the walls alongside paintings of forest scenes and bunches of flowers. It is thoroughly cosy. For a while we watch the rolling news from Ukraine – Piotr has been watching it on his iPad all day – shaking our heads in dismay and disbelief at the emerging pictures of horror on the screen. As the light fades, Teresa's husband goes outside to load up a wheelbarrow with meats, cheeses, nuts and sweet baked morsels, ready for the evening ahead. There is a huge loaf baked by Krystoph, who takes great pride in his breadmaking. Some of the snacks are a little less tempting. There are strings of soft pig hide complete with bristles and fat, and even the odd ear nestled amongst the other delicacies. There is vodka flavoured with berries, blackcurrant wine, and red wine in cartons. A collection of torches and headlamps is assembled, and we wind our way from the house in a little procession, past an ancient barn with studded doors and cartwheels leaning against it, past a well and into the trees. In the distant dark I can make out a large hut. Inside, it is old and very beautiful. There is a small room with patterns carved into its wooden walls, and a fire burning in a little stove. It is like walking into a fairy tale. We unload the goodies from the wheelbarrow onto the little table, and pour drinks as tea lights in little glass storm lanterns are lit. Within minutes, the place is glowing, with candles lining the window sill and mantelpiece, and marking a path down the jetty into the great dark lake beyond. The men strip off; the women, including me, opt for bathing suits; and then a great heavy door is opened next to the fireplace into the sauna room. There is much hilarity and shrieking, as we all adjust to the temperature and the pungent smell of pine and eucalyptus.

The evening grows increasingly raucous. Piotr breaks into song, rough, loud and thoroughly heartfelt. These are soulful Ukrainian folk tunes, and we sing along, picking up the tune as we go. Then Emilia sings, a pure, fluty contralto, from inside the sauna, and the shouting and laughing stops as everyone listens, in thrall to her. Under duress I sing a folksong from Somerset. To my delight, Emilia knows the tune, so we duet together through the open door.

It is apparently my turn for the 'special treatment of a visitor'. I am to lie down on the top shelf of the sauna, while Teresa's husband sprinkles me with hot water, and flaps and squeezes the bundle of hot wet rags that he dips into a bucket of hot water onto my back, shoulders, feet. Then a bucket of cold water, which makes me shriek, then the hot rags again. It's both delightful and a challenge of endurance.

I'm not going to give in. But eventually, when he's cooked my feet to the point that I'm imagining blisters in the morning, I cave, to a round of applause and shoulder thumping from the others. Apparently I've done well. I'm in the club. Once we are dripping with sweat and can't take the heat any more, everyone pours out of the sauna, and into the forest, icy leaf mould crunching beneath bare feet. The candles placed at intervals between the trees light a path a few yards into the dark, and we hold hands to find our way. Squelching through the bracken and moss, onto the wooden jetty, trying to gauge where the black wood turns abruptly into black water, then, with a yell, jumping in. The water is perishingly cold, and wonderful. Large pieces of ice float on the surface, and the moon's reflection fragments about us as we splash. In the distance, the silhouetted shapes of the forest line the further shores.

⁓

It has been a magical detour, despite the dire news from nearby Ukraine, but I must return to my cello-related travels. I am due to go to Paris, to resume my search for traces of Pál Hermann's story. So early next morning, after a bowl of hot noodles and blueberry soup, Sebastian and Emilia drive me through the forest to the station at Augusta. I remark on how few houses we pass. The nearest village, Kukle, has a population of seventy-five people. 'Nobody even in Poland knows this area,' Sebastian says, 'but it is wonderful. So much beauty.' He explains that my visit has been a welcome distraction – there's been very little to relieve the monotony of the cold winter, and they've enjoyed my unexpected visit as much as I have. I stagger onto the train at 7 a.m., ready for two days of travelling before I hope to end up in Paris. Sitting back in one of the old-fashioned compartments, complete with its own curtains and sliding door, I fall asleep immediately.

Paris – Pál Hermann

After a brief stopover in Berlin to retrieve my cello from the Philharmonie (where the archivists had become attached to its benign presence and seemed almost sad to see it go), we are now travelling back to Paris together. I am going to see if I can find any trace of Pál Hermann's Gagliano cello, which has been lost since 1952. Paris is the last place it was known to have been taken. As the train cuts through the flat, square fields of northern France, I put my headphones on, settle back in my seat and listen to Bach's B minor Mass. The recording transports me back to a performance of the Mass I had taken part in before I left England. My husband was conducting, so I had decided at the last minute to join in and sing in the chorus. It is a piece I love, possibly above all others, and one I have played so many times I know most of the continuo line by heart. On this occasion it was performed by a period instrument ensemble. By coincidence, the continuo cellist was someone to whom, a few years before when my arm was particularly painful and I felt I couldn't bear to play anymore, I had given my own beautiful Baroque cello.

In the Agnus Dei, notes fall like tears. As the violins answer the cello, all the condensed sorrow and hope of the world seem woven into the fabric of the piece. Listening, unprepared for the experience, to my own cello's plaintive sound echoing around the concert hall, it was as much as I could do not to sob, and to pretend to keep singing. I felt every movement that the cellist made, knew every fingering decision, knew how it felt to touch the mottled walnut wood of the fingerboard, and to stroke the bow across the gut of the strings. The familiarity was agonizing.

This cello had been made for me, and for twenty years had been my companion through music college and years of freelance performance when my arm was still too unreliable to play a modern instrument. Until the point when I loaned it to my cellist friend, Tom, I had been the only one ever to play it. I had completely forgotten he would be playing in this performance. Something deep inside me both recoiled from and pulled painfully towards its sound, as if I had pressed on a bruise I didn't know I had, or stumbled across a recording of the voice of someone recently dead.

In that moment, I unwittingly experienced first hand how much of ourselves can be gathered up in the sound of our instruments. The experience made me all the more determined to recover what I could of Pál Hermann's voice, in the form of his lost instrument. Its silence is one I am not prepared to accept without a fight. And if I could recover his voice, perhaps I could finally commit to finding mine, and take control of my own story as a cellist.

❧

There is a lovely concept in Māori culture known as *whakapapa*: an expanded understanding of genealogy. It acknowledges the ties between relatives and descendants and, in the same breath, the bond between people and important objects. It is this deep kinship that joins an instrument and its multiple players across time and place, united by their patterns of touch and their shared physical knowledge. Finding Pál's Gagliano will not bring him back, but it would allow his family to hear a sound so familiar to him that, were he there to hear it, it would elicit as visceral a reaction as the one that overcame me during that Bach performance.

Writing the stories of objects is about loss and death as much as it is about life and connection. Pál's missing cello is loud in its silence, present in its absence. Despite being lost, it is at the very centre of his narrative, like a taped police silhouette of a body. And yet the cello itself has been separated from its own story. The neurologist Oliver Sacks once described a client with amnesia as being 'isolated in a single moment of

being, with a moat or lacuna of forgetting all round him [...]
He is a man without a past (or future), stuck in a constantly
changing, meaningless moment.'[1] While a cello separated from
its provenance may have forgotten what it knows, it still holds
the voice of the dead. And this isn't just a fanciful metaphor.
We know that instruments are shaped by their players. They
absorb their body heat and sweat, and the resonance of the
wood is changed by the way in which a player performs. Over
years of repeated patterns of practice, the cello comes to hold
something of a player's distinctive personality. If I can find the
missing Gagliano cello, I can find something of Pál Hermann.

❧

At the Gare du Nord, I follow the other passengers out onto
pavements stippled with discarded chewing gum. Weaving a
path between departing taxis, I find a pavement table in a
café-bar where I can get my maps in order. I wind my cello
strap around my ankle and unfold a street map of Paris. It
feels reassuring to be tethered to my instrument like this, as
much the cello's job to protect me as it is mine to guard its
safety. My plan is to trace a route between the different luthiers' shops to which Pál's cello was taken in 1952, before all
record of it disappears. But before I embark on my search for
the cello, I need to piece together what happened to it before
it was brought to Paris.

❧

When Pál Hermann walked out of his rooms on the Rue de
Gorp in Toulouse, in April 1944 to make his way to Place
Wilson, he left his cello behind. On his arrest, the Gestapo
sealed the flat, itemized his few belongings, which included
the precious Gagliano, and stationed guards to keep a regular
watch on the street outside. Pál had quickly scribbled a note
and given it to someone before the train he had been put
on had left for Drancy. We do not know how Tik's father

338

Jan Weevers managed to receive the note in Monguilhem, or indeed whether the note was to Pál's landlady, who then wrote to Jan to tell him of her lodger's fate. Either way, it was clear to Jan that, if he could not save Pál himself, he could at least try to rescue his cello.

Never one to be held back by potential risk, Jan formulated a plan, with the help of two friends in Toulouse, one of whom was a luthier. His name is not mentioned but it is likely that he was Charles Voiry, the city's principal instrument maker and restorer, whose workshop represented Pál's nearest supply of strings and other accessories. Once Jan had enlisted his help, Voiry sourced the poorest-quality student cello he could find. Under cover of darkness, the three men assembled outside Pál's apartment block. They ran a huge risk of being seen by a police patrol, being apprehended by one of the neighbours, or caught by a passing official. In fact, the plan was so impossibly dangerous that Tik thinks her father must have risked his life to bribe the guards.

Their plan was to break into the apartment, but the front door of Pál's flat had been boarded shut after his arrest, and the only way in was through a little window between two buildings. Jan somehow managed to open or perhaps break it, and shimmied through. The other two men pushed the cello in after him, leaving the case outside. Once inside, Jan substituted Pál's cello for the unfortunate body-double, carefully eased the Gagliano back through the little window, and quickly followed himself. What happened next is unclear. Tik presumes that the luthier then took the Gagliano back to his workshop and hid it there, although, knowing her father's character, she believes it equally possible that Jan cycled the 150 kilometres back to his home at Le Moulin Neuf on blacked-out streets and country lanes, with the cello strapped to his back.

In 1944 all international mail was impossible. Corrie and her aunt Loes only heard about Pál's death and the rescue of his cello after the war. Even after 1945, European borders remained very strictly guarded, preventing any attempt to transport the Gagliano from Toulouse to Holland. Though the family had saved it, Corrie never saw her father's cello again.

Jan's rescue of the Gagliano was the nearest thing he could have done to saving Pál's life, but in 1952 the family decided to try to sell the instrument that had, until that point, been kept safely with Jan in Monguilhem. I tried to find out from Tik why they had made this decision. 'Corrie wanted to be a medic, and there was no money for her to study. She had nothing. What could the family do? The cello was the only thing her parents had left her. No one played the cello, and a great instrument like that deserves to be played.' More practically, owning an instrument of that value when no one used it felt like an unwanted responsibility. It needed maintenance, and insurance. The family knew that Zoltán Székely's Hungarian Quartet was in Paris for a concert in the winter of 1952, and would be travelling on to Holland afterwards. All four players of the quartet had known Pál well, so Jan determined to take the Gagliano up to Paris, to get advice from the quartet's cellist, Vilmos Palotai, as to how to sell it.

Fortunately for me, Jan Weevers was a man who, as Corrie and Tik both put it, never limited himself to a few words when a hundred would do. True to form, on 15 December 1952 he wrote an extremely detailed account of his Parisian exploits with the Gagliano. He described how, on arriving in Paris, he met up with Tik, who was studying there at the time, and father and daughter together took the cello to the Hotel Cambon, where three of the four members of the Hungarian Quartet were staying. Then as now, the hotel is an upmarket residence on the historic Rue Cambon, between the Place de la Concorde and the Louvre, and a stone's throw from the River Seine. Jan and Tik were shown to the room of Vilmos Palotai, who was resting, in preparation for the concert that evening. Jan and Palotai discussed the cello, and Palotai instructed him to take it to several luthiers, to get their opinion on what would be a reasonable price.

Jan and Tik attended the Hungarian Quartet's concert that night, which was, Jan reported, a 'resounding and beautiful success', and greatly appreciated by the audience, who called for two encores. Perhaps, given the presence of Pál's cello, their absent friend might have been present in the quartet's thoughts as they played the repertoire that he himself had performed so many times.

The morning after the concert, Jan set off on his first visits, to consult two luthiers on the Rue de Rome: Ernest Maucotel and then Louis Billottet. His first stop was the workshop of Maucotel & Deschamps. There was already a connection between Maucotel and Pál Hermann's patron Jaap de Graaff, as it was to Maucotel's workshop that Jaap had gone in order to acquire Székely's Stradivari, back in the 1920s. Ernest Maucotel inspected the Gagliano, and mentioned to Jan a price of one million francs.

Armed with the confidence that Maucotel's high estimate of the cello's worth had given him, Jan picked up the case once more and proceeded down the road to Louis Billottet's workshop.[2] Pál had taken his cello to Billottet for repairs while he was living in Paris in 1940. As Billottet was already familiar with the instrument, Jan was hopeful he would buy it.

But when he arrived, Jan was told that Billottet had died five years earlier, and his wife was now running the workshop. She did not seem surprised when he mentioned Maucotel's estimate of the cello's value, but she was not in a position to buy the instrument herself. Instead, she offered to sell it on his behalf, for a 10 per cent commission. One million francs was considerably more than the average price of Gaglianos sold at the time.[3] Back in the 1920s, de Graaff had bought it for £800, although there are no records to show where he had originally purchased it. To buy Pál's cello for one million francs in 1952 would be the equivalent of spending £35,500 on it today. It places it at the absolute top end of the Gagliano family's instruments.

Jan offered to consider Mme Billottet's offer, and proceeded to the Millant brothers, also in the Rue de Rome. They 'found it a beautiful instrument in excellent condition (there is only a small piece of the soul [pièce d'âme] under the top above the soundpost) without any doubt a Nicolò Gagliano, with original scroll. With them I mentioned the same [price] as with Billottet.'[4]

Jan's final stop was 12 Rue Parilys, the shop of Marcel Vatelot, one of the foremost instrument makers and dealers.

In a thorough examination, removal of strings and bridge, Vatelot noticed that the soundpost was crooked. [...] So I had him put in a new soundpost and left the cello with him until 12 o'clock the following morning. He had told Vilmos Palotai, who had informed him a few days earlier about prices, that a Gagliano Nicolo was well worth 800 thousand [francs] in good condition, but when he had seen it he said to me: 'Je ne savais pas qu'il s'agissait d'un instrument si beau et le prix d'un million ne me paraît pas exageré' ['I didn't know that it was such a beautiful instrument and the price of one million didn't seem excessive']. But he is not a candidate for that price. At the moment all luthiers in Paris are full of beautiful instruments, also a lot of cellos, so no buyer is interested if not for a low price. So it is certainly not the right time to get a decent price from a luthier.

At this point, Jan was running out of options. He was unable to sell the cello to a dealer, and it did not look as if Vilmos Palotai was interested in buying it for himself, although he greatly admired the instrument. Vilmos pointed out that it was all very well for Billottet to agree that the cello was indeed worth in the region of a million francs, but was he, M. Billottet, prepared to buy it for that? It turned out that he was not. 'Now you see, this does not mean anything at all!' he declared. Jan was temporarily outmanoeuvred, but he was not deterred.

࿔

In the early 1950s, with so many stolen and looted instruments circulating around Europe, there was a rule that only professional musicians were allowed to travel with multiple instruments. Jan's fallback plan all along may well have been to give Palotai the cello to take to relatives in Holland, should he fail to find a buyer in Paris. According to the family, Palotai did indeed take the cello back to Amsterdam, where Corrie's uncle collected it from him at the station and took it to the finest instrument shop in the city, owned by Max Möller. Corrie believes it was sold for around 10,000 Dutch guilders, which she then used to pay for her university degree. But when I tracked down Cornelie Möller, Max Möller's daughter-in-law, she maintained that there is no record of any sale. Lack of documentation was quite common owing to the confusion of the time, she told me. If it was sold for cash, there would be no listing in the books for it. Like so many objects, and indeed people in the post-war period, it had disappeared.

࿔

Jan's letter, written in Dutch in minuscule handwriting, is in front of me on my café table alongside my street map, and will be my guide across the city. It gives the exact addresses of all the luthiers to whom he took the cello, and these are now marked on my map. Realistically, I know that I'm most likely to be undertaking a journey of homage to the cello rather than finding any new clues. I am paying my respects to the

Gagliano before the trail goes cold. But I can't help hoping I might unearth some crucial fact or archival gem. I hoist up my own cello once more, leave a couple of euros on the café table, and head for the Métro, with Jan's letter firmly in my hand. He and I share a strange kind of kinship, as we lug a cello case across the metropolis, seventy years apart.

Following Jan's example, I set off for the ninth arrondissement, in search of the Rue de Rome. It is still at the heart of the luthier industry in Paris. On the short walk from the Gare St Lazare I pass gloriously archaic luthiers' shop windows. In one, violins hang by their peg boxes in illuminated glass and wooden cabinets. Above them, stowed as if in a luggage rack in an aeroplane, more violins lie on their sides, little white price tags dangling from their pegs like fish on the end of diminutive fishing rods. Violins hang suspended from the ceiling in rows, and the scrolls and ribs of instruments adorn every surface in a confusion of wooden curves. In another window, stocky double bass bridges are lined up against the glass, their wooden legs akimbo.

My first stop is the workshop of Maucotel and Deschamps, where Jan got his valuation of the Gagliano. Both Ernest Maucotel and Paul Deschamps died in the early 1960s, but instrument dealers' businesses are often passed down to assistants, so I have high hopes of finding the famous workshop, until it turns out that the premises it once occupied is now a burger restaurant. The firm, I learn, died with them. As a result, no one knows the whereabouts of the business records that might mention the Gagliano. I can find no trace of Billottet's workshop, and so move on to number 56, the address Jan gave for the brothers Max and Roger Millant. Their business no longer exists under their name, but the premises is still a luthier's workshop, looking discreet and even dowdy, in comparison with the flamboyantly bedecked florists next door.[5] Max Millant's son Bernard took on the business in the 1950s, and died as recently as 2017, so I rather hoped that this trail might not be as cold as the others, but when I enquire inside, I find the current proprietors are not at all inclined to help. They believe the records they inherited from Millant do not date as far back as the 1950s, so there is no way of finding out any more information about the brothers' examination of the Gagliano.

~

My only real hope for information now lies in the archives of Marcel Vatelot, the last luthier visited by Jan. Today, Vatelot's business has been taken on by Jean-Jacques Rampal, who studied and worked with Vatelot. However, despite the director's first-hand connection to the past, I know that previous attempts to extract historical information from Vatelot-Rampal have not met with success. The company has, on multiple occasions, insisted that there are no archives or records. Undaunted, I ring the bell, and wait.

Although the woman on reception seems sympathetic and friendly as I try to explain why I am here, when she summons Jean-Jacques Rampal I cannot be ushered out fast enough. I am starting to feel like the unwelcome flower seller or accordion player working tables at a restaurant, as I drag my story from shop to shop. I have seen how detailed the records of British instrument dealers are, and I know there are obligations for French dealers and makers to keep records for tax purposes. Could it really be true that none of these luthiers have any archives at all? Or is it simply that there is an inbuilt suspicion of any lost instrument whose fate is tied up with a potential Holocaust story? Have they assumed I represent one of many Jewish families, wanting the money that is rightfully theirs to compensate for a looted instrument? I try to reassure Rampal that whatever it is that I'm after, it isn't money. But the story doesn't translate into my rudimentary French very well, and I know I'm not going to get beyond his initial suspicion.

However, just as I am leaving, I encounter Rampal's young business partner and one-time apprentice, Jonathan Marrolle. He is part of a new, younger generation of dealers, for whom the aftermath of the war, and the many lost instruments that are still to be found, are a matter of historical interest. Perhaps he will be less defensive. I try, one last time, to ask for information. 'Are there any records of Vatelot's workshops from the 1950s?' 'Of course,' he says, and promises to look out for any record of a Gagliano having been in the shop in December 1952. But when I receive his scans of the workshop diary pages, I can find no mention of it at all.

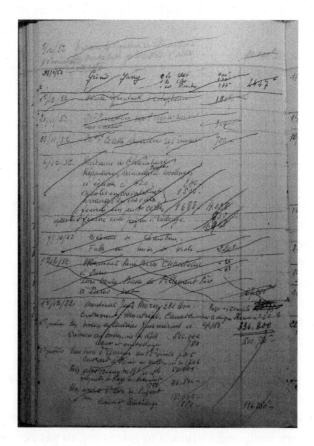

Marcel Vatelot's workshop diary.

❧

Lives are tethered to objects, but when the object is severed from the life, something of both are lost. Would a cello as magnificent as a Gagliano simply fall into disuse, or is it more likely that it has continued to be played? If so, would it be possible to stumble upon it at a concert or rehearsal? A Gagliano is very valuable, but not quite in the league of a Stradivari, and so less likely to have ended up in a bank vault locked away as an investment. Maybe there are cellists sitting next to it in orchestras, pupils listening to it demonstrating phrases to them in lessons, even recordings of its voice in circulation. In my imagination, I create counternarratives for it, making its way around Europe, even playing alongside Anita's lost Ventapane.

❧

In 1936, before he could have had any idea of the scale of displaced Jewish objects that was to come, philosopher Walter Benjamin wrote that 'the authenticity of a thing is the essence of all that is transmissible from its beginning, ranging from its substantive duration to its testimony to the history which it has experienced. [...] What is really jeopardized when the historical testimony is affected is the authority of the object.'[6]

Provenance is the history of ownership or possession of a material object such as a manuscript or an instrument. Provenance illuminates the cultural, social and historical context of a creative work. It is the portal to the object's biography and to the lives connected to it. But knowing a cello's provenance necessarily changes the current owner's relationship to their instrument. I talked recently to Shulamit Sarid, a young Jewish cellist from Israel, and asked her what instrument she played. She said it was a German cello, about two hundred years old, and that she loved it. But there was something about it that had always disconcerted her. There was no record of where it had been during the Second World War, or whose hands it had fallen into. Was she playing an instrument that had been taken from another Jewish cellist, or one played by a Nazi Party member?

Sometimes, knowing the provenance of an instrument makes it impossible to play it. Actively chosen silences in the context of the Holocaust can be the means of mental survival. Anita cannot afford to be reunited with her childhood cello. It has to remain in the past for her present to be possible. Shulamit cannot afford to know which side her cello was on during the war. The one option would make it unbearable to play, the other would contaminate it for her.

It has long been the custom amongst auction houses and dealers that provenance is not disclosed, with the result that there is little transparency about prior ownership and possession. Instruments changed hands frequently during the war, often with the only record on their paperwork being 'property of a gentleman'. The identity of owners in such cases is impossible to ascertain. Recently, UNESCO has put pressure on the museum community to write a voluntary pledge that they will not acquire a new object if they can't prove its ownership before 1970. Museums in Austria are re-examining their public art collections to find out whether they contain artefacts that were looted. But objects and instruments in private collections are infinitely harder to trace. Owners may have no idea they are in possession of a looted instrument, and even if they do suspect it, the cello is now rightfully theirs in law. The past is the past. Perhaps.

～

Objects define us. They are the outward expression of our identity; they hold and trigger our memories; and they provide physical proof that we exist. But they are also the interface between us and others. They evoke people, and past and present relationships; they help us understand where we begin and others end; and they can embody the complexity of a relationship.

We come and go, are destroyed, celebrated or forgotten in our turn. These instruments survive, to build relationships with new players, to play future repertoire that we can't imagine. Like the trees from which they are cut, their solidity endures, while the landscape around them changes. Even when separated from its story, a cello remains a still point in a turbulent, transient world.

London –
The 'Mara' Stradivari

March 2022

Every so often, the world presents you with an image that is impossible to forget. When I was in Trieste, Marco Zanettovich had shown me one particular photograph of his father Renato with the other two members of the Trieste Trio. The trio stand in borrowed suits, solemnly facing the camera, their backs to the rounded contours of a 1960s aeroplane on the runway in Buenos Aires. They are about to ascend the steps, to take their precious cargo back to Europe. Only a few days before, they were holding on to the rope around the floats that saved their lives. Now, between them, Renato Zanettovich and Amedeo Baldovino hold a rectangular box the size of a modest trunk, gripping the box by the parcel string that holds its lid in place. I looked at the image in silence for a moment, before Marco said, reverently, 'In that little box are the remains of the 'Mara'. They are bringing it home.'

Another image, this one not captured on camera: Amedeo is at the naval base with Renato looking on, surrounded by fragments of sodden wood, trying to piece together the shape of the instrument he had known so intimately. The journalists are standing awkwardly by, having rushed to interview him, now not knowing what to say.

Everyone agreed that the naval base was not the place to lay out the body of the cello, but what else could they do? At this point the trio's host Jeannette Arata de Erize arrived at the base and took over.[7] She brought the men and their sad bundle of wood to her home and laid out the pieces of the 'Mara' on a clean bedsheet to dry out. The room was closed. This is the point at which Amedeo's narrative of the events of the shipwreck ends. What he doesn't tell us is what happened to Renato's violin. This part of the story Marco fills in for me. His father had been travelling with his Guadagnini violin in a double case, knowing that he was to collect an instrument from relatives after a concert. As a result, when the Guadagnini ended up overboard, it did so with another violin, as well as Renato's music, which he had stored in one end of his case. Unfortunately, he had chosen the end with the precious Guadagnini in, and the weight of it meant that the case floated with the Guadagnini in the water, and the cheap student violin preserved above water level. When the case was finally washed up on a shore some distance away, the Guadagnini was found to be irreparably destroyed.

The 'Mara's' remains were destined for W. E. Hill & Sons, one of the few instrument makers in the world with the skills required to repair such a mess of an instrument. If it had been anything other than an irreplaceable Stradivari, such expensive life-saving surgery would never have been embarked on. As it was, the box was taken to their workshop in Hanwell, on the western edge of London, in what is now the borough of Ealing. The building has long since been turned into flats.

What was the reaction on opening that box of fragments? Who was it who untied the string, and first picked out piece after piece, to lay them gingerly on the workbench, where they would be worked on for nearly a year, until one of the greatest instruments of the world left the building once again? One of the frustrations of research into instrument making is that the names of the repairers are often not recorded. As one of the current employees puts it, Hill & Sons was an institution that liked 'to give the impression of miracles taking place, an instrument is shaped, and repaired as if by magic, and appears fully formed'. None of the names of the highly skilled team of workers who devoted a year of their time to the project remain in their records.

It took the luthiers at Hill's 700 hours over nine months, at a cost of £1,000 (over £23,000 today), to restore the 'Mara' to its former glory. In fact it was not exactly its former glory, for the resurrected 'Mara' was, in part at least, a new instrument. At some point between lying in state on Jeannette's bed in Buenos Aires, and being placed on the Hills' workbench, key pieces of the instrument had disappeared. Rumour has it that they were lost at customs, but there is no way of proving it.

~

The 'Mara' had led a colourful life ever since it had left Stradivari's care in 1711. Amedeo Baldovino had loved it, and treated it with great reverence, but it had taken a battering at the hands of a previous owner, Giovanni Mara. He was the husband of a great German singer, Gertrude Elisabeth Schmöhling, until she left him, unable to tolerate his alcoholism and moods. Both she and the cello suffered from his abuse and bore scars that he had inflicted upon them. On one occasion, Gertrude was supposed to sing before the music-loving Frederick the Great of Prussia, but cancelled the performance as she did not wish the severe bruising on her face to be seen in public.[8] On being told of this, the king was so furious that he sent for her violent husband and told him that, as he was so fond of beating, he could serve as a drummer in one of his regiments for a month.[9] When W. E. Hill & Sons came to own his cello in the late 1880s, they were horrified to see the damage Mara had caused, recording in their diaries: 'Unfortunately his violoncello seems to have suffered somewhat from his viciousness. Traces of alcoholic liquor having been upset and allowed to drip from the top to the bottom sides, removing the beautiful varnish on its downwards course, are still discernible.'

In the leather-bound Hill registers, I discover to my fascination that the 'Mara''s shipwreck in the River Plate was not the first time it had travelled to Buenos Aires. A neatly written note from 1910 records that the Hill brothers had sold the 'Mara' to a wealthy Argentine banker, a Señor Carlos

A. Tornquist of Buenos Aires, who owned it from 1910 until 1934, when he sold it back to the Hills, from whom 'Mr. Murray Lees, a very cautious Scottish man', purchased it that November.[10] Twenty years later, in 1954, it was bought by Amedeo Baldovino, who by this point was already internationally famous. For almost forty-two years it appeared on stages with him throughout the world, and he continued playing it until shortly before his death. When the teenage Raphael Wallfisch had been studying with Amedeo, he was both intrigued and overawed by the battle-scarred 'Mara'. 'I saw the cello every day. Once I put a bow on it when Baldovino wasn't looking – perhaps he'd gone out that day. Then I heard he was selling it. It was a time I was looking for a sponsor to help me buy a great cello. I was desperate to have it, but Baldovino warned me against it. "You shouldn't have that millstone round your neck," he said. "Don't bother with it." At the time, I was not really sure what he meant, but after tripping up with Amaryllis Fleming's Stradivari, I began to understand.'

Reading Amedeo's account of his reunion with his cello after the shipwreck, I am inclined to believe that he knew better than anyone what a great responsibility it was to be the caretaker of such an instrument. Nine years into his relationship with the cello, he had inadvertently been responsible for its destruction. The scars might have been concealed so skilfully by the Hill workshop that they are hardly visible now, but they could not erase Amedeo's memories of that night.

In Trieste, Marco Zanettovich told me that his father believed the 'Mara' was salvageable only because it was a Stradivari, whereas the damage to his Guadagnini was irreparable. There is some evidence to suggest that Stradivari, unlike other makers, used ground glass in a solution painted immediately onto the wood, which might have helped to waterproof it. I'm interested to hear what other makers think of the theory. Could this be why the wood of the 'Mara' survived its soaking? I'd asked Stefan-Peter Greiner when I attended his instrument workshops in Cremona. 'It's possible,' he said. 'There are many different theories. Ground glass was a common filler used to thicken paint. It was possibly more waterproof than other common binders and fillers. You do find silica in old instruments, and whether ground glass is the root of that, or whether it is more waterproof, we just don't know.' He thinks it's a theory that is heading in the right direction, but the truth is it's still a mystery. What we do know for certain, however, is that the 'Mara' survived, and has since outlived two owners. It now belongs to a Swiss cellist, Christian Poltera, and he has agreed to meet me in a smart hotel in central London.

～

Christian has a few hours free before he has to rehearse with his sextet for two chamber music performances at the Wigmore Hall. His schedule is exacting – a different European city almost every night – and I'm lucky to be able to get some time with him. The lift in the hotel lobby whirs and pings and Christian emerges, neat and well dressed, his dark eyes thoughtful behind frameless glasses. We find a quiet sofa and begin to talk. He begins with an apology – for the first time in ten years, the 'Mara' is not with him! He had been suffering from a frozen shoulder, and the narrow body of the 'Mara' requires him to lean in and over it. So, temporarily, he's playing on his own cello, which is much broader-shouldered and allows him to sit back, easing the pressure on his upper body. Of course I'm disappointed, but I have so much I want to ask him about the instrument, and I'm already planning to include a detour to Switzerland to see him and the cello on another occasion. I tell him as quickly as I can about my book project and sit back to listen as he begins to tell me the story of his relationship with one of the greatest instruments ever made, from the moment it left Amedeo Baldovino's hands to the present day.

In 1996, Christian's teacher, Heinrich Schiff, asked him and a group of his fellow students at the Mozarteum in Salzburg whether they knew anything about the 'Mara' Stradivari. He had heard that the elderly Baldovino was no longer able to play, and the dealer Charles Beare was selling it in London. Schiff was scheduled to play the Brahms Double Concerto in London in a few days' time, so the coincidence of his being there, and the iconic cello being suddenly (and only briefly) available, was too tempting to resist. Nineteen-year-old Christian didn't know anything about the 'Mara' beyond its reputation, but a friend of his had a life-size poster of the cello decorating the wall of their shared student flat. To cello students, the 'Mara' was the equivalent of a gorgeous celebrity pin-up. Schiff announced that he would come to join them in their flat that evening, throwing his students into a frenzy of tidying. When he arrived, his eyes turned to the poster. The next day he boarded a plane for London.

As it turned out, Amedeo Baldovino had not handed the cello over to Charles Beare with permission to sell to anyone he wished. Instead, he had written a document stipulating which cellists were to be considered for future ownership. No person on the list of the chosen was allowed to know who else was on it but, in the light of this, a curious little coda that sits oddly at the end of Amedeo's account of the shipwreck makes sense. 'The Mara was my master and trusty friend for almost 42 years. Now my wish is that it will continue to have the same significance for the new person who is going to play it. It is a precious thing for whoever may own it.' Amedeo's document recounting the details of the Mara's rescue was his attempt to write the cello's future by describing their shared past: will, blessing, and eulogy, all in one. It was important that the future servant of his 'master' understood exactly what he and the 'Mara' had been through together. Unlike Pál's Gagliano and Anita's Ventapane, the 'Mara' would, Amedeo hoped, never be separated from its story.[11]

There were at least two players on his list – Yo-Yo Ma and Heinrich Schiff – but Yo-Yo Ma was already the custodian of Jacqueline du Pré's 'Davidoff' Stradivari. Christian Poltera isn't sure whether Heinrich had been told of Amedeo's wishes, or whether he was simply drawn to the legendary instrument, as it was so rare for such a cello to be on the market. Either way, when Heinrich sat down in the London sales room and put his bow to the 'Mara''s strings, he knew he could not imagine leaving without it. In fact, he asked to borrow the cello there and then, took it to his hotel and settled in, with a bottle of red wine for sustenance, to unlock the many mysteries and idiosyncrasies of the instrument.

Usually, understanding the workings of a Stradivari takes time, as player and instrument gradually build a relationship. But Heinrich played Brahms through the night, and the next day turned up at the concert hall with the 'Mara' (and a slight hangover) to greet violinist Frank Peter Zimmerman, with whom he was to record the double concerto. Zimmerman was horrified – they had rehearsed already, and Heinrich had been playing his own instrument. This would be totally different. The colours, sound quality, balance – everything would be changed with the 'Mara'. Heinrich was adamant and the recording went ahead, with him playing his new cello as if he were taming a stallion bareback, as Zimmerman later recalled. It was a huge risk, but the recording betrays no sense of how young the partnership between cello and player was, and it even went on to win the Deutsche Schallplattenpreis.

After that, there was no going back. Heinrich could not contemplate the 'Mara' falling into other hands; neither could he begin to raise enough money to buy it himself. He contacted a concert promoter who admired his playing. The promoter was a keen amateur cellist and was very taken with the idea. The next morning he had his answer – it would be purchased for him to play.

From this point on, the young Christian Poltera saw the 'Mara' in most of his lessons. He watched Heinrich play it – 'always fabulously', he adds – and got to know its sound. When his own cello, a lesser Stradivari from 1698, was reclaimed by the foundation who had loaned it to him, Christian found himself with no instrument. He was booked to play the Shostakovich cello concerto, so Heinrich, always free and easy with the 'Mara', simply lent it to him for a month.

I wondered how such a petite, old instrument would stand up against the battering of Shostakovich's twentieth-century anger, but Christian explains that this is one of the many curiosities about the cello: 'You'd think that Beethoven sonatas would be perfect for it, and that you might choose a more robust modern instrument, that had been constructed with heavy-duty steel strings in mind, for more modern repertoire. But no – the "Mara" moulds itself to whatever you play on it, even though Stradivari could have had no idea of the demands that modern cellists would make on it in future centuries.'

Christian's serious face lights up as he remembers his first lengthy encounter with the 'Mara'. Like his teacher, but without the red wine, he unclipped the case in a hotel room, and tentatively began the process of taming the instrument, a note at a time. He vividly recalls how the room around him seemed to change as he played. Surrounded by carpets and thick curtains – an acoustic-free square of a bedroom – and yet, instead of the notes falling dead into the soft furnishings, the 'Mara' seemed to create its own acoustic. Christian felt as if he had been transported into a cathedral, the sound reverberating from everywhere and nowhere simultaneously. This, he tells me, is one of the unique properties of the 'Mara'. If you stand at the back of a concert hall and listen to another great cello, say Heinrich Schiff's other instrument, the 'Sleeping Beauty'

Montagnana that was once owned by Gregor Piatigorsky, you can identify concretely the specific place from where the music originates. The sound is transmitted from cello to listener in a way that is solid, quantifiable and very present. Not so for the 'Mara'. Defying all laws of physics, its sound seems to have no single source, creating the impression of a golden halo, a cloud of glowing resonance, translucent and opaque. The varnish of the cello itself has an orange-golden shine. I wonder if, had it been a darker varnish, Christian would identify the same golden glow in the sound. He thinks for a moment. 'It just couldn't be dark,' he says, with certainty. 'I'm a great believer in cellos sounding as they look. And that cello is made of sunshine, both inside and out.'

Heinrich Schiff had always lived dangerously, being, in Christian's memorable words, a 'chain-smoking, espresso-sipping, madly alive tempest of a man'. His blood pressure, unsurprisingly, was worryingly high. It was as if he played just as his heart beat, Christian believes. His vibrato was fast and not relaxing, and his playing, like every aspect of his character, was driven and intense. As his health failed, he could no longer manage to play the 'Mara'. Mstislav Rostropovich had a similar experience in the last ten years of his life, when the 'Duport' Stradivari, made in the same year as the 'Mara', finally became too much for him.

'These great Stradivari are not easy instruments,' Christian explains. 'When you pick up a modern cello, or even another great older instrument, it's a relief compared to the unpredictable wrestling you undertake with a Stradivari. That's why I've never believed in these blind testings, where a Stradivari is played, and then another cello, and people conclude that the Stradivari is no more special than the other. In order to coax the best out of it, you have to live with the instrument, get to know its foibles, adapt how you play. It's like a long-term relationship with someone absolutely extraordinary, and complex.'

To forge a relationship with a great instrument requires a profound sense of humility. The cellist Murray Welsh remembers how everyone loved it when Rostropovich came to London to play the 'Duport' Stradivari in concert, but that it was the 'Duport' the audience heard, not Rostropovich. Christian nods. 'A great Stradivari is not for every player. It isn't a vehicle for your own voice, it has its own discrete identity. You have to fit your ideas around it – you are show-casing it, you are its carer, presenting it to the public for it to sing. There are two voices duetting on stage – yours and your Stradivari.'

&

The last time Heinrich Schiff appeared with the 'Mara' was to play Beethoven sonatas. It was 25 April 2010, and he was on stage in the Mozart Hall of the Vienna Konzerthaus. It was only during the concert that he realized that his performing career was finally at an end. He could not hold the bow. His arm was causing him agony, but he could not bring himself to admit to the audience that the extraordinary powers he had spent years perfecting had left him. He pretended the fault was with the bow, the spike, anything but admit the truth in public. Heinrich had become accustomed to ignoring the pain he often experienced in his bowing arm, but now it was clear he could not continue. It would be the last time he would play in public.

When Christian was due to play near Salzburg in 2012, he visited his old teacher, who was by now terminally ill. He found him in a sorry state. The 'Sleeping Beauty' had been sold to a collector in Taiwan, where it would not be played, or even seen. It was a great source of sorrow for him, even though he was no longer able to play it himself. When Christian arrived, the 'Mara' was standing in a corner of the room, due to be sold in two weeks' time. It, too, was not going to remain in Europe, or go to a player who would perform on it. It was as if it were lined up, waiting stoically for its execution. Both instruments would, as far as European cellists and concert goers were concerned, be silenced for a generation. Christian said his goodbyes to Heinrich, and returned for the pre-concert rehearsal, troubled and thoughtful. When pressed, he relayed the situation to the other members of the chamber group. They all had instruments procured for them by a sponsor. As soon as the rehearsal was over, they called their instruments' owner, who agreed to buy the 'Mara' then and there for Christian, even though he had no personal connection to either instrument or player. The idea of such great instruments being lost to Europe and to the public was sufficient incentive. After only a couple of phone calls, the cello was Christian's.

When Christian broke the news to Heinrich, he was overjoyed at the Mara's last-minute reprieve, and took to his grave the knowledge that it would now be cared for by his own pupil, who had loved it for so many years. One of Christian's first engagements was with his trio member Frank Peter Zimmerman, the violinist who had been so thrown by the Mara's sudden appearance with Heinrich, years before. Now, Christian appeared for the trio's concert and proudly produced the recently procured 'Mara' from his case. Zimmerman rolled his eyes. Not again!

From that moment onwards, Christian has played the 'Mara' for almost every concert, except, as bad luck would have it, for his brief London appearance this week. Frustrating though it is, there is something fitting about the Mara's absence today. A cello that so nearly ended its life in the 1960s, that died and was resurrected, is always both present and in part absent.

〜

After Christian and I have talked for a couple of hours, we are joined by Robert Brewer Young, with a violin case under one arm. He is one of the five directors of the twenty-first-century incarnation of W. E. Hill & Sons, exuding energy and intelligence, originally American but speaking every language you can name. He tells us how the 'Mara' passed through the hands of the Hill family four times between 1885 and 1954, before it ended up on the workbench of what is now his company, in soggy pieces in a cardboard box, in 1963.

According to Robert, the Hill diaries report that the instrument was not just restored but *improved* by their work. It's a bold statement. But, when reunited with it, Amedeo also claimed that it sounded better than ever. Could the 'Mara' really have been improved? I wonder whether the memory of its sound had simply faded a little for Amedeo during his year of waiting for its return. Christian is sceptical. When I ask him why, his answer isn't quite what I expect. It isn't that he doubts an instrument can undergo such wholesale destruction and come out better, it's that he doubts that the 'Mara''s voice could in fact ever really *be* destroyed. Even in an accident so extreme. I am fascinated by this theory, akin to our hazy but comforting sense that someone's soul lives on independently from the body after death. Christian expands on his theory. 'The "Mara" has such a strong identity, such a strong voice. It can't be destroyed, and it can't be improved.' What he loves – and Robert agrees – is its quasi-mystical ability to wrong-foot everyone, to overturn every assumption luthiers might make about it. Is its secret in the varnish or in the wood? The varnish was largely washed off in the river; what was left was carefully diluted by the workmen and spread over the reconstructed body, like a watery skin graft. And the wood isn't even all the original. The ribs at the bottom of one side of the instrument had to be recreated, a transplant to stop up a hole. In short, the 'Mara' resolutely refuses to disclose where its secret lies, and yet, there it is – a translucent, glowing voice that transcends shipwrecks, disaster and time itself.

Marylebone, London – W. E. Hill & Sons

Centuries of history appear to condense into the present moment, in the actions of the luthiers in a workshop. The planing of wood, turning pegs to make them fit a peg box, and stringing and tuning an instrument have not changed. These loving ministrations to the temperamental string family have been undertaken ever since the instruments were invented. There is something timeless about these rituals, and equally about the historic institution W. E. Hill & Sons. In the spring of 1660 Samuel Pepys wrote in his diary 'In ye morning came Mr. Hill, ye instrument maker, & I consulted with him about ye altering my lute & my viall (17 February).' And a month later, on 5 March, 'Early in ye morning Mr. Hill comes to string my theorbo, which we were about till past ten o'clock, with a great deal of pleasure.'

In 1939 Alfred and Arthur Hill donated a priceless collection of instruments to the Ashmolean Museum in Oxford. They reside in their glass cases only a short cycle ride away from my college. I have spent many hours looking at them, trying to hear their stories, willing their voices to whisper through the glass. It is only when I visit the Hill workshop in the company of Robert Brewer Young that I learn that these instruments were originally war evacuees, sent away from London to the cloistered safety of the Ashmolean, carefully preserved during the same conflict that would claim Anita's Ventapane and separate Pál Hermann from his Gagliano. And there they still hang, silent, but undamaged.

I follow Robert up the staircase to Hill's London office, where he pulls down from the shelf a weighty volume, beautifully bound with marbled endpapers. This register is a Who's Who of the world's greatest instruments. The sound of a violin wafts up the staircase from a lower room. He opens the Register of Sales and shows me name after name, listed in copperplate writing, with the dates and instruments purchased. Taking 1921 as a specimen year, I see that, in the space of three months, Gaglianos, Stradivari and many other famous cellos were changing hands. My eye stops on an Amati purchased from the Medici family, along with a list of the repairs carried out on it. It is possible to trace each instrument's appearance and reappearance through these registers, as owners die or their fortunes change, and the instruments are returned to Hill & Sons a generation later to be sold again.

I am hoping to find the Gagliano's first appearance, when Pál Hermann's patron Jaap de Graaff acquired it, but I wonder if I might be able to trace it further back, finding vestiges of its life before. Even if these huge leather volumes tell me only the barest details, the diaries that the Hill brothers also kept might reveal something. The entries in the ledger are written in a deliberately cryptic shorthand devised by the Hill family. Even with magnification I cannot make sense of all the indecipherable hieroglyphs. There are only two people alive now who are able to decode it. Handily for me, one of them is Robert.

This shorthand is a form of instrumental DNA, holding the key to recognizing and identifying what is unique about each violin, viola or cello. The Hill brothers developed their secret code to prevent others from reading it and to safeguard the secrets of these valuable instruments. But the Hill shorthand was also designed to help them identify individual instruments. Like a dentist noting down details of teeth during a check-up, the Hills could assess an instrument and commit all the essential information to paper in seconds. With the aid of the code, they would always be able to recognize the same instrument when it returned to their shop.

In their shorthand, the Hill brothers always looked at an instrument in the same order – back, sides, head, front, varnish. 'This is because the back wood is usually more interesting than the front,' Robert explains. 'There's not much variation with pine, but spruce or maple has more personality. You can tell a lot about the maker and how affluent they were from the wood, not just the instrument. For instance, highly flamed maple is expensive, less flamed is cheaper.' Robert points at random to one entry, and deciphers it for me: 'Medium flames, good amount of orange varnish, dark wood, fine curl plus very fine widening towards the flanks, head plainer.' It is a cross between a book of secret spells and the shipping forecast.

Robert and I are both hoping that some further indication as to the fate of the Gagliano resides here, in one of these little treasure hunt clues. I tell him about one passage in Jan Weever's 1952 letter from Paris, that might, I hope, be the key to identifying the instrument.

> I came in contact with a certain M. Sand, photographer and publisher of a very expensive fashion magazine, for which he makes all the photos: 'L'art et la Mode', and I went to visit him with the cello on Sunday afternoon. At first I did not mention a price, let him quietly measure it and look at it and when he had found that the instrument was beautiful and that it had only a burnt-in text on the rim, put the instrument back into his case.

A burnt-in text on the rim. When I had first examined this letter, Tik, Paul, Corrie and I had puzzled over the translation of this key phrase. It is the most hopeful lead I have, and might just provide the key to finding the cello. The Gagliano has some kind of tattoo, but what is it? And what size?

The phrase Jan wrote in Dutch is *ingebrandde spreuk op de randen*. This, I am told, alludes to a signature made by a kind of little poker, heated and then used to inscribe or decorate wood. Not only is this mysterious 'burnt-in text' intriguing, but Mr Sand was 'disappointed' by it. What could be disappointing about an inscription? If it were tiny and insignificant, why would it be a cause of such dismay? When I had worried away at the Dutch translation with Corrie, she had pointed out two accents – the equivalent of capitals – which indicate that he was VERY disappointed to discover it. Conversely, I am delighted. It must be a significant enough feature to make an impact on the instrument. And therefore someone must recognize it. If we're to find it, it will be this inscription that helps us. With this, we could put a call out across the luthier community, describing the Gagliano's birthmark. But what could the inscription possibly say?

If Pál Hermann's Gagliano had ever passed through the hands of W. E. Hill & Sons, one of the makers would have written a detailed entry for it in this book. And they would not have failed to comment on such a curious feature. As we hunt through the pages of the diaries, the same names appear again and again. Wealthy businessmen who turn to Hill & Sons to sell or purchase valuable instruments for investment – Baron Knoop, Blagrove, and Richard Bennett, an amateur violinist who made a fortune in bleach and spent it building up one of the world's largest collections of Stradivari violins. You can chart the patterns of their lives through the Hill books: the years of wealth, or financial collapse.

W. E. Hill & Sons issue authenticity certificates for the instruments they sell, so we hunt for a historic record of one for our Gagliano, but we're out of luck – the books turn out to list only instruments made by Stradivari and Guarneri 'del Gesù'. The Hills would have had a book of Gagliano certificates but it appears to have been lost. There are other gaps in the archive as well. We find a certificate for the 'Cristiani' Stradivari, but it refers the reader to a Letter Book, F. 545, a mysterious volume whose whereabouts no one knows.

So we try another tack, turning to a huge book of sales, with its marbled flyleaves and textured leather binding. The Hill brothers used to give the instruments they sold a serial number, etched onto the end of the fingerboard. If we can find a record of the sale of the Gagliano in their sales book, it will bear that distinctive number, assuming of course that its fingerboard has not been replaced. In some cases, hopeful sellers have faked these numbers, or claimed they have them when they don't, in order to raise the price. The serial number is the first piece of information entered for almost all the instruments listed in the book, on page after page of entries.

The Gagliano family created hundreds of instruments, and many of them appear in Hill's magnificent sales book. Between 1925 and 1929 alone, fifteen Gagliano cellos were sold by Hill's, and even more violins. Wurlitzer, the New York dealers, seemed particularly to favour them, buying multiple instruments in one sale. But nowhere do we find the names Jaap de Graaff or Louise Bachiene amongst the purchasers. Or any reference to their address. I am just about to turn the page, when Robert suddenly points to an entry near the top. 'There it is! That's your cello!' The entry states that on 14 January 1925, an N. Gagliano cello was sold by Hill's to Ernest Maucotel, in Paris. Is it a coincidence that, in 1952, Maucotel was the first dealer Jan called on when he was trying to sell the cello, or did he already know that the Gagliano had a connection with the shop? Maucotel was the dealer from whom Jaap de Graaff had bought Zoltán Székely's Stradivari violin in 1928. De Graaff was looking for a suitable cello for Pál Hermann at the same time and this Gagliano sold to Maucotel by Hill & Sons would have been there in the shop. It would be too much of a coincidence if the cello, moving from London to Paris and back again, was not to become Pál's.

I look more closely, studying the entry for further clues. Maddeningly, it is one of the very few listings that don't record a serial number. Why is this? There is a little note next to the entry – '1/2 purchase'– which means, I find out, that the Hill's owned a share of it, and Maucotel bought them out of their interest in the instrument for £150. It seems a paltry amount for such a good cello. Did Maucotel own the other half, or someone else? De Graaff bought it for £800 – a lot more than two times £150.

Robert and I keep returning to the tiny writing, as if the letters will loop and curl and rearrange themselves into further information. That must be our cello. It must. If we can find the Maucotel archives, we might have the information we need to find the cello, even without a serial number. But, as I discovered on my trip to Paris, there are no traces left of the empire that was once Maucotel and Deschamps, or its archives. It's a dead end, for now at least.

∼

Once we have exhausted all that W. E. Hill & Sons' archives have to offer us, we turn to the instrument itself. I arrange all the photographs I have of Pál playing his Gagliano on the desk in front of us. This is the first time Robert has seen them, and he examines them intently, tracing his finger across the smooth surface of the image as if reading an impossible braille.

When he eventually looks up, he is glowing with excitement. 'This is wonderful. More than I could have dared hope for,' he says. 'If this is what I think it is, then it is something really extraordinary. And I think it is the key to finding the cello.'

In the south of Italy, where Neapolitan makers such as the generations of the Gagliano family worked, spruce is extremely expensive and rare. Robert has been studying one particular spruce tree for many years. Imported from northern Italy, it found its way to the Gagliano workshop, and from that same tree, between roughly 1720 and 1820, three generations of the Gagliano family created cellos. The wood is very distinctive, with a trademark pattern known in German as *Haselfichte*, which literally means 'hazel spruce' but is rendered more poetically as 'bear claw'. This is because it is as if a bear has carved its claw marks across the surface in a gnarled swirl, a result of the peculiar way in which the particular spruce trunk has grown.

'I have been all across Europe tracing five cellos made from that one tree, that all bear the same mark,' says Robert, barely able to contain his excitement. 'Now. There, look there.' He points at the left side of the front of Pál's cello, just beyond the fingerboard. 'That's the *Haselfichte*. I think this is the sixth cello!'

This mark alone ought to be enough to identify the instrument. No luthier would forget seeing this cello on their workbench. But this still doesn't solve the mystery of the 'burnt-in inscription' on the cello's side. What does Robert make of that? He tells me that it was not uncommon for makers to inscribe a stringed instrument. Stradivari did it, and so did Amati. The 'San Lorenzo' Stradivari violin of 1718 has *in domo eius* ('in his house') inscribed on it, suggesting it might have been a wedding present. The instruments made by Andrea Amati in the mid-sixteenth century for King Charles IX of France were all painted with the fleur-de-lys of the royal household, in the style of Limoges porcelain. If Pál Hermann's Gagliano bears an inscription, it could be an indication that the instrument had been made for an important commission.

Looking again at the photographs of the Gagliano, Robert notes how beautifully and carefully made the instrument is. The wood is exquisite, and the craftsmanship superb. It sets it apart from some of the Gaglianos' other instruments, which were considerably more rustic than this, made for musicians on a very tight budget, with poor-quality wood. But this cello is really quite special. Robert thinks it would have combined everything the Gaglianos had learnt from working particularly closely with musicians in Naples to perfect the sound of their instruments, as well as using the best wood, cutting into their precious spruce. It would have been a very special commission, maybe even a court instrument. From what we can see from the photographs, the cello's purfling (the thin edging around the instrument's front and back) is made of the thinnest imaginable strips of white beech and paper, framing the fabulous spruce top, its back and ribs cut from broad-flamed maple. None of these materials would have been easy to obtain in Naples at the time the Gaglianos made the cello.

The Hills' workshop diaries are highly disparaging of south Italian makers, whom they regarded as distinctly 'Not Our Class, Dear'; 'All the rough southerners think about is food', sneers the diary. Their private prejudices manifest in wood-snobbery. They are sniffy about the beech wood that they used, suggesting they might have recycled fish crates, and the paper used for the purfling might have wrapped pasta.

But the Hills' prejudices were based on ignorant assumptions. In northern Italy, where beech is very common, it was used for furniture (and fish crates); in the south, however, it was very slow-growing, and so an enormous luxury, usually having to be imported to the area. Only the noblest houses had beech mouldings around them. Furniture made of average wood but inlaid with beech was ennobled, raised to a higher level by the rich association it brought. Paper, too, was rare and expensive, and black papers were indeed used for wrapping the most expensive pasta. 'To edge a cello with paper takes a phenomenal degree of skill,' Robert explains. 'Two channels must be carved with a knife, then meticulously laid with the paper. It's fiendishly difficult, and something few luthiers today could achieve.'

∽

I know more about the instrument itself, and would be able to identify it if I find it, but I still do not know its whereabouts. For as long as I've known Pál Hermann's story, I have been trying to find his cello. The more I've spoken to players and come to understand their relationship to their instruments, the more convinced I have become that the nearest we can ever get to restoring him to his family is to find that cello and play his compositions on it. I have searched through every auction house's catalogues for mention of a sale of a Gagliano that fits its description, contacting the seller on each occasion to find out about the provenance of the instrument. I have talked to dealers, to makers and to players. I have placed articles in specialist magazines, and broadcast on the BBC. I have hounded numerous players who own, or even might possibly own, a Gagliano. So far, nothing has come of it.

It's time to turn my attention to where Pál's cello might have gone in 1952, if it did indeed end up in Amsterdam. Jan Weevers's letter mentioned one Dutch dealer, a character called Max Möller. Both Pál's relatives and I had been told that there were no records of such a sale, but after my experience with Vatelot-Rampal, I have learnt not to take the statement that all records had vanished at face value. Having now run out of all other options, I decide to try pleading with Möller's relatives one last time. Were there any records, anything at all, that they could share with me about the workshop's activities after the war? If not, then where did they generally sell instruments, and to whom? Is there any record of sales, particularly around the winter and spring of 1952–3? 'No, nothing,' Cornelie, his daughter-in-law, replied. Again. And she declined to talk to me on Zoom, or even over the phone, as she didn't want to have any contact with the media. I assured her, doing my best not to sound too desperate, that I was not the media, but a harmless cellist and writer, eager to restore something of the soul of the murdered Pál Hermann to his ninety-year-old daughter, before it was too late. The reply was unexpected, and shocking. Her own husband, she told me, had been 'murdered by burglars'. After that, she talked to no one, and that was to include me. But perhaps something in my impassioned plea for solace for the bereaved daughter of a murdered father struck a chord.

Eventually, after a few more petitions on my part, she wrote to me again. 'I can't help you,' she said. 'You have the wrong dealer, it was a company named Gebr. Müller [Müller brothers] who probably sold it from a different shop, and definitely not us. The family is mistaken. Max Möller had no part in it.' So that was that. I could not press her any further without legitimately being accused of stalking.

Late the same evening I glance again at her strangely abrupt message. I notice for the first time that there is a jpeg attached to the email. When I open it, I find a photograph of a typed document from September 1953, written in Dutch. I puzzle over it for a while, then send it to Paul van Gastel, Pál's grandson and my untiring provider of Dutch translations. Within minutes the phone starts to ring. When I pick it up, I hear Paul's voice on the other end, choked with emotion. 'You did it!' he exclaims. 'You've found Pál's soul – his spirit – you've brought him back to us!'

I don't know what he is talking about, but a moment later he emails me his translation of the document, and we read it aloud together, laughing and weeping:

4 September 1953

Herewith we guarantee that the cello in the possession of Mr Kurt Herzbruch, Cologne, is the work of the late Neapolitan Master Nicolò Gagliano, whose label, dated 1730, is in the instrument.

Description: Floor: jointed, from very beautiful maple wood. Deck: really fine mature resonance. Piebald spruce: really fine and characteristic cut ('stung'), the darkening on the splay is still richly present. Varnish: original, fine transparent light brown to gold-yellow. The instrument is a fine and characteristic example of the work of this Master and is in good shape.

Attached are three photograph details in order to identify the instrument.

This cello is a first-class concert instrument, was for years in the possession of a performing artist and was in 1928 sold by Maucotel & Deschamps to Mr de Graaff in London.

It's our cello all right. But then comes the gift I could not have dared to hope for. The soul of Pál Hermann. For right at the bottom of the page, separated from the preceding words by a blank space – almost as if the form of the document itself understood the import of its words and accorded the statement a respectful silence – I read the following:

The frame of the instrument bears an incision with the following words:

Ego sum Anima Musicae (I am the soul of music).

1117   4 september 1953

Hierdurch garantieren wir,dasz das Cello im Besitze des
Herrn Kurt Herzbruch,Köln,eine Arbeit ist des alt-neapoli-
tanischen Meisters,Nicola Gagliano,dessen Etikette,datiert
1730,sich im Instrumente befindet.

Beschreibung;Boden; geteilt,aus sehr schön geflammtem Ahorn
holz. Decke; sehr fein jährige Resonnans.Ficht-Schecke;
sehr fein und karakteristisch gestochen,die Schwärzung auf
der Abkantung noch reichlich erhalten.Lack;original,feines
durchsichtiges hell-braun bis goldgelb. Das Instrument ist
ein feines und karakteristisches Beispiel für die Arbeit
dieses Meisters und in guter Erhaltung.
Nebenstehend drei Detail Photographieen sur Identifizierung
dieses instrumentes.
Dieses Cello das ein Konzertinstrument ersten Ranges ist,war
Jahre lang im Besitze konzertierender Künstler und wurde
1928 von Maucotel & Deschamp,Paris an Herrn de Graaff,London
verkauft.

Die Zargen des Instrumentes sind graviert und von dem Sinn-
spruche:Ego sum Anima Musical,(ich bin die Seel der Musik.)
versehen.

Kurt Herzbruch (far right) and the Schäffer Quartet.

Despite Möller's daughter-in-law outwardly maintaining that the company had had nothing to do with the sale, here is the proof that the Gagliano had indeed passed through their hands. Finally I have a lead – the name of an individual known to have owned the Gagliano after it was sold in Amsterdam. I need to track down Mr Kurt Herzbruch of Cologne, who left Möller's shop with this very special instrument, with no idea who it was who had previously owned it. After some digging, I find that Herzbruch was a well-known German cellist, who made many recordings of Beethoven and Mozart quartets, Schubert trios and Boccherini quintets, mostly with the Schäffer Quartet in Cologne in the 1950s. Some of these might presumably have been made with his new Gagliano.

I am struck by the fact that he was a chamber musician like Pál Hermann. Does this instrument lend itself specifically to quartet repertoire, and the very particular demands it places

373

on a player? Had Kurt Herzbruch any way of knowing that the works he was performing and recording were well known to this instrument, which had only stopped playing them under the fingers of the anonymous 'well-known performing artist' a few years before?

It seems like it will be an easy task to track down Herzbruch's descendants and find out whether they still have his cello. People rarely throw away paperwork relating to an instrument of this value. But when I succeed in contacting his widow and daughter, they tell me that Herzbruch did not keep the cello for more than a year. They have no idea where or when he sold the Gagliano.

No luthiers in Cologne have a record of its purchase, and only one or two of Kurt's pupils remember hearing him mention it. None of them even saw the Gagliano as he never took an instrument with him to teach, preferring to borrow his pupils' instruments if he wanted to demonstrate something.

∽

Armed with the information I have gained from Robert, and now from Cornelie Möller, I renew my international search for the Gagliano, contacting makers, joining online cellist groups and putting out calls on radio stations across Europe and America. Many players get in touch with helpful suggestions and possible leads, all of which come to nothing. One intriguing cello surfaces in America, which had been owned by a cellist from the Metropolitan Opera Orchestra. Gerald Kagan had walked past a pawn shop in Portugal, and seen the ribs and back of a cello hanging in the window. He made enquiries and found that the front of the instrument was intact in another part of the shop. He purchased the pieces of the cello, took them home to America and spent years restoring the instrument, which he then played from time to time at the Met. The feature that had attracted him to this wreck was some large, ornately painted writing that curved its way round its ribs: 'Ego sum Anima Musicae'. I want to believe it is Pál's cello. What are the chances of two instruments with the same inscription and no provenance? But after the owner obligingly takes it to a luthier for identification, it turns out that the instrument is indisputably French. Someone else's soul, another lost instrument, separated from its story.

But I haven't drawn a complete blank. I can now trace the Gagliano from one particular spruce tree in Naples to London and Paris in the 1920s. I have found Jaap de Graaff purchasing the cello in Paris in 1928. Was he attracted by its romantic inscription? Perhaps he even took the two young Hungarians with him as he examined the instruments available at Maucotel's. Did Pál select the cello himself, hearing his own sound, his own soul, in its sonorous voice, or was it presented to him back in London when he returned for his next concert? We cannot know. But the sale in Paris marked the beginning of its 'years in the possession of a performing artist'.

Pál Hermann's name was erased from his Gagliano's story when Möller typed up the sales certificate in 1953, but that anonymous 'artist', buried in an unknown grave, indelibly left something of himself in the patterns of wear and tear on his cello's wooden body. And hours of his life were shaped by it, as he perfected his own technique in partnership with it. His name might be forgotten, but their performances, their artistry, are not.

And the cello has not forgotten him either. 'I am the soul of music', it tells us. But 'anima' is not simply 'soul'. It positions itself in a space somewhere between 'breath', 'life' and 'spirit'. In this little inscription, these few words, lies a resurrection. The cello holds the life, the breath of its player, and it reassures us that, while it breathes and plays, his spirit is not lost.

The Cello Through Silence to Sound I

As I renew my determination to find ways to play despite my injury, I discover that there is great inspiration to be had from cellists who have refused to be silenced, or have found the strength to accept their silencing with dignity, when it is inevitable. Amaryllis Fleming struggled to play all her life, but she was one of the greatest teachers of the twentieth century. Cigarette in mouth, she was by turns gracious and unpredictable, riotous and seraphic. My teacher Nick Roberts adored her. To me she has long been a name that hovered over the Royal College of Music – in whose Amaryllis Fleming recital hall I often played. I was always intrigued by her Christian name – that exotic, gramophone trumpet of a flower. Nick remembers that she had to practise in the most disciplined of routines every day of her career to be the great player she was. On some days she could play divinely. On others it was a titanic battle, and she combatted the stress of this lifelong fight with her instrument with nicotine and gin (with only a dash of tonic).

Eventually, Amo suffered a series of mini-strokes. The prognosis was that she would never walk again, and would remain in bed, in need of constant care. The thought must have been unimaginable to someone with such a fiery spirit. She hated the idea of being so curtailed, and of being separated from her cello. Rather than finding the sight of her cello in the corner of the room unbearable, she would lie in bed gazing at it, unreachable yet so tantalizingly close. Gradually she taught herself to sit up. Bit by bit, over weeks and months, she managed to recover some ability to walk. And muscle by muscle, she began the agonizing process of teaching her wasted and recalcitrant arms what her brain knew so well – how to play. Open strings at first, then gradually coaxing her fingers down, building up their strength, until she could play relatively well in tune. The bowing arm was harder, the bow shaking as it moved further away from the control of her hand, often juddering and dropping to the floor. But little by little, recognizable melodies emerged. She had triumphed. And to celebrate her victory, reclaiming herself and her music from near death, she invited all her doctors and carers to a private concert, as her way of thanking them for the help they had given her in her long struggle. She played pieces that a year or so before she would have considered easy, encore repertoire: Saint-Saëns's *The Swan*; some short Mendelssohn lollipops, including Cristiani's 'Song without Words'.

But the sense of triumph was enormous. Those who were there remember it as the most emotional playing they had ever witnessed. The concert nearly ended in tragedy when, as she played, she suffered at least two small heart attacks. Not to be deterred, she managed to regain control over her wavering bow, pushing onwards through the pain and dizziness to finish her last little recital.

The luthier Charles Beare recalled his final visit to her in hospital. She was a pitiful sight, wired up to monitors, unable to move. She clearly wanted to whisper to him, so he leant towards her. 'Cigarette,' she rasped. 'In my handbag, under the bed.' 'I remonstrated with her', he said. 'After all, it was a hospital.' But there was never any arguing with Amaryllis. 'So I found the packet, placed one between her lips, and lit it. I don't believe I've ever seen anyone look so content. Shortly after, a nurse came in, exclaimed in horror at the wreaths of smoke coming from her bed, and chased me out of the ward. I never saw Amo again.'

When I visited Charles, and he had proudly shown me his portrait of Amaryllis by Augustus John, we turned our attention to the opposite wall, where a photograph of Jacqueline du Pré hangs. His expression was nothing short of adoration. 'I *loved* Jackie,' he says. 'She used to call me from her hotel room, wherever she was. "Hello, Charles," she'd say. "What are you doing? How are things?" "They're fine, Jackie, but this is the middle of the night." She had no idea what time zone she was in, and she'd always be mortified. But I could never be cross with her for her nocturnal chats. And I could always guarantee it would happen again.' He smiled up at her, as if sharing a secret joke.

Jacqueline du Pré's career is one of the most beguiling, poignant stories in classical music. She was a legend to me as I grew up with her recordings, and leafed through the CD booklets with their pictures of her and her husband Daniel Barenboim laughing at the piano, or of her hair streaming as she threw herself at her cello.

There has rarely if ever been a player so naturally at ease with their instrument. Of course what appears natural is muscular effort; behind that spontaneity are thousands of hours of technical studies: Feuillard, Sevcik, Popper; scales; Bach; keeping in shape just as an athlete would. This is the analogy Natalie Clein uses to describe her consciousness of herself as a player: an athlete needing to be in peak performance condition, an identity completely separate from the one so often foisted upon a young and 'natural' female cellist.

When Jacqueline du Pré was offered the 'Davidoff' Stradivari by her wealthy godmother, her teacher, William Pleeth, told her it is 'one of the really great instruments of the world. The only thing is whether it suits you, and that you must decide for yourself.' She quickly fell in love with it, finding that it responded 'in a completely different way from any other cello she had played before. She loved experimenting with the way it produced sound and found that with the right kind of gentle coaxing it could offer an incredibly fine palette of colours.'[12]

Long before it was owned by Jacqueline du Pré and then by Yo-Yo Ma, the 'Davidoff' had come into the possession of the cellist Karl Davidoff in an extraordinary way:

> The late Czar, Alexander II used to give musical entertainments at his palace. On one occasion, Rubinstein, Wieniawsky, and Davidoff were present. A certain Count Wielhorsky (noted for his love of art and his absent-mindedness), received the artistes, when Davidoff at once noticed that the Count

was very nervous and excited. Asking what the matter was, Davidoff received the following answer: 'Today I celebrate my seventieth birthday, and in a way of my own, I present you with my Stradivarius violoncello.' Davidoff took this for a joke, but he very soon found out that the Count was quite in earnest. The music began, and after the first trio the emperor spoke to Wieniawsky, remarking upon the lovely tone of his violin, and asking him what make it was. 'A Stradivarius, your Majesty,' was Wieniawsky's answer, whereupon the emperor remarked to Wielhorsky 'You have also a Strad, have you not?' The count said 'No, your Majesty, I used to have one, but I gave it to-night to Carl Davidoff.' The new owner of the violoncello now saw that the count had indeed not been joking.[13]

Whatever cello Jacqueline du Pré played, her idiosyncratic technique and her absolute commitment to finding the colours she wanted meant that she brought her own sound to the instrument. But between 1965 and 1968, she played almost exclusively on the 'Davidoff'. In those recordings, her biographer Elisabeth Wilson believes that 'we can hear an extra luminous sheen in the cello sound, a result of the combination of an outstanding player and an incomparable instrument'.[14]

Jacqueline du Pré's playing was characterized by its spontaneity and fearless risk-taking, and the unpredictable 'Davidoff' was a perfect match for her. By 1970, however, she had begun to find the cello too much to manage. The instrument that had previously been a thrilling challenge had now become just too difficult and risky. Daniel Barenboim bought her a newly made cello by luthier Sergio Peresson. There was no way it could compare to one of the greatest instruments ever made, but she found herself preferring it to her beloved 'Davidoff'. No one could understand why she would forsake such an instrument. Can the relationship between player and cello be so sensitive that the instrument can detect an illness years before the player herself is aware of it? Later, she realized that her relationship with the 'Davidoff' had fallen apart when the beginnings of multiple sclerosis had set in. By the time she was twenty-eight, she had fallen silent.

Yo-Yo Ma believes that 'Jackie's unbridled dark qualities went against the "Davidoff". You have to coax the instrument. The more you attack it, the less it returns.' When I talked to the cellist Sebastian Comberti about Jacqueline du Pré's relationship to the 'Davidoff', he said his theory is that she simply made too many demands on the instrument, and as playing became more of a physical struggle for her this increased. There is only so much a cello can take, and her playing was so enthusiastic and full-blooded that a modern instrument, even if it was inferior, was better able to withstand the onslaught.

Jacqueline du Pré was an inspiration to me as a young teenage cellist, but the first cello I ever heard, aside from my own and my teacher's, was Julian Lloyd Webber's 'Barjansky' Stradivari. There was a preponderance of his recordings in my local library, and I used to take home armfuls of them, to make my own copies, labelling tapes wonkily with thin little stickers – 'Julian L-W – cello'. In tiny letters I wrote names that were hardly known to me as I copied them: Elgar, Dvořák, Shostakovich. One tape I recorded was a compilation of songs from Julian's brother's shows, adapted for cello – I had no concept that melodies from *Cats* were in any way different from the great concertos, only that the tunes were shorter than movements. I had neither been to a concert nor heard of a thing called a musical. Later on, when I found that Andrew Lloyd Webber's music actually had words and wasn't the exclusive domain of the cello, I was rather affronted.

After a forty-year career as a soloist, Julian finds his cello is now silent. To him, at any rate. When he experienced, mid-performance, a sudden loss of power in his right arm which was so bad that he could hardly hold onto his bow, he knew that his career as a cellist was over. He also knew that, for him, there was no middle ground between making his cello sing to the best of his ability, and its total silence.

The wear and tear of Julian's performing career on his body had resulted in a herniated disc in his neck. He learnt that it was pressing on a nerve, which was causing a loss of power in his arm. Doctors told him that he could have an operation, but with little guarantee of success and with high risks attached. He might lose his voice, they said, as they would have to cut through next to his voice box. He weighed up this impossible choice: to lose his career, and his voice as a cellist; or to risk his speaking voice, possibly even his life. He has a young daughter, a wife, responsibilities. He chose to sacrifice the cello.

When I go to talk to him about his cello, I am led into his office by his secretary, where I find Julian and his cellist wife waiting for me. Jiaxin Lloyd Webber is quietly spoken and shy, unassumingly elegant in a fur gilet. Julian greets me, and I am struck by the extraordinary quality of his piercingly blue eyes. They are an intriguing couple, hushed and thoughtful, gently welcoming. I begin the interview by asking them to introduce themselves in their own words. It's a little artificial, but I'm visiting them ostensibly to make a recording for the BBC, and it's always useful to splice an 'intro' into a recording. They dutifully do so. 'I'm Jiaxin, and I'm a cellist.' 'I'm Julian Lloyd Webber, and I'm an *ex*-cellist.' Julian gives a wan smile. He emphasizes the 'ex' with pragmatic courage, speaking briskly. It almost physically hurts me to hear it. I wonder how it must sound to them.

It is hardly surprising that Julian became a musician, being born to a composer and piano teacher, but he was the first string player in the family. He never got on with the piano, but when he was four he was taken to an orchestral children's concert at the Festival Hall, where he was transfixed by the cellos. It was love at first sight, and he appealed to his parents to let him have his own cello. When a tenth-size instrument was delivered to the house, it was a grave disappointment. He had expected a magnificent beast just like the ones he had seen on stage. This was practically a viola with a spike.

In 1983 a listing appeared in Sotheby's auction catalogue, with the picture of an exquisitely carved scroll next to it, akin to a side-on, head-and-shoulders mug shot. It was the famous 'Barjansky' Stradivari (dated on its label as 1684, though believed to have been made around 1690), and as soon as Julian saw it was for sale, he felt he had to try it.[15]

When he began to play the cello, he knew it was better than any instrument he'd ever touched. It was prohibitively expensive, but he decided he'd do anything to secure it. Almost overnight, the cello became his life, his passion, his identity. He mortgaged the house and put in his bid. Julian believes that he and the 'Barjansky' were destined to be together.

He found it quite hard to play in the early days, he tells me. It had so much personality, and every time he took it out of the case it was different. With the cello having languished in a bank vault for fifty years, he quickly realized that it was a matter of gently coaxing out the sound, waking it up day by day, winning its confidence and taming it as musician and instrument got used to each other.

The 'Barjansky' was to be his constant companion for the next thirty-one years. 'Being on stage under immense pressure after hundreds of hours of preparation is as intense as it gets. These are the moments that you share with your cello alone. Your metaphorical and actual travelling companion; you two against the world. There is a kind of supernatural relationship with the instrument: times when the cello carries you and tries to help you; times when you might not be on the best form, but the cello is. There were times when I would come off stage, put the cello back in its case and whisper "well done" to it as I wrapped it up for the night.'

Jiaxin sees her relationship with her own cello as a marriage. 'He might not be the best man...' (Julian interrupts her with a laugh) 'but he's yours, and you stick with him.'

Julian feels that his 'Barjansky' is a male instrument, with a masculine sound. Jiaxin's cello has a more feminine personality. When they played duets, their cellos fitted together. It was like a man and a woman talking to each other, Jiaxin remarks: their sounds are so different, and they had to work on blending them. Their cellos were two compatible but contrasting figures.

Jiaxin misses this aspect of their relationship – they can no longer play their marriage out through their music. Now Julian conducts her as a soloist, and she feels he understands her playing better than anyone else, but sometimes it's difficult: he's a very strong personality, she says. He denies this vehemently, but with a smile.

When he was forced to stop playing in 2014, Julian quickly realized that not only could he not bear to touch the 'Barjansky' again but that he would have to sell it. 'It was a very strange moment – to go from the good earnings of a successful soloist to being unemployed was quite frightening. Of course the cello was a financial asset, as well as a partner. And it should be played. The public has a right to hear its voice; it *needed* to be played.' The partnership between a cello and its player may be a marriage, but it is not for better or for worse, and it should last only as long as the player can offer the instrument what it needs.

I ask Julian to tell me when he first knew he had a problem.
'The problem first occurred in the middle of a recital. It

was during the first movement of John Ireland's Sonata – a work I love dearly. Suddenly I lost power in my right arm – I thought I was going to drop the bow. I had never experienced anything like it. I didn't know what was wrong or what to do. I was genuinely frightened. I struggled through to the end of the first half and immediately told my wonderful pianist, Rebeca Omordia, that I didn't think I could go on. Rebeca dealt with it in a clever and challenging way. She said "You can be an awkward bastard – don't tell me you can't even hold your bow!" But I still had to go to the concert organizer and tell him that I wasn't sure if I could complete the second half – after all, it was the Rachmaninov Sonata, where the cellist has to play "flat out" most of the time! That was a totally humiliating moment. Anyway, somehow I got through to the end and immediately phoned home to Jiaxin. She thought I might have been overplaying (I had just returned from a lengthy tour of China) but in my heart I knew it was something far worse than that.'

Meanwhile, Julian tried to pretend everything was normal. His manager was calling him with engagements he had always wanted to undertake, such as a performance of Shostakovich's First Cello Concerto in Moscow. 'I felt a fraud accepting the concerts but I was always hoping to find a cure.' By April 2014 he had to accept defeat when, during a rehearsal of the comparatively gentle Haydn C major Cello Concerto in St George's Hall, Bradford, he realized he wouldn't be able to get through the performance. 'My wife was with me – she cried more than I did. I called my manager and that was it. Our silent drive back from Bradford to London was emotionally shattering for both of us.'

At this point he falls silent. He wants me to hear Jiaxin's point of view, he says at last, but he is not yet ready to hear her talk about it. He gets up, and quietly leaves the room.

Jiaxin explains to me that they have still never discussed what happened that evening. When she relives it, she clutches at her arms spontaneously. 'It was a terrible night,' she says earnestly. Julian had explained to her that they had to leave in the interval, and they loaded their two cellos into the back of the car. They drove home in silence. There was nothing to say. Both knew that it was the end of everything for him.

Julian's final performance as a cellist was on 2 May 2014 in Malvern with the English Chamber Orchestra. After the concert, he went through the motions that every cellist has undertaken countless times before. The opening of the case ready to receive its inhabitant, wrapping the cello's body lovingly in the cloth that protects it from scratches, swaddling it, enshrouding it. Putting the instrument away is part of the ritual of ending practice or performance. These actions are often automatic, the marking of the distinction between the sounds of music-making and the silence after the instrument has been put down. This time, the rituals took on a dream-like significance. He could not yet face talking to anyone about what he now knew to be his future. He had not even articulated it to himself, but knew from the subtle, felt relationship between his own body and his Stradivari that his injury was simply too great a barrier, and that he no longer had the strength to play. Only his cello shared his secret for that moment. He wrapped it slowly, carefully, and laid it in the case for the last time. 'Sleep well,' he said. He has never heard it or seen it since, nor has he played again.

Jiaxin has to practise at home when he's around. I ask her whether it's hard for him to hear her, when she can express herself through her cello but he can no longer do the same.

She thinks about it. 'He just shuts the door when I'm practising,' she says. 'He hides his emotions very well.'

At that moment, Julian rejoins us. The three of us sit in thoughtful silence. Eventually, I ask him whether he ever wonders where his cello is now, or who is playing it.

No, he doesn't know where his 'Barjansky' is now. He chokes on its name and a tear makes its way slowly down his cheek. He doesn't know who has it, or even if it is being played.

Such a famous Stradivari would not be hard to track down, I point out.

He agrees. He believes it might be in New York.

But does he want to know?

He pauses to think about it. 'No,' he says quietly. He'd rather not. He played his part in its life, and now it would sound different in new hands. It would not be his sound anymore. 'It's like your partner has moved on to a new relationship. It's too painful to know whether they're happy or not, or whether they're missing you. They've got their own new life, but you're left with the silence where they used to be.' However unbearable the thought of hearing it again, the thought of it not being played is worse.

Hampstead, London –
The 'Open-String' Cello

April 2022

All through my travels I have asked myself who we are without our instruments. Now, with the help of Robert Brewer Young and the resources of the Hills's workshop, I have the opportunity to bring instruments to players who have never had them. The cellos we are hoping these children will be able to make will hold a story not of the past but of their future. The 'Open-String cello' is a strange hybrid: a modern-day resurrection that uses new technology alongside ancient instrument patterns, and recycled pieces of other instruments.

Fifty years ago, the fragments of the 'Mara' were laid out on the workbenches of W. E. Hill & Sons. Today, the luthiers at Hill's are drawing up plans to map out a new kind of cello that can be shipped to Rosario in pieces. In Argentina, only 300 kilometres from where the 'Mara' was reduced to fragments, there is a youth orchestra in desperate need of good-quality instruments. Rosario is the city the Trieste Piano Trio were heading for when fate intervened. From fragments of other derelict and destroyed instruments, Robert Brewer Young and Jason Reitenberger (head technician and engineer at Hill's) hope to create something new – a flat-pack cello that is designed in such a way that it will have the sound of a superb-quality instrument.

∽

The youth orchestra in Rosario is drawn from players in one of the roughest areas of the city. Drug use and gun warfare

are part of the fabric of a harsh and impoverished existence. The children who join the orchestra must pledge not to get involved in gang conflict. In return, they and their families become part of a larger, safer community. As one teacher put it, having an instrument case slung over your shoulder is like 'wearing a bullet-proof vest'. However, there are few resources. One cello is shared between multiple children – they have to book their turn on it to practise.

Alongside his day job working with the most valuable instruments in the world, Robert has gone from luthier to luthier, looking for pieces of wood to be repurposed. He turns up with an empty box and leaves with old fingerboards, bridges, tailpieces and gently used strings, the stray old bones of instruments. He then goes to tree fellers and takes away spare tone wood, storing up his foraged spoils ready to recycle them for new instruments for the Rosario orchestra. The cellos will have a front and back manufactured by machine. Robert and Jason worked with the Engineering Faculty at Cambridge on their five-axis Computer Navigated Cutting machine to be able to cut out and reproduce their designs for parts of the new cellos. The meticulously precise axes are controlled by computer. From their coordinates they can punch out the front and back of the instruments. These machines can be manufactured relatively cheaply and sent to Argentina, so that with a minimum of training the students in Rosario can start to make the cellos themselves, crafting their own instruments.

The 'Open-String' cellos are odd-looking prefabs, more chimera than cello. They are guitar-shaped, as rounded sides are cheaper and simpler to produce than a cello's pointed, scalloped sides. And the new cellos have flat backs like guitars to simplify the design and save money. As with every design alteration, there is a historical precedent for this feature: there is in fact a Stradivari cello – known, unimaginatively, as 'the Flat-back Stradivari' – which might originally have been intended as a five-stringed instrument or a viola da gamba. It's still played today, albeit with a curved back that Hill & Sons made for it some years ago.

One of the great boasts of this new generation of instruments is that, from their position at the cutting edge of engineering, they reach a hand back through time. While the reasons for radically redesigning the string family are cost-driven and practical, all have a foot in history, and a rationale. The result is an instrument that looks space-age. Alongside the rounded sides and flat back, the scroll is one of the most distinctive changes. The bottom of the scroll, known as the peg box, is now hollow, leaving the pegs visible from both back and front, like the structure of a leaf skeleton. This backless peg box is a feature of some historic instruments. In this context, it makes it easier for young hands to string the cello, the pegs being more accessible. Above them, instead of a scroll curled like a snail or fern-head, there is a simple but elegant carved shape, rather like the opening out of a square trumpet bell. It wouldn't look out of place in a contemporary art gallery, but the design is not in fact modern, being inspired by Stradivari's drawings in the Museo del Violino of a viola d'amore's pyramid-shaped scroll. In Berlin I saw a similar scroll on an arpeggione (an early bowed instrument that looks like a guitar, with six strings and frets).[16]

What *is* new, however, is that these cellos will be so carefully designed that they will not sound like cheap, self-assembled instruments, but will be conservatoire quality, good enough for the children to play professionally, if they choose to. Robert is adamant that the young players should not be limited by poor-quality factory instruments with pegs that pop out and lose their tuning, and from which it's impossible to coax a good sound.

Two prototypes have already been made: a violin and a cello. But the large-scale production of this new species must wait until we can be sure that the design is perfect. 'We make these instruments with no idea how they're going to work,' admits Robert. 'But what has surprised us most with the two instruments we have so far, is how good they sound. *Disruptively* good.'

There are women in the orchestral programme who have already been taught how to make and re-hair bows, and bamboo planted locally could grow within four years to be strong enough for bow sticks. The aim is for the orchestra to become self-sufficient, the wood for their instruments foraged or home-grown. The young cellists will be able to punch out the front and back pieces of their cellos and create their own instruments in a matter of weeks. However, until we have tried and tested the new model, it is impossible to know what these strange new instruments will sound like, or how hard it will be for someone with no training to construct them. And this is where I come in. Under the very close supervision of Robert and Jason, I will attempt to make my own Open-String cello, the very first made by a non-professional from start to finish.

～

The workshop of W. E. Hill & Sons is tucked away on a little cobbled street in leafy Hampstead. In the attic, under great triangular windows, are the benches of the luthiers. Huge piles of wood shavings like cut hair at a barber's are swept into a corner. Chamber music bubbles from a transistor radio on a shelf. At the workbench, Jason is carving a shape out of a rectangle of wood. He puts down his chisel and hands the wood to me. He claims it is spruce, but it feels all wrong – the weight not tessellating with what I see. 'It's been compressed,' he explains, delighted by my confusion. He says that he is trying to make a sustainable alternative to ebony, which is particularly dense. By squashing spruce, he can make it strong enough to carve a cello's fingerboard out of it. But before we can think about perfecting the fingerboard, we need to create the front and back of our new cello.

It takes roughly three hundred hours to make a standard cello and a hundred and fifty hours to make a violin. Varnishing can take up to a further hundred hours, depending on how obsessive you are about the antiquing process. With the machine that Jason and the Cambridge engineers have developed, we are able to produce a cello plate for our new instrument in less than four hours. Had we carved it by hand this might have taken us a week. The shapes of the F holes have been cut by the machine, but at this stage they are still just outlines full of wood. This cello is waiting to be born, its eyes shut and its wood wrinkled, with the grain and the thin lines from the machine implanted on its surface.

The cello's front and back need to become completely smooth, and so I set to work in my denim pinafore apron, with little rounded brass planes that fit neatly between thumb and forefinger, and vary in size from a tiny to a substantial mouse. When Jason and Robert demonstrate, their hands sweep effortlessly over the front of the instrument. When I try, the blade catches or hardly makes a connection. I have to learn to feel what the wood wants me to do, and listen to what it's telling me. The cello guides the process of its own birth. A cello can tell you things you didn't already know, and this one is communicating both through touch and through sound. After a while I find that when the plane judders, it's just like a tense bowing arm that is not free, preventing flow and movement. If I had understood what my instrument and my body were telling me, all those years ago, would I have sustained such a serious injury? Instead of a bow, I hold a plane in my right hand, and in the stroking movements as I guide it across the body of the cello I am finding a new way of existing in harmony with the instrument. But it is still surprisingly difficult to get this right, and I am shocked to find how de-skilled I am. In a language of up and down bow strokes, I have suddenly become a stumbling, stuttering foreigner.

Soon it is time to add the purfling: thin black and white strips that wind round the outline of the cello's body. The purfling's purpose is largely decorative, but it also acts as a buffer to stop any cracks at the fragile edges from reaching further into the heart of the instrument. In effect, it is a highly attractive firebreak. Jason holds up three unprepossessing lumps of wood – two pear and one poplar. These are planed and then shaved into thin, noodle-like strips. The two pear strips are dyed black or dark blue, and sandwiched together with the poplar to make a black–white–black sandwich of wood, so thin it could be paper (indeed, in the case of Pál Hermann's Gagliano, it actually is).

We measure how many of these brittle strands it will take to get around the cello, and Jason shows me how to cut the ends at an angle with a sharp little knife, so they will interlock. It is similar to the technique of grafting a cutting from a plant or tree. I half expect him to tell me that we dip the little strips in rooting powder before planting.

Next we embark on something that resembles questionable cookery more than gardening. A little copper pan forms a bain-marie for a jam jar of disgustingly yellow glue (a pungent combination of bones and cow hide). As this bubbles on the primus, Jason shows me how to stroke the purfling strips with a fragment of washing-up sponge, coaxing them into remembering their innate, wooden flexibility. Once damp they become more pliable, though also more likely to separate into soggy threads, so we need to work quickly. We take it in turns, one of us running a pipette of hot bone glue along the little channel prepared for the purfling, while the other squeezes in the strip as quickly and as accurately as possible, then taps it into its groove with what resembles a little toffee hammer.

The children in Rosario who make these cellos will be learning to glue and hammer traditional purfling, or indeed any other material they would like to use, such as copper wire, but the whole process is a world away from the complications of making a standard cello. Normally, you would have to cut the thin purfling strips to fit the points of the body of the instrument, but with our simple rounded sides we just coax and bend them into a smooth pear shape, no difficult spikes to negotiate. I am delighted to learn that the sharp points at the side of a traditional cello's purfling are known as the 'bee sting'. I am taken back momentarily to the buzz of the bees circling around my bow as I played them Bach.

Once the purfling is in place, we head down to the workshop kitchen to wash the cello's front: a baptismal ritual to welcome it into the world, with the practical result of removing the excess wet glue. When it is dry, I stroke carefully round it with a little curved chisel, my face almost level with the front of the instrument as I carve off the tiny black and white peelings, until the purfling is absolutely flush with the wood of the instrument. What until an hour ago was only a suggestion of a cello, a shapely piece of tree lying flat on a bench, has suddenly transformed into a piece of art, delineated and set apart by the thinnest of black and white frames.

Although our curved cello face looks great from the front, inside it is still thick and flat, and needs hollowing out in order for its sound to have any resonance. As a player, I am intimately acquainted with the sloping surfaces of the exterior of a cello's front and back. But it is only as I chisel away that I start to understand the curving of the wood differently, experiencing it anew and intimately through the motions of my arms, shaping the unseen inside of its body.

I am using a vast, neanderthal chisel, with a great rugged handle the width of the neck of a cello. It looks like it would be more at home in a museum of hunter-gatherers' tools than a twenty-first-century workshop. Moving my whole body from the hips, holding the chisel into my torso and twisting it to curl out swirls of great wood chips is extremely hard

work, at least if you are as inexperienced as I am. And it's nerve-wracking. You must trust in your judgement, and in your understanding of the curvature of the wood. Once the front is upside down and lying in a brace, you cannot see how deep the curve is. And if you dig fractionally too far and stick the chisel through the front, the cello is ruined. I must stop millimetres away from the outside of the wood, leaving it flexible but sturdy.

Now it's time to 'tune' the front, a process that is one of the most nebulous and intriguing elements of instrument making. In my world, the process of tuning your cello involves listening to an A and tweaking the strings until they are a perfect A, D, G and C. To a luthier working on a half-finished instrument, it means something entirely different, as they listen to the sound of the wood as it is tapped and knocked. No one can really agree what pitch they are listening for when they undertake this mystical process, but they think they know when they've found it. The most I can get from Robert and Jason is that tapping an F sharp around the shoulders tends to be promising. At the moment, when I tap, the resonant knocking is nearer a G. I scrape away a fraction more of the inside of the front, until I've lowered it by a semitone. The hips reveal a lower note, a B flat to my ears. The pitch that we might tap changes depending on how big the instrument is, but most luthiers will have an idea of the range of pitch they are looking for. Others, however, will be more interested in how the wood bounces when you hold it on different node lines. Either way, it's all rather academic, because when you glue the ribs on to the front, the pitch will change.

When we create an instrument, we hone the sound to resemble the one we imagine for it, invariably that of the human voice. And the voices we are surrounded by are those that we will emulate. Different languages focus on different vowel sounds. And so do instruments. In Cremona I had watched a luthier shifting the soundpost of a particularly nasal French violin. He lowered it for a minute and looked at me. 'Did you know that European instruments have European accents? A French instrument sounds nasal, a German one is harsher, with more consonants, and Italian instruments sing *bel canto*.'

It's possible to run a pitch through a piece of wood, and watch tea leaves or iron filings jump into patterns. Those patterns will change if you shave the wood a little on one side. But which pattern means a good-sounding instrument? No one knows. To complicate matters further, every piece of wood has a different voice, even if they are from the same tree: a piece from higher up will have a different diameter, and the grain will be smaller. The 'tuning' process makes us feel we have some purchase over its sound, but the wood isn't going to reveal its voice that easily. It is only when we finally play the finished instrument that we really learn what music the wood holds within it.

                         ~

I have sanded and smoothed the back, and it is time to fit the ribs. The machine has cut two little channels around the front and back for them to slot into. This is a Flemish technique, making it much easier to assemble. I am intrigued by whether the thickness of the wood is related to the sound quality of the instrument. The cello ribs used by Guarneri 'del Gesù' were very thick compared to Stradivari's, and Brescian ribs were even more so. It's all to be experimented with. Our cello's ribs seem almost horrifyingly thin to me. I feel I don't know my own cello as well as I thought I did. It is impossible to tell from the outside of a cello just how flimsy these solid-seeming pieces are.

I hold up the two wooden shapes that will become the ribs, which look like scarves waving perpetually in the wind. They need some coaxing to be slotted into the grooves around the cello's back. This coaxing takes the form of a sponge bath, followed by careful bending around a curling tong, which has been heating up on the corner of the bench. They sizzle like burning hair, but smell pleasingly like the pine wood of a sauna, transporting me for a moment back to the snowy forests of Suwalki.

When the wood and glue are dry, we add the first of many coats of varnish. The children's varnish will be a simple recipe, with none of the rare ingredients I encountered in Cremona, basting their handiwork in a queasy concoction of egg white, walnut oil and meat preserver.

                         ~

When I was in Cremona, the luthiers Massimo and Abraham opened up a little instrument museum at the heart of the violin-making school to show me the treasures hidden inside.

Alongside the expected gambas and viols, ornately decorated and hanging in their glass cases, were some of the most unusual instruments in existence: violins with no F holes; violins with the F holes in the back; triangular instruments – a freak show of mutants made over the years by the school's teachers and students. Some are modern experiments, but many are actual historical instruments, from the medieval rebec onwards. None of them, in Abraham's view, is better than Stradivari's cellos and violins. When I asked him why this was, Abraham looked at me as if I were quite mad. 'It's like asking why the violin has stopped evolving. It's because it's the perfect model. It can't be bettered.'

I run this theory past Robert and Jason. Are there elements of our new Open-String design that have improved on the design of the conventional cello? The purfling is infinitely simpler to fit, the pegs easier to turn; the front and back take far less time to create; and the instrument can be made available to people who could never dream of owning an old Italian cello. Have we actually bettered the hitherto unimprovable?

Robert puts down his chisel and thinks for a moment. 'The question really is, what is a cello *for*? What purpose are we serving in making one, and how does that relate to the construction? By taking the cello's corners away, we've improved on the design from the point of view of the maker, but what about the player?'

I think back to the serpentine experience of playing the curvy prototype. In terms of an improvement, the traditional cello cannot serve communities without access to resources in the way that this one can. In terms of construction, we're trying to open up the specialist process of instrument making to non-professionals. That could be called an improvement. But are we improving aesthetics or acoustics, or a combination of both?

Perhaps Stradivari has the last word, but on what? Certainly not on making music more accessible, as he himself worked for the wealthiest members of the church and for royalty. If it is all about sound, then it's difficult to explain away the fact that modern instruments frequently beat older ones in a blind listening contest. But do we agree on what it is we're listening for? We can be moved in a different way by a great old instrument, as I found when I heard the 'Cristiani'. We are hearing its story, as well as its sound.

⌇

Even if a cello is separated from its biography, as in the case of Pál Hermann's Gagliano, it carries its own story within its wood. It tells of the place it grew, of the climate, of the shocks it endured. The knots in the wood tell us about how low or high the tree's branches were, whether or not it was in a thick canopy and had to reach high for the sun.

What stories will our new hybrid cellos tell? Using block chain technology, Robert and Jason want to be able to follow the lives of these cellos, given for free and never sold, as they accumulate their own stories. The technology can communicate the information to make the instrument, but it also has the capacity for the player to log their relationship to their cello, like a digital diary. How has the instrument affected them? What is their life together with their newly constructed companion like? The cello's biography travels with it as it is handed on to its next player. 'It will be the equivalent of an instrument passport,' says Jason. These instruments can, hopefully, never be separated from their story, or the story of their maker and players. I can't help thinking that if Anita's Ventapane or Pál Hermann's Gagliano had had such 'instrument passports', and had carried their block chain stories with them, I would be able to track them. 'But maybe the mystery and the appeal would vanish?' suggests Jason. On reflection, perhaps he's right.

We leave our nearly finished cello resting on its side in the workshop, and I imagine the children who will be making the next ones, shaped in its image. They will plane and polish, learning to use their hands in a new way, following their cellos from lumps of timber to crafted instruments. As players we often feel we're custodians, not owners, of our instruments. When the top is taken off a cello, we're glimpsing a different world – the world of their makers. But these young musicians will have a deep, physical understanding of the fragility and craftsmanship of their instruments, tuning the cellos' sound to reflect their own voices, carving themselves indelibly into the bodies of their new creations. They will be both makers and players.

Sanding and planing at my workbench, I find myself reflecting on the photo session, months ago now, that was part of the stimulus for this book. My initial gaucheness, and the sudden ease I felt once I was united with my cello. Since that afternoon, I have travelled, played and listened. I have come to realize that my silhouette has been missing the shape of a cello for most of my adult life. Now, as I leave the Hampstead workshop, I feel I have begun to understand the cello from the inside out, from the beginnings of design to the final varnish strokes. I might not yet have succeeded in finding Pál Hermann's Gagliano, but in making the Open-String cello I have begun to create a new soul, a cello that will become the locus for future stories and connections through its music. The instrument I leave on the workbench is waiting to become another player's shadow. Over the last few months, I have come closer to completing the cello-shaped hole in my own.

Coda

Oxford – The Sand Cello

The Canadian neuroscientist Professor Robert Zatorre has researched how we experience music in silence, and our ability to continue a phrase in our minds even after the actual music has stopped. This, he explains, is because neural activity takes place in the auditory cortex when anyone imagines a piece of music. We have our own internal concerts, our personal stock of repertoire we can perform silently to ourselves at any time. But for instrumentalists, there is another layer of response when music is imagined. By mapping the activity in the brain when a musician imagines a piece they have played, he found that the physical experience of playing is replicated in the brain, even if the body remains still.[17] Specific activity in the primary motor regions of the brain sends messages to the fingers that would play each note, to the muscles that would control the movement of the bow. In other words, our instruments and the experience of playing them are hardwired into our brains.[18] I think of Jacqueline du Pré, in her wheelchair, her brain still sending the signals to her arms whenever she imagined the opening chords of the Elgar.

And Prof. Zatorre has discovered something else, still more extraordinary. He has found that when a musician has a close relationship to a specific instrument, as Pál Hermann had to his Gagliano, they imagine the *specific* sound of that instrument in its absence. Even when physically separated, a musician's instrument is embedded in the connections between brain and limbs, enabling it to be played at any time in their imagination. I am deeply moved by this thought. It means that, even after Pál Hermann was separated from his cello, right up until his death his cello was with him. Even in silence there is music, resistance, resurrection.

⁓

With the greatest reluctance, I have to admit to myself that, for now at least, I cannot find the Gagliano. I will not give up. I believe it is being played somewhere, but I feel I must write to Corrie Hermann to tell her that, after a year of searching, I have not been able to trace her father's cello. This was a letter I had hoped never to have to send. Her reply, however, is unexpected. She acknowledges my efforts with her usual generosity and warmth, but in addition sends me a photograph of a little sculpture made by the Belarussian-French artist Ossip Zadkine (1888–1967). It is not a sculpture that can be found in any auction house catalogue or museum. It exists in this image only. It is a sculpture made from sand, capturing a moment in its shapes and gestures, but never intended to last.

Ossip Zadkine probably met Pál Hermann and the de Graaff family when he was exhibiting his paintings and sculptures in Roots Gallery in London in 1928, the same year that Jaap de Graaff purchased the Gagliano for Pál. He became friendly with the family, and was staying at the beach house in Ouddorp in 1937, where he watched Pál practise. This was four years after Ada had died following the accident on Ouddorp beach. Taking mud and sand from the beach, Zadkine sculpted a maquette of Pál and his Gagliano, perfectly capturing the swaying movement, the rounded embrace of instrument and player in the moment of making music together.

The sand sculpture, photographed by Louise Bachiene.

A decade later, Ossip Zadkine's work would come to sym-
bolize all that nearby Rotterdam had lost in the war. His
anguished sculpture *De Verwoeste Stad* (The Demolished
City), stands 6.5 metres high, and features a man with his
arms flailing outstretched, his heart missing. It has been in the
Centre of Rotterdam since 1953, a monument for a city, but
also for the talented young Jewish man he had known there,
who, unlike Ossip himself, did not escape in time.

Ossip's beach sculpture of Pál was a shaping of sound and
movement into something solid, but still transient. Like the
maquette, Pál himself and now his cello have vanished, as
if they too were made of nothing more solid than grains of
sand. But when, in 1941, Ossip thought back to Pál and that
pre-war summer, he made another statue, this time one that
was intended to last.[19] Forced into exile in America by the

Nazi occupation, Ossip returned repeatedly to the figure of a harlequin to express his sorrow and frustration at the destruction of the Europe he and Pál had known. 'I had roared like a harlequin in my solitude, and no one heeded me.'[20]

Looking at Corrie's photograph of the sand cello, I can see that Zadkine's terracotta statue known as *Le second personage* or *Arlequin assis au violoncelle*, is so clearly influenced

Arlequin assis au violoncelle.

by his original impression of Pál Hermann as to be almost a copy. I think what Corrie is trying to tell me is that, through Ossip Zadkine's art, something of the sound and movement of her father's cello playing will remain animated forever. As Ossip himself said:

The object, whether it is a book, a bottle, or a human body, once it is visualised and expressed by means of clay, stone, or wood, ceases to be a document and becomes an animated object in stone, wood or bronze, and lives its independent life [...] These animated, independent objects are meant to vibrate through their plastic and poetic symbolism.[21]

I must finally make my peace with the absence of Pál Hermann's Gagliano.

INTERLUDE

The Cello Through Silence
to Sound II

Silence is a collective abbreviation for a whole array of musical absences: the absence of sound, sounds never made, the absence of those who should have made them, sounds too quiet to be heard, sounds delayed or postponed indefinitely. Silence is the opposite of music, but it is also its lifeblood – the breaths between the phrases, the drama, the anticipation, and the quality of the breathless hush between final note and applause. Music embraces calm silences, pregnant silences, animated or aggressive silences. Musical silence can be temporal, gestural or spatial. In some cases, such as John Cage's famously curated silence, *4 Minutes 33 Seconds*, silence even *becomes* music. Without sound there cannot be silence, and vice versa.

A cello implies by its mere existence the capacity for sound. It is shaped to contain resonating air, its F holes exist to allow the sound out. The beauty we perceive when we look at it as a work of craftsmanship is not that of a cabinet or sculpture, but of an object designed to be heard. But for the majority of the time a cello is silent. There is the graveyard silence surrounding a dusty old instrument abandoned in an attic, entirely different from that of an instrument put down temporarily in a music room but shortly to be played again. Then there is the silence of a house where a cello used to be played, the canvas cello case left behind in Breslau, whose owner had been deported.

Trying to listen to musical silence is like 'deliberately studying the spaces between trees in a forest: somewhat perverse at first, until one realizes that these spaces contribute to the perceived character of the forest itself, and enable us to speak coherently of "dense" growth or "sparse" vegetation'.[22] But it is precisely this silence that Yo-Yo Ma listens to when he plays Bach.

On 25 June 2020, Yo-Yo Ma came to Oxford to hear students play chamber music. He was without his cello – he had brought his ability to listen, not his ability to play. After he had made the generous, encouraging comments that are typical of him, he told the students about his Silk Road Project, which had involved travelling across six continents to take the Bach unaccompanied Cello Suites to deeply troubled communities. This was far from a standard recital tour. He played in war zones, at contested borders, and for communities who struggled to find a language with which to communicate. He intended to offer his music as a way of opening up a conversation. 'This is what I do, can we sit down and talk? It is a listening tour. I like to listen to what people say, and then we find the communalities.'

For Ma, Bach is the vehicle for these kinds of conversations. An accompanied piece is a dialogue between piano and cello. But unaccompanied Bach is a duet between cello and silence. The cello shapes the silence, frames it, presents it between its phrases, paints its quality – restful, surprising, active, expectant. The many-coloured silences that Ma creates during the kaleidoscope of short dances pass by, and at the end, as he lowers his bow, the silence that settles becomes his. He then puts down his cello to listen.

Yo-Yo Ma is describing a very particular kind of silence, shaped by his sound. Susan Sontag maintains that,

> A genuine emptiness, a pure silence is not feasible – either conceptually or in fact. If only because the artwork exists in a world furnished with many other things, the artist who creates silence or emptiness must produce something dialectical: a full void, an enriching emptiness, a resonating or eloquent silence. Silence remains, inescapably, a form of speech (in many instances, of complaint or indictment) and an element in a dialogue.[23]

Yo-Yo Ma's silence, like Susan Sontag's, is one that invites connection and conversation, a form of speech, and even a form of music, perhaps. Jacqueline du Pré repeatedly returned to another kind of celloistic silence in her teaching. It was towards the end of her life, and she was already confined to her wheelchair, trapped both within her own silence and with the sounds of her disability. 'Don't let the sound of your wheels drive you mad', she wrote in her notebook. She listened to others' sound, helping to shape their playing. While she taught, she sang and tried to shape through her gestures the music that she would herself have made. Cellist Matthew Sharp was one of her pupils, brought to play to her at the age of twelve.

'Make the note stretch into infinity', she told him, and he has never forgotten it. When I met up with him, I asked Matthew what he thought she meant. He picked up his cello and demonstrated what she showed him. A negative space, as the silences in music are sometimes described, became for Jacqueline du Pré a positive one. She was refusing to distinguish between the end of the note and the silence beyond.

The Cellist, a ballet inspired by Jacqueline's life and created by choreographer Cathy Marston for the Royal Ballet, has at its centre a shattering absence both of sound and of movement. The crisis point comes when the dancer depicting Jacqueline stands upstage with her back to us, ready to begin a recital. At this point the orchestra falls silent, for the first time in the performance. Their silence carves out a palpable, pregnant hush. We watch the dancer as she holds her bowing arm out, fully extended, as if she were to begin the recital on a long up bow. Everyone's attention, both on stage and in the 'real' audience, is focused on that arm. Her silence is observed from all sides. But she does not move. And for a matter of seconds that seem like minutes, she remains in that pose, her imagined bow frozen in the air, unable to begin the music, or break the silence. Then her arm begins to shake, and she lowers it awkwardly to her side.

The silence before the shaking begins is carefully curated. In the rehearsal studio I watch as Cathy Marston and her prima ballerina experiment with the length of this crucial moment. How long can an audience be held breathless, and how long can dancers remain motionless? I think back to the real Jacqueline du Pré's advice to the young Matthew Sharp. The irony of this note is that infinity is what begins it, and it is never heard.

Matthew and I experiment with playing in silence. Bows poised over the strings, trying to listen to the music after the sound has ended. Looking at a cellist with their bow held in stasis above the instrument, our eyes see sound, or at least its potential, even when our ears hear silence. This, I realize, is why the audience watching the ballet cannot bear for the shaking of the dancer's arm to begin. It must be postponed as long as possible, not only for extra dramatic effect, but because once the terrible movements of uncontrolled muscles begin, and trigger the orchestra's anguished wails, the infinite possibilities that the poised, unplaying bowing arm represent are shut down for ever. The writer Adrienne Rich once said that 'The impulse to create begins – often terribly and fearfully – in a tunnel of silence.'[24]

Thinking back once again to Jacqueline du Pré's words to Matthew, I cannot shake off the impression that, in adversity, she found a way of using silence as a resistance to *being* silenced. Silence 'never ceases to imply its opposite and to depend on its presence'.[25] Jacqueline's insistence on silence, travelling on into infinity, cannot exist without sound, its opposite. If the bow never stops moving, the music can never end, even when the strings are still.

When I first lost the use of my arm, I often thought of my fascination as a young girl with the story of the early twentieth-century British cellist Beatrice Harrison. I had found her memoir in my local library alongside Jacqueline du Pré's recordings, and read, transfixed, as she described how she had once continued playing a concert despite a terrible hand injury, her fingers bleeding onto the neck of the cello, slipping in her own blood as she shifted between notes. It was both ghoulish and compelling. I wanted to push past my injury, to show I too could be as resilient as Beatrice. But whenever I put my hand on the neck of the cello and tried to depress the strings, the sensation of weakness and the burning through my arm were simply too much.

Now I find that the more I talk to musicians who have struggled, the more I understand that even having the possibility of continuing to play is a privilege. Some cellists are permanently silenced. For others, to play is a continual struggle, but a struggle that is an inspiration, and one that I can learn from.

While in Berlin, I spent an afternoon playing to the first principal cellist of the Berlin Philharmonic Orchestra. Ludwig Quandt has a deep understanding of cello technique, but also of how to adapt it creatively when playing is a challenge.

In 2008, after some heavy gardening, cutting and digging, he started to experience a sharp pain in the palm of his right hand. A brief period of rest did not help it. Eventually, he had exploratory surgery and was told that the median nerve was damaged. After two years of going from one specialist to another, and being given multiple diagnoses, it was too late for it to regain its function. It had been dead for too long.

The median nerve controls the muscles that allow you to flex the thumb, so he couldn't hold the bow. 'I tried to play,' he explains to me, 'but it flew out of my hand. Sometimes in louder passages I tried to grab it in a fist. But it was hopeless. Really dreadful. I didn't know whether I had to give everything up. And I had twenty years still ahead of me leading this fabulous orchestra.'

Eventually, he found an ingenious way of working around his injury. 'Once I realized the answer was in a Japanese bike shop, I could rebuild my life.'

'I'm sorry – what?' He holds out his bow to me by way of explanation. On it are loops of stretchy pink rubber, the same thickness as spaghetti, and very strong.

'I found my system to survive on the cello. Japanese bicycle rubber. It's very primitive, but it's also cheap. You have to buy it in Japan, in strips of two metres. I cut it to length. It's from the valve to stop the air escaping. Between the pump and the inner tyre.'

I asked him how on earth he found it. 'I was touring around to find rubber, in more or less the same colour as skin, that lasts for more than a couple of days. I tried everything. Then a fan of the orchestra wrote to me after an Asian tour, and suggested this stuff, from the bicycle department of the shop Tokyo Hands. She sent me a box. I loop it round the frog of the bow, and tie my last two fingers into it.'

I try it, looping the rubber around the bow with Ludwig's help, then winding three loops around my two last fingers. It forces my hand backwards, taking the control away from the first finger. It feels very disempowering, the bow controlling the hand, not the other way round. There is no pressure on my thumb, with the result that the bow skates around uncontrolled on the string when I try to play.

'To start with it hurt to play like this,' says Ludwig, 'and the balance had to be refound, but now, it works. You get used to it.'

I ask him how different playing feels since his injury.

'In the past, when I played, I had the feeling that wow, it was flying. Sometimes you feel that it is *beherrschen* – it feels light, you can do something in a really good way. But after the injury, never. There is always this limitation, that kills a lot of the joy of playing. But I love the music itself. For me, it doesn't matter what instrument I play. It is not "the cello the cello, the cello" for me. It is about the music, and I can still express it, I can still make the variety of colours and voices, the characters I want to create. I've survived fourteen years like this, and have another six years left with the orchestra. What comes after, I don't know. But it won't be gardening.'

I tell him about my own arm injury, and how I have never found a really satisfactory way of working around it. Playing a baroque cello helped evade it, but its limitation has always been a cloud hanging over me, and for periods in my life has stopped me playing altogether. I explain that, finally, I'm determined to try to overcome it.

'It's never too late,' Ludwig says. 'I was forty-seven when I had my injury.' He hands me his Rogeri cello to play. It's a rich chestnut colour, with a sound that seems to leap out of it as soon as the bow touches the string.

As I play, Ludwig walks slowly around me, as if I'm an exhibit in a museum. Eventually he speaks. 'What I see in every down bow is that you lift your shoulder. There is no reason for it. Down bows don't require your shoulder to move.'

Have I always done this? I don't know. I played instinctively when I was younger.

'It is a lot of extra work for the body, with no justification. Sabotage, basically. And it will affect your left arm also.'

I play again. Apparently it's much better. As soon as I bring my awareness to it, it stops. But now when I change bow, there is apparently a sudden extraneous movement. It's so odd. Why do our bodies behave in these ways, thinking there are movements that are necessary when they aren't?

The tension in my shoulders affects all the nerves down my arms. Ludwig observes that, when I play, my head and shoulder are trying to come together, as if they are being pulled by shortened muscles. 'It feels like your back is looking for, I don't know. Stability?'

I mention that I was born with a scoliosis in my spine, which I hadn't known about until it was diagnosed in my mid-twenties.

'Ah!' he says. 'Maybe that's the deeper reason of this whole problem.' Even when I speak, he observes, my shoulder is working all the time. 'I see it, and I wonder. Because that's the region where the pain comes from.'

With the right specialist help, and a programme of muscle stretches and strengthening, he believes I can learn to manage my injury, and finally find a way of playing that works with my unstable spine, without trapping the nerves and disabling me. There's a long way to go, but not everyone has a second chance. Perhaps my silencing might not be as final as I have often feared.

Encore

London – 'The Soul of Music'

June 2022

One day, out of the blue, Robert Brewer Young calls to say he
has a surprise for me. I catch the train to London and meet him
at the Wigmore Hall. The historic recital venue, just off Bond
Street, is the location of Pál Hermann's premiere of his 'Grand'
Second Duo on 15 March 1930. Today, without any audience, the auditorium has its own peculiar, velvety hush. Robert
greets me at the door. I can tell he's excited, but I have no idea
what he has planned. Alone on stage is a solitary cello case,
lying on its side. I am momentarily reminded of the 'Cristiani',
propped up alone on stage in Berlin, waiting for Lise to join it.

'Go on, open the case,' urges Robert.

I undo the clips and swing the case open. Inside is a cello
swathed in a silk cloth. I can see from the pyramid scroll that it
is our own Open-String cello. I have never yet played it, as its
varnish was still wet when I last saw it in the workshop. When
I lift it out and remove the cloth, I find to my amazement that
the cello I thought I knew so intimately is now alien and new.
Robert has had it covered in writing. Its body has been made to
speak, inscribed like Anita's tattooed arm, like Pál Hermann's
Gagliano. It's beautiful. Breathtaking. I don't know what to say.

As I examine it more closely, I find that the words he has
chosen are from a poem I love, and that I had often returned to

on my travels. Ursula Wood, the second wife of Ralph Vaughan Williams, wrote 'To a 'Cellist' to explore her fascination with the composite being that is the cello and its player. Merman, centaur: a cellist with bow in hand is grafted to their instrument, and together they become something more than mortal.

Composite being, man's intelligence
And tautened strings on wooden shell, sets free
Voice beyond speech or words' close boundary
To shape a world in logic of pure sense,
To comprehend beyond experience
Silence and sound in measured harmony.

Now our 'composite being', this strange mixture of old and new, has come to embody Ursula's words, and I see that Robert's decision to inscribe the poem's second stanza across our cello is perfect. As I follow the swirl of writing around the cello's body, Robert tells me that the calligrapher Brody Nuenschwander had taken the curves of the cello's F holes as his inspiration for the font. The cello's own shape is inscribed onto itself, as the words sweep across the cello like the movement of a bow.

It is time to complete the final part of our cello's journey into the world. We must find out what it sounds like. Robert hands me a bow, but I am suddenly filled with a sense of panic. What if I don't like its voice? A player's relationship to a cello's sound is deeply personal, partly influenced by what instruments they're used to, and how they studied. The first cellos we hear are the ones that will be ingrained in our minds, and to a certain extent, subtly dictate the shapes, sounds and feelings we look for in an instrument.

But this is only part of the story. Whether we're scientifically measuring the peaks of resonance in the sound, or whether we're making filings jump into vibratory patterns on a cello's front, it always comes back to the fact that the relationship between our own voice and an instrument's is an almost mystical combination of science and emotion. Rational explanation can only go so far, before we're faced with the connection that cannot be quantified: the understanding between a cello and its player.

༄

The Open-String cello feels insecure to hold, its pear-shaped, heavy hips slipping between my knees, and I realize how much I rely on the sharper edges of the inverted C shapes of my own cello's sides to grip it. When I begin to play, I find the lower two strings are warm, resonant, and have a surprising quality. I hardly have to try to coax out the sound – it's eager, responsive and fresh. The upper register feels a little more like a new instrument, and has the green wetness of a sapling. With more playing, the sound will grow and flourish, bed itself in, whereas the lower half feels at least fifty years old. It's a curious mix, almost as if the cello's dual identity as modern and ancient, new and reclaimed, is reflected across its sound. I play Pál Hermann, Bach, Mendelssohn, anything I can think of.

Only when I finally stop playing do I realize that, without knowing it, I have found what I have been looking for. I may never recover Pál Hermann's Gagliano, or indeed Anita's Ventapane, but since my cello and I had first set out from Oxford, I have found a way to reshape what had been a broken world for me. I have begun a lifelong journey to learn how to hold 'silence and sound in measured harmony'.

∽

In the course of writing this book, I have come to see my own cello as a completely new object – a part of my life as essential and present to me as my partner or my children, rather than a closed case in the corner of the room. My eyes no longer move on from it with a dim sense of unease. I have my cello next to me as I write, ready to be picked up at any moment. I play in between typing, for hours at a time. Instead of feeling a punch of loss whenever friends talk about their professional playing, I now have a diary full of rehearsals and concert dates. Like the 'Mara', I feel something of myself has been pieced back together. And playing has never felt so natural, so joyful. The word that springs to mind, thanks to Zoltán Székely, is *vlot*.

I have struggled for years to comprehend my own silencing. But the bee cello, alone and seemingly silent in its orchard, could have told me that silence is never entire, and rarely final. If you listen differently, there is resonance, and music. Always. Even when no one is there to elicit it. Now, as I cradle the newly inscribed cello in my arms, a work of craftsmanship with a voice that is all its own, it seems to me an apt image: the wonderfully strange relationship between the human and the transcendental that meet in the body of a cello. I think back to little Corrie Hermann being jealous of her father's cello – the body he was so close to for hours on end, to the exclusion of his daughter, who perceived something of the intensity and exclusivity of that relationship. The cello was the body his fingers touched more than any human, and that still, somewhere, preserves something of that touch.

Things are never simply things, and cellos, more than most, are the loci around which ghosts converge. A cello can be home, can provide the roots for a player who does not know where home is. Pál Hermann, Lise Cristiani, Anita Lasker-Wallfisch and Amedeo Baldovino were nomadic whether through the demands of their concert schedules, or because they were forced from home. Their instruments, and their voices as cellists were the one thing they could be certain of, as borders opened and closed, countries excluded them or convention stifled them. In Trieste, Marco Zanettovich talked about his father and Amedeo surviving because they were Musicians 'with a capital M'. For me – and for many of the community of cellists I have encountered during my travels – security, identity and voice all lie in the Cello with a capital C.

As Pál Hermann's Gagliano tells us, wherever it is, whoever is playing it now:

Ego sum Anima Musicae.
I am the soul of music.

Listening

For these recordings below and more:
https://drkatekennedy.wordpress.com/cello-a-journey/listening-page/

Bach, J. S., Double Violin Concerto, Arnold Rosé and Alma Rosé with Rosé String Quartet (Biddulph Recordings, 2019)

Bach, J. S., Suite no. 2 for Solo Cello, Amaryllis Fleming (BBC live broadcast, 1974), https://www.youtube.com/watch?v=A5AbOf UOIV4

Boccherini, Luigi, Cello Concerto in B flat major, Jaqueline du Pré with the English Chamber Orchestra (including Anita Lasker-Wallfisch), conducted by Daniel Barenboim (EMI, 1967)

Elgar, Edward, Cello Concerto, Jacqueline du Pré, with Sir John Barbirolli and the London Symphony Orchestra (Warner Classics, 1995, Parlophone Records Ltd)

Hermann, Pál, Cello Concerto, reconstructed by Fabio Conti, Clive Greensmith with the Lviv International Symphony Orchestra, conducted by Theodore Kuchar (Toccata Classics, 2021)

Hermann, Pál, Grand Duo for Violin and Cello, Marko Komonko and Denys Lytvynenko (Toccata Classics, 2022)

Lely, John, The Harmonics of Real Strings, Anton Lukoszevieze (2014), https://anothertimbre.bandcamp.com/album/the-harmonics-of-real-strings

Mendelssohn, Felix, 'Song without Words', in D major, op. 109, Christian Poltera (on the 'Mara' Stradivari) and Ronald Brautigam (BIS 2187, 2019)

Pergolesi, Giovanni Battista, 'Dolorosa' from *Stabat Mater*, arranged for cellos, Julian and Jiaxin Lloyd Webber, from their album *A Tale of Two Cellos* (Naxos Classics 8.573251, 2013)

Schumann, Robert, **Trio in F major**, op. 80, Trieste Piano Trio, recorded live in Buenos Aires, August 1973 (MZ Digital Audio, MZ 7096-201)

Select Bibliography

Agamben, Giorgio, *Remnants of Auschwitz: The Witness and the Archive,* trans. Daniel Heller-Roazen (New York: Zone Books, 1999).

Appadurai, A. (ed.), *The Social Life of Things: Commodities in Cultural Perspective* (Cambridge: Cambridge University Press, 1986).

Attali, Jacques, *Noise: The Political Economy of Music* (Minneapolis: University of Minnesota Press, 1985).

Attlee, Helena, *Lev's Violin: An Italian Adventure* (London: Penguin Books, 2001).

Becker, Sarah, 'Sexual Sonorities: Gender Implications in Eighteenth- and Nineteenth-Century Viola da Gamba and Violoncello Performance Practices' (Music Honors thesis, Trinity University, 2013), http://digitalcommons.trinity.edu/music_honors/6; accessed 10 Jan. 2024.

Benedetti, Evangeline, *Cello, Bow and You: Putting it All Together* (Oxford: Oxford University Press, 2017).

Bucklow, Spike, *The Alchemy of Paint: Art, Science, and Secrets from the Middle Ages* (London: Marion Boyars, 2009).

Boyden, David, *The Hill Collection of Musical Instruments in the Ashmolean Museum, Oxford* (Oxford: Oxford University Press, 1969).

Brent, Francis, *The Lost Cellos of Lev Aronson* (New York: Atlas, 2009).

Brandmair, Brigitte, and Stefan-Peter Greiner, *Stradivari Varnish: Scientific Analysis of his Finishing Technique on Various Instruments* ([Vienna]: n.p., 2010).

Brown, Bill, 'Thing Theory', *Critical Inquiry*, 28 (2001), pp. 1–22.

Campbell, Margaret, *The Great Cellists* (London: Faber, 1988).

Campbell, Murray, Clive Greated and Arnold Myers (eds.), *Musical Instruments: History, technology, and performance of instruments of Western music* (Oxford: Oxford University Press, 2004).

Cander, Chris, *The Weight of a Piano* (New York: Knopf, 2019).

Chazan, Michael, *The Reality of Artifacts: An Archaeological Perspective* (London: Routledge, 2019).

Citron, Marcia J., *Gender and the Musical Canon* (Cambridge: Cambridge University Press, 1993).

Corredor, J. Ma., *Conversations with Casals* (London: Hutchinson, 1956).

Cowling, Elizabeth, *The Cello* (London and Sydney: Batsford, 1975).

Crome, Robert, *The Compleat Tutor for the Violoncello* (London: 1765).

Davies, Norman, and Roger Moorhouse, *Microcosm: A Portrait of a Central European City* (London: Jonathan Cape, 2003).

Denis, François, *Traité de Lutherie: The Violin and the Art of Measurement*, trans. Adrian Shaw (Aladfi, 2006).

Deserno, Katharina, *Cellistinnen. Transformationen von Weiblichkeit in der Instrumentalkunst* (Göttingen: Vandenhoeck & Ruprecht, 2019).

Dondi, P., et al., 'Automatic Identification of Varnish Wear on Historical Instruments: The Case of Antonio Stradivari Violins', *Journal of Culture Heritage*, 22 (2016), pp. 968–73.

Doubleday, Veronica, 'Sounds of Power: An Overview of Musical Instruments and Gender', *Ethnomusicology Forum* 17 (2008), pp. 3–39.

Downes, Stephanie, Sally Holloway, and Sarah Randles (eds), *Feeling Things: Objects and Emotions through History* (Oxford: Oxford University Press, 2018).

Duchesneau, Michel, *L'Avant-garde musicale à Paris de 1871 à 1939* (Sprimont: Mardaga, 1997).

Dunicz-Niwińska, Helena, *One of the Girls in the Band: The Memoirs of a Violinist from Birkenau*, trans. William Brand (Oświęcim: Auschwitz-Birkenau State Museum, 2014).

Easton, Carol, *Jacqueline du Pré: A Biography* (Cambridge: Da Capo Press, 1989).

Echard, Jean-Philippe, and Bertrand Lavédrine, 'Review on the

Characterisation of Ancient Stringed Musical Instruments, Varnishes and Implementation of an Analytical Strategy', *Journal of Cultural Heritage*, 9 (2008), pp. 420–9.

Echard, Jean-Philippe, et al., 'The Nature of the Extraordinary Finish of Stradivari's Instruments', *Angewandte Chemie*, 49 (2010), pp. 197–201.

Faber, Tony, *Stradivarius: Five Violins, One Cello and a Genius* (London: Macmillan, 2004).

Faitelson, Aleks, *The Truth and Nothing but the Truth: Jewish Resistance in Lithuania* (Jerusalem: Gefen, 2006).

Felman, Shoshana and Laub, Dori, *Testimony – Crises of Witnessing in Literature, Psychoanalysis and History* (Abingdon: Taylor & Francis, 2013).

Felstiner, Mary, 'Commandant of Drancy: Alois Brunner and the Jews of France', *Holocaust and Genocide Studies*, 2 (1987), pp. 21–47.

Forsee, Aylesa, *Pablo Casals: Cellist for Freedom* (New York: Thomas Y. Crowell Company, 1965).

Forty, Adrian, *Objects of Desire: Design and Society since 1750* (London: Thames and Hudson, 1986).

Gell, Alfred, *Art and Agency: An Anthropological Theory* (Oxford: Clarendon Press, 1998).

Gill, Dominic (ed.), *The Book of the Violin* (Oxford: Phaidon Press, 1984).

Gaskell, Ivan, 'The Life of Things', in Michelle Henning (ed.), *Museum Media* (Chichester: John Wiley and Sons, 2015), pp. 167–90.

Goethe, Johann Wolfgang von, Theory of Colours, trans. Charles Lock Eastlake (Cambridge, MA: MIT Press, 1970).

Gold, Dina, 'The Stars of David that Aren't', *Moment*, 27 April 2021, https://momentmag.com/violins-stars-of-david; accessed 10 Jan. 2024.

Gold, Dina, *Stolen Legacy: Nazi Theft and the Quest for Justice at Krausenstrasse 17/18, Berlin* (Chicago: American Bar Association, 2016).

Gray, Anne, *The World of Women in Classical Music* (San Diego: WordWorld, 2007).

Grymes, James A., *Violins of Hope* (New York: Harper Perennial, 2014).

Gunderson, Frank, Robert C. Lancefield and Bret Woods (eds), *The Oxford Handbook of Musical Repatriation* (Oxford: Oxford University Press, 2019).

Harrison, Beatrice, *The Cello and the Nightingales: The Autobiography of Beatrice Harrison*, ed. Patricia Cleveland-Peck (London: J. Murray, 1985, re-issued Canongate Books, 2024).

Haueisen, Jens, and Thomas R. Knösche, 'Involuntary Motor Activity in Pianists Evoked by Music Perception', *Journal of Cognitive Neuroscience*, 13 (2001), pp. 786–92.

Hoffmann, Freia (ed.), *Reiseberichte von Musikerinnen des 19. Jahrhunderts. Quellentexte, Biographien, Kommentare* (Travel Reports by Female Musicians of the 19th Century: Sources, Biographies, Commentaries) (Hildesheim: Olms, 2011).

Hoskins, Janet, *Biographical Objects: How Things Tell the Stories of People's Lives* (New York: Routledge, 1998).

Isserlis, Steven, *The Bach Cello Suites: A Companion* (London: Faber, 2021).

Kater, Michael H., *The Twisted Muse: Musicians and Their Music in the Third Reich* (New York: Oxford University Press, 1997).

Kennaway, George, 'The Manly Cello?' and 'Gender in Action: Performing the Cello', in *Playing the Cello, 1780–1930* (New York: Routledge, 2014), pp. 171–205, 207–33.

Kirkham, Pat, and Judy Attfield, *The Gendered Object* (Manchester: Manchester University Press, 1996).

Kinel, Lola, *Under Five Eagles: My Life in Russia, Poland, Austria, Germany and America, 1916–1936* (London: Putnam, 1937).

Heike Fricke (ed.), *Musikschule 'Paul Hindemith'. 75 Jahre Musikschule Neukölln* (Saarbrücken: Pfau, 2002).

Kowalski, Wojciech, *Liquidation of the Effects of World War Two in the Area of Culture* (Institute of Culture, Poland, 1994).

Knorr, Ernst-Lothar von, *Lebenserinnerungen. Erlebtes Musikalisches Geschehen in Deutschland* (Cologne: P. J. Tonger, 1996).

Lachendro, Jacek, 'The Orchestras in KL Auschwitz', *Auschwitz Studies*, 27 (2015), pp. 7–148.

Laks, Simon, *Gry Oświęcimskie* (1979, pub. Oswiecim: Auschwitz-Birkenau State Museum, 1998).

Lasker-Wallfisch, Anita, *Inherit the Truth, 1939–1945* (London: Giles de la Mare, 1996).

Lazzaro, Federico, *Écoles de Paris en Musique 1920–1950: Identités,*

Nationalisme, Cosmopolitisme (Paris: Librairie Philosophique J. Vrin, 2018).

Jacques Lusseyran, *Against the Pollution of the I: On the Gifts of Blindness, the Power of Poetry, and the Urgency of Awareness* (Novato, CA: New World Library, 2015).

Lwowski, Marcin, *Orkiestra z Auschwitz* (Warsaw: Wydawnictwo Swiat Ksiazki, 2021).

Mairson, Harry, 'Secrets of Stradivari', *Stanford Magazine*, 29 January 2018, https://medium.com/stanford-magazine/computer-science-professor-makes-modern-day-proportioned-version-of-stradivarius-cristiani-cello-374c05d58a6e; accessed 10 Jan. 2024.

Marrus, Michael R., and Robert O. Paxton, *Vichy France and the Jews* (New York: Basic Books, 1981).

Mercier, Anita, *Guilhermina Suggia: Cellist* (London: Routledge, 2017).

Milosch, Jane C., and Nick Pearce, *Collecting and Provenance: A Multidisciplinary Approach* (New York: Rowman & Littlefield, 2019).

Neumann, Arianna, *When Time Stopped: A Memoir of My Father's War and What Remains* (London: Scribner, 2020).

Phipps, Elena, *Cochineal Red: The Art History of a Color* (New York: Metropolitan Museum of Art, 2010).

Piatigorsky, Gregor, *Cellist* (Garden City, NY: Doubleday, 1965).

Pollens, Stewart, *The Manual of Musical Instrument Conservation* (Cambridge: Cambridge University Press, 2015).

Pollens, Stewart, *Stradivari* (Cambridge: Cambridge University Press, 2010).

Prieto, Carlos, *The Adventures of a Cello* (Austin: University of Texas Press, 2006).

Pukánszky, Béla, '"Cellist Woman in a Paris Salon!" Lisa Cristiani's (1827–1853) Career as a Performer in Contemporary Publicism', www.academia.edu/49129929/_Cellist_woman_in_a_Paris_salon_Lisa_Cristianis_1827_1853_career_as_a_performer_in_contemporary_publicism; accessed 20 Dec. 2023.

Remnant, Mary, *English Bowed Instruments from Anglo-Saxon to Tudor Times* (Oxford: Clarendon Press, 1986).

Rich, Adrienne, *Arts of the Possible: Essays and Conversations* (New York: W.W. Norton, 2001).

Roberts, Sophie, *The Lost Pianos of Siberia* (London: Doubleday, 2020).

Russell, Tilden A. 'The Development of the Cello Endpin', *Imago Musicae*, 4 (January 1987), pp. 335–56.

Sacks, Oliver, *The Man Who Mistook His Wife for a Hat* (New York: Summit Books, 1985).

Sacks, Oliver, *Musicophilia: Tales of Music and the Brain* (London: Picador, 2008).

Sandys, William and Simon Andrew Forster, *The History of the Violin and Other Instruments Played on with the Bow from the Remotest Times to the Present* (London: William Reeves, 1864).

Schafer, Murray, *Soundscape: Our Sonic Environment and the Tuning of the World* (Rochester, VT: Destiny Books, 1994).

Shapreau, Carla, 'The Loss of French Musical Property during World War II: Post-War Repatriations, Restitutions, and 21st Century Ramifications', Institute of European Studies, University of California, Berkeley, 2013, https://escholarship.org/uc/item/9jnop8k6; accessed 10 Jan. 2024.

Siblin, Eric, *The Cello Suites: In Search of a Baroque Masterpiece* (London: Vintage, 2011).

Sontag, Susan, *Styles of Radical Will* (New York: Picador, 2002).

Straeten, Edmund S. J. van der, *History of the Violoncello, the Viol da Gamba, Their Precursors and Collateral Instruments: With Biographies of All the Most Eminent Players of Every Country* (London: William Reeves, 1971; first published 1914).

Stowell, Robin (ed.), *The Cambridge Companion to the Cello* (Cambridge: Cambridge University Press, 1999).

Szczepanski, Ignacy, *Häftlingskapelle* (Warsaw: Książka i Wiedza, 1990).

Veil, Simone, *A Life: A Memoir*, trans. Tamsin Black (London: Haus Publishing, 2009).

Vries, Rene de, *Met een cello door Siberie. Het avontuurlijke leven van Lise Christiani (1827–1853) en haar Stradivariuscello (1700–heden)* (*Travelling with a Cello through Siberia: The Adventurous Life of Lise Cristiani (1827–1853) and her Stradivarius Cello (1700–now)*) (Delft: Elmar, 2014).

Vries, Willem de, *Commando Musik. Comment les Nazis ont Spolié l'Europe Musicale* (Paris: Buchet-Chastal, 2019).

Walden, Valerie, *One Hundred Years of Violoncello: A History of*

Technique and Performance Practice, 1740–1840 (Cambridge: Cambridge University Press, 1998).

Wasielewski, Wilhelm Joseph von, *The Violoncello and Its History* (London and New York: Da Capo Press, 1968; first published 1894).

Waugh, Alexander, *The House of Wittgenstein: A Family at War* (London: Bloomsbury, 2009).

Wilson, Elizabeth, *Jacqueline du Pré: her Life, her Music, her Legend* (New York: Arcade Publishing, 2013).

Wordsworth, William (ed.), *Jacqueline du Pré: Impressions* (London: Granada, 1983).

Zatorre, R. J., and A. R. Halpern, 'Mental Concerts: Musical Imagery and Auditory Cortex', *Neuron*, 47 (2005), pp. 9–12.

Archives

Anita Lasker-Wallfisch's archive, Imperial War Museum, London

Auschwitz-Birkenau Memorial Museum

Berlin Philharmonic Orchestra archives, Philharmonie Hall, Berlin

Clifford Curzon archive, British Library, London

Kaunas Ninth Fort museum, Kaunas

Musikschule Paul Hindemith festschrifts, Zentral- und Landesbibliothek, Berlin

Philharmonie de Paris archives, Musée de la Musique, Paris

Royal College of Music archives, London

Shoah Memorial Archives, Paris

W. E. Hill & Sons, Queens Street, London

Wiener Holocaust Museum archives

Wigmore Hall, London

Acknowledgements

I have many people to thank, new friends and old, who have helped shape this book: Corrie Hermann, Ada-Louise and Paul van Gastel in the Netherlands and France; Andrea Nocerini, Min Kym, Stefan-Peter Greiner, Massimo Ardoli and Abraham Díaz Romero in Cremona; Kuba Stankiewicz, Rafał Motriuk, Ola Rupocińska and Bente Kahan in Wrocław; Marco Zanettovich in Trieste; Emilia Melon, Sebastian Szkota, Krystoph Dostępnya, Max and Piotyr in Suwalki; Vytautas Petrikenas in Kaunas; Katarzyna Kuszaj-Jarnot in Oświęcim; Anita Lasker-Wallfisch, Raphael Wallfisch, Robert Brewer Young, Sam Blade, Jason Reitenberger, Charles Beare, Freddie Beare, Robin Lustig, John Topham, Christian Poltera, Steven Isserlis, Sebastian Comberti and Matthew Sharp in London; Martin and Deirdre Bencsik in Nottingham; Yo-Yo Ma, Nick Roberts and Bruno Guastalla in Oxford; Robert Zatorre in Canada; Shulamit Sarid in Israel; Julian and Jiaxin Lloyd Webber in Birmingham; Ludwig Quandt, Natalie Clein and Verena Alves in Berlin, and Clive Greensmith, Carla Shapreau and Bob Elias at the Colburn Institute of Music in Los Angeles. Others have been of great assistance behind the scenes: historians Julian Wright, Rebecca Abrams and Percy Leung for careful reading, advice and research, and Dame Hermione Lee and Simon Over for their unstinting support. This book would not have been possible without them.

I have been generously supported by the Authors' Foundation, by Words by Design, and by Oxford University, in particular the Oxford Centre for Life-Writing at Wolfson College. I am also very grateful both to Charles Beare and to W. E. Hill & Sons for access to their archives.

Notes

Prelude

1. Adapted from Eric Siblin, *The Cello Suites*, p. 255.
2. There is some confusion over the date of Lise Cristiani's birth, which is listed variously as 1824, 1825 and 1827. See Katharina Deserno, *Cellistinnen. Transformationen von Weiblichkeit in der Instrumentalkunst* (Göttingen: Vandenhoeck & Ruprecht, 2019).

1st Movement – Cello

1. Although arguably the first few hours and weeks, even up to the end of the first year, are the time when a cello will change and develop the most.
2. Archived programmes record performances by Baldovino in: the Singakademie with the Berlin Philharmonic Orchestra on 14 November 1931; recitals on 16 April 1932, 14 December 1940, 10 April 1941, and 7 and 14 September 1941 at the Beethovensaal; 18 December 1940 at the Philharmonie with the Städtisches Orchester Berlin; 1 February 1942 at the Konzertsaal der Staatlichen Hochschule für Musik, again with the Städtisches Orchester Berlin; and a return visit with the Trieste Piano Trio on 5 April 1962.
3. Pál Hermann's concerts at the Singakademie include 2 February 1928, with Alice Ehlers (harpsichord), a chamber orchestra conducted by Michael Taube, and a recital, accompanied by V. Ernst Wolff, on 17 December 1929.
4. On 21 September 1928 with the Magdeburger Domchor, conducted by Bernhard Henking and the organist Erwin Zillinger.
5. Cristiani's performances in Berlin in 1846 were reviewed in the *Allgemeine Musikalische Zeitung*, 1846, pp. 289–91.
6. For more discussion of such stories, see Jan Alber, 'What Commodities Have to Say about Consumerism: The Eighteenth-Century Novel "The Adventures of a Black Coat"', *Material Culture*, 48, 1, special issue: *Consumer Goods* (2016), pp. 55–66.

7. Ivan Gaskell, 'The Life of Things', in Michelle Henning (ed.), *Museum Media* (Chichester: John Wiley and Sons, 2015), p. 169.
8. Both concerts were presented by the Freunde alter Musik with Alice Ehlers (harpsichord). On 24 November 1926, Pál Hermann was joined by Marianne Mathy (singer) and Annie Steiger-Betzak and Nora Williamson (violin); on 15 February 1927, the other musicians were Adelheid Armhold and Georg Kulenkampff. See www.concertprogrammes.org.uk/html/search/verb/GetRecord/4407/; accessed 19 Dec. 2023.
9. Alexander Pope, 'An Essay On Criticism', 1709, p. 98, in *The Works of Alexander Pope Esq*, with notes and illustrations by himself and others (London: 1824).
10. Review in the *Pesti Napló*, Budapest, 12 December 1923. Taken from a document in which a selection of Pál Hermann's reviews are collated, owned by Corrie Hermann.
11. Described as such in a review in the *Nieuwe Rotterdammer Courant*, 22 August 1923.
12. Although the cello is now missing, I make the claim as to the quality of its sound based on reviews of Pál Hermann's performances on it, but also based on the recordings he went on to make with it in Berlin.
13. On 27 March 1902 the Hill diaries record: 'We learn that Sig. Pezze has sold his Strad cello to Mr. Gardiner for £1,200. This is the Strad cello which I used to see when I was a boy in the possession of the late Mr. Whitmore Isaacs, a Worcester banker. It formerly belonged to Mara, the husband of the famous singer. Mara ill-treated the instrument very much, and the stains of the wine that he spilt down it are still visible. We finely repaired the cello, and sold it for £400 to Mr. Tarn who let Pezze have it for the same amount. It is still a fine cello, but £1,200 is a high value to place upon it. The prices artists now get for instruments are far beyond anything we can do, and they are mainly responsible for the high prices that are now ruling. Only the other day Whitehouse insisted on insuring his Ruggeri cello for £600; he thinks it well worth this, but it certainly is not. I think he gave us £130 for it.'
14. In 1927, Erich had invited his closest musical friends to attend the first-ever performance of Bach's *The Art of Fugue* in Leipzig. The guests were Pál Hermann, Alice Ehlers, a harpsichordist who had often played and analysed *The Art of Fugue* for the Mendelsohns, and Hans Erich Riebensahm, a pianist and professor at the Hochschule für Musik in Berlin. The Mendelsohns flew their guests from Berlin, a journey that took two hours. Few people flew in those days, and while the Mendelsohns were used to

flying, Erich recalls that it was a new experience for his three guests, who 'had to struggle with nausea'.

I would see Mendelsohn's name again, this time in Breslau, his modernist design for a huge shop made of curved glass panels creating a landmark in the city centre that would have been well known to the young Anita Lasker.

15. This quote is from Franz Schreker, then the director of Berlin's Hochschule für Musik, in a note of recommendation, written for Pál Hermann, and in the family's private collection of documents.

16. Dorothea Kolland, 'Zwischen Salonmief und Reformgeist: Musikschulen in Rixdorf und Neukölln', in Heike Fricke (ed.), *Musikschule 'Paul Hindemith'. 75 Jahre Musikschule Neukölln* (Saarbrücken: Pfau, 2002), p. 89.

17. According to W. E. Hill & Sons' diaries, Albert Einstein visited Hill's when in London on 4 October 1933. 'The Professor proved a delightful acquaintance, his face beaming with a smile which bespoke a genial nature. He brought with him a German violin for our inspection. It proved, alas! to be a very badly constructed instrument which had been fitted up to produce an easy speaking tone, utterly lacking in power however, and imbued with an ugly nasal quality. Alfred, who, thanks to his political activities, has become an able debater, soon convinced Einstein that the vaunted improvement effected by his friend, Dr. Levine, was an illusory one, and if the tone of the fiddle appealed to him, it was because he had become accustomed to it. We showed him the "Messie" [the 'Messiah' Stradivari, now in the Ashmolean's collection] and allowed him to draw the bow across it: he is not a great player, and the tone he produces is small, though of a sympathetic quality. He expressed himself well pleased with his visit to us, and we parted good friends. I asked him for his visiting card that I might add it to my collection. He, however, said he had none! but expressed his readiness to write a few lines on a card for me, and the following is a translation of this memento: "In remembrance of a visit to the firm of Hill 4th X 33. I admired the virgin [pure] Stradivari [the Messie]. Albert Einstein."'

18. There are also recordings, found after much hunting through sound archives, of Pál playing Mozart and Beethoven quartets with the Wittenberg Quartet. Alfred Wittenberg was a Jewish violinist born to one of the musical families of Breslau, who escaped Nazi Germany with his parents to make his home in Shanghai.

19. The *Volkssturm* ('people's storm') was a militia established by the Nazis towards the end of the Second World War, consisting of male civilians between the ages of sixteen and sixty.

20. Looking back on the events of 1933–4, Knorr wrote in his memoir: 'The first inevitable sacrifices had already been made to the "new era", which a little later brought us blood, tears and destruction in an unimaginable way: Paul Hindemith had stopped teaching under the duress of circumstances and my cello teacher Hermann, as a Jew, was no longer allowed to teach.' Ernst-Lothar von Knorr, *Lebenserinnerungen. Erlebtes musikalisches Geschehen in Deutschland* (Cologne: P. J. Tonger, 1996), p. 166.

21. Evangeline Benedetti, *Cello, Bow and You: Putting It All Together* (Oxford: Oxford University Press, 2017), pp. 22–3.

22. Susan Sontag, 'The Aesthetics of Silence' (first published 1967), in *Styles of Radical Will* (New York: Picador, 2002), p. 9.

23. Gregor Piatigorsky, *Cellist* (Garden City, NY: Doubleday, 1965), ch. 27.

24. For instance, a Francesco Pressanda cello made in Turin is identified by its owner as being generously covered with 'a rich fiery red-orange varnish' (quoted in Elizabeth Cowling, *The Cello* (London and Sydney: Batsford, 1975) p. 38; and W. E. Hill & Sons frequently describe instruments in their records by their flames.

25. Regula Qureshi, 'The Indian Sarangi: Sound of Affect, Site of Contest', *Yearbook for Traditional Music*, 29 (1997), p. 4.

26. Piatigorsky, *Cellist*, ch. 29.

27. Alfred Gell, *Art and Agency: An Anthropological Theory* (Oxford: Clarendon Press, 1998), pp. 16–17.

28. Cited in Tony Faber, *Stradivarius: Five Violins, One Cello and a Genius* (London: Macmillan, 2004), p. xvi.

29. Nancy C. Lutkehaus, cited in Veronica Doubleday, 'Sounds of Power: An Overview of Musical Instruments and Gender', *Ethnomusicology Forum*, 17/1 (2008), p. 12.

30. Piatigorsky, *Cellist*, ch. 29.

31. Ivan Gaskell, 'The Life of Things', *Museum Media*, 2015, p.169.

32. With thanks to the many cellists in the International Cello Society for their willingness to introduce me to their cellos. These names are taken from a far larger selection.

33. Piatigorsky, *Cellist*, ch. 25.

34. This is the opus 109 'Song without Words' in D major. In fact, Mendelssohn also dedicated an Andante Pastorale in C major for piano to her, and Arnaud Dancla dedicated his *Le Signal du pâtre* for violoncello and piano op. 4 to Cristiani.

35. For more information on Pain, who was described as an excellent 'amateur', and devoted her life to chamber music, see Alexandre Sorel, 'Madame Pain (Thérèse-Rosalie Sézille de Montarlet)', *Bulletin de la Société historique de Compiègne*, 8 (1895), pp. 48–68.

36. According to the announcement of the inaugural concert in the music journal *Le Ménestrel*, 9 December 1838, p. 3, which advises people who want tickets to apply to M. Herz at 38 Rue de la Victoire.
37. *Le Ménestrel*, 16 February 1845.
38. *La France Theatrale*, 16 February 1845.
39. Nicolas-Alexandre was a painter; his son Jules-Paul, a playwright and librettist.
40. In his article 'Cellist Woman in a Paris Salon: Lisa Cristiani's (1827–1853) Career as a Performer in Contemporary Publicism' (available at www.academia.edu/49129929/_Cellist_woman_in_a_Paris_salon_Lisa_Cristianis_1827_1853_career_as_a_performer_in_contemporary_publicism; accessed 20 Dec. 2023), Béla Pukánszky tells us that other critics of the young Cristiani commented on this link between women cellists and art: 'The authors of several reports point out that "the cellos in the hands of women" is not a new phenomenon, as there are examples of female figures with cello in painting from previous centuries' (p. 7).
41. *La Revue et Gazette Musicale*, 1845, p. 61, probaby written by Henri Blanchard, one of the most eminent music critics in France at the time.
42. *La Revue et Gazette Musicale*, 1845, p. 61.
43. *Wiener Zeitschrift fur Kunst, Literatur, Theater und Mode*, 1845, pp. 391–2.
44. *Berlin Musical Times*, 3 January 1846.
45. *Allgemeine Musikalische Zeitung*, 42 (October 1845), pp. 749–50, written by 'L. R'.
46. *Allgemeine Musikalische Zeitung*, 1846, p. 249.
47. *Allgemeine Musikalische Zeitung*, April 1846, pp. 289–91.
48. *Sonntagsblätter* (Vienna), 18 May 1845, p. 479, written by Joseph Plank. He also mentions that her Vienna performance included the Mayseder Trio in A flat, a Donizetti aria and his 'Liebestranke' from *L'Elisir d'Amore*, Schubert's 'Ständchen' and Offenbach's *Bolero* and *Prière*.
49. *Der Sammler*, 27 May 1845.
50. *Die Grenzboten Zeitschrift für Politik und Literatur*, semester 1, vol. 2 (1845), p. 539.
51. 'Song without Words', or 'Lied ohne Worte', op. 109.
52. This is a view shared by Prof. Douglass Seaton, reviewing Larry Todd's edition of Mendelssohn's 'Song without Words' in *Nineteenth-Century Music Review*, 15 (2018), pp. 145–8: 'The Romance sans Paroles op. 109 (MWV Q 34), for Lisa Cristiani, was a tribute from the composer to a brilliant player, presumably

intended to feature her famously elegant style and in its "feminine" lyricism possibly also a nod to contemporary gender images.'

53. *Wiener Allgemeine Musik-Zeitung*, 17 May 1845, pp. 234–5, written by Ugnaz Lewinsky.

54. These were the *Kammersonate* and *Quatre Épigrammes*. Pàl Hermann also mentions in a letter of 10 August 1933 how positive the publishers Hug Zurich were about the possibility of publishing his *Divertimento*.

55. 'Wij gaan om 1/2 9 weer naar L. [Lerenz] toe en spelen daar drie stukken van mij (duo, solosonate + quartett)' ('We are going to L. at around 8.30 and [will] play three pieces by me (duo, solo sonata + quartet)'). From a letter written in Brussels, 27 October 1933. The London performance was at 19 Wigmore Street, in a shared recital with composer-pianist Roy Agnew, on 13 February 1932.

56. Italian composer Fabio Conti has completed the orchestration, and the piece was recorded alongside Conti's orchestration of Pàl Hermann's cello concerto in Lviv in 2018.

57. 'Of particular note was [...] the rather rare presence of some foreign formations presenting, among others, works by their compatriots (the Winterthur Quartet, the Hungarian New Quartet, the Heidelberg Chamber Orchestra and the Strub Quartet in Berlin).' Lazzaro, Triton Society and the 'School of Paris'.

58. Lazzaro, 1932, The Triton Society and the 'School of Paris'.

59. Salle Cortot, http://www.sallecortot.com/la_salle.htm; accessed 20 Dec. 2023.

60. See Pat Kirkham and Judy Attfield, *The Gendered Object* (Manchester University Press), 1996 for a detailed discussion of the ways in which gender relations operate through material goods, and shape our sense of social identity.

61. For a detailed discussion of the many terms by which a cello is described see Brenda Neece, 'The Cello in Britain: A Technical and Social History', *Galpin Society Journal*, 56 (2003), pp. 77–115.

62. Valerie Walden, in her book *One Hundred Years of Violoncello: A History of Technique and Performance Practice, 1740–1840* (Cambridge: Cambridge University Press, 1998), tells us that few players before the mid-eighteenth century were expected to specialize in one instrument above another.

63. For instance, in Robert Crome's *The Compleat Tutor for the Violoncello* (London, 1765).

64. Crome, *Compleat Tutor for the Violoncello*.

65. According to the blind French author and activist Jacques Lusseyran, *Against the Pollution of the I: On the Gifts of*

Blindness, the Power of Poetry, and the Urgency of Awareness
(Novato, CA: New World Library, 2015).

2nd Movement – Journeys

1. From Pál Hermann's manuscript diary.
2. Jaap de Graaff and Louise Bachiene had been well connected in the art world in London before the war, and had bought a considerable collection, including pieces by Ethel Walker. They had also sat for portrait artist Robin Guthrie, who now has a number of his portraits displayed at the National Portrait Gallery.
3. In a previous postcard he mentions a Dominican church in which he was playing, but it is not clear whether his performance was under his own name, or whether it was a public concert. It may be that this is the same church mentioned in his last correspondence.
4. Archive document CDXXVIII-94, Shoah Memorial Archive, Paris. In a letter dated 30 June, it is clear that the building was being sold (XVIIIb-115(1260)).
5. The information about the pass to perform is taken from Limore Yagil, *Au nom de l'art, 1933–1945. Exils, solidarités et engagements* (Paris: Fayard, 2015).
6. Pages from this document can be viewed in Carla Shapreau, 'The Austrian Copyright Society and Blacklisting during the Nazi Era', 2014, http://orelfoundation.org/journal/journalArticle/the_austrian_copyright_society_and_blacklisting_during_the_nazi_era; accessed 20 Dec. 2023.
7. Simone Veil was to survive Auschwitz and Bergen-Belsen, and to go on to become the first President of the European Union. Her autobiography, *A Life*, was published in 2009.
8. All these details are taken from eye-witness accounts, recorded in interview and held at the Drancy Memorial Museum.
9. Gregor Piatigorsky, *Cellist*, ch. 26.
10. There is very little research to investigate exactly what happens when wood ages, but dendrochronologist John Topham agrees that, potentially, the crispness of old wood might improve the sound. (In conversation with the author, 2023.)
11. Robb Report, *The Theft, Recovery, and Legend of Joshua Bell's Red Stradivarius Violin*, 2 November 2018, YouTube, www.youtube.com/watch?v=Q9aVKP4jG8o; accessed 20 Dec. 2023.
12. Carla Shapreau, 'The Thief, his Wife, and the Huberman Strad', *The Strad*, 8 February 2019.

13. The experiment took place in June 2012. It included violins made by the most respected modern makers, by Stradivari between 1710 and 1730, and by Guarneri 'del Gesù' (*c*.1740). The results were recorded in Claudia Fritz et al., 'Soloist Evaluations of Six Old Italian and Six New Violins', *PNAS*, 111 (2014), pp. 7224–9, https://doi.org/10.1073/pnas.1323367111.

14. From a summary of her journey, printed in *Le Tour du monde*. There are two sources for 'quotes' from Lise Cristiani's travels. In 1860 her grandfather Nicolas-Alexandre Barbier published his account of Lise's journey in the *Journal des Débats Politiques et Littéraires, 26 September 1860,* "Voyage d'un Stradivarius à travers la Sibérie, le Kamtchatka et le Caucase (1848–1853)", p. 1f. This was followed three years later by 'Extraits de la correspondence d'une artiste', an extensive article written by a M. de Lanoye that documents Cristiani's travels in the Parisian journal *Le Tour du monde 1863 I,* "Voyage dans la Sibérie Orientale. Notes Extraites de la Correspondance d'une Artiste (Mlle Lise Cristiani) 1849–1853", pp. 385–400. The voice on the page is one that has been filtered and carefully presented to suit the purposes of the authors. The order of her travels is doctored to end her life with a dramatic journey for the sake of a fitting denouement. It is also not clear whether these quotes are her letters being directly quoted, or, as Barbier claimed, excerpts from a travel journal. Lise's voice exists unadulterated only in a handful of letters in archives such as the Staatsbibliothek in Berlin, and the University and State Library in Bonn, but the only substantial first-hand account of her travels is what Barbier and de Lanoye chose to give us. All quotations in this section are drawn from these two sources, unless otherwise noted. The quotations have been translated by Percy Leung for this book.

15. *Wiener Zeitschrift für Kunst, Literatur, Theater und Mode,* 1845, pp. 391–2.

16. Franzeva Istoricheskiy Vestnik, writing in 1888.

17. According to a travel report in the *Journal des débats.*

18. *The Private Diary of Leo Tolstoy 1853–1857,* ed. Aymer Maude (London: Heinemann, 1927), p. 17.

19. Katharina Deserno gives an excellent account of Lise Cristiani in *Cellistinnen. Transformationen von Weiblichkeit in der Instrumentalkunst* (Göttingen: Vandenhoeck & Ruprecht, 2018).

20. In an interview with Graham Young, for *Business Live,* 29 January 2015.

21. See Min Kym's memoir, *Gone: A Girl, a Violin, a Life Unstrung* (London: Viking, 2017).

22. Ivan Gaskell, 'The Life of Things', in Michelle Henning (ed.), *Museum Media* (Chichester: John Wiley and Sons, 2015), p. 171.

23. Murray Schafer was inspired by Petrarch's fourteenth-century example in the fourteenth century, making up the term 'landscape' in answer to his desire to describe the view from the top of a mountain, and being frustrated by the lack of language for the expansive magnificence he saw beneath him.

24. Murray Schafer, *A Sound Education: 100 Exercises in Listening and Sound-Making* (Indian River, Ontario: Arcana Editions, 1992).

25. The substantial scratches on the side of the cello are still visible on historic photographs in the W. E. Hill & Sons archive.

26. Muriel Handley, letter to the Editor, *Violin Times* (London), April 1898; excerpt available at https://tarisio.com/cozio-archive/property/?ID=40712; accessed 21 Dec. 2023.

27. Eugene Polonaski, 'Celebrated Violins and Their Owners', *Violin Times* (London), February 1898; excerpt available at https://tarisio.com/cozio-archive/property/?ID=40712; accessed 21 Dec. 2023.

28. It is only recently, on the discovery of his will, that a date has been established for Stradivari's birth.

29. Casein, a milk protein powder, like a baby's formula, is generally used now for inlay instead of the mammoth bone paste.

30. Gum lac is the resin encrustation formed when the *Coccus lacca* insect infests the branches of trees. It is found in south and southeast Asia.

31. Sacconi had a lifelong obsession with Stradivari's varnish. His seminal study, *I 'Segreti' di Stradivari* (Cremona: Libreria del Convegno, 1972), translated into English as *The 'Secrets' of Stradivari* (1979), was the result.

32. The identification of the ingredients in Stradivari's varnish has been the result of years of research, by scientists and instrument makers Louis Condax, C. Y. Barlow and J. Woodhouse, amongst others. The two most comprehensive studies on the subject are Brigitte Brandmair and Stefan-Peter Greiner's *Stradivari Varnish: Scientific Analysis of his Finishing Technique on Various Instruments* (Vienna: 2010), and Jean-Philippe Echard et al., 'The Nature of the Extraordinary Finish of Stradivari's Instruments', *Angewandte Chemie*, 49 (2010), pp. 197–201, https://doi.org/10.1002/anie.200905131 (accessed 21 Dec. 2023), which assesses the varnish on Stradivari's instruments at the Cité de la Musique in Paris.

33. Taken from a typescript of the conversation in Charles Beare's personal archive.

34. Pathé footage of the sinking ship and the arrival of rescued passengers on dry land can be seen at www.youtube.com/watch?v=m_edDZ-65NQ (accessed 21 Dec. 2023).

35. *The Times*, 12 July 1963, p. 10. The Emmaus Foundation records how Abbé Pierre survived by clinging to a wooden part of the boat, while around him the passengers drowned. Later on, while on a trip to Algiers, he showed the pocket knife that had enabled him to survive this ordeal.

36. Robert Macfarlane describes his visit to the Carso and its tunnels in *Underland: A Deep Time Journey* (London: Penguin, 2020).

37. The composer and violinist Giuseppe Tartini was born further along the peninsula, near the border with Slovenia, in 1692.

38. Marina Rossi, *Soldati dell'Armata Rossa al confine orientale 1941–1945* (Gorizia: Libreria Editrice Goriziana, 2014).

3rd Movement – Silence

1. From Fritz Lustig's unpublished memoir, with thanks to Robin Lustig for permission to use his father's words.

2. For a detailed discussion of the events of that night, see Martin Gilbert, *Kristallnacht: Prelude to Destruction* (New York: Harper Press, 2006).

3. This was the Latvian Ambassador.

4. Fritz's future wife, from Breslau, was also given a visa to the UK, but her mother, only forty years old, was considered too elderly; she was rounded up, taken from Breslau to Kaunas, and shot at the Ninth Fort, a prison fortress taken over by the Nazis for mass killings. For Robin's published account of his father's early life, see Robin Lustig 'Eighty Years after Kristallnacht, Why My Family Has Become German Again', *Guardian*, 10 Nov. 2018, https://www.theguardian.com/news/2018/nov/10/eighty-years-after-kristallnacht-family-german-robin-lustig; accessed 3 Jan. 2024.

5. To put this in context, in Dresden, which was synonymous with destruction, the number was four out of every ten. Richard Hargreaves, *Hitler's Final Fortress: Breslau 1945* (Barnsley: Pen and Sword Military Books, 2011), p. 10. See also Norman Davies and Roger Moorhouse, *Microcosm: Portrait of a Central European City* (London: Jonathan Cape, 2002).

6. The correspondence, along with many letters from Anita and Renate to Marianne in England, is held at the Imperial War Museum in London.

7. There is also a copy of the documentation in the Wiener Library, London, now part of Anita's archive there, collection ref: 1040.

The term 'holocaust' comes from the Latin, which is a translation of the Greek term *holocaustos*, 'completely burned'. It was used by the church fathers to translate the complex sacrificial doctrine of the Bible in books such as Leviticus and Deuteronomy. It is criticized for giving a sense of martyrdom, of purpose, to the deaths that did not exist, thereby misrepresenting them. And so the term *so'ah*, or Shoah, which translates as a devastation or catastrophe, has been adopted to convey the senselessness of the genocide. I choose, with caveats, to use the term 'holocaust' rather than 'Shoah', during the course of this book, because, as Primo Levi said, it may be inaccurate, but it is a term people understand.

8. The song was written by Mark Warshawsky (1848–1907), and is one of the most well-remembered songs from before the Holocaust, having been taught in kindergartens.

9. 'Shtetl' is the name for a small, usually Ashkenazi, Jewish town.

10. Anita's friends, Ruth and Werner Krumme, were both taken to Auschwitz for their part in Anita's escape attempt. Ruth was killed on arrival. Werner survived, helping as many people as he could in the camp during his incarceration.

11. Primo Levi, *If This Is a Man*, trans. Stuart Woolf (New York: Orion Press, 1959).

12. There was a bass player at one point, Yvette Assael-Lennon, but Maria and then Anita were the only two cellists of the orchestra.

13. Giorgio Agamben, *Remnants of Auschwitz: The Witness and the Archive*, trans. Daniel Heller-Roazen (New York: Zone Books, 1999), p. 104.

14. Auschwitz-Birkenau State Museum (APMA-B), Statements Collection, vol. 76, p. 204 and p. 43, account by Henryk Król.

15. These storehouses were known as 'Kanada' (the land of plenty), and were located between Auschwitz I and Birkenau, which are three kilometres apart.

16. Szymon Laks, *Gry Oświęcimskie*, p. 94.

17. APMA -B, Statements Collection, vol. 56, p. 43, account by Adam Kopyciński.

18. Anita Lasker-Wallfisch, *Inherit the Truth, 1939–1945* (London: Giles de la Mare, 1996), p. 76.

19. APMA-B, Statements Collection, vol. 160, pp. 27–8, account by Marian Kołodziej.

20. APMA-B, Memoirs Collection, vol. 136, p. 248, from an account by Anatol Adamczyk, who was one of the few who survived these working parties. All accounts of the orchestra quoted here were given later by survivors.

21. APMA-B, Memoirs Collection, vol. 130, p. 31, report by

Witold Pilecki, quoted in Jacek Lachendro, 'The Orchestras in KL Auschwitz', *Auschwitz Studies*, 27 (2015), p. 37. For other, similarly bitter accounts of the orchestra and the marching labourers' opinion of it, see APMA-B, Memoirs Collection, vol. 2, p. 278, account by Stanisław Kobylański, and APMA-B, Memoirs Collection, vol. 110, p. 21, account by Kazimierz Gwidka.

22. Szymon Laks, *Gry Oświęcimskie*, pp. 60, 85–6.

23. Anita Lasker-Wallfisch, *Inherit the Truth*, p. 77.

24. The 'stage' is described in Maria Zarębińska-Broniewska, 'Koncert', in *Opowiadania Oświęcimskie* (Warsaw: Książka, 1948), p. 63.

25. Dr Margarita Schwalbová, 'A Doctor Gives Her Account of Auschwitz-Birkenau', in *Eleven Women's True Experiences of Auschwitz-Birkenau, 1942–1945*.

26. Quoted in Lachendro, 'The Orchestras in KL Auschwitz', p. 137.

27. APMA-B, Statements Collection, vol. 56, p. 47, account by Adam Koyciński, and Ignacy Szczepański, *Häftlingskapelle* (Warsaw: Książka i Wiedza, 1990), p. 17, both quoted in Lachendro, 'The Orchestras in KL Auschwitz', p. 34.

28. Laks, *Gry Oświęcimskie*, p. 72.

29. *Träumerei* ('Dreaming') is one of Robert Schumann's thirteen piano pieces known as *Kinderszenen* (*Scenes from Childhood*), op. 15, which has also been arranged for cello.

30. Schwalbová, 'A Doctor Gives Her Account of Auschwitz-Birkenau'.

31. Katarzyna Naliwajek writes about this phenomenon in various chapters of her recent book *Sounds of Apocalypse: Music in Poland under German Occupation* (Frankfurt-am-Main: Peter Lang, 2023).

32. Margo Větrovcová remembers this, see Lachendro, 'The Orchestras in KL Auschwitz', p. 107.

33. David Dubal, *Conversations with Menuhin* (New York: Harcourt Brace Jovanovich, 1991), p. 26.

34. Benjamin Britten to Peter Pears, 1 August 1945, in Donald Mitchell and Philip Reed (eds), *Letters from a Life: The Selected Letters and Diaries of Benjamin Britten 1913–1976, Volume 2: 1939–45* (Berkeley and Los Angeles: University of California Press, 1991), Letter 505, p. 1272.

35. Yehudi Menuhin, *Unfinished Journey: Twenty Years Later* (Fromm International, 1997), p. 186.

36. Britten to Pears, 1 August 1945. Letter 505, 1 August 1945, from *Letters From a Life, vol. 2, 1939–1945*, Donald Mitchell and Philip Reed (eds) (London, Faber and Faber).

37. There is currently only one recording of the work, made by

Toccata Classics with the Lviv International Symphony Orchestra and cellist Clive Greensmith.

38. Mention of the twenty-two survivors can be found in 'Searching for Any Family Members of Convoy #73', https://www.holocaustchild.org/2000/12/searching-for-any-family-members-of-convoy-73/ (accessed 4 Jan. 2024), written by Eve Line Blum-Cherchevsky, the daughter of one of the members of the convoy. At least one of these survivors was 'liberated' by the Soviet troops, only to be taken to the gulag and killed.

39. Aleks Faitelson, *The Truth and Nothing but the Truth: Jewish Resistance in Lithuania* (Jerusalem: Gefen, 2006), p. 485. 'Emes' translates as 'truth' in Yiddish, the equivalent being 'emet' in Hebrew. It is a difficult word to translate accurately, as it can also be used in the sense of 'reality'. To complicate matters, it is a word with enormous resonance in Jewish culture and comes with a great deal of biblical and Talmudic weight attached.

40. Levi, *If This is a Man*, pp. 215–16.

41. Agamben, *Remnants of Auschwitz*, p. 34. Holocaust scholars Giorgio Agamben and Shoshana Felman try to find a space within the lacuna, within the impossibility of bearing witness both on behalf of the dead, and through language. Felman suggests that song might take the place of speech, and that something within rhythm and melody can transcend the limitations of language. Agamben disagrees, criticizing this approach for aestheticizing testimony. See also Felman, Shoshana and Laub, Dori, *Testimony – Crises of Witnessing in Literature, Psychoanalysis and History* (London, Taylor & Francis, 2013).

42. Simone Veil, *A Life: A Memoir*, trans. Tamsin Black (London: Haus Publishing, 2009), p. 37. The theory that the few who went on to Estonia might have been kept alive for corpse burning can also be found in the volumes of relatives' memories, compiled and privately published by Eve Line Blum-Cherchevsky as *Nous Sommes 900 Français* (2012). Vytautas does not believe it can be substantiated.

43. Faitelson, *The Truth and Nothing but the Truth*, p. 489.

44. A glissando is the process of joining notes together – in the case of a cello, not taking your finger off the string between notes, so there is a sliding sound between them.

45. Robert Crome, *The Compleat Tutor for the Violoncello* (London, 1765), p. 15.

46. Jean-Baptiste Bréval, *Traité du Violoncelle* (Paris, 1804), p. 3.

47. Jacques Attali, *Noise: The Political Economy of Music* (Minneapolis: University of Minnesota Press, 1985), p. 3.

4th Movement – Sound

1. Oliver Sacks, *The Man Who Mistook His Wife for a Hat* (New York: Summit Books, 1985), p. 29.
2. It is unclear whether the Billottet business records have survived.
3. The prices I find on the books of W. E. Hill & Sons for 1952 are much lower, the highest being £750 for a Ferdinand Gagliano (approximately £20,000 today). The estimate given by Maucotel was in 'old francs'. The franc was revalued in 1960, with 100 old francs becoming 1 nouveau franc.
4. The *pièce d'âme* is a small wooden patch used to mend a crack in the instrument's soundpost.
5. Max's son Bernard, born in 1929, took over the family business when the brothers retired, and became a master bow maker. He had begun his apprenticeship in 1946, and set up his workshop at 56 Rue de Rome when he was only twenty-one.
6. Walter Benjamin, 'L'œuvre d'art à l'époque de sa reproduction mécanisée' ('The Work of Art in the Age of Mechanical Reproduction'), *Zeitschrift für Sozialforschung*, 5 (1936), pp. 40–68.
7. Jeannette Arata de Erize was the president of the Mozarteum in Argentina from 1955 until her death in 2013, having held concerts in her own home before the Mozarteum expanded to stage concerts in the museums of Buenos Aires, and, later, in the Teatro Colón.
8. William Sandys and Simon Andrew Forster, *The History of the Violin: And Other Instruments Played on with the Bow from the Remotest Times to the Present* (London: William Reeves, 1864).
9. This is the version of the story found in Sandys and Forster, *The History of the Violin*, p. 228.
10. From the Hill diaries, 7 November 1934.
11. There was one cellist Amedeo could not countenance owning his 'Mara'; apparently, he considered their playing too violent. The instrument had been through enough. Despite my best attempts to extract the information from him, Christian Poltera was far too professional to tell me who this cellist was.
12. As Elizabeth Wilson records in her biography, *Jacqueline du Pré: Her Life, her Music, her Legend* (New York: Arcade Publishing, 2013), p. 134.
13. Carl Fuchs, 'Carl Davidoff', *The Strad*, March 1892.
14. Wilson, *Jacqueline du Pré*, p. 135.
15. Henley wrote the label date, but Tarisios have since dated it more accurately. See 'Antonio Stradivari, Cremona, 1690, the

"Barjansky"', https://tarisio.com/cozio-archive/property/?ID=41607; accessed 10 Jan. 2024.

16. This particular arpeggione was made in the 1800s by Czech luthier Anton Mitteis and is displayed in the instrument museum of the Philharmonie in Berlin.

17. Zatorre cites a study from 2001, in which pianists were monitored, and connections were found between the experience of imagining music they knew and motor signals being sent to specific fingers. Jens Haueisen and Thomas R. Knösche, 'Involuntary Motor Activity in Pianists Evoked by Music Perception', *Journal of Cognitive Neuroscience*, 13 (2001), pp. 786–92.

18. For more discussion of 'silent concerts', see Robert Zatorre and Andrea R. Halpern, 'Mental Concerts: Musical Imagery and Auditory Cortex', *Neuron*, 47 (2005), pp. 9–12.

19. *'Arlequin assis au violoncelle'* was owned originally by American ceramicist Carol Janeway, whom Zadkine had known, and whom he was to use as a model for a bust in 1943. Six bronze casts of the original were made during Zadkine's lifetime. The original is now in the Phoenix Art Museum.

20. Quoted in Ionel Jianou, *Zadkine* (Paris: Arted, 1964), p. 47.

21. Quoted in Robert Goldwater and Marco Treves (eds), *Artists on Art from the XIV to the XX Century*, third edition (New York: Pantheon Books, 1958), p. 430.

22. Thomas Clifton, 'The Poetics of Musical Silence', *Musical Quarterly*, 62 (1976), p. 163.

23. Susan Sontag, 'The Aesthetics of Silence', pp. 9–10.

24. Adrienne Rich, 'Arts of the Possible', lecture given in 1997, in *Arts of the Possible: Essays and Conversations* (New York: W.W. Norton, 2001), p. 150.

25. Sontag, 'The Aesthetics of Silence', p. 10.

Illustrations

Index

Illustrations are indicated by numbers in *italics*.